Inside Microsoft® Windows® SharePoint® Services 3.0

Ted Pattison
Daniel Larson

PUBLISHED BY
Microsoft Press
A Division of Microsoft Corporation
One Microsoft Way
Redmond, Washington 98052-6399

Library of Congress Control Number: 2007920382

Printed and bound in the United States of America.

2 3 4 5 6 7 8 9   QWT   2 1 0 9 8 7

Distributed in Canada by H.B. Fenn and Company Ltd.

A CIP catalogue record for this book is available from the British Library.

Microsoft Press books are available through booksellers and distributors worldwide. For further information about international editions, contact your local Microsoft Corporation office or contact Microsoft Press International directly at fax (425) 936-7329. Visit our Web site at www.microsoft.com/mspress. Send comments to mspinput@microsoft.com.

Acquisitions Editor: Ben Ryan
Project Editor: Kathleen Atkins
Editorial and Production Services: Custom Editorial Productions, Inc.
Technical Reviewer: David Robinson; Technical Review services provided by Content Master, a member of CM Group, Ltd.

Body Part No. X13-23792

To Annabelle, Daisy, Sophie, and Amy. You are the only components that my farm will always want to run with Full Trust and Unconditional Love.

—Ted Pattison

To Sallina. You are my passion, my inspiration, my muse, and my love. To our unborn child, you are loved more than words can express.

—Daniel Larson

Contents at a Glance

Acknowledgments. ix

Foreword. xiii

Introduction xv

1   Getting Started. 1

2   SharePoint Architecture 29

3   Pages and Design. 63

4   Web Parts 99

5   AJAX Web Parts 133

6   Lists and Content Types 175

7   Document Libraries 217

8   SharePoint Workflows. 253

9   Solutions and Deployment. 311

10   Application Security 351

Table of Contents

Acknowledgments. ix

Foreword. xiii

Introduction xv

1   Getting Started. 1

    Site Provisioning 1

    Site Customization 11

    WSS as a Development Platform 15

    Creating Your First Feature 21

    Summary 28

2   SharePoint Architecture 29

    IIS and ASP.NET 2.0 Primer 29

    ASP.NET 2.0 Framework 33

    WSS Integration with ASP.NET 40

    Creating Custom Application Pages 49

    Summary 61

3   Pages and Design. 63

    Site Page Fundamentals 63

    Designing Site Pages by Using Controls 74

    Master Pages 83

    Branding WSS Sites by Using CSS Files 95

    Summary 98

4   Web Parts 99

    Web Parts. 99

    Summary 131

5   AJAX Web Parts 133

    Introduction. 133

    Building Rich Internet Applications with ASP.NET AJAX. 136

What do you think of this book? We want to hear from you!

Microsoft is interested in hearing your feedback so we can continually improve our books and learning resources for you. To participate in a brief online survey, please visit:

www.microsoft.com/learning/booksurvey/

Building AJAX Web Part Parts for WSS. 155
Summary. 173

6   Lists and Content Types 175
Lists and Content Types 175
Event Receivers. 209
Summary. 215

7   Document Libraries 217
Working with Document Libraries 217
Forms Libraries and Microsoft Office InfoPath 229
Office Open XML File Formats. 233
Summary. 252

8   SharePoint Workflows. 253
Windows Workflow Foundation 253
SharePoint Workflows. 264
Developing Custom Workflow Templates 271
Integrating Workflow Input Forms 291
Summary. 309

9   Solutions and Deployment. 311
Introduction 311
Site Definitions 312
Application Deployment Through Features 324
WSS Globalization and Localization 327
Deployment Using Solution Packages 331
Language Packs 346
Summary. 350

10   Application Security 351
Introduction 351
Trust Levels and Code Access Security 352
Authentication, Authorization, and Identities 361
User Impersonation with the User Token 371
Summary. 378

Index. 379

What do you think of this book? We want to hear from you!

Microsoft is interested in hearing your feedback so we can continually improve our books and learning resources for you. To participate in a brief online survey, please visit:

www.microsoft.com/learning/booksurvey/

Acknowledgments

Ted's Acknowledgments

I guess I should start at the beginning. It was Mike Fitzmaurice (aka Fitz) who invited me up to the Microsoft campus in Redmond in June of 2005. On the phone, Fitz told me I was going to get a sneak peak at some of their "new stuff" that was still in a top-secret alpha cycle. While I was in town, Fitz introduced me to a handful of program managers on the SharePoint team who turned out to be invaluable resources as Dan and I did the research to write this book. Of all the helpful people who took time to answer our questions, we would especially like to thank Mike Ammerlaan, the ultimate answer man, who seems to possess an all-encompassing and infinite understanding of how Windows SharePoint Services works from the inside out.

Later in the summer of 2005, I began work on a project with the Microsoft Developer Platform Evangelism group to author and teach a developer-focused training course on SharePoint 2007 technology. I was teamed and became good friends with the legendary Patrick Tisseghem of U2U to create slides and lab exercises. I would like to thank Mauricio Ordonez and Scott Burmester for giving me the opportunity to work on this project. I would also like to thank those I worked with, including Rob Barker, Chris Predeek, Doug Mahugh, Christin Boyd, and Don Campbell; all of these people helped to build my understanding of Windows SharePoint Services and the surrounding technologies.

I would also like to thank all those who contributed their time to reviewing chapters. David Robinson technically reviewed all the chapters and provided some great insights. I was lucky enough to have some of the industry's finest reviewing my workflow chapter, including Eilene Hao, Dharma Shuklaa, Gabe Hall, Scot Hillier, Robert Bogue, and Ken Getz. We were also very fortunate to have Morgan Everett, Mark Collins, and Stephen Terlecki perform in-depth and very timely reviews of Dan's chapter on AJAX Web Parts.

I owe a large debt of gratitude to the SharePoint MVP community. First, I want to acknowledge what an excellent job that Lawrence Liu and April Dalke have done to bring this community together. We have a private distribution list where we all share our experiences with one another on a daily basis. I'd like to thank those SharePoint MVPs who post regularly and have taught me so much, including Adam Buenz, Amanda Murphy, Andrew Connell, Bob Fox, Bil Simser, Bill English, Bob Mixon, Carlos Segura Sanz, Cornelius J van Dyk, Darrin Bishop, Brad Smith, Dustin Miller, Eli Robillard, Erol Giraudy, Gary Bushey, Göran Husman, Heather Solomon, Jan Tielens, Jason Medero, Joel Ward, John Holliday, Joris Poelmans, Kevin Laahs, Loke Kit Kai, Luis Du Solier Grinda, Mads Nissen, Mark Kruger, Matthew McDermott, Mei Ying Lim, Michael Greth, Michael Noel, Mike "the Enforcer" Walsh, Nick Swan, Renaud Comte, Robert Bogue, Shane Perran, Shane Young, Spencer Harbar, Stacy Draper, Stephane Cordonnier, Stephen Cummins, Steve Smith, Steven Collier, Todd Baginski, Todd Bleeker, Todd O. Klindt, Pierre Vivier-Merle, Woody Windischman, and Xi Chen.

I must also thank my technical peer group known as the DevelopMentor alumni crowd. I will always fondly remember my time at DevelopMentor back in the mid-to-late 1990s when Don Box was in charge, COM was still loved, and the Internet bubble was growing bigger with each and every day. I had the good fortune to forge friendships and become technically engaged with true geniuses, such as Don Box, Chris Sells, Tim Ewald, Brent Rector, John Lam, Ingo Rammer, Aaron Skonnard, Ian Griffiths, Keith Brown, Fritz Onion, Jon Flanders, Mike Woodring, Ted Neward, Andrew Gayter, Bob Beauchemin, Brian A. Randell, Brian Maso, Brock Allen, Cal Caldwell, Craig Andera, Dan Sullivan, Dan Weston, Daniel Sinclair, Dominick Baier, Doug Turnure, Dr. Joe Hummel, George Shepherd, Henk de Koning, Jason Masterman, Jason Whittington, Jim Wilson, Kent Tegels, Kevin Jones, Kirk Fertitta, Marcus Heege, Mark Taparauskas, Matt Milner, Niels Berglund, Scott Bloom, Simon Horrell, Steve Rodgers, and Martin Gudgin. And all of us are very grateful that Craig Andera was willing to run the mail server with the DevelopMentor alumni distribution list out of his basement for the first few years, just to keep this peer group connected with its technical insights and its unique brand of humor.

I would like to thank all those at Microsoft Press who helped me publish this book. I was lucky enough to work with Ben Ryan as my acquisitions editor and Kathleen Atkins as my production editor. As future would have it, these are the same two people I worked with in the previous millennium when I published my first Microsoft Press book on VB and COM in 1998.

Finally, I would like to thank Dan Larson, my partner in crime. Thanks for your willingness to jump into the mix and help me ship this book in 2007. Thanks for your insights into list schemas, site definitions, and CAS security settings and for significantly improving the final manuscript. I was particular impressed with your mastery of WSS integration with AJAX extensions for ASP.NET and your ability to write about it without any substantial resources and get it into our book in such a timely fashion. You, sir, have truly earned the nickname, "Captain AJAX."

Dan's Acknowledgments

Although many of my acknowledgments remain the same as Ted's, I owe a great deal of my experience to Microsoft Consulting and the developer community in Denver, Colorado. Anthony Petro and Marcus Hass were instrumental in providing guidance and in-depth knowledge of the WSS platform early on, including some of the first large-scale Internet-facing deployments of WSS and SharePoint Portal Server. We learned a lot in those days about stripping WSS down to its core platform elements and building new experiences based on that; many of those concepts will come through in this book.

I would also like to thank the Microsoft Consulting teams I've worked with, including Scott Short. Scott was particularly instrumental in teaching me to write SDK components for developers, a key theme that has resounded in many of my projects and will come through in this book as well. He taught me to write frameworks instead of applications and to work with developer teams to ensure successful technology adoption.

The clients we worked with over the years have also provided the real-world experience that this book builds on, and I'd like to thank David Levstik, David Weinstein, John Daniels, Lei Yu, Jack Deverter, and the rest of the client teams I've worked with over the years.

The Denver developer community that includes Joe Mayo and Roy Ogborn has been instrumental in mentoring me throughout my career and teaching me most of what I know about C#, ASP.NET, and the Microsoft technology stack, and I'd like to thank you in particular. Chris Wallace and the Denver Visual Studio .NET User Group have also been instrumental in providing those early opportunities to speak on .NET and SharePoint technologies, as well as the Rocky Mountain SharePoint User Group, including Kris Syverstad and Matt Passannante.

I would also like to thank my developer team at *NewsGator* for providing a lot of real-world experience and feedback into the AJAX architecture patterns we present in this book. A special thanks to Lane Mohler, Brian Agnes, Sherstin Lauman, Darrin Long, Josh Aragon, and Tom McIntyre.

I also owe my wife Sallina a great deal of gratitude for her patience and support throughout the book's development cycle. Sallina, I could not have written this book without you.

Finally, I would also like to thank Ted for his contributions to my content and for the collaboration we did throughout the book. We truly had a great time writing together, and we hope that shows throughout the book! We hope you enjoy this book as much as we enjoyed writing it.

Foreword

Ted Pattison's arrival on the SharePoint technology scene back in 2004 marked a particularly nice milestone: A popular developer trainer with serious .NET development credentials realized the developer potential of Windows SharePoint Services. Ted started writing about developing with SharePoint products and technologies in his *MSDN Magazine* column. He developed training materials. He taught classes. He delivered high-quality conference presentations. We noticed.

Ted was one of a handful of people we brought in to work with our engineering teams very, very early in the development of Windows SharePoint Services 3.0 to write preliminary white papers for early beta customers, all of which were turned into SDK articles. He developed and delivered training to customers and partners in our early adopter programs, and the experiences with training many, many developers along the way has given him particularly good insight as to what they want and what they need to learn to make use of SharePoint technology.

Most important, we don't regard Ted as a "SharePoint developer." Ted is a .NET developer who has figured out how to incorporate SharePoint technology into his repertoire of skills and tools. He knows when to make use of our technology and how to do so in a way that meshes with standard practices developers have come to adopt for .NET in general and ASP.NET in particular. His time spent training for DevelopMentor and his time spent since then at his own company established his skills both in explaining technology and translating that understanding into practical "hands-on" activity.

Together with Patrick Tisseghem (who has conveniently written a Microsoft Press book on developing with Microsoft Office SharePoint Server 2007—the perfect companion to this book), with whom Ted frequently collaborates, you won't find people who've spent more time thinking about, teaching courses about, and speaking about developing with SharePoint products and technologies.

Daniel Larson is the perfect coauthor for Ted, with a background to complement Ted's. Dan has been involved with our technology going back five years, and blogs about developing with SharePoint technology on a regular basis. He spends time with our engineering team finding ways to incorporate the latest ASP.NET developments into the pages we serve up in SharePoint sites, and is passionate about Internet- and community-targeted technologies like RSS and OPML.

But more important than any of that is that Dan practices what he preaches. At NewsGator, he creates world-class portal applications using SharePoint products and technologies integrated with RSS, AJAX, and social computing. He's seen what works and what doesn't and has personally figured out how to get from pain to payoff when it comes to creating great products with SharePoint technology.

You'll see a lot of valuable content in this book. It covers our Web user interface, our storage technology for documents and data, and our ready-to-use application facilities like workflow and content types. Most important, it advocates a style of organizing code projects that makes the task of writing, maintaining, deploying, and updating code a lot more productive.

When you develop for Windows SharePoint Services, you're really creating extensions and assets to be used by a preexisting Web application. Ted and Dan have figured this out and have geared their examples and guidance to that reality. The results are great—happy reading!

Derek Burney

General Manager, Windows SharePoint Services

Microsoft Corporation

Introduction

If you look around at what's been happening on the Windows platform lately, it would be hard to miss that this "SharePoint" thing has been growing in popularity. SharePoint technologies provide an effective solution for creating team sites to facilitate collaboration in a LAN-based environment. At the opposite end of the spectrum, SharePoint technologies also make it easier to manage content in an Internet-facing site that can scale to accommodate thousands of users in a Web farm environment. And while SharePoint technologies provide significant value with out-of-the-box functionality, there's far more you can accomplish if you are prepared to embrace Windows SharePoint Services as a development platform.

The purpose of this book is to help you design and develop custom business solutions for Windows SharePoint Services 3.0 (WSS). Our goal is to teach you how to create, debug, and deploy the fundamental building blocks such as Features, Site Definitions, Page Templates, Web Parts, List Schemas, Content Types, Event Handlers, and Workflow Templates. Once you apply yourself and become comfortable developing with these building blocks, there's no limit to the types of applications and solutions you can create on the Windows SharePoint Services platform. In addition, you will gain the skills you need to extend the out-of-the-box functionality that is included with Microsoft Office SharePoint Server 2007 (MOSS).

Who This Book Is For

This book is written for software developers who are proficient with Visual Studio 2005, the Microsoft .NET 2.0 Framework, and ASP.NET. The code samples in this book are written in C#. This book will provide a comprehensive overview of Windows SharePoint Services 3.0 for software developers and architects and provide expert guidance on developing applications on this platform. Developers who are new to Windows SharePoint Services as well as experienced WSS developers will benefit from this book.

System Requirements

You'll need the following hardware and software to build and run the code samples for this book:

- Microsoft Windows Server 2003 with Service Pack 1 or Microsoft Windows Server 2003 R2 (native install or Virtual Machine environments)
- Microsoft Windows SharePoint Services 3.0
- Microsoft Visual Studio 2005 Standard Edition or Microsoft Visual Studio 2005 Professional Edition or Microsoft Visual Studio 2005 Team Suite
- For a native installation, we recommend at least a 1 GHz Pentium processor and 1 GB of RAM
- For an installation on a Virtual PC image, we recommend a host computer with at least a 2 GHz Pentium processor and 2 GB of RAM

Code Samples

All of the code samples discussed in this book can be downloaded from the book's companion content page at the following address:

http://www.microsoft.com/mspress/companion/9780735623200/

Support for This Book

Every effort has been made to ensure the accuracy of this book and the companion content. Microsoft Press provides support for books and companion content at the following Web site:

http://www.microsoft.com/learning/support/books/

You can also look for code updates and a list of errata at the following Web site:

http://www.TedPattison.net/InsideWSS

Questions and Comments

If you have comments, questions, or ideas regarding the book or the companion content, or questions that are not answered by visiting the sites above, please send them to Microsoft Press via e-mail to

mspinput@microsoft.com

Or via postal mail to

Microsoft Press

Attn: *Inside Microsoft® Windows® SharePoint® Services 3.0* Editor

One Microsoft Way

Redmond, WA 98052-6399

Please note that Microsoft software product support is not offered through the preceding addresses.

Chapter 1
Getting Started

- Learn about fundamental Windows SharePoint Services (WSS) concepts and terminology.
- Learn about the principles of site provisioning.
- Learn about customization opportunities with WSS.
- Explore the out-of-the-box collaboration features of WSS.
- Learn about development opportunities for extending WSS.

Site Provisioning

Looking back a decade ago, many companies were just learning about the World Wide Web and discovering their ability to reach customers using HTML-based content. Back then, most companies maintained a single public-facing Web site. That's all they needed for the purposes of advertising their products and services.

Times certainly have changed since then. Today companies are using Web sites not just to reach customers, but also to provide applications for vendors, employees, and top-level management. It's not uncommon for a large company to create hundreds or even thousands of Web sites. For example, a large corporation could require a new Web site to be created for each new marketing campaign or each new employee.

In a world without SharePoint products and technologies, it can be expensive and time consuming for a company to keep up with its need to continually create and manage Web sites. For example, let's walk through what is required to create a Web site designed to track sales leads and customers.

First, the process requires a database administrator to create a new database and the required tables in SQL Server or some other DBMS system to track sales data. Next, a developer must create an ASP.NET Web site with Web pages and the required code to view and edit the sales data. Once the ASP.NET Web site is ready for deployment, a system administrator must then copy the ASP.NET application files to the target Web server and configure Internet Information Services 6.0 (IIS) to create a new virtual directory. If the ASP.NET application is to be deployed in a Web farm environment, the requirements increase because these administrative procedures must be duplicated across each front-end Web server in the farm.

As you can imagine, using this approach to get a new Web site up and running usually takes weeks, or sometimes even months, because of the need to coordinate efforts between a database administrator, a Web developer, and a system administrator. WSS was designed from the ground up to make the creation of Web sites faster and more cost effective. As a WSS developer, you will learn to develop components that others will use to create sites and workspaces.

At its core, WSS is a site provisioning engine. The architecture of WSS was specifically designed to operate in a Web farm environment. The act of provisioning (a fancy word for creating) a site in WSS can be accomplished by any member of the IT department in less than a minute by filling in the required information in a browser-based form and clicking the OK button. There's no need for a database administrator to create a new database or any new tables. There's no need for an ASP.NET developer to create a new ASP.NET Web site. There's no need for a system administrator to copy any files or configure any IIS settings on the front-end Web server.

The WSS site provisioning engine is based on an integrated storage model that involves multiple SQL Server databases to store content and configuration data. When you install WSS, you can elect to use SQL Server 2005 or SQL Server 2000. For simple deployments and development scenarios, you can also use SQL Express, which eliminates the need to purchase a licensed copy of SQL Server.

Microsoft Office SharePoint Server 2007

It is important that you know the difference between Windows SharePoint Services (WSS) and Microsoft Office SharePoint Server 2007 (MOSS). While WSS and MOSS are both pieces of software built by the Microsoft Office team, WSS is included as a part of the Windows Server 2003 operating system while MOSS is a separate product with its own SKU. You should think of WSS as the underlying platform and think of MOSS as a value-added set of components and services that has been built on top of this platform.

WSS does not have its own licensing model. Instead, the use of WSS is controlled through Windows Server 2003 licenses. This makes it very cost effective for companies to roll out applications that have been designed and built on top of the WSS platform. MOSS, on the other hand, has its own licensing model that includes server-side licenses and client access licenses (CALs). The MOSS licensing model is further broken out into a Standard Edition and an Enterprise Edition.

Every deployment of WSS is based on the concept of a farm. Simply stated, a *farm* is a set of one or more server computers working together to provide WSS functionality to clients. In the simplest deployment scenario, a WSS farm consists of a single server computer that acts as both the front-end Web server and the SQL Server database server. A more complicated WSS farm would consist of several front-end Web server computers and a dedicated database server, as shown in Figure 1-1.

Each WSS farm runs a single SQL Server database known as the *configuration database*. The configuration database tracks important farm-wide information. For example, the configuration database tracks which front-end Web servers are associated with the farm as well as which users have been assigned administrative permissions within WSS at the farm level.

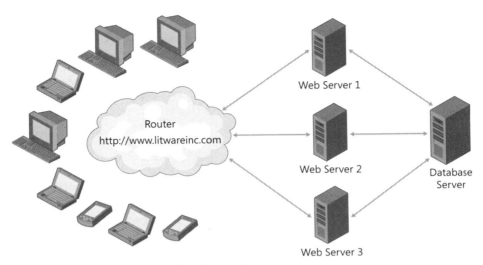

Figure 1-1   A WSS farm provides Web applications.

WSS is built on top of Internet Information Services 6.0 (IIS). In particular, WSS relies on IIS Web sites to handle incoming HTTP requests. Therefore, you need to understand exactly what an IIS Web site really is. An *IIS Web site* provides an entry point into the IIS Web server infrastructure. For example, the Default Web Site created automatically by IIS listens for incoming HTTP requests on port 80. You can create additional IIS Web sites to provide additional entry points using different port numbers, different IP addresses, or different host headers.

An important characteristic of an IIS Web site is that its security settings are configured independently of other IIS Web sites. For example, you can configure the Default Web Site as a public-facing site that might involve using Basic Authentication and allowing anonymous access. You can create a second IIS Web site intended for use within the corporate LAN on a different port such as port 1000. Once you have created this intranet Web site in IIS, you can configure it to require integrated Windows authentication and to disallow anonymous access.

An IIS Web site must be specially configured when it is used to serve up WSS sites. We are going to defer discussing the technical details of this configuration until the next chapter. At this point, we want to introduce some important concepts and terminology.

An IIS Web site that has been specially configured to run WSS sites is known as a *Web application*. Every WSS site runs in the context of a specific Web application. This is important because the hosting Web application for a WSS site provides many important aspects of the WSS environment including the security configuration for user authentication.

The installation of WSS creates and configures a Web application named the *WSS 3.0 Central Administration* application. The WSS 3.0 Central Administration application provides pages that allow you to perform administrative chores such as converting a standard IIS Web site into a WSS Web application. The WSS Central Administration application also provides the option to create a new IIS Web site and automatically configure it to be a WSS Web application as well, all without having to use any of the IIS administration tools directly.

Web Applications Versus Virtual Servers

In the last version of WSS, the product team used the term *virtual server* to describe an IIS Web site that has been extended with WSS functionality. In the current version of WSS and its supporting documentation, the term *virtual server* has been replaced with the term *Web application* mainly to avoid confusion with another Microsoft product of the same name. However, as a WSS developer you must remember that the new term *Web application* and the old term *virtual server* are often used interchangeably. For example, the WSS object model provides the SPVirtualServer class to program against Web application objects.

Within a typical WSS farm, there are usually several different Web applications. The WSS Central Administration application is configured during installation as its own separate Web application. You then need one or more other Web applications to create and manage the sites that will be accessible to end users. For example, the Default Web Site can be configured as a WSS Web application to make WSS sites available through the standard HTTP port 80. You might decide to create additional Web applications within the farm such as an intranet Web application on port 1000. WSS configuration data is stored on a farm-wide basis in the configuration database, and the data associated with WSS sites is tracked in another type of database known as a *content database*. When you create a new Web application with the WSS 3.0 Central Administration application, WSS creates a new content database. If you stick with a simple deployment model, your farm will include one content database for each Web application, as shown in Figure 1-2. In scenarios that require higher levels of security or more granular storage planning, it is possible to use more sophisticated administrative procedures to distribute the sites within a Web application across multiple content databases.

Figure 1-2   A WSS farm provides Web applications that store their data in content databases.

Tip   When developing for Windows SharePoint Services, you are not permitted to directly access the configuration database or any of the content databases. For example, you must resist any temptation to write ADO.NET code that reads or writes data from the tables inside these databases. Instead, you should write code against the WSS programming APIs, which results in WSS running system code that accesses the configuration database and/or a content database on your behalf.

Sites and Site Collections

Let's take a step back and ask a fundamental question—what is a WSS site? First, a *WSS site* is a storage container for content. Site content is primarily stored in the form of lists, document libraries, and child sites. Second, a site is a securable entity whose content is accessible to a configurable set of users. A site can either define its own set of users, or it can inherit the users of its parent site. A site also contains a configurable set of groups and permissions that define the level of accessibility that various users have on the site's lists and document libraries.

Note that WSS doesn't actually perform user authentication. Instead, WSS relies on the underlying layers within IIS and the ASP.NET authentication provider infrastructure to accomplish that. However, WSS does take charge when it comes to authorization. WSS provides user interface elements and supporting code that allows privileged users to configure authorization to various elements within their sites. WSS 3.0 also introduces valuable security trimming features so that commands and links to site elements are only shown to users who are authorized to access them.

Third, a site is an application with an extensible, fully customizable user interface. A site administrator can create pages and customize their layout and appearance. A site administrator can also modify a site's navigation structure using the browser.

Finally, a site is the foundation for using the Microsoft Web Part Page and Web Part technology. Site administrators can customize Web Part Pages by adding and configuring Web Parts. A user can further personalize a Web Part Page by modifying, adding, and/or removing Web Parts. All the customization data and personalization data associated with the Web Parts on a Web Part Page are automatically stored in the content database.

Every WSS site must be provisioned within the scope of an existing Web application. However, a site cannot exist as an independent entity within a Web application. Instead, every WSS site must also be created inside the scope of a *site collection*. A site collection is a container of WSS sites. Each site collection requires a top-level site. In addition to the required top-level site, a site collection can contain a hierarchy of child sites. Figure 1-3 shows several possible site collections. The first site collection contains just a top-level site. The second site collection contains one level of child sites below the top-level site. The third site collection contains a more complex hierarchy of child sites.

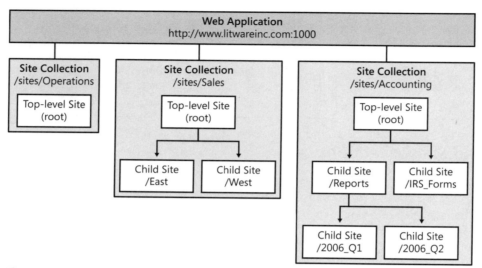

Figure 1-3   Sites exist within site collections. Each site collection must have a top-level site and can contain a hierarchy of child sites.

When a company first begins using WSS or MOSS, one of the first questions that comes up is how to partition sites across site collections. For example, should you create one big site collection with lots of child sites, or should you create many individual site collections? These decisions are usually best made after thinking through all the relevant issues discussed in the next few paragraphs. You must gain an understanding of how partitioning sites into site collections affects the scope of administrative privileges, security boundaries, backup and restore operations, and site design.

You should be asking yourself why the WSS architecture requires this special container to hold its sites. For starters, site collections represent a scope for administrative privileges. If you have been assigned as a site collection administrator, you have full administrative permissions within any existing site and any future site created inside that site collection.

Think about the requirements of site management in a large corporation that's provisioning thousands of sites per year. The administrative burden posed by all these sites is going to be more than most IT departments can deal with in a timely manner. The concept of the site collection is important because it allows an IT department to hand off the administrative burden to the business divisions that own the sites.

Let's walk through an example. In many companies using WSS, someone in the IT department is responsible for provisioning site collections upon request from one of the business divisions. During the provisioning process, the IT department assigns one or more users from the business division with administrative permissions at the level of the new site collection. After that point in time, administrative users from the business division can add users as well as create site elements such as lists and document libraries without any assistance from the IT department.

They can also add child sites below the top-level site. This allows them to grow the hierarchy of child sites and configure security for these child sites any way they see fit.

> ## The WSS Decoder Ring
>
> When developers begin to use WSS, there is often confusion surrounding different terminology used between WSS and its version 1.0 predecessor SharePoint Team Services (STS). For example, the WSS term *Site Collection* is the equivalent of the old STS term *Site*. The new WSS term *Site* is the equivalent of the old STS term *Web*. The new WSS term *Top-level Site* is the equivalent of the old STS term *Root Web*.
>
> Though the WSS team has been consistent using the new WSS terminology in the product documentation, there are still many places that use the term *Web* when you expect *Site* and that use the term *Site* when you expect *Site Collection*.
>
> For example, the names of classes in the WSS object model are based on the old STS terms. As a result, you program against a site collection using an SPSite object, and you program against a site using a SPWeb object. An SPSite object provides a public property named RootWeb that returns an SPWeb object representing the site collection's top-level site. Once you understand this potential point of confusion, getting up to speed on various aspects of WSS becomes less confusing.

A second motivation for site collections is that they provide a scope for membership and security authorization. By design, every site collection is independent of any other site collection with respect to what security groups are defined, which users have been added as members, and which users are authorized to do what.

For example, imagine that the IT department at Litware, Inc. has provisioned one site collection for the Sales department and a second site collection for the Accounting department. Even though there are users within the Accounting department that have administrative permissions within their own site collection, there is nothing they can do that will have any effect upon the security configuration of the Sales site collection. That is because the WSS architecture sees each site collection as an island with respect to security configuration.

A third motivation for site collections is that they provide a convenient scope for backup and restore operations. You can back up a site collection and later restore it with full fidelity. The restoration of a site collection can take place in the same location where backup was made. Alternatively, a site collection can be restored in a different location and even inside a different farm. This technique for backing up a site collection and restoring it in another location provides a strategy for moving WSS sites from a development environment to a staging environment and then to a production environment.

The STSADM.EXE Command Line Utility

WSS ships with a handy command-line utility named STSADM.EXE. This utility allows you to run interactive commands from the Windows command line and to script batch files that accomplish administrative tasks such as creating, backing up, and restoring site collections. When you run this utility from the command line or from a batch file, you must pass the –o parameter followed by one of the supported operations. Here's an example of a command line instruction to create a new site collection at a specific URL.

```
STSADM.EXE -o CreateSite -url http://localhost/sites/Sales
                         -ownerlogin LitwareServer\BrianC
                         -owneremail brianc@litwareinc.com
                         -sitetemplate STS#0
```

Note that this example has introduced line breaks between the parameters to make things more readable. However, you cannot actually use line breaks between the parameters when running the STSADM utility from the command line or from a batch file.

Keep in mind that the installation of WSS adds the STSADM.EXE utility to a WSS system directory deep within the Windows Program Files directory. If you want to be able to call this utility directly from the command line on your development workstation, you should add the following path to your configured System path.

```
c:\program files\common files\microsoft shared\web server extensions\12\bin\
```

When you write a batch file, you should also assume that it might be run on a machine that does not have the proper System path configured. Therefore, you should write batch files that explicitly specify the location of the STSADM.EXE utility.

```
@SET STSADM="c:\program files\common files\microsoft shared\
            web server extensions\12\bin\stsadm"

%STSADM% -o CreateSite -url http://localhost/sites/Sales
                       -ownerlogin LitwareServer\BrianC
                       -owneremail brianc@litwareinc.com
                       -sitetemplate STS#0
```

Once again, the line breaks in the preceding example are only for readability. You will want to remove them when writing an actual batch file.

A final motivation for you to start thinking in terms of site collections is that they provide a scope for many types of site elements and custom queries. For example, the WSS object model provides the means for you to run queries that span all the lists within a site collection. However, this convenient query mechanism does not span across site collections. Therefore, if your application design calls for running queries to aggregate list data from several different sites, you have an added motivation to design these sites as child sites within the same site collection.

Users can also create several types of custom site elements for reuse across all the sites within a site collection. For example, if you create a site column within a top-level site, then this site column is reusable in all the child sites down below. This allows you to define the column characteristics such as formatting, validation, or a choice list one time and then to use this reusable column type across many lists within the site collection. Later, you can update the site column and have this update affect all the lists when the site column is used. Site columns are new to WSS 3.0 and are discussed more fully in Chapter 6, "Lists and Content Types."

Provisioning a Site Collection

You cannot really appreciate the simplicity of WSS until you have provisioned your first site collection. We are now going to walk you through the steps of doing exactly that. You will play the role of a SharePoint farm administrator. Therefore, you will need the proper permissions.

- Under the Windows Start menu, find the Administrative Tools group and then select the SharePoint 3.0 Central Administration menu to launch the WSS Central Administration application. Over the next few steps you will use this application to create a new site.

- At the top of the home page of the Central Administration application, there are three tabs: Home, Operations, and Application Management. Select the Application Management tab.

- On the Application Management page, locate and click the link titled Create Site Collection in the SharePoint Site Management section. This will take you to a page where you will enter the details that WSS requires whenever you want to create a new site collection.

- Take a look at Figure 1-4, which shows the top half of the WSS Create Site Collection page. This figure shows an example of filling in the Title, Description, URL, and Site Collection Administrator fields when provisioning a new site collection.

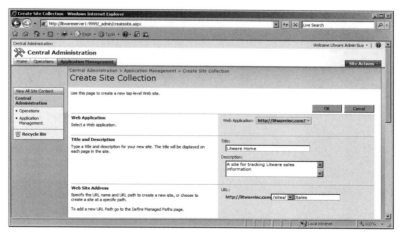

Figure 1-4   When creating a new site collection, you are required to specify the name, the target URL, and user account information for one or two site collection administrators.

■ Figure 1-5 shows the bottom half of the WSS Create Site Collection page. You can see that this page allows the user to select a site template to use when creating the top-level site. As you can see, you can select from several different site templates including Team Site and Blank Site. Select the Blank Site template.

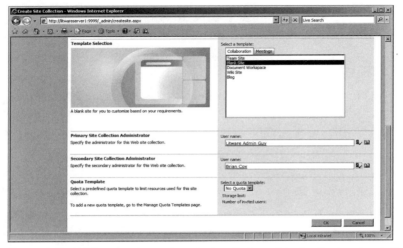

Figure 1-5 WSS prompts you to select a site template for the top-level site.

■ After you have filled in all the required information, you can click the OK button to start the provisioning process. WSS will provision a new site collection containing a top-level site. The top-level site will be created using the site template you selected. When the provisioning process has completed successfully, WSS will display the page shown in Figure 1-6.

Figure 1-6 WSS displays a success message—the new site collection has been created.

■ Congratulations. You have now created a new WSS site collection which includes a top-level site created from the Blank Site site template. You can now click on the link *http://LitwareServer/sites/Sales* to navigate to the home page of this top-level site, as shown in Figure 1-7. The site doesn't contain any lists yet because it was created from the Blank Site site template. However, adding new lists and document libraries is very simple.

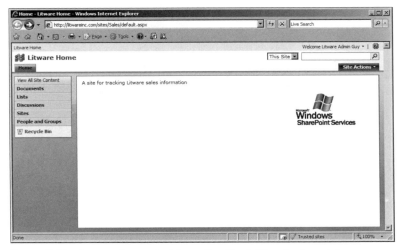

Figure 1-7   A new site created from the Blank Site site template

Site Customization

Now that you have created your first site collection, you must decide how to configure it and how to customize its top-level site. WSS provides many options for configuring and customizing sites. We will start by exploring the various options that are available to users who have been assigned administrative privileges at the site collection level.

In the top-right corner of the page, you can see the Site Actions menu. This menu provides commands that allow you to create new site elements, customize the current page, and navigate to the Site Settings page. It is important to note that this is a menu that provides security trimming. That means that although someone with administrative privileges will see all the Site Actions menu commands, less privileged users will see a reduced set of commands. For site visitors with read-only access, the Site Actions menu will be completely hidden.

The Site Settings Page

The Site Settings page provides links to pages that allow you to perform various administrative and customization tasks. The standard Site Settings page for a top-level site is shown in Figure 1-8.

If you are new to WSS, you should take some time to explore all of the administrative pages that are accessible through the Site Settings page. Note that the Site Settings page for a top-level site contains one section for Site Administration and a second section for Site Collection Administration. The Site Settings page for child sites will not include the section for Site Collection Administration.

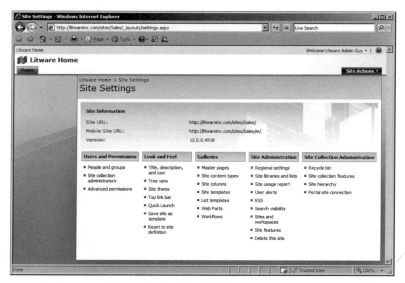

Figure 1-8 Each site provides a Site Settings page that provides various configuration and customization options.

You can see that there is a Users And Permissions section dedicated to security configuration as well as a Look And Feel section for changing the appearance of the user interface and navigation options. There is also a Galleries section that allows you to see and configure various elements within the current site such as master pages, site columns, and content types. Over the next few chapters, we will explore each of these galleries in depth.

The Create Page

The Site Actions menu also provides the Create menu command, which takes you to the Create Page, as shown in Figure 1-9. The functionality provided to users by the Create Page is one of the most enabling aspects of WSS. That is because the Create Page allows users to customize the current site by creating new site elements on demand such as lists, document libraries, Web Part Pages, and child sites.

The Create Page shown in Figure 1-9 contains links for the standard element types that are available out-of-the-box with WSS. These standard element types have been designed to facilitate team-level collaboration. They include list types for collaborating on list-based items such as announcements, contacts, links, calendar events, tasks, and issue tracking.

The standard collaboration features of WSS also include support for creating several different types of document libraries. In addition to the standard document library type, there are also more specialized document library types for picture libraries and wikis.

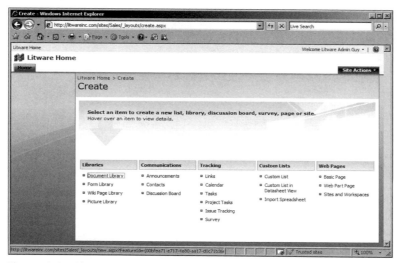

Figure 1-9   The Create Page allows users to provision new site elements on demand.

While the Create Page is great for users with site administrator privileges, it will interest developers as well. The set of creatable element types seen by the user on the Create Page is completely extensible. Throughout this book, you will see several different techniques you can use to add custom element types, such as your own list types and document library types that have been designed to solve a unique business problem. What's nice about this is that your custom element types will show up right alongside the standard WSS element types, presenting a very consistent experience for users as they provision new elements within their sites.

Creating Lists and Document Libraries

WSS makes it extremely easy for a user with the proper permissions to customize a site by creating new lists and document libraries. The user simply clicks on the link for the desired list type on the Create Page and is then taken to another page and prompted to enter a name and description for the list. Note that the names of lists and document libraries must be unique within the scope of the current site.

Once a list or a document library has been created, it is ready for use. Each list and document library provides a set of pages that allows users to add, view, modify, and delete items and documents. You should now create one or more lists in your new blank site so you can continue to follow along with the next section.

Customizing Lists with the List Settings Command

WSS is very flexible in that it allows users to customize many aspects of an existing list or document library. Each list provides a toolbar with a Settings menu. The Settings menu provides a List Settings command that takes the user to a special page, shown in Figure 1-10.

The resulting page has a title with the word *Customize* and then the name of the list. For example, the title generated by List Settings for the Announcements list will be *Customize Announcements*.

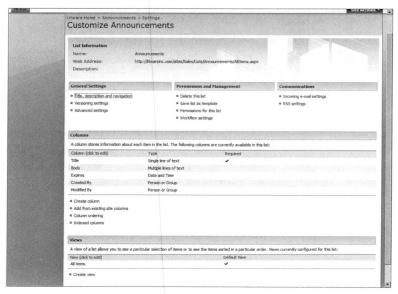

Figure 1-10   The List Settings command displays a page allowing users to customize a list.

The List Settings command allows the user to customize a list's properties such as its name and whether it is shown as a link in the Quick Launch navigation section. This Settings page also allows the user to configure other important aspects of the list including security and versioning. The List Settings page also provides users with the flexibility to customize a list or document library by adding, removing, and modifying columns and views.

Site Customization and Personalization Using Web Parts

The inclusion of Web Part technology is one of the most powerful aspects of WSS. Web Part Pages provide each site with an extensible HTML-based user interface.

Let's take a moment and examine a Web Part Page from the perspective of a Web Part consumer. If you are a site administrator, you can select the Edit Page command from the Site Actions menu on the home page of a site to enter into a customization mode where you can move, add, modify, or delete Web Parts. Changes made to Web Parts in this mode are referred to as customizations because they are seen by all the users of the site.

WSS also provides less privileged users with the ability to personalize Web Part Pages by adding and modifying Web Parts. Keep in mind that WSS uses the terms *customization* and *personalization* to mean different things. Customization changes are seen by all users.

Personalization changes are seen by only the user who made them. WSS is smart enough to store the shared customization data and private personalization data separately in the content database. In code, you will see this referred to as shared storage and personal storage. A Web Part page is laid out in terms of Web Part zones. A Web Part is added to a Web Part page by being placed within a Web Part zone. WSS allows users to create new Web Part pages using a preprovided set of templates. With the browser, you can use one of these Web Part page templates to create a new Web Part page with a predefined layout of zones. When a user creates a new Web Part page using the browser, the resulting Web Part page must be created within the context of a document library.

WSS as a Development Platform

In one sense, WSS works against professional software developers because it empowers users to create and customize their own sites. In minutes, a user can create a WSS site, add several lists and document libraries, and customize the site's appearance to meet the needs of a particular business situation. An identical solution created using ASP.NET would likely take a developer weeks or months to complete.

In another sense, WSS provides professional developers with new and exciting development opportunities. As with any other framework, the out-of-the-box experience with WSS will only take you so far. At some point, you will find yourself needing to create custom list types and write code for custom WSS components such as Web Parts, event handlers, and workflows. What's incredibly attractive about WSS as a development platform is that it was designed from the ground up with developer extensibility in mind. The WSS developer platform includes the object model, Web Part framework, Web services, and site provisioning model, providing a comprehensive framework for scalable portal applications.

Customization Versus Development

As you begin to design software for the WSS platform, it is critical that you differentiate between customization and development. WSS is very flexible for users because it was designed to support high levels of customization. As we have pointed out, you no longer need to be a developer to build a complex and highly functional site.

A sophisticated user can create and customize lists and document libraries. Users can also customize and personalize the appearance of their pages through the use of Web Parts. Advanced users can even provide an effective branding solution by using the SharePoint Designer to customize the master pages and Cascading Styles Sheets associated with sites.

You should remember that WSS records every site customization by modifying data within the content database. This is true whenever you create a new list or whenever you customize an existing list by adding new columns and views. It's also true for all types of site customization you can perform using Microsoft Office SharePoint Designer.

The fact that all site customization is recorded as modifications to the content database is both a strength and a weakness for WSS. It is a strength because it provides so much flexibility to users and site administrators with respect to performing ad hoc customization. It is a weakness for professional software development because customization changes are hard to version and to make repeatable across multiple sites.

Think about a standard ASP.NET development project where all the source files you are working with live within a single directory on your development machine. Once you have finished the site's initial design and implementation, you can add all the site's source files to a source control management system such as Microsoft Visual SourceSafe. This makes it possible to have a very disciplined approach to deploying and updating the site after it has gone into production. You can also elect to push changes out to a staging environment where your site's pages and code can be thoroughly tested before they are finally pushed out to the production environment.

As a developer, you should ask yourself the following questions: How do you conduct source control management of customization changes? How do you make a customization change to a list definition or a page instance and then move this change from a development environment to a staging environment and finally to a production environment? How do you make a customization change within a site and then reuse it across a hundred different sites? Unfortunately, these questions have very tough answers, and usually you will find that a possible solution isn't worth the trouble.

Fortunately, as a developer you can work at a level underneath the WSS customization infrastructure. To be more specific, you can work with the low-level source files to create underlying definitions for things like lists and page templates. These low-level source files do not live inside the content database, but instead they live within the file system of the front-end Web server. Working at this level is more complex and has a steeper learning curve. However, it lets you centralize source code management and have a more disciplined approach involving code sign-off when moving pages and code from development to staging to production. This approach also makes versioning and reuse of code far more manageable across multiple sites, Web applications, and farms.

For the remainder of this book, we will differentiate between customization and development according to these criteria. WSS customizations are updates to a site accomplished by making changes to the content database, generally through the Web browser or the SharePoint Designer. A site customization never requires touching the front-end Web server. WSS development, on the other hand, involves working with files that must be deployed to the file system of the front-end Web server. WSS development includes creating page templates and list definitions, as well as creating components deployed in compiled assemblies such as custom Web Parts, event handlers, and workflow templates. WSS development at this level is also referred to as *developing provisioning components*.

Keep in mind that development requires a degree of control over the front-end Web server because of the need to push out files such as page templates and assemblies. If you work in a WSS environment where you are not permitted to make any changes to front-end Web servers, you will not be able to deploy any of your development efforts. In such an environment, you will be restricted to using only customization techniques that can be accomplished by making changes to the content database.

Although customization provides users with a great deal of flexibility, development is far more powerful. It's a much better approach for creating reusable WSS solutions, as well as the best way to optimize the response times and throughput for high-traffic sites. Developing provisioning components with WSS is the primary focus of this book, whereas discussions of customization and related tools such as the SharePoint Designer will be secondary.

Development Opportunities

As a developer, you have many different avenues for extending WSS. Over the next two chapters, we will discuss how you can create custom application pages and page templates to add functionality to a business solution. As you will see, some types of pages in a WSS site allow you to write managed code directly behind them; other types do not. However, even with the types of pages that do not directly support code, you still have the ability to write code in Web Parts and ASP.NET User Controls and then to use these components in your pages.

Enhancements to WSS 3.0 have added rich integration with ASP.NET master pages and Cascading Style Sheets (CSS). This provides a good deal of control when you need to brand a site that will be seen by customers or top-level management. There's also tight integration with the ASP.NET navigation provider framework that makes it possible to create any type of custom navigation structure that you can create for a standard ASP.NET 2.0 application.

You can also develop many types of custom components for use within WSS sites. These components include standard ASP.NET server controls, Web Parts, event handlers, custom field types, and custom policies. The why and how of developing these types of components will be discussed throughout the course of this book.

As a developer, you also have control over how you store content within a custom site. WSS lets you define custom types for lists and document libraries, giving you control over which columns they contain and which views are available to users.

WSS 3.0 has added a valuable new innovation known as the *site column*. A site column is a reusable column definition that can be used across multiple lists. A site column defines the name for a column, its underlying field type, and other characteristics such as the default value, formatting, and validation. Once you have defined a site column, you can then use it as you define the schema for custom lists and document libraries. An obvious advantage is that you can update the site column in a single place and have that update affect all the lists where the site column has been used.

WSS 3.0 adds a second powerful innovation focused on content storage. It is known as a *content type*. A content type is a flexible and reusable WSS type definition that defines the columns and behavior for an item in a list or a document in a document library. For example, you can create a content type for a customer presentation document with a unique set of columns, an event handler, and its own document template. You can create a second content type for a customer proposal document with a different set of columns, a workflow, and a different document template. Then you can create a new document library and configure it to support both of these content types. The introduction of content types is very significant to WSS 3.0 because it provides an ability that did not exist in WSS 2.0 to deal with heterogeneous types of content in lists and document libraries.

Another great new development opportunity is to work with the new Office Open XML file formats. This new technology introduced with Microsoft Office 2007 provides you with the ability to generate and/or manipulate Microsoft Office Word documents and Microsoft Office Excel documents from server-side code within custom components such as event handlers and workflows. What's nice is that the Office Open XML file formats eliminate the need to install and run a version of a Microsoft Office desktop application such as Office Word or Office Excel on the server. Everything can be done by programming against server-side libraries, which provide high degrees of scalability and robustness.

One of the most exciting areas of extending WSS 3.0 is in the area of workflow. WSS is built on top of Microsoft's new Windows Workflow Foundation that is part of the .NET Framework 3.0. WSS adds an extra dimension on top of the Windows Workflow Foundation to provide a foundation for attaching business logic to list items and documents in a WSS site. WSS extends the basic model of the Windows Workflow Foundation by associating a task list and a history list with each workflow. This adds a degree of responsibility and accountability to workflows that are human-oriented in nature, such as a workflow for reviewing or approving a document.

Both WSS and MOSS ship with workflows that are installed and ready to use. WSS includes a simple routing workflow for things such as moderation and approval. MOSS supplies workflows that are more complex and are used to support features such as their Web Content Management approval process.

The creation of custom workflows represents an obvious extensibility point for developers creating business solutions with WSS and with MOSS. In addition to the standard support of the Visual Studio Extensions for the Windows Workflow Foundation, the Office team provides a WSS-specific workflow Software Development Kit (SDK) and a workflow starter kit including Visual Studio project templates for creating custom workflows targeted at WSS sites.

Security and site membership are two other areas that provide developers with opportunities for extending the standard WSS infrastructure. Previous versions of WSS were tightly coupled to Windows accounts and Microsoft Active Directory, making SharePoint technologies undesirable for Internet-facing sites. This is no longer the case with WSS 3.0. The new infrastructure for user authentication has been redesigned to sit on top of the authentication provider infrastructure introduced in ASP.NET 2.0.

If you don't want to maintain user accounts for WSS users inside Active Directory, you simply need to build or acquire an ASP.NET authentication provider that's been designed to store and manage user accounts in an alternative identity repository such as a SQL Server database. This architectural enhancement has led WSS 3.0 to gain much wider adoption as a platform for building Internet-facing sites.

For example, ASP.NET 2.0 ships with the forms authentication provider that allows you to maintain user accounts inside a SQL Server database. This authentication provider can be configured for use in a WSS 3.0 site. With little effort on your part, you can put a WSS site on the Internet that allows unknown users to register themselves as members. ASP.NET 2.0 provides you with convenient support for creating and maintaining user accounts, and even allows users to change and reset their passwords. When you use forms authentication, you can use the same programming techniques to manage user accounts in a WSS solution as you would in an ASP.NET 2.0 solution.

Introduction to Features

Though there are many different avenues for custom development in WSS, you should start off by learning about *features*. Features are a new developer-focused innovation that has been added to WSS 3.0. Features provide a mechanism for defining site elements and adding them to a target site or site collection through a process known as *feature activation*. The element types that can be defined by a feature include menu commands, link commands, page templates, page instances, list definitions, list instances, event handlers, and workflows.

At a physical level, a feature consists of a directory created within a special WSS system directory located within the file system of each front-end Web server. The directory for a feature contains one or more XML-based files that contain Collaborative Application Markup Language (CAML). By convention, each feature directory contains a manifest file named feature.xml that defines the high-level attributes of the feature, such as its ID and its user-friendly Title.

Besides the feature.xml file, a feature usually contains one or more additional XML files (for example, elements.xml) that define the actual elements that make up the feature. The directory for a feature can also contain several other types of files for things like list definitions and page templates, as well as other kinds of resources such as graphics files, Cascading Style Sheets, and JavaScript files.

One valuable technique for getting up to speed on features is to examine the standard set of features that ships as part of the basic WSS installation. An example of what the FEATURES directory looks like after you have installed WSS is shown in Figure 1-11. As you can see, each feature has its own directory. Also note that the Site Features page will look very different if you have installed MOSS because there will be more than 100 features.

At the end of this chapter, you will see how to create and deploy your first custom feature. Once you have created a feature, you then must install it with WSS at a farm-level scope. Once a feature has been installed with WSS, it can then be activated within the context of a site or a site collection using an administrative page accessible through the Site Settings page.

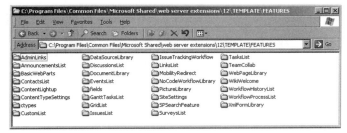

Figure 1-11   Many stock aspects of WSS, such as collaboration lists, are implemented as features.

Throughout this book, we will continually introduce new features to solve a particular problem such as branding a site with a custom master page and Cascading Style Sheet. Other features will demonstrate how to provision new page instances and how to make components such as Web Parts and custom workflows accessible within a site.

While a custom feature allows a developer to define one or more elements that can be activated inside the context of a site or site collection, WSS also provides a developer with the ability to define the entire blueprint for a site by creating a custom *site definition*. The development of custom site definitions allows a developer to take control over every aspect of a new site such as its branding, its initial set of lists, and which features it uses. Chapter 9, "Solutions and Deployment," is dedicated to working with site definitions.

Programming Against the WSS Object Model

Another important aspect of WSS development is programming against the WSS object model. The core types provided by the WSS programming model are exposed through a standard WSS assembly named Microsoft.SharePoint.dll.

Let's look at a simple example. Imagine you have just created a console application, and you have added a reference to Microsoft.SharePoint.dll. The WSS object model exposes an SPSite class that serves as an entry point into the WSS object model at the site collection level. Each site within a site collection is represented as an SPWeb object. Each list within a site is represented as an SPList object. Here's a simple example using the WSS object model to access the top-level site within a target site collection and discover all its lists.

```
using Microsoft.SharePoint;

namespace Hello_WSS_OM {
  class Program {
    static void Main() {
      string sitePath = "http://litwareinc.com";
      // enter object model through site collection.
      SPSite siteCollection = new SPSite(sitePath);
      // obtain reference to top-level site.
      SPWeb site = siteCollection.RootWeb;
      // enumerate through lists of site
```

```
      foreach (SPList list in site.Lists) {
        Console.WriteLine(list.Title);
      }
      // clean up by calling Dispose.
      site.Dispose();
      siteCollection.Dispose();
    }
  }
}
```

You should observe the two calls to the Dispose method at the end of this code example. Several object types in the WSS object model, such as SPSite and SPWeb, use unmanaged resources and must be disposed of in a timely manner. If you fail to do this and simply rely on the garbage collector of the .NET Framework to reclaim memory, your code can cause problems by consuming far more memory than it needs. As a rule of thumb, when you create a disposable object, you are also responsible for calling Dispose on it. However, object references obtained through the WSS Web application's SPContext should not be disposed.

Creating Your First Feature

There's no better way to end the first chapter than to dive in and create a simple Hello World feature from the ground up. This exercise will step you through the fundamental aspects of creating, deploying, and testing a feature. To make things more interesting, at the end of this exercise, we will also add event handlers that will fire whenever the feature is activated and deactivated. The code inside these event handlers will use the WSS object model to change some characteristics of the target site.

In this walk-through, we are going to use Microsoft Visual Studio 2005 to create a new development project for the feature. Using Visual Studio 2005 will provide color coding of XML and ASP.NET tags. Visual Studio 2005 will also provide the convenience of IntelliSense when working with the XML files required to define a feature.

Let's start off by creating a new Class Library DLL project named **HelloWorld**. We are going to create a C# project in our example, but you can create a Visual Basic .NET project instead if you prefer. Eventually, we will add code that will be compiled into the output DLL for the feature's event handlers. However, first we will get started by creating the feature.xml file.

Before creating the feature.xml file, consider that the files for this feature must be deployed in their own special directory inside the WSS system directory named FEATURES. The FEATURES directory is located inside another WSS system directory named TEMPLATE.

```
c:\Program Files\Common Files\Microsoft Shared\web server extensions\12\TEMPLATE\FEATURES
```

Given the requirements of feature deployment, it makes sense to create a parallel hierarchy of folders within a Visual Studio project used to develop a WSS feature. This will make it easier to copy the feature files to the correct location and test them as you do your development work.

Start by adding a folder named TEMPLATE to the root directory of the current project. Once you have created the TEMPLATE directory, create another directory inside that named FEATURES. Finally, create another directory inside the FEATURES directory using the same name as the name of the feature project. In this case the name of this directory is HelloWorld, as shown in Figure 1-12.

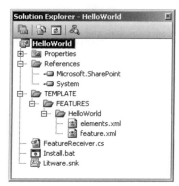

Figure 1-12   A Visual Studio project for developing a WSS feature

Next, create an XML file named feature.xml inside the HelloWorld directory. This is where you will added the XML-based information that defines the high-level attributes of the feature itself. Add the following XML to the feature.xml file to add a top-level Feature element along with attributes that define the feature itself.

```
<Feature
  Id="B2CB42E2-4F0A-4380-AABA-1EF9CD526F20"
  Title="Hello World Feature"
  Description="This is my very first custom feature"
  Scope="Web"
  Hidden="FALSE"
  ImageUrl="menuprofile.gif"
  xmlns="http://schemas.microsoft.com/sharepoint/">

  <ElementManifests>
    <ElementManifest Location="elements.xml" />
  </ElementManifests>

</Feature>
```

You see that a feature is defined using a Feature element containing attributes such as Id, Title, Description, Version, Scope, Hidden and ImageUrl. You must create a new GUID for the Id attribute so that your feature can be uniquely identified. You create the feature's Title and Description attributes using user-friendly text. These attributes will be shown directly to the users on the WSS administrative pages used to activate and deactivate features.

The Scope defines the context in which the feature can be activated and deactivated. The feature we are creating has a scope equal to Web, which means it can be activated and deactivated within the context of the site. If you assign a Scope value of Site, your feature will then be activated and deactivated within the scope of a site collection. The two other possible scopes for defining a feature are WebApplication scope and Farm scope.

As you can see, the Hidden attribute has a value of FALSE. This means that, once installed within the farm, our feature can be seen by users who might want to activate it. You can also create a feature where the Hidden attribute has a value of TRUE. This has the effect of hiding the feature in the list of available features shown to users. Hidden features must be activated from the command line, through custom code, or through an activation dependency with another feature. Activation dependencies will be discussed in more detail later in Chapter 9.

You will also notice that the ImageUrl attribute has a value that points to one of the graphic images that is part of the basic WSS installation. This image will be shown next to the feature in the user interface.

The last part of the feature.xml file shown previously is the ElementManifests element. This element contains inner ElementManifest elements that reference other XML files where you will define the elements that make up the feature. In our case, there is a single ElementManifest element that uses the location attribute to point to a file named element.xml.

Enabling IntelliSense in Visual Studio

Inside the TEMPLATE directory there is a directory named XML that contains several XML schemas, including one named wss.xsd. If you associate this schema file with feature files such as feature.xml and elements.xml, Visual Studio will provide IntelliSense, which makes it much easier to author a custom feature. You may also copy these XSD files into C:\Program Files\Microsoft Visual Studio 8\Xml\Schemas\.

Now it's time to create the element.xml file and define a single CustomAction element that will be used to add a simple menu command to the Site Actions menu. Add the following XML, which defines a CustomAction element to elements.xml.

```
<Elements xmlns="http://schemas.microsoft.com/sharepoint/">
  <CustomAction
    Id="SiteActionsToolbar"
    GroupId="SiteActions"
    Location="Microsoft.SharePoint.StandardMenu"
    Sequence="100"
    Title="Hello World"
    Description="A custom menu item added using a feature"
    ImageUrl="_layouts/images/menuprofile.gif" >
      <UrlAction Url="http://msdn.microsoft.com"/>

  </CustomAction>
</Elements>
```

This CustomActions element has been designed to add a menu command to the Site Actions menu. It provides a user-friendly Title and Description as well as a URL that will be used to redirect the user when the Menu command is selected. While this example of a feature with a single element does not go very far into what can be done with features, it provides us with a simple starting point for going through the steps of installing and testing a feature.

Now that we have created the feature.xml file and the elements.xml file to define the HelloWorld feature, there are three steps involved in installing it for testing purposes. First, you must copy the HelloWorld feature directory to the WSS system FEATURES directory. Second, you must run a STSADM.EXE operation to install the feature with WSS. Finally, you must activate the feature inside the context of a WSS site. You can automate the first two steps by creating a batch file named install.bat at the root directory of the HelloWorld project and adding the following command line instructions.

```
REM - Remember to remove line breaks from first two lines
@SET TEMPLATEDIR="c:\program files\common files\microsoft shared\
                web server extensions\12\Template"
@SET STSADM="c:\program files\common files\microsoft shared\
            web server extensions\12\bin\stsadm"


Echo Copying files
xcopy /e /y TEMPLATE\* %TEMPLATEDIR%

Echo Installing feature
%STSADM% -o InstallFeature -filename  HelloWorld\feature.xml -force

Echo Restart IIS Worker Process
IISRESET
```

Actually, you can also automate the final step of activating the feature within a specific site by running the ActivateFeature operation with the STSADM utility. However, we have avoided this in our example because we want you to go through the process of explicitly activating the feature as users will do through the WSS user interface.

Once you have added the install.bat file, you can configure Visual Studio to run it each time you rebuild the HelloWorld project by going to the Build Events tab within the Project Properties and adding the following post-build event command line instructions.

```
cd $(ProjectDir)
Install.bat
```

The first line with *cd $(ProjectDir)* is required to change the current directory to that of the project directory. The second line runs the batch file to copy the feature files to the correct location and install the feature with the InstallFeature operation of the command-line STSADM.EXE utility.

Once the feature has been properly installed, you should be able to activate it within the context of a site. Within the top-level site of the site collection you created earlier this chapter, navigate to the Site Settings page. In the Site Administration section, click the link with the title Site Features. This should take you to a page like the one shown in Figure 1-13. Note that if you are working within a farm that has MOSS installed, you will see many more features than if you are working within a farm with just WSS.

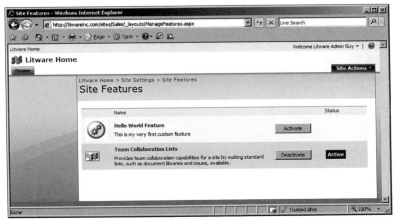

Figure 1-13 Once a feature is installed, it can be activated and deactivated by users.

You should be able to locate the HelloWorld feature on the Site Features page. You can then go through the act of clicking the button to activate the feature. Once you have done this, you should be able to drop down the Site Actions menu and see the custom menu item, as shown in Figure 1-14. If you select this custom menu item, you will be redirected to the URL that was defined by the Url attribute of the UrlAction element within the elements.xml file.

Figure 1-14 A CustomAction element can be used to add custom menu commands to the site actions menu.

After you have successfully activated the feature and tested the custom menu command, you should also experiment by returning to the Site Features page and deactivating the feature. Once you have deactivated the HelloWorld feature, you should be able to verify that the custom menu has been removed from the Site Actions menu.

You have now witnessed the fundamental principle behind features. Developers create various types of site elements that can be added or removed from a site through the process of activation and deactivation.

Adding an Event Handler to a Feature

Now it's time to take the example of the HelloWorld feature a little further by adding event handlers and programming against the WSS object model. First, start by adding a project reference to Microsoft.SharePoint.dll. Next, locate the source file named Class1.cs and rename it to FeatureReceiver.cs. Next, add the following code.

```
using System;
using Microsoft.SharePoint;

namespace HelloWorld{
  public class FeatureReceiver : SPFeatureReceiver {
    public override void FeatureInstalled(
                          SPFeatureReceiverProperties properties){}
    public override void FeatureUninstalling(
                          SPFeatureReceiverProperties properties) { }

    public override void FeatureActivated(
                          SPFeatureReceiverProperties properties){
      SPWeb site = (SPWeb)properties.Feature.Parent;
      // track original site Title using SPWeb property bag
      site.Properties["OriginalTitle"] = site.Title;
      site.Properties.Update();
      // update site title
      site.Title = "Hello World";
      site.Update();
    }

    public override void FeatureDeactivating(
                          SPFeatureReceiverProperties properties) {
      // reset site Title back to its original value
      SPWeb site = (SPWeb)properties.Feature.Parent;
      site.Title = site.Properties["OriginalTitle"];
      site.Update();
    }
  }
}
```

The first thing you should notice is how you create an event handler that fires when a feature is activated or deactivated. You do this by creating a class that inherits from the SPFeatureReceiver class. As you can see, you handle events by overriding virtual methods in the base class such as FeatureActivated and FeatureDeactivating. There are also two other event handlers that fire when a feature is installed or uninstalled, but we are not going to use them in this introductory example.

The FeatureActivated method has been written to update the title of the current site using the WSS object model. Note the technique used to obtain a reference to the current site–the properties parameter is used to acquire a reference to an SPWeb object. The properties parameter is based on the SPFeatureReceiverProperties class that exposes a Feature property that, in turn, exposes a Parent property that holds a reference to the current site. The site title is changed by assigning a new value to the Title property of the SPWeb object and then calling the Update method.

Also note that this feature has been designed to store the original value of the site Title so that it can be restored whenever the feature is deactivated. This is accomplished by using a persistent property bag scoped to the site that is accessible through an SPWeb object's Properties collection. Note that many of the objects in the WSS object model have a similar Properties property, which can be used to track name-value pairs using a persistent property bag. WSS handles persisting these named value pairs to the content database and retrieving them on demand.

Now that we have written the code for the feature's two event handlers, it's time to think about what's required to deploy the HelloWorld.dll assembly. The first thing to consider is that this assembly DLL must be deployed in the Global Assembly Cache (GAC), which means you must add a key file to the project in order to sign the resulting output DLL during compilation with a strong name.

Once you have added the key file and configured the HelloWorld project to build Hello-World.dll with a strong name, you can also add another instruction line to the post-event build command line to install (or overwrite) the assembly in the GAC each time you build the current project. The command line instructions for the post-event build should now look like this:

```
"%programfiles%\Microsoft Visual Studio 8\SDK\v2.0\Bin\gacutil.exe" -if $(TargetPath)
cd $(ProjectDir)
Install.bat
```

The next step is to update the feature.xml file with two new attributes so that WSS knows that there are event handlers that should be fired whenever the feature is activated or deactivated. This can be accomplished by adding the ReceiverAssembly attribute and the ReceiverClass attribute, as shown here.

```
<Feature
  Id="B2CB42E2-4F0A-4380-AABA-1EF9CD526F20"
  Title="Hello World Feature"
  Description="This is my very first custom feature"
  Version="1.0.0.0"
  Scope="Web"
  Hidden="FALSE"
  ImageUrl="menuprofile.gif"
  ReceiverAssembly="HelloWorld, Version=1.0.0.0, Culture=neutral,
                    PublicKeyToken=b59ad8f489c4a334"
  ReceiverClass="HelloWorld.FeatureReciever"
  xmlns="http://schemas.microsoft.com/sharepoint/">

  <ElementManifests>
    <ElementManifest Location="elements.xml" />
  </ElementManifests>

</Feature>
```

The ReceiverAssembly attribute should contain the four-part name of an assembly that has already been installed in the GAC. The ReceiverClass attribute should contain the namespace-qualified name of a public class within the receiver assembly that inherits SPFeatureReceiver.

Once you have made these changes to the feature.xml file, you should be able to test your work. When you rebuild the HelloWorld project, Visual Studio should run the install.bat file to copy the updated version of the feature.xml file to the WSS FEATURES directory and to install the updated version of feature.xml with WSS. The build process should also compile Hello-World.dll with a strong name and install it in the GAC. Note that you will likely be required to run an IISRESET command to restart the IIS worker process. This is due to the fact that features and assemblies loaded from the GAC are cached by WSS within the IIS worker process.

At this point, you should be able to test your work by activating and deactivating the feature within the context of a WSS site. When you activate the site, it should change the Title of the site to "Hello World." When you deactivate the feature, it should restore the Title of the site to the original value.

If you have successfully completed these steps, you are well on your way to becoming an accomplished WSS developer. That's because creating features and programming against the WSS object model are the two most basic skills you need to acquire.

Summary

WSS represents different things to different types of people. To users, WSS provides the foundation for Web-based business solutions that scale from simple team collaboration sites to enterprise-level applications. To site collection administrators, WSS provides the instant gratification of being able to customize sites by adding lists and document libraries and by customizing many aspects of a site's appearance through the browser or by using a customization tool such as the SharePoint Designer.

To a company's IT department, WSS provides a scalable and cost-effective solution for provisioning and managing a large number of sites in a Web farm environment. It also provides a reliable mechanism to roll out applications and to version them over time.

To a developer, WSS represents a rich development platform that adds a tremendous amount of value on top of the underlying ASP.NET platform. Developers build WSS-based software solutions using features, site definitions, and components such as Web Parts, event handlers, workflows, and custom policies. There is enough to the WSS development story that it will take us the rest of this book to describe how it all fits together.

Chapter 2
SharePoint Architecture

- Review important concepts and terms for IIS and ASP.NET.
- Understand how Windows SharePoint Services (WSS) extends the ASP.NET routing infrastructure.
- Understand the difference between site pages and application pages.
- Learn to create custom application pages.

IIS and ASP.NET 2.0 Primer

This chapter examines the core architectural details of how WSS integrates with Microsoft Internet Information Services (IIS) and ASP.NET. We'll start by reviewing some of the fundamental concepts and terms used with IIS and ASP.NET. We'll then describe how the WSS team designed and implemented WSS 3.0 to sit on top of IIS and extend the ASP.NET Framework.

The primary goal of this chapter is for you to understand the internal workings of a Web application and how it initializes the WSS runtime environment. As you will see, the WSS team has extended ASP.NET by replacing many of the standard components with their own.

At the end of this chapter, we will introduce application pages and discuss why they become a fundamental aspect of WSS architecture. We will also walk you through the process of creating your own application pages for a custom solution and writing code behind them that accesses the WSS object model.

IIS Web Sites and Virtual Directories

Both ASP.NET and WSS rely on IIS 6.0 to supply the underlying listening mechanism to process incoming HTTP requests and supply a management infrastructure for launching and running worker processes on the Web server. Your understanding of how all of the pieces fit together should start with the basic concepts of an IIS Web site and virtual directories.

An *IIS Web site* provides an entry point into the IIS Web server infrastructure. Each IIS Web site is configured to listen for and process incoming HTTP requests that meet certain criteria. For example, an IIS Web site can be configured to handle requests coming in over a specific IP address or port number or can be routed to the Web server by using a specific host header, such as *http://Extranet.Litwareinc.com*.

IIS automatically creates and configures an IIS Web site named Default Web Site that listens for HTTP requests coming in over port 80 on any of the IP addresses supported on the local Web server. It is also possible to create and configure additional IIS Web sites by using the IIS Administration tool.

Each IIS Web site defines a specific *URL space*. For example, the standard Default Web Site defines a URL space to handle any incoming request whose URL maps to the following pattern: *http://www.Litwareinc.com/**. As you can imagine, an unlimited number of URLs can be created within this URL space. IIS processes incoming requests targeted to one of these URLs by routing them to the Default Web Site.

Each IIS Web site is configured to map to a *root directory*, which is a physical directory on the file system of the hosting Web server. For example, standard configuration for IIS maps the Default Web Site to a root directory located at C:\Inetpub\wwwroot. In the most straightforward routing scenarios, IIS maps incoming HTTP requests to physical files inside the root directory. For example, IIS will respond to a request for *http://www.Litwareinc.com/page1.htm* by simply loading the contents of the file located at c:\Inetpub\wwwroot\page1.htm into memory and streaming it back to the client.

One important aspect of an IIS Web site is that it controls whether incoming requests require authentication and, if so, which authentication protocols to use. For example, the Default Web Site might be intended as a public-facing Web site for Internet users. As such, it might be configured to allow anonymous access and to support Basic Authentication. A secondary IIS Web site intended exclusively for employee use within the corporate LAN might be configured to disallow anonymous access and to support Integrated Windows Authentication instead of Basic Authentication.

In addition to IIS Web sites, IIS supports the creation and configuration of virtual directories. A *virtual directory* is an entity that defines a child URL space nested within the URL space of its parent IIS Web site. Like an IIS Web site, a virtual directory is configured with a root directory on the file system of the hosting Web server. IIS provides the flexibility of defining the root directory for a virtual directory at any location. For example, you could create a virtual directory within the Default Web Site with a URL space such as *http://www.Litwareinc.com/Sales*. When you create this virtual directory, you can configure its root directory as a file system directory such as C:\WebApps\Site1.

IIS provides an administration utility named Internet Information Services (IIS) Manager", shown in Figure 2-1. This utility allows you to inspect, create, and configure IIS Web sites and virtual directories on the current machine. It can be started by using the shortcut Start | Administrative Tools | Internet Information Services (IIS) Manager. If you are not already familiar with this utility, you can launch it to learn how it is used to inspect and configure the properties of IIS Web sites and virtual directories.

Note that IIS tracks configuration information about its IIS Web sites and virtual directories in a repository known as the *IIS metabase*. The IIS metabase lives on the file system of each front-end Web server running IIS. For example, when you create and configure an IIS Web site using the IIS administration utility, IIS tracks these changes by writing entries to the local IIS metabase.

Figure 2-1   IIS provides an administration utility to inspect and configure IIS Web sites and virtual directories.

Instead of using the IIS administration utility, you can also automate the process of creating and configuring IIS Web sites and virtual directories by writing scripts or by writing managed code that programs against the IIS object model. This process is commonly done in Web farm environments when rolling out new Web sites because the identical IIS metabase setting must be applied across each front-end Web server in the farm.

ISAPI Extensions and ISAPI Filters

In the most straightforward routing scenarios, IIS simply maps an incoming request to a physical file within the root directory of an IIS Web site or virtual directory. However, IIS also supports the Internet Server Application Programming Interface (ISAPI) programming model, which provides the opportunity for more sophisticated routing scenarios. In particular, the *ISAPI programming model* allows you to configure an IIS Web site or virtual directory so that incoming requests trigger the execution of custom code on the Web server.

The ISAPI programming model was introduced with the original version of IIS and continues to provide the lowest level for creating custom components for IIS. The ISAPI programming model consists of two primary component types: ISAPI extensions and ISAPI filters.

An *ISAPI extension* is a component DLL that plays the role of an endpoint for an incoming request. The fundamental concept is that IIS can map incoming requests to a set of endpoints that trigger the execution of code within an ISAPI extension DLL. An ISAPI extension DLL must be installed on the Web server and configured at the level of either an IIS Web site or virtual directory. Configuration commonly involves associating specific file extensions with the ISAPI extensions by using an IIS *application map*.

While an ISAPI extension serves as an endpoint, an *ISAPI filter* plays the role of an interceptor. An ISAPI filter is installed and configured at the level of the IIS Web site. Once installed, an ISAPI filter intercepts all incoming requests targeting that IIS Web site. The fundamental concept is that an ISAPI filter can provide pre-processing and post-processing for each and every incoming request. ISAPI filters are typically created to provide low-level functionality for an IIS Web site, such as custom authentication and request logging.

Custom development of ISAPI components isn't very popular these days for several reasons. First, custom ISAPI components are difficult to design, develop, and debug because they must be written in unmanaged C++ and require complicated coding techniques for things such as thread synchronization. Most developers work a level above ISAPI and utilize frameworks such as ASP and ASP.NET. While it is likely that you will never be required to write an ISAPI component, it is still important that you understand how ISAPI components fit into the big picture.

Application Pools and the IIS Worker Process

IIS provides a flexible infrastructure for managing worker processes by using application pools. An *application pool* is a configurable entity that allows you to control how IIS maps IIS Web sites and virtual directories to instances of the IIS worker process. Note that instances of the IIS worker process are launched using an executable named w3wp.exe, as shown in Figure 2-2.

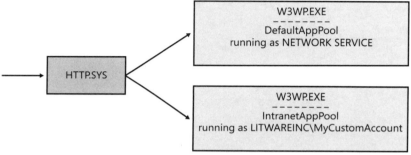

Figure 2-2   IIS uses a device driver named HTTP.SYS to route incoming requests to the proper application pool.

The routing architecture of IIS is controlled by a kernel-level device driver named http.sys. This device driver listens for incoming HTTP requests and uses information in the IIS metabase to route them to whatever instance of w3wp.exe is associated with the target application pool. If http.sys determines that the target application pool doesn't have a running instance of w3wp.exe, it launches a new instance on demand to process the request.

Each IIS Web site and virtual directory can be configured to run in its own isolated application pool. Conversely, you can configure many different IIS Web sites and virtual directories to run in the same application pool for greater efficiency. The key observation you should make is that a tradeoff exists between isolation and efficiency. To achieve greater isolation means you must run more instances of w3wp.exe, which compromises efficiency. To achieve greater efficiency means you must map multiple IIS Web sites and virtual directories to fewer instances of the IIS worker process, which compromises isolation.

Every application pool has an important setting known as the application pool identity. The *application pool identity* is configured with a specific Windows user account that is either a local account on the Web server or a domain account within an Active Directory directory service domain. When http.sys launches a new instance of w3wp.exe for a specific application pool, it uses the application pool identity to initialize a Windows security token that serves as the process token. This is important because it establishes the "runs as" identity for code that runs within the IIS worker process.

By default, IIS uses the identity of the local Network Service account when you create a new application pool. However, you can configure the application pool identity by using any other user account you like. When deploying Web sites based on ASP.NET and WSS, it is recommended that you configure the application pool identity with a domain account instead of the Network Service account. This is especially true in a Web farm environment when you need to synchronize the identity of an application pool across multiple front-end Web servers in the farm.

Restarting an Application Pool

When developing for ASP.NET and WSS, you will occasionally find it necessary to restart the application pool that you are using to test your code. This might be the case when you need to refresh an XML file within a feature definition you are developing, or you might need to reload a new version of an assembly DLL from the Global Assembly Cache. You can restart all of the processes associated with IIS by running the following command from the command line:

```
IISRESET
```

You can alternatively restart just the process associated with a specific application pool by running a VB Script macro named iisapp.vbs that has been a standard part of the IIS 6.0 installation since Windows Server 2003 Service Pack 1. You must run this script by using a scripting host, such as cscript.exe. When you call cscript.exe and then include the path to iisapp.vbs, you can restart a specific application pool by passing the /a parameter along with the name of the IIS application pool.

```
cscript.exe c:\windows\system32\iisapp.vbs /a "DefaultAppPool"
```

The main advantage of using this technique is that it is faster than a full IISRESET command, which restarts all processes associated with IIS. Using this command instead of an IISRESET command can save you a few seconds here and there.

ASP.NET 2.0 Framework

The ASP.NET Framework represents a significant productivity layer on top of IIS and the ISAPI programming model. If you are familiar with ASP.NET development, you know that it provides the convenience of writing your application logic in a managed language, such as C# or Visual Basic .NET, and working with all productivity-oriented visual designers provided by Microsoft Visual Studio. The ASP.NET Framework also provides many other valuable abstractions that assist developers in areas such as state management, data binding, navigation, and data caching.

The ASP.NET Framework is implemented as an ISAPI extension named aspnet_isapi.dll. The basic configuration for ASP.NET involves registering application maps for common ASP.NET file extensions including .aspx, .ascx, .ashx, and .asmx at the level of an IIS Web site or virtual directory. When IIS sees an incoming request targeting a file with one of these extensions, it forwards the request to aspnet_isapi.dll, which effectively passes control over to the ASP.NET Framework. The way in which the ASP.NET Framework processes a request largely depends on the extension of the target file.

The ASP.NET Framework executes the requests targeted for each IIS Web site and each virtual directory as its own independent ASP.NET application. Behind every ASP.NET application is a root directory containing a set of files. This architecture promotes a very simple x-copy style for deploying an ASP.NET application. You simply create a new virtual directory on the Web server computer and copy the ASP.NET application files into the root directory. Of course, this is a little more tedious in a Web farm environment because of the creation of a virtual directory, and the copying of the files must be duplicated over each front-end Web server in the farm.

Each ASP.NET application can be configured independently by adding a web.config file at its root directory. The *web.config* file is an XML-based file with configuration elements that control the behavior of various features of the ASP.NET Framework such as compilation, page rendering, and state management. A simple web.config file looks like this:

```
<configuration>

  <system.web>
    <customErrors mode="On" />
    <httpRuntime maxRequestLength="51200" />
    <authentication mode="Windows" />
    <identity impersonate="true" />
    <authorization>
      <allow users="*" />
    </authorization>
  </system.web>

</configuration>
```

It is important to note that the ASP.NET Framework runs each ASP.NET application with a certain level of isolation. This is true even in a scenario when you have configured multiple ASP.NET applications to run within the same IIS application pool. The ASP.NET Framework provides isolation between ASP.NET applications running inside the same instance of the IIS worker process by loading each of them into a separate .NET Framework AppDomain.

ASP.NET Pages

The *page* is one of the most valuable abstractions in the ASP.NET Framework. Developers building ASP.NET applications typically construct pages by dragging and dropping server controls onto a visual design surface in Visual Studio and modifying the properties of pages and controls by using standard property sheets. The ASP.NET Framework and Visual Studio also make it relatively simple to add logic to pages by writing managed code that executes in response to page-level and control-level events.

At a physical level, a page in an ASP.NET application is a file with an .aspx extension that resides on the Web server and is compiled into a DLL on demand by the ASP.NET runtime. Consider the following .aspx page definition that contains a server-side control and a simple event handler.

```
<%@ Page Language="C#" %>

<script runat="server">
  protected override void OnLoad(EventArgs e)  {
    lblDisplay.Text = "Hello, ASP.NET";
  }
</script>

<html>
<body>
  <form id="frmMain" runat="server">
    <asp:Label runat="server" ID="lblDisplay" />
  </form>
</body>
</html>
```

Behind the scenes, the ASP.NET Framework does quite a bit of work to compile an .aspx file into a DLL. First, it must parse the .aspx file to generate a C# (or Visual Basic .NET) source file containing a public class that inherits from the Page class that is defined within the System.Web.UI namespace inside the system.web.dll assembly. When the ASP.NET page parser generates this Page-derived class, it builds a control tree containing all of the server-side controls defined within the page file. The page parser also adds the required code to hook up any event handlers that are defined within the page.

Once the ASP.NET page parser builds the source file for an .aspx page, it can then compile it into a DLL. This compilation occurs automatically the first time the .aspx file is requested. Once the ASP.NET runtime has compiled an .aspx file into a DLL, that copy of the DLL can be used for all subsequent requests that target the same .aspx file. However, the ASP.NET runtime monitors the datetime stamp on the .aspx file and retriggers the compilation process to rebuild the DLL if it sees that the associated .aspx file has been updated.

One reason the ASP.NET Framework is so popular has to do with the convenience of server-side controls. It's very easy to compose pages using out-of-the-box controls that ship with the ASP.NET Framework such as the validation controls, the calendar control, and controls that support data binding, such as the GridView control and the Repeater controls. Furthermore, it's relatively simple for a developer to author custom controls and use them on pages.

Master Pages

ASP.NET 2.0 introduced master pages, which provide a very effective approach to page templating. In particular, a *master page* defines common elements that are to be used across many different pages (such as the top banner) as well as site navigation controls. The layout defined in a master page can then be used across many different pages that link to it. In ASP.NET terminology, a page that links to a master page is known as a *content page*. The basic relationship between a master page and its associated content pages is shown in Figure 2-3.

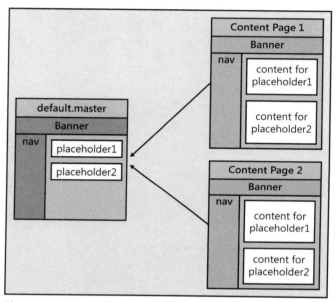

Figure 2-3   A master page defines a common layout and named placeholders that can be replaced within the content pages that link to the master page.

For example, assume that you want to create a master page that defines the HTML layout with a banner at the top of the page. You start by creating a file with a .master extension, such as default.master. Next, you add the @*Master* directive at the top of the page. Below that, you define the HTML layout of the page and add in named placeholders, such as the following example.

```
<%@ Master %>
<html>
<body>
  <form id="frmMain" runat="server">
    <table width="100%">
      <tr>
        <td> <!-- Display Litware Banner -->
          <h1>Litware Inc.</h1><hr />
        </td>
      </tr>
```

```
      <tr>
        <td> <!-- Display Main Body of Page -->
          <asp:contentplaceholder id="PlaceHolderMain" runat="server" />
        </td>
      </tr>
    </table>
  </form>
</body>
</html>
```

When you want to create a content page, you create an .aspx file and add an *@Page* directive that contains a MasterPageFile attribute. Once you decide which of the named placeholders from the master page you would like to replace, you then define Content elements for each one. The following is a simple example of a content page that links to the default.master page shown in the preceding code and replaces the content in the placeholder named PlaceHolderMain.

```
<%@ Page Language="C#" MasterPageFile="~/default.master" %>

<script runat="server">
  protected override void OnLoad(EventArgs e)  {
    lblDisplay.Text = "Hello World";
  }
</script>

<asp:Content ID="main" Runat="Server"
             ContentPlaceHolderID="PlaceHolderMain" >
  <asp:Label ID="lblDisplay" runat="server" />
</asp:Content>
```

Note that when you create a content page that links to a master page, any HTML you would like to add must be written inside a Content element that points to a specific named placeholder. The page will not compile if you try to add HTML or server-side controls outside of a Content element. However, as you can see from the previous example, you can add a script block outside of a Content element and add whatever code you like.

When a master page defines a named placeholder, you are not required to replace it within a content page. Therefore, a master page can create a placeholder with default content inside. Any content page that links to that master page and does not include that named placeholder will get the default content. Another content page that links to the same master page and does include that named placeholder will override the default content, replacing it with its own custom content.

Finally, note that whoever creates a master page decides what the named placeholders will be and which contain default content. This is important when it comes to designing pages for a WSS site because you will be creating content pages that link to master pages created by the WSS team. In this case, you must learn what placeholders the WSS team has defined and what types of content are replaceable.

HTTP Request Pipeline

Underneath the productivity-centered architecture for pages and server-side controls, the ASP.NET Framework exposes the *HTTP Request Pipeline* for developers who like to work at a lower level. It provides the developer with a degree of control comparable with the ISAPI programming model. However, when you create a component for the HTTP Request Pipeline, you are able to write your code in a managed language such as C# or Visual Basic .NET. You can also use APIs provided by the ASP.NET Framework, which is much easier than using the ISAPI programming model.

Figure 2-4 displays a picture of the HTTP Request Pipeline and its three replaceable component types: HttpHandler, HttpApplication, and HttpModule. As requests come in, they are queued up and assigned to a worker thread that then processes the request by interacting with each of these component types.

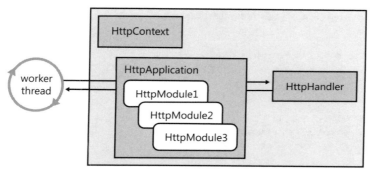

Figure 2-4   The HTTP Request Pipeline allows developers to replace components such as HttpHandler, HttpApplication, and HttpModule.

The ultimate destination of any request is the endpoint, which is modeled in the HTTP Request Pipeline by using an HttpHandler class, which implements the IHttpHandler interface. As a developer, you can create a custom HttpHandler component and plug it into the HTTP Request Pipeline by adding configuration elements to the web.config file.

The HTTP Request Pipeline places an HttpApplication component in front of the HttpHandler. On an application-wide basis, incoming requests are always routed through the HttpApplication before they reach the target HttpHandler, thus giving the HttpApplication the ability to preprocess any request no matter which HttpHandler it is being routed to. This preprocessing stage is handled through a series of events that are defined inside the HttpApplication class such as BeginRequest, AuthenticateRequest, and AuthorizeRequest.

In situations when you don't want to use a custom HttpApplication component, the ASP.NET Framework initializes the HTTP Request Pipeline with a standard HttpApplication object that provides default behavior. However, you can replace this standard component by creating a file named global.asax and placing it in the root directory of the hosting ASP.NET application. For example, you can create a global.asax that looks like the following:

```
<%@ Application Language="C#" %>

<script runat="server">

  protected void Application_AuthenticateRequest(object sender, EventArgs e) {
    // your code goes here for request authentication
  }


  protected void Application_AuthorizeRequest(object sender, EventArgs e)  {
    // your code goes here for request authorization
  }

</script>
```

The third replaceable component type in the HTTP Request Pipeline is the HttpModule. The HttpModule is similar to the HttpApplication component in that it is designed to handle events defined by the HttpApplication class and is processed before control is passed to any HttpHandler classes. For example, you can create a custom HttpModule component to handle request-level events such as BeginRequest, AuthenticateRequest, and AuthorizeRequest. As with the HttpHandler, an HttpModule class is defined with an interface. You can create a class that implements the IHttpModule interface and plug it into the HTTP Request Pipeline by adding configuration elements to the web.config file.

Whereas custom HttpApplication components can be defined as simple text files with an .asax extension, custom HttpModule components are always compiled as classes within assembly DLLs. To add a custom HttpModule component into the HTTP Request Pipeline, you then add entries into a web.config file.

While an HttpApplication component and an HttpModule component are similar in what they do, the HttpModule contains a few noteworthy differences. First, you are not limited to one HttpModule per application as you are with the HttpApplication components. The web.config file for an ASP.NET application can add in several different HttpModule components. Second, HttpModule components can be configured at the machine level. In fact, the ASP.NET Framework ships with several different HttpModule components that are automatically configured at the machine level to provide ASP.NET functionality for things such as Windows authentication, Forms authentication, and output caching.

The final component that we want to discuss with respect to the HTTP Request Pipeline is HttpContext. As ASP.NET initializes a request to send to the HTTP Request Pipeline, it creates an object from the HttpContext class and initializes it with important contextual information.

From a timing perspective, it's important to see that ASP.NET creates this object before any custom code inside the HTTP Request Pipeline has a chance to begin execution. This means that you can always program against the HttpContext object and the child objects that it contains, such as Request, User, and Response. Whenever you are authoring a component that is to execute within the HTTP Request Pipeline, you can write code that looks like the following:

```
HttpContext currentContext = HttpContext.Current;
string incomingUrl = currentContext.Request.Url;
string currentUser = currentContext.User.Identity.Name;
currentContext.Response.Write("Hello world");
```

Further Reading About ASP.NET

We encourage you to learn as much as you can about ASP.NET 2.0 because it will make you a stronger WSS 3.0 developer. Many advanced ASP.NET techniques are readily available when you are creating solutions for WSS 3.0. The following list presents a few of our favorite titles.

- *Programming ASP.NET 2.0: Core Reference,* by Dino Esposito (Microsoft Press, 2006)

- *Programming ASP.NET 2.0 Applications: Advanced Topics,* by Dino Esposito (Microsoft Press, 2006)

- *Essential ASP.NET 2.0, 2nd Edition,* by Fritz Onion and Keith Brown (Addison-Wesley Professional, 2007)

WSS Integration with ASP.NET

As you build your understanding of how WSS integrates with ASP.NET, you should begin by thinking through the high-level WSS design goals that were created to add value on top of the ASP.NET Framework. WSS adds significant value on top of ASP.NET in environments that require sites to be continuously created, updated, and deleted. WSS also adds a dimension of site element provisioning on top of ASP.NET that allows site administrators to quickly create pages, lists, and document libraries within the context of a site.

WSS integrates with ASP.NET at the level of the IIS Web site. Each IIS Web site in which you intend to host WSS sites must go through a one-time transformation process in which it is configured to become what WSS terminology refers to as a *Web application*. This transformation process involves adding IIS metabase entries and a WSS-specific web.config file to the root directory of the hosting IIS Web site. Once the transformation is completed, WSS extends the routing architecture of IIS and ASP.NET to properly route all incoming requests through the WSS runtime.

The next section of this chapter discusses the nuts and bolts of how a Web application is configured. However, before you dive into these details, we want you to make an important observation. In particular, we want you to consider how the Web application as a whole fits into the bigger picture of WSS architecture from the perspective of manageability and scalability.

The creation of a WSS Web application is a significant administration task that requires farm-level administrative privileges. Creating a Web application requires a significant number of changes to the file system and the IIS metabase on each front-end Web server. In a Web farm environment, these changes are automatically mirrored across each front-end Web server in the farm by the WSS runtime. This step of creating a Web application is only required when initially installing and configuring WSS.

Once a Web application is created, it is no longer necessary to touch the file system or IIS metabase of the front-end Web server when creating, updating, and deleting sites or site collections. The WSS architecture makes it possible to provision new sites and site collections simply by adding entries to the configuration database and a content database. It is this aspect of the WSS architecture that gives it significant management and provisioning advantages over ASP.NET. This added level of manageability is even more pronounced in a Web farm environment.

Web Applications

Two primary ways exist to create a Web application by using either the WSS Central Administration Application or the stsadm.exe command-line utility. First, you can create a Web application by converting an existing IIS Web site. Alternatively, you can create a new Web application from scratch and let WSS create the new IIS Web site for you behind the scenes. In either case, WSS configures the resulting IIS Web site by adding an IIS application map and creating several virtual directories. WSS also copies a global.asax file and web.config file to the root directory of the hosting IIS Web site.

WSS must add an IIS application map to each Web application to ensure that each and every incoming request is initially routed to the ASP.NET runtime. Remember that the default configuration for ASP.NET only registers application maps for requests with well-known ASP.NET file extensions such as .aspx, ascx, .ashx, and .asmx. Therefore, WSS configures the hosting IIS Web site with a wildcard application map to route all incoming requests to aspnet_isapi.dll, including those requests with non-ASP.NET extensions such as .doc, .docx, and .pdf.

Because every request targeting a Web application is routed through aspnet_isapi.dll, the request gets fully initialized with ASP.NET context. Furthermore, its processing behavior can be controlled by using a custom HttpApplication object and adding configuration elements to the web.config file. The WSS team uses standard ASP.NET techniques to extend the HTTP Request Pipeline by using several custom components, as shown in Figure 2-5.

First, you can see that WSS configures each Web application with a custom HttpApplication object by using the SPHttpApplication class. Note that this class is deployed in the WSS system assembly Microsoft.SharePoint.dll. WSS integrates this custom application class by creating a custom global.asax file at the root of the Web application that inherits from SPHttpApplication.

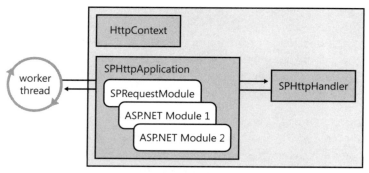

Figure 2-5 WSS extends the standard ASP.NET HTTP Request Pipeline with its own custom components.

```
<@Application Inherits="Microsoft.SharePoint.ApplicationRuntime.SPHttpApplication" >
```

In addition to including a custom HttpApplication object, the WSS architecture uses a custom HttpHandler and a custom HttpModule. These two WSS-specific components are integrated into the HTTP Request Pipeline for a Web application using standard entries in the web.config file. Examine the following XML fragment that is taken from the standard web.config file used by a WSS 3.0 Web application.

```
<configuration>
  <system.web>

    <httpHandlers>
      <remove verb="GET,HEAD,POST" path="*" />
      <add verb="GET,HEAD,POST" path="*"
          type="Microsoft.SharePoint.ApplicationRuntime.SPHttpHandler, ..." />
    </httpHandlers>

    <httpModules>
      <clear />
      <add name="SPRequest"
          type="Microsoft.SharePoint.ApplicationRuntime.SPRequestModule, ..." />
      <!-- other standard ASP.NET httpModules added back in -->
    </httpModules>

  </system.web>
</configuration>
```

The WSS team members have created their own HttpModule named SPRequestModule to initialize various aspects of the WSS runtime environment. You can see that the standard WSS web.config file configures SPRequestModule so that it is the first HttpModule to respond to application-level events in the HTTP Request Pipeline of ASP.NET. If you examine the web.config file for a WSS Web application, you will see that WSS adds back in several of the standard HttpModule components from the ASP.NET Framework that deal with things such as output caching and various types of authentication.

The standard WSS web.config file also registers an HttpHandler named SPHttpHandler and configures it with a path of "*". This allows WSS to provide the SPHttpHandler class as a single endpoint for all incoming requests.

As you can see, the architecture of WSS is made possible through extending the HTTP Request Pipeline. This allows WSS to fully leverage the underlying capabilities of the ASP.NET Framework while also taking over control of each and every request that targets a Web application.

Standard web.config File for a Web Application

In the previous section of this chapter, you saw that the web.config file for a Web application contains standard ASP.NET configuration elements. However, WSS goes further by extending the standard ASP.NET web.config file format with a custom SharePoint section. Examine the following XML fragment that shows the SharePoint section of the web.config file and the elements within the configSections element that are required by ASP.NET for extended configuration information.

```xml
<configuration>

  <configSections>
    <sectionGroup name="SharePoint">
      <section name="SafeControls" type="..." />
      <section name="RuntimeFilter" type="..." />
      <section name="WebPartLimits" type="..." />
      <section name="WebPartCache" type="..." />
      <section name="WebPartWorkItem" type="..." />
      <section name="WebPartControls" type="..." />
      <section name="SafeMode" type="..." />
      <section name="MergedActions" type="..." />
      <section name="PeoplePickerWildcards" type="..." />
    </sectionGroup>
  </configSections>

  <SharePoint>
    <SafeMode />
    <WebPartLimits />
    <WebPartCache />
    <WebPartControls />
    <SafeControls />
    <PeoplePickerWildcards />
    <MergedActions />
    <BlobCache  />
    <RuntimeFilter />
  </SharePoint>
</configuration>
```

The configuration elements that are nested within the SharePoint section are read by various components of the WSS runtime. For each element nested within the SharePoint section, there is a section element inside the configSections element that defines what configuration class is used to read this information at run time. This makes it possible for various components of the WSS runtime to read this WSS-specific configuration information while processing a request. You will see several development techniques throughout this book that require adding or changing elements within the SharePoint section of the web.config file.

SPVirtualPathProvider

One of the strengths of WSS over ASP.NET is its ability to provision and customize pages within a site without having to make any changes to the local file system of the front-end Web server. This capability of WSS to provision and customize pages is made possible by storing customized versions of .aspx files and .master files inside the content database and retrieving them on demand when they are needed to process an incoming page request.

Consider a simple example of how page customization works in WSS. Imagine that you would like to modify the HTML layout of the home page (default.aspx) for a particular site by using the Microsoft Office SharePoint Designer. When you modify and save a page using SharePoint Designer, WSS writes the entire contents of this customized page definition to the content database. After that point, when the same page is requested, WSS must retrieve the contents of this customized page definition from the content database and pass it along to the ASP.NET runtime for parsing. We will now explain the architectural details that make this possible.

ASP.NET 2.0 introduced a new pluggable component type known as a virtual path provider. The idea behind a *virtual path provider* is that it abstracts the details of where page files are stored away from the ASP.NET runtime. By creating a custom virtual path provider, a developer can write a custom component that retrieves ASP.NET file types, such as .aspx and .master files, from a remote location, such as a Microsoft SQL Server database. Once a virtual path provider retrieves the contents of an .aspx page, it can pass it along to the ASP.NET runtime for parsing.

The WSS team created a virtual path provider named SPVirtualPathProvider that is integrated into every Web application. The SPVirtualPathProvider class is integrated into the ASP.NET request handling infrastructure by the SPRequestModule. More specifically, the SPRequestModule component contains code to register the SPVirtualPathProvider class with the ASP.NET Framework as it does its work to initialize a Web application. Figure 2-6 displays a diagram that depicts the role of the SPVirtualPathProvider.

As you can see, the SPVirtualPathProvider is able to retrieve an ASP.NET page file from the content database, such as default.aspx, and then pass it along to the ASP.NET page parser. The SPVirtualPathProvider class works together with another class named the SPPageParserFilter to supply processing instructions to the ASP.NET page parser. For example, the SPPageParserFilter component controls whether the ASP.NET page parser compiles the ASP.NET page into an assembly DLL or whether it processes the page in a no-compile mode that is introduced with ASP.NET 2.0. In the next chapter, you will see how to add an entry into the web.config file that tells the SPPageParserFilter how to process pages.

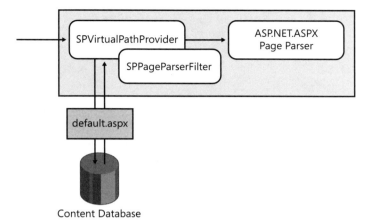

Content Database

Figure 2-6   WSS employs a custom virtual path provider to employ the .aspx page parser supplied by ASP.NET 2.0.

The SPVirtualPathProvider component plays a critical role in the overall WSS architecture. As you can see, it provides the foundation for supporting page customization. It also supports an important optimization known as *page ghosting,* which is a key factor in allowing a WSS farm to scale out to tens of thousands of pages across all the sites within a farm. Let me provide a quick example to illustrate how page ghosting works.

Imagine that you have just created 100 new WSS sites from the Blank Site template. If none of these sites requires a customized version of its home page (default.aspx), would it still make sense to copy the exact same page definition file into the content database 100 times? The answer to this question is obviously no. Fortunately, pages within a WSS site such as default.aspx are based on *page templates* that live on the file system of the front-end Web server. Page templates are used to provision *page instances* within the context of a site, such as the page that is accessible through a specific URL like *http://litwareinc.com/default.aspx.*

When a page instance is initially provisioned from a page template, WSS doesn't need to store a copy of it in the content database because WSS can load the page template from the file system of the Web server and use it to process any request for an uncustomized page instance. Therefore, you can say that page ghosting describes the act of processing a request for an uncustomized page instance by using a page template loaded into memory from the file system of the front-end Web server.

Page ghosting is valuable because it eliminates the need to transfer the contents of a page definition file from the SQL Server computer with the content database to the front-end Web server computer. Page ghosting also makes it possible to process the home pages for thousands of different sites by using a single page template that is compiled into an assembly DLL and loaded into memory in the IIS worker process just once per Web application. Both of these optimizations are key factors in the scalability of WSS in high-traffic environments running thousands or tens of thousands of sites.

When you modify a page and save a customized version of it in the content database using SharePoint Designer, you eliminate the possibility of page ghosting. Instead, the provided SPVirtualPathProvider must retrieve the customized version of the page from the content database, as shown in Figure 2-6. For this reason, customized pages are sometimes referred to as *unghosted pages*.

Now that you understand how WSS processes requests for both ghosted and unghosted pages, you should observe the important role that is played by the SPVirtualPathProvider. It is the SPVirtualPathProvider that determines whether the page being requested has been customized. The SPVirtualPathProvider makes the decision whether to process a page as a ghosted or an unghosted page. Furthermore, all aspects of page ghosting and unghosting are hidden from the ASP.NET runtime and represent a value-added dimension of WSS.

Page Parsing in WSS V2

The previous version of WSS was based on ASP.NET 1.1, which did not provide any equivalent to the virtual path provider model introduced in ASP.NET 2.0. Consequently, the WSS team created their own .aspx page parser to parse customized .aspx files after they are retrieved from the content database. Unfortunately, the .aspx parser created by the WSS team for WSS 2.0 does not support many of the richer features offered by the ASP.NET page parser, such as the ability to host user controls. The new architecture introduced in WSS 3.0, which includes the SPVirtualPathProvider and the ASP.Net page parser, should be seen as one of the more significant architectural enhancements over WSS 2.0.

Virtual Directories Within a Web Application

When WSS converts an IIS Web site into a Web application, it creates several virtual directories. These virtual directories, including the _controltemplates directory, the _layouts directory, the _vti_bin directory, and the _wpresources directory, are used by various aspects of the WSS runtime. These virtual directories can be seen by examining a Web application using the IIS Manager tool, as shown in Figure 2-7.

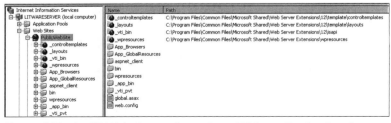

Figure 2-7   An IIS Web site configured as a Web application has four standard virtual directories including the _layouts directory.

As you can see from the image in Figure 2-7, each of the virtual directories within a Web application maps to a physical directory on the file system of the front-end Web server under the following path:

```
c:\program files\common files\microsoft shared\web server extensions
```

Each of these virtual directories plays a special role in the overall WSS architecture. For example, the _vit_bin directory provides WSS with a way to expose DLLs and .asmx Web service files at a path within the URL space of a Web application. The _controltemplates directory provides a dedicated repository for deploying ASP.NET user controls that can be used within pages. The _wpresources virtual directory provides a repository for resource files that are deployed along with Web Parts.

The one virtual directory of a Web application that we want to discuss in greater depth in this chapter is the _layouts directory because it provides the foundation for a special type of page known as an application page. *Application pages* are served up from the _layouts directory and provide a special type of functionality that is discussed in the next section.

Site Pages versus Application Pages

Some pages in a WSS site, such as the home page (default.aspx), support user customization by using tools such as the SharePoint Designer. Pages that support user customization are known as *site pages*. While the support for the customization of site pages provides a great deal of flexibility, it also has a downside. To support page customization without adversely affecting scalability, WSS must employ the page ghosting scheme discussed earlier in this chapter. However, page customization can still have a measurable impact on scalability.

Imagine a large WSS environment with a Web application running thousands of sites. What would happen if the site administrator of each site modified the site's home page with the SharePoint Designer? Every one of these site pages would become unghosted. This would negatively impact scalability by forcing the front-end Web server to retrieve each page separately from the content database. Each page would also have to be individually parsed and loaded into memory.

Also consider the fact that once a site page has been customized, a copy must be stored in the content database. This brings up a security concern. Imagine a situation in which a malicious user who has been granted site administrator permissions within a site collection tries to mount an attack by writing in-line code within a customized version of a site page. This security concern is mitigated in WSS by having a default policy that prohibits in-line scripting in site pages. The default policy also runs site pages in a no-compile mode, which means they are not compiled into DLLs.

The key point here is that customization support for site pages brings with it performance concerns and security issues. As noted earlier, the WSS architecture provides another type of page known as an application page. One of the key characteristics of an application page is that it does not support customization. Therefore, application pages can circumvent some of the main performance concerns and security issues associated with site pages.

The standard Site Settings page (settings.aspx) is a good example of an application page. It can be accessed from any site, yet it does not support customization. Application pages, such as settings.aspx, are deployed as physical files on the file system of the front-end Web server in a directory at the following path:

```
c:\program files\common files\microsoft shared
   \web server extensions\12\TEMPLATE\LAYOUTS
```

Note that the physical \LAYOUTS directory is mapped to the virtual _layouts directory whenever WSS creates a new Web application. By using this mapping scheme along with some additional processing logic, the WSS runtime can make each application page accessible within the context of any site in the farm. For example, assume that there are three different sites in a WSS farm accessible through the following three URLs:

```
http://Litwareinc.com
http://Litwareinc.com/sites/Vendors
http://Litwareinc.com:1001/sites/Accounting
```

An application page, such as settings.aspx, can be accessed by adding its relative path within the _layouts directory to the end of a site's URL. For example, you can access the Site Setting page by using any of the following three URLs:

```
http://Litwareinc.com/_layouts/settings.aspx
http://Litwareinc.com/sites/Vendors/_layouts/settings.aspx
http://Litwareinc.com:1001/sites/Accounting/_layouts/settings.aspx
```

Because there is only one version of an application page scoped at the farm level, it can be compiled into a single DLL and loaded into memory once for each Web application. You never have to worry about the existence of different versions of an application page for different sites. Furthermore, application pages are not subject to attack from users who have permissions to customize site pages. Therefore, WSS does not prohibit them from containing in-line code.

Application pages are used extensively by the WSS team to supply much of the standard functionality for provisioning and administrating sites as well as the elements inside them. Figure 2-8 displays an image of the physical \LAYOUTS directory on the front-end Web server that WSS maps to the _layouts directory. As you can see, the standard installation of WSS 3.0 includes many different application pages, including settings.aspx.

If you open and inspect the source code for one of the standard WSS application pages, you see that it links to a master page in the _layouts directory named application.master. In the next section, we will discuss the creation of custom application pages. When you create your own custom application pages, you might want to follow suit and create them to link to the application.master file as well.

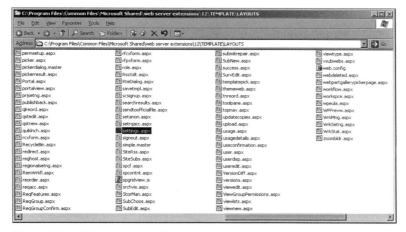

Figure 2-8 The \LAYOUTS directory contains application pages that are accessible from within any site in the farm.

Let us now summarize the difference between site pages and application pages. Site pages support page customization. Examples of site pages include the home page (default.aspx) for a site as well as the pages associated with lists and document libraries, such as AllItems.aspx, NewForm.aspx, and EditForm.aspx. The fact that site pages support customization provides flexibility but can also impact performance and scalability. Site pages do not support in-line code under the default security policy enforced by WSS.

Application pages do not support customization, which gives them two distinct advantages over site pages. First, each application page is always compiled into a single DLL so that it performs and scales better than a site page. Second, application pages are allowed to have in-line code. Now that you have a basic understand of what constitutes an application page, it will be worthwhile to see what is involved in creating your own application pages for a custom solution.

Creating Custom Application Pages

This chapter is accompanied by a sample Visual Studio project named CustomApplicationPages. This project contains several different examples of application pages such as Hello.aspx, ApplicationPage1.aspx, ApplicationPage2.aspx, and ApplicationPage3.aspx. This Visual Studio project also has a post-build event that runs a batch file named install.bat, which copies the application pages to where they need to be deployed inside the \LAYOUTS directory. The install.bat file also installs a feature named CustomApplicationPages, which adds menu items to the Site Actions menu of the current site and allows users to navigate the project's application pages.

Once you open the CustomApplicationPages project, you should build it. This will run the install.bat file. After that point, you should be able to go to any site and activate the site-level feature named CustomApplicationPages, which will then allow you to follow along with the examples throughout the remainder of this chapter.

Note that while it is possible to deploy your application pages directly inside the \LAYOUTS directory, this can cause problems due to potential file name conflicts between your application pages and those created by Microsoft and other companies. It is a best practice to deploy your application pages inside a company-specific or project-specific directory that is nested within the \LAYOUTS directory. The application pages in the sample project discussed here are deployed within a project-specific directory located at the path \LAYOUTS \CustomApplicationPages.

As a rule, application pages should derive from a base class in the Microsoft.SharePoint assembly named LayoutsPageBase. For example, assume that you want to create a custom application page to display some information about the current site. In our first example, we will work with an application page named Hello.aspx, which does exactly that.

Application pages are usually created as content pages that link to the master page named application.master that resides in the \LAYOUTS directory. This master page file can be referenced in a custom application page using a virtual path of ~/_layouts/application.master. The definition for the application page named Hello.aspx shown in Listing 2-1 shows the starting point for creating your own application pages.

Listing 2-1   A custom application page can contain HTML layout and in-line code.

```
Custom Application Page
<%@ Assembly Name="Microsoft.SharePoint, [full 4-part assembly name]"%>
<%@ Page Language="C#" MasterPageFile="~/_layouts/application.master"
        Inherits="Microsoft.SharePoint.WebControls.LayoutsPageBase"  %>

<%@ Import Namespace="Microsoft.SharePoint" %>

<script runat="server">
  protected override void OnLoad(EventArgs e) {
    SPWeb site = this.Web;
    lblSiteTitle.Text = site.Title;
    lblSiteID.Text = site.ID.ToString().ToUpper();
  }
</script>

<asp:Content ID="Main" contentplaceholderid="PlaceHolderMain" runat="server">
  <table border="1" cellpadding="4" cellspacing="0" style="font-size:12">
    <tr>
      <td>Site Title:</td>
      <td><asp:Label ID="lblSiteTitle" runat="server" /></td>
    </tr>
    <tr>
      <td>Site ID:</td>
      <td><asp:Label ID="lblSiteID" runat="server" /></td>
    </tr>
  </table>
</asp:Content>
```

```
<asp:Content ID="PageTitle" runat="server"
             contentplaceholderid="PlaceHolderPageTitle" >
  Hello World
</asp:Content>

<asp:Content ID="PageTitleInTitleArea" runat="server"
             contentplaceholderid="PlaceHolderPageTitleInTitleArea" >
  The Quintessential 'Hello World' Application Page
</asp:Content>
```

Note that the application page example shown in Listing 2-1 adds three Content tags to add HTML content to the resulting page. In particular, this page replaces placeholders defined inside application.master named PlaceHolderMain, PlaceHolderPageTitle, and PlaceHolder-PageTitleInTitleArea. However, these are just three of the many different placeholders defined inside application.master that you can choose to replace.

Also note that the version of Hello.aspx shown in Listing 2-1 has a script block at the top containing code that programs against the WSS object model. When you are programming a page like this within Visual Studio 2005, you are able to benefit from conveniences such as color-coding and IntelliSense. However, you must be sure to add the correct @Assembly directive to the top of the page. You should modify the @Assembly directive shown in Listing 2-1 with the assembly information for the Microsoft.SharePoint assembly shown here:

```
Microsoft.SharePoint,
Version=12.0.0.0,
Culture=neutral,
PublicKeyToken=71E9BCE111E9429C
```

We have added line breaks here to make this information more readable. However, you should make sure that you add all of the assembly information in a single line whenever you add an @Assembly directive to an .aspx file.

Application pages are handy because they provide quick and easy access to the WSS object. Once you have created an application page and provided an overridden implementation of the OnLoad method, as shown in Listing 2-1, you can obtain entry points into the WSS object model in a site-specific context using the following code, which uses properties exposed by underlying LayoutsPageBase base class:

```
SPSite siteCollection = this.Site;
SPWeb site = this.Web;
```

The ability to obtain site-relative as well as site collection-relative context makes writing application pages far more powerful. An application page can behave differently depending on which site you go through to access it. When you navigate to an application page through the context of one site, it will typically appear and behave differently when you navigate to it through the context of another site.

Our example of Hello.aspx uses WSS object model code in the OnLoad method to obtain information about the current site and then to display that information on labels that are defined on the placeholder named PlaceHolderMain.

```
protected override void OnLoad(EventArgs e) {
  SPWeb site = this.Web;
  lblSiteTitle.Text = site.Title;
  lblSiteID.Text = site.ID.ToString().ToUpper();
}
```

When you access Hello.aspx through the context of a particular site, it displays relative information about the current site, as shown in Figure 2-9.

Figure 2-9 A custom application page can easily be programmed against the WSS object model.

The Code-Behind Approach in Application Pages

While you have just seen it is possible and fairly easy to add in-line code inside the .aspx file for a custom application page, you can also use a different approach in which your code is maintained in a code-behind style supported by ASP.NET. All the example application pages in the CustomApplicationPages sample project use this approach, with the exception of the one application page you have already seen named Hello.aspx. You might prefer this code-behind approach because it provides a separation between your code and the user interface layout details. The code-behind approach can also improve your design time experience when writing the code for application pages.

Let's start by examining ApplicationPage1.aspx, which has two server control tags and output that is identical to Hello.aspx. The big difference is that the code for ApplicationPage1.aspx is maintained in a source file named ApplicationPage1.cs, which is compiled into an assembly named CustomApplicationPages.dll that it installed in the Global Assembly Cache (GAC). If you examine the definition for ApplicationPage1.aspx in Listing 2-2, you can see that it contains the same HTML markup and control tags as Hello.aspx, but the code has been removed.

Listing 2-2 A custom application page can reference a code-behind base class.

```
<%@ Assembly Name="Microsoft.SharePoint, [full 4-part assembly name]" %>
<%@ Assembly Name="CustomApplicationPages, [full 4-part assembly name]" %>

<%@ Page Language="C#" MasterPageFile="~/_layouts/application.master"
        Inherits="CustomApplicationPages.ApplicationPage1"
        EnableViewState="false" EnableViewStateMac="false" %>

<asp:Content ID="Main" contentplaceholderid="PlaceHolderMain" runat="server">
  <table border="1" cellpadding="4" cellspacing="0" style="font-size:12">
    <tr>
      <td>Site Title:</td>
      <td><asp:Label ID="lblSiteTitle" runat="server" /></td>
    </tr>
    <tr>
      <td>Site ID:</td>
      <td><asp:Label ID="lblSiteID" runat="server" /></td>
    </tr>
  </table>
</asp:Content>

<asp:Content ID="PageTitle" runat="server"
             contentplaceholderid="PlaceHolderPageTitle" >
  Hello World
</asp:Content>

<asp:Content ID="PageTitleInTitleArea" runat="server"
             contentplaceholderid="PlaceHolderPageTitleInTitleArea" >
  Application Page 1: 'Hello World' with code behind
</asp:Content>
```

There are two other important differences between Hello.aspx and ApplicationPage1.aspx. First, ApplicationPage1.aspx contains a second assembly directive which references the output assembly for the current project named CustomApplicationPages.dll. Second, ApplicationPage1.aspx does not inherit directly from LayoutsPageBase; instead it inherits from a code-behind class named ApplicationPage1, which is defined in the namespace CustomApplicationPages. Now let's examine Listing 2-3, which shows the definition for this code-behind class inside the source file ApplicationPage1.cs, which has been written to inherit from LayoutsPageBase.

Listing 2-3 A code-behind class for an application page should inherit from LayoutsPageBase.

```
using System;
using System.Web;
using System.Web.UI;
using System.Web.UI.WebControls;
using Microsoft.SharePoint;
using Microsoft.SharePoint.WebControls;

namespace CustomApplicationPages {

  public class ApplicationPage1 : LayoutsPageBase {
```

```
        // add control fields to match controls tags on .aspx page
        protected Label lblSiteTitle;
        protected Label lblSiteID;

        protected override void OnLoad(EventArgs e) {

            // get current site and web
            SPSite siteCollection = this.Site;
            SPWeb site = this.Web;

            // program against controls on .aspx page
            lblSiteTitle.Text = site.Title;
            lblSiteID.Text = site.ID.ToString().ToUpper();
        }

    }
}
```

When you have an .aspx file and a code-behind class, there is a handy technique in ASP.NET programming where the code-behind class defines a control field using the same name as a control instance in the .aspx page. When the ASP.NET runtime compiles the .aspx file, it adds support to create the control instance and assign a reference to the control field in the code-behind class. This makes it possible for methods within the code-behind class to access the control instances defined inside the .aspx file. For example, the ApplicationPage1 class defines control fields named lblSiteTitle and lblSiteID to match the control tags defined in ApplicationPage1.aspx. This makes it possible for code within the OnLoad event handler method inside ApplicationPage1.cs to access these controls through the control fields named lblSiteTitle and lblSiteID.

Debugging WSS Components

Under normal conditions, WSS provides error messages intended for end users in a production environment. This means that WSS doesn't automatically provide rich diagnostic information or helpful error messages to assist you when you are debugging your code. While you are developing WSS components such as custom application pages, you must modify the web.config file for the current Web application to enable debugging support and error messages that contain stack traces. Here's a fragment of the web.config file that shows the three important attributes that have been changed from their default values to enable rich debugging support.

```
<configuration>
  <SharePoint>
    <SafeMode CallStack="true" />
  </SharePoint>
  <system.web>
    <customErrors mode="Off" />
    <compilation debug="true" />
  </system.web>
</configuration>
```

While it is essential to modify the web.config file as shown here to enable debugging support, you will also find it occasionally necessary to return the web.config file to its original state. For example, you might create an application page that throws an exception or an event handler that cancels a user's actions. By returning the web.config file to its original state, you can see how your code will actually behave in a production environment. Therefore, you should become comfortable with the act of changing the web.config file back and forth between debugging mode and standard end user mode.

Navigation Support for Application Pages

Now that you have seen how to create an application page, let's complement it by adding a feature that adds a menu item to the Site Actions menu. This menu item will be created to allow the user to navigate to ApplicationPage1.aspx. In the last chapter, we demonstrated a technique for creating a custom feature with a CustomAction element. We will now create another CustomAction with a slight variation. Take a look at the following CustomAction element.

```
<!-- Add Command to Site Actions Dropdown -->
<CustomAction Id="SiteActionsToolbar"
  GroupId="SiteActions"
  Location="Microsoft.SharePoint.StandardMenu"
  Sequence="2001"
  Title="Application Page 1"
  Description="Check out some typical site properties"
  ImageUrl="/_layouts/images/DECISION.GIF">
    <UrlAction Url="~site/_layouts/CustomApplicationPages/ApplicationPage1.aspx"/>
</CustomAction>
```

You should see that this CustomAction element is almost identical to the one we demonstrated in the last chapter. The difference rests in the string used for the URL attribute of the inner UrlAction element. The URL attribute in this example begins with ~site. This is a dynamic token that is replaced by WSS with the actual URL to the current site. By using this technique, you can provide a menu item within the Site Actions menu, such as the one shown in Figure 2-10, that allows the user to navigate to your custom application pages with the correct site-relative context.

Figure 2-10   A menu item created with a CustomAction element makes it easy for the user to navigate to a custom application page.

When creating a CustomAction element, you can configure the URL attribute of the inner UrlAction element by using the ~site token, as you have just seen. You should note that WSS also supports the ~sitecollection token in cases in which your application page should always be executed within a URL associated with the current site collection and its top-level site.

Creating an Application Page with the SPGridView Control

ApplicationPage2.aspx demonstrates the technique of employing a handy server-side control created by the WSS team, named SPGridView. SPGridView is an enhanced version of the ASP.NET GridView control that integrates with the WSS Cascading Style Sheet (CSS) files so that it picks up the same look and feel as its surrounding environment.

The SPGridView control is defined inside the Microsoft.SharePoint assembly in the Microsoft.SharePoint.WebControls namespace. In order to use this control inside an application page, you must add an @Assembly directive referencing the Microsoft.SharePoint assembly; in addition, you must add an @Register directive to import the control's namespace and define a Tagprefix attribute that will be used when creating a control tag. Here's an example of the @Register directive that is used in ApplicationPage2.aspx.

```
<%@ Register Tagprefix="SharePoint"
             Namespace="Microsoft.SharePoint.WebControls"
             Assembly="Microsoft.SharePoint, [full 4-part assembly name]" %>
```

As you can see, this @Register directive imports the Microsoft.SharePoint.WebControls namespace with a Tagprefix value of SharePoint. That makes it possible to create an instance of the SPGridView control using a control tag that looks like this.

```
<SharePoint:SPGridView runat="server"
                       ID="grdPropertyValues"
                       AutoGenerateColumns="false"
                       RowStyle-BackColor="#DDDDDD"
                       AlternatingRowStyle-BackColor="#EEEEEE" />
```

Take a moment and examine the complete application page definition in the source file named ApplicationPage2.aspx. After you have done that, open the source file named ApplicationPage2.cs and examine the code-behind class for this application page. You can see that the class named ApplicationPage2 works together with a custom helper class named PropertyCollectionBinder to create an ADO.NET DataTable object filled with information about the current site and site collection. The DataTable object is being used in this example because its contents can be used to populate SPGridView by using standard ASP.NET data binding techniques.

Restricting Application Pages to Site Administrators

The application pages and supporting menu items in the Site Actions menu shown so far have been created in a manner so that they are accessible to all users of a site. However, that isn't always desirable. Application pages are often designed to provide information and functionality that should only be accessible to site administrators. We will discuss how to do this by examining our next sample application page, named ApplicationPage3.aspx.

Let's start by revisiting the creation of a CustomAction element within a feature. You can add an attribute named RequireSiteAdministrator and assign it a value of true so that the menu item only displays to those users who are also site administrators.

```
<!-- Add Command to Site Actions Dropdown -->
<CustomAction Id="SiteActionsToolbar"
  GroupId="SiteActions"
  Location="Microsoft.SharePoint.StandardMenu"
  Sequence="1003"
  Title="Application Page 3"
  Description="Admin-only Application page"
  RequireSiteAdministrator="True"
  ImageUrl="/_layouts/images/DECISION.GIF">
    <UrlAction Url="~site/_layouts/CustomApplicationPages/ApplicationPage3.aspx"/>
</CustomAction>
```

While this provides a good start by hiding the menu item from users who are not site administrators, it doesn't provide a truly secure solution. The application page itself will still be accessible to any user who knows the URL. When you want to lock down an application page in a secure manner, you can accomplish this by overriding the RequireSiteAdministrator property of the LayoutsPageBase base class as shown in the following code.

```
public class ApplicationPage3 : LayoutsPageBase {

  protected override bool RequireSiteAdministrator {
    get { return true; }
  }

  protected override void OnLoad(EventArgs e) {
    // your code goes here
  }
}
```

Once you add this code to an application page, you truly make it secure. When a user who is not a site administrator tries to navigate to this application page, the user is redirected to the standard WSS Access Denied page.

Adding a Custom Menu Item to the ECB Menu

We will now take the idea of creating a custom application page even further by examining one that displays information about a particular document in a document library. In our example, we will look at the application page named ApplicationPage4.aspx. We begin by creating a new CustomAction element. However, this CustomAction element does not add a menu item in the Site Actions menu. Instead, it is designed to add a new menu item to the

ECB menu for each document within a document library. Examine the following XML fragment that defines a CustomAction.

```
<!-- Per Item Dropdown (ECB) Link -->
<CustomAction Id="ApplicationPage4.ECBItemMenu"
  RegistrationType="List"
  RegistrationId="101"
  ImageUrl="/_layouts/images/GORTL.GIF"
  Location="EditControlBlock"
  Sequence="105"
  Title="Application Page 4" >

  <UrlAction Url="~site/_layouts/CustomApplicationPages/ApplicationPage4.aspx
              ?ItemId={ItemId}&amp;ListId={ListId}"
  />
</CustomAction>
```

This CustomAction element is different than what you have seen before because it has a RegistrationType attribute that is assigned a value of List. It also is configured with a RegstrationID attribute that is assigned a value of 101. Note that 101 is a list type identifier that applies to all document libraries. You should also notice that the Location attribute has a value of EditControlBlock, which creates the effect of adding the menu item to the ECB menu of documents within a document library, as shown in Figure 2-11.

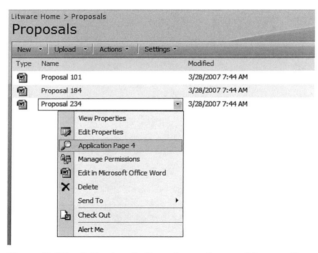

Figure 2-11   A CustomAction element can add menu items to the ECB menu for items in a list or documents in a document library.

If you look at the CustomAction element in this example, you see that the ActionUrl element is configured with a URL attribute that points to ApplicationPage4.aspx and appends the following QueryString.

```
../ApplicationPage4.aspx?ItemId={ItemId}&amp;ListId={ListId}
```

Note the existence of the {ListId} token and the {ItemId} token within the QueryString that is appended to the end of the URL used to navigate to ApplicationPage4.aspx. WSS dynamically replaces the {ListId} token with the identifying GUID for the current list or document library. WSS dynamically replaces the {ItemId} token with the integer identifier for the current list item or document.

The code inside ApplicationPage4.cs is written under the assumption that there is information in the query string that can be used to identify a specific document and its hosting document library. Examine the following code to see how it pulls the required information out of the query string and uses it to create an SPList object and an SPListItem object.

```
// get current site and web
SPSite siteCollection = this.Site;
SPWeb site = this.Web;

// access current list or document library
string ListId = Request.QueryString["ListId"];
SPList list = site.Lists[new Guid(ListId)];

// access current list item or document
string ItemId = Request.QueryString["ItemId"];
SPListItem item = list.Items.GetItemById(Convert.ToInt32(ItemId));
```

In cases such as this one, you can assume that you are dealing with a document library and not simply a standard list type. In these situations, you can add code that converts the SPList object into a SPDocumentLibrary object. You can also access the document in question directly by creating an SPFile object as shown in the following sample.

```
// get current site and web
SPSite siteCollection = this.Site;
SPWeb site = this.Web;

// access current list or document library
string ListId = Request.QueryString["ListId"];
SPList list = site.Lists[new Guid(ListId)];
lblListTile.Text = list.Title;
lblRootFolderUrl.Text = list.RootFolder.Url;

// if current list is a document library...
SPDocumentLibrary documentLibrary = (SPDocumentLibrary)list;
lblDocumentTemplateUrl.Text = documentLibrary.DocumentTemplateUrl;

// access current list item or document
string ItemId = Request.QueryString["ItemId"];
lblDocumentID.Text = ItemId;
SPListItem item = list.Items.GetItemById(Convert.ToInt32(ItemId));
lblDocumentName.Text = item.Name;
lblDocumentUrl.Text = item.Url;
```

```
// if current list is a document library...
SPFile file = site.GetFile(item.Url);
lblFileAuthor.Text = file.Author.Name;
lblFileSize.Text = file.TotalLength.ToString("0,###") + " bits";
lblFileLastModified.Text = "By " + file.ModifiedBy.Name +
                           " on " + file.TimeLastModified.ToLocalTime().ToString();
lblFileCheckOutStatus.Text = file.CheckOutStatus.ToString();
```

The code you see in ApplicationPage4.cs uses the WSS object model to discover information about a particular document and its document library. When you navigate to this page from the ECB menu item of a document within a document library, it displays the types of information shown in Figure 2-12.

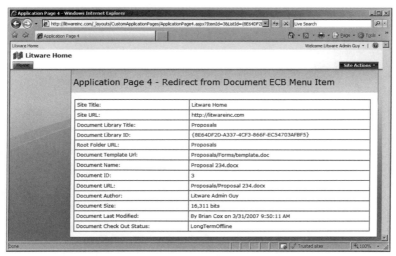

Figure 2-12   An application page can be designed to display information about a specific list item or document.

From the few examples we have presented, you should be able to see that creating custom application pages can be very valuable in a custom solution. You should also understand that what we have demonstrated here only scratches the surface of what is possible. You can create custom application pages to provide custom administration at the level of a site collection, site, list, item, document library, or document. You can also create a custom application page to provide a custom user interface for a list with user interface elements geared toward item entry, display, updating, or deletion. In summary, custom application pages can often provide the foundation of a custom WSS solution.

Summary

This chapter began by reviewing important concepts and terminology used in IIS and ASP.NET. As you begin to learn how WSS works internally, it is critical that you have a firm grasp of these topics. You have seen that WSS converts an IIS Web site into a Web application by replacing several components within the HTTP Request Pipeline. You have also seen that the SPVirtualPathProvider component plays an essential role in the overall WSS architecture because it provides the foundation for page customization.

This chapter also discussed the difference between site pages and application pages. While application pages do not support customization, they have a few key advantages over site pages. Namely, they perform better and can contain in-line code or code-behind. In this chapter, you have observed an approach for creating custom application pages and integrating them into the menus of a site by using CustomAction elements.

Now that you have a basic understanding of what can be done with custom application pages, it's time to turn our attention back to site pages. The next chapter examines the processing model for site pages in greater depth and discusses the creation of custom page templates, as well as how to provision them into page instances within a site.

Chapter 3

Pages and Design

- Understand the benefits and restrictions of safe mode processing.
- Learn how to design site pages with controls and Web Part zones.
- Learn how to customize the master page used by site pages.
- Learn how to customize the Windows SharePoint Services (WSS) navigation infrastructure.
- Learn best practices for branding WSS sites.

Site Page Fundamentals

Chapter 2, "SharePoint Architecture," introduced you to the key differences between application pages and site pages. You learned that application pages have an advantage over site pages in that they perform better and provide a developer with the ability to add in-line code. You also learned that site pages have some key advantages over application pages because they can be created dynamically and can also be customized by users on a site-by-site basis.

Chapter 2 discussed the role of the SPVirtualPathProvider component and introduced the principles of page ghosting and unghosting. As you remember, page ghosting is an optimization used with site pages in which a single page template can be used to process multiple page instances across many different sites. For example, the home page for every team site in a Microsoft Windows SharePoint Services (WSS) farm is based on an underlying page template named default.aspx that resides on the file system of the front-end Web server. A page template, such as default.aspx, is compiled into an assembly dynamic-link library (DLL) and loaded into memory just once per Web application. However, this page template and its efficient usage of memory can still be used to serve up pages for thousands of sites. This is an obvious advantage toward scalability.

When a user customizes a site page by using the SharePoint Designer and then saves those changes, a customized version of the page definition is stored in the content database. While this provides flexibility from a customization standpoint, it also can have a negative impact on performance and scalability. When the customized page is requested, its page definition must be retrieved from the Backend database server by the SPVirtualPathProvider component and then fed to the ASP.NET compiler, where it is parsed and loaded into memory. You can imagine that a Web application with thousands of customized pages requires more memory because each customized page definition must be separately parsed and loaded into memory within the application pool that is hosting the current Web application.

You should note that customized pages are not processed by using the standard ASP.NET model in which a page is compiled into an assembly DLL. Instead, customized pages are parsed by the ASP.NET page parser and then processed using the no-compile mode feature that was introduced with ASP.NET 2.0.

As a developer, your initial reaction to this might be to question why customized pages are processed in no-compile mode. Your instincts likely tell you that compiled pages run faster than no-compile pages. However, no-compile pages can be more efficient and more scalable in certain scenarios. This is especially true in a large WSS environment where the number of customized pages can reach into the thousands or tens of thousands.

No-compile pages can be loaded into memory and then unloaded in a manner that is not possible for compiled pages because the .NET Framework doesn't really support the concept of unloading an assembly DLL from memory. The closest equivalent would be to recycle the current Windows process or the current .NET AppDomain. However, this type of recycling involves unloading all assembly DLLs from memory, not just those assembly DLLs that haven't been used recently. Furthermore, the .NET Framework places an upper limit on the number of assembly DLLs that can be loaded into a .NET AppDomain.

No-compile pages provide higher levels of scalability because they do not require loading new assembly DLLs or managed classes into memory. Instead, the processing of no-compile pages involves loading control trees into memory. WSS can manage the memory usage for the control trees associated with customized pages more efficiently because they are not compiled into assembly DLLs. For example, once WSS has finished processing a customized page, it can unload the page's control tree to free up memory for other purposes. Furthermore, no-compile pages eliminate the need to go through the compilation process, which actually provides faster response times for pages upon first access.

Programming with SPFile Objects

WSS tracks each site page as a file within the content database. You can access a site page through the WSS object model by using the SPFile object. For example, assume that you want to program against the home page for a site. You can obtain a reference to the required SPFile object by using the GetFile method of a SPWeb object.

```
SPWeb site = SPContext.Current.Web;
SPFile homePage = site.GetFile("default.aspx");
```

The SPFile class makes it possible to read and write to the contents of a site page. For example, the OpenBinary method of an SPFile object returns a binary array containing the page contents. The OpenBinaryStream method returns a System.IO.Stream object. Each of these methods provides an approach for reading the contents of a site page. An SPFile object also provides a SaveBinary method that allows you to update the contents of a site page as well. Note that updating the contents of a site page by using this method customizes the page and moves it into an customized or *unghosted* state.

The SPFile class provides several other methods for managing site pages within a site such as Delete, MoveTo, and CopyTo. The Delete method, as its name implies, removes the target file from the site. MoveTo makes it possible to move a file, such as a site page, to another location so that it's accessible through a different URL. CopyTo allows you to clone a site page with a copy. Note that if you call CopyTo on an uncustomized page, it creates another uncustomized page. Likewise, if you call CopyTo on an customized page, it results in the creation of a customized page in an unghosted state.

> **Tip**   *Ghosted* and *uncustomized* are terms used to describe site pages served up using file system templates. *Unghosted* and *customized* both refer to pages that exist entirely in the database, which no longer depend on a file system template.

The SPWeb object for a site also exposes a Files property with a public Add method that allows you to add new site pages. There is an overloaded version of the Add method that allows you to pass a stream object with the contents of the new page. The following example demonstrates writing the contents of a new page to a MemoryStream object and then using it to create a new site page named Hello.htm.

```
// write out new page in memory stream
MemoryStream stream = new MemoryStream();
StreamWriter writer = new StreamWriter(stream);
writer.WriteLine("<html><body>");
writer.WriteLine("Hello, World");
writer.WriteLine("</body></html>");
writer.Flush();

// add new page to site
SPWeb site = SPContext.Current.Web;
site.Files.Add("hello.htm", stream);
```

Note that the Add method doesn't support adding a new site page that is associated with an underlying page template. Therefore, site pages created by using the Add method are always created as customized pages in an unghosted state.

The SPFile class provides a CustomizedPageStatus property that makes it possible to determine whether a site page has been customized and placed in an unghosted state. The Customized-PageStatus property is based on an enumeration type named SPCustomizedPageStatus. If a SPFile object for a site page has a CustomizedPageStatus property value of Uncustomized, it means that the page is still in a ghosted state. A site page with a CustomizedPageStatus property value of Customized has been customized and is in an unghosted state. The SPFile object also provides a method named RevertContentStream that removes any customizations and returns an unghosted page to its initial ghosted state.

SPFolder Objects

The files within a WSS site are structured within a hierarchy of folders. Each folder is represented in the WSS object model with an SPFolder object. Each SPFolder object contains a

Files property that allows you to enumerate through its files. If you want to enumerate through all of the files at the root folder of a site, you can access the RootFolder property of a SPWeb object and then use a foreach loop to enumerate through all of its files.

```
SPWeb site = SPContext.Current.Web;
SPFolder rootFolder = site.RootFolder;

foreach (SPFile file in rootFolder.Files){
  // process each file
}
```

The WSS object model also makes it possible to enumerate through the folders within a folder. This, in turn, makes it possible to write code that enumerates through all of the folders within a site to discover all existing files. The following code displays an example of custom code that starts at the root folder of a site and uses recursion to populate an ASP.NET TreeView control.

```
const string SITE_IMG = @"\_layouts\images\FPWEB16.GIF";
const string FOLDER_IMG = @"\_layouts\images\FOLDER16.GIF";
const string GHOSTED_FILE_IMG = @"\_layouts\images\NEWDOC.GIF";
const string UNGHOSTED_FILE_IMG = @"\_layouts\images\RAT16.GIF";

protected override void OnLoad(EventArgs e) {
  SPWeb site = SPContext.Current.Web;
  SPFolder rootFolder = site.RootFolder;
  TreeNode rootNode = new TreeNode(site.Url, site.Url, SITE_IMG);
  LoadFolderNodes(rootFolder, rootNode);
  treeSiteFiles.Nodes.Add(rootNode);
  treeSiteFiles.ExpandDepth = 1;
}

protected void LoadFolderNodes(SPFolder folder, TreeNode folderNode) {
  foreach (SPFolder childFolder in folder.SubFolders) {
    TreeNode childFolderNode = new TreeNode(childFolder.Name,
                                            childFolder.Name,
                                            FOLDER_IMG);
    LoadFolderNodes(childFolder, childFolderNode);
    folderNode.ChildNodes.Add(childFolderNode);
  }

  foreach (SPFile file in folder.Files) {
    TreeNode fileNode;
    if (file.CustomizedPageStatus == SPCustomizedPageStatus.Uncustomized) {
      fileNode = new TreeNode(file.Name, file.Name, GHOSTED_FILE_IMG);
    }
    else {
      fileNode = new TreeNode(file.Name, file.Name, UNGHOSTED_FILE_IMG);
    }
    folderNode.ChildNodes.Add(fileNode);
  }
}
```

Note that this code is also written to provide different images that allow the user to distinguish between pages that are customized and those that are uncustomized. A graphic of the resulting TreeView control is shown in Figure 3-1.

Figure 3-1   A WSS site contains a hierarchy of folders and files. Files such as .aspx and .htm pages can either be in an uncustomized or customized state.

Working with Page Templates

Up to this point, the discussion of page templates has revolved around using the standard page templates that are built into WSS. It is now time to explore how to create your own page templates and integrate them into a custom business solution. You can create and integrate custom page templates by using either a feature or a site definition. Because we have not yet discussed site definitions, this chapter focuses on the use of custom page templates within the context of a feature.

Examples of using page templates in this chapter are based on a Microsoft Visual Studio project named CustomSitePages that contains a feature of the same name. (The project is included on the companion Web site for this book.) Figure 3-2 displays the Solution Explorer window for this project. As you can see, the project contains a feature.xml and an elements.xml file like the other features that we built in earlier chapters. However, this feature also contains several .aspx files that are used to define site page templates, such as Page01.aspx and Page02.aspx. The CustomSitePages project also contains several ASP.NET user controls as well as the code for an ASP.NET custom control that will be discussed later in this chapter.

If you open and build the CustomSitePages project, you find a post-build event that runs a batch file named Install.bat. This batch file copies the feature files along with the page templates into the proper location within the TEMPLATE directory and then installs the CustomSitePages feature by using the stsadm.exe command-line utility. Note that the CustomSitePages feature is designed to activate within the context of a site. After the feature is installed, you can activate it within any site in the current farm and follow along with these examples.

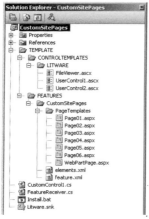

Figure 3-2 The CustomSitePages project demonstrates how to build a feature with custom site page templates.

When the CustomSitePages feature is activated, it contains declarative logic in elements.xml to provision site page instances from its page templates. The code in the FeatureActivated event extends the navigation components of a WSS site by adding two new drop-down menus to the top link bar with menu items to navigate to the newly provisioned site page instance. The technique for adding these drop-down menus to the top link bar is explained later in this chapter.

Let's start with a simple definition for a page template. Examine the following definition for the page template named Page01.aspx.

```
<%@ Page MasterPageFile="~masterurl/default.master"
    meta:progid="SharePoint.WebPartPage.Document"  %>

<asp:Content runat="server" ContentPlaceHolderID="PlaceHolderMain">

  <h3>Hello World</h3>

  A simple page template used to create site pages

</asp:Content>
```

The Page directive at the top of this page template assigns a value of ~masterurl/default .master to the MasterPageFile attribute to link to the standard master page used by site pages within WSS sites. We will defer a more detailed discussion of master pages and the MasterPageFile attribute until later in this chapter. For now, simply assume that this site page template is designed to link to the standard master page.

You should also notice that the Page directive in the previous example contains a meta:progid attribute with a value of SharePoint.WebPartPage.Document. This attribute is included to make that page compatible with the SharePoint Designer, and is also available in the SPFile object's ProgID property. Once site page instances have been provisioned by using this page template, users can open these pages with the SharePoint Designer and customize their content.

This simple example demonstrates the power and elegance of master pages in WSS development. You should be impressed at how little text is needed to define a simple page template. All that's really required for a simple page template is to link to a master page and supply some unique content for the placeholder named PlaceHolderMain. As you learn more about how WSS uses master pages, you will discover that there are many more named placeholders that you can optionally override within your page templates to enrich them with all types of content such as controls, scripts, and styles.

Now that you've seen how to create a simple page template, it's time to put it to use. Keep in mind that a page template, such as Page01.aspx, serves no purpose until you begin using it to provision site page instances. This can be done by creating a feature that contains a special type of element known as a *Module*.

A Module element can be thought of as a file set. When you create a Module, you add one or more inner File elements. The key point is that each File element is used to provision an instance of a file from a file template. Remember that the file template exists on the file system of the front-end Web server, whereas the file instance being provisioned is being created inside the context of a particular site.

In this particular case, we want to provision an instance of a site page from the page template named Page01.aspx. Note that the top-level directory of the CustomSitePages feature contains a nested directory named PageTemplates that contains all of the page templates. When you define a Module element, you can specify a Path attribute that points to a source directory, such as PageTemplates. You can also specify a Url element if you would like to instantiate the resulting site page instance within an inner folder instead of at the root folder of the target site.

```
<Elements xmlns="http://schemas.microsoft.com/sharepoint/">
  <Module Path="PageTemplates" Url="SitePages" >
    <File Url="Page01.aspx" Type="Ghostable" />
  </Module>
</Elements>
```

Note that the File element within this example is created with a Url attribute that points to the source file for the page template. When you activate a feature that contains this Module element, WSS provisions a site page instance within the target site at the following relative path.

```
SitePages/Page01.aspx
```

The user can navigate to this page by using the Site Pages drop-down menu and clicking on the menu item with a caption of Site Page 1. Figure 3-3 depicts the resulting site page instance.

Figure 3-3   A Module element allows you to provision a site page instance from page templates.

Note that the File element in the previous example contains a Type attribute with a value of Ghostable. When a site page instance, such as Page01.aspx, is provisioned, it initially exists in an uncustomized state and benefits from the principles of page ghosting. This means that you can activate this feature in a thousand different sites within a Web application and that all sites use a single compiled version of the page. Page ghosting also makes it possible to make changes to the page template on the file system of the front-end Web server and have those changes affect all of the sites that have pages provisioned from this page template.

Only two possible settings exist for the Type attribute: Ghostable and GhostableInLibrary. These two settings are used to differentiate between files that are provisioned inside a document library and those that are not. In this case, the site page instance has a Type of Ghostable because it is not being provisioned inside a document library. Later in the chapter, you will encounter an example of a File element whose Type attribute value will be defined as GhostableInLibrary.

You should also note that when defining a File element, you can optionally include the Name element. This makes it possible to provision a site page instance with a name that differs from the name of the underlying page template. This technique wasn't used in the previous example, so the resulting site page instance was provisioned with the same name as the page template. However, you can extend the Module element shown earlier to provision several different site page instances from a single page template and give them all different names.

```
<Elements xmlns="http://schemas.microsoft.com/sharepoint/">
  <Module Path="PageTemplates" Url="SitePages" >
    <File Url="Page01.aspx" Name="PageA.aspx Type="Ghostable" />
    <File Url="Page01.aspx" Name="PageB.aspx Type="Ghostable" />
    <File Url="Page01.aspx" Name="PageC.aspx Type="Ghostable" />
  </Module>
</Elements>
```

Safe Mode Processing

It's important to understand that all customized site pages are parsed and processed in a special mode known as safe mode. The primary motivation for safe mode involves the fact that standard users can modify the contents of site pages. In other words, a user (such as a site owner) possessing no administrator privileges within the farm can make any modifications to a page within a site. Consider a scenario in a large farm in which a site administrator attempts to mount an attack on the Web server by writing C# code within a customized site page inside an in-line script block. Safe mode prevents this type of attack by disallowing in-line script in any customized source.

Examine the code in the page template named Page02.aspx. It contains a simple in-line script to write a message back to the browser.

```
<%@ Page Language="C#" MasterPageFile="~masterurl/default.master"
    meta:progid="SharePoint.WebPartPage.Document"  %>

<asp:Content ID="main" runat="server"
            ContentPlaceHolderID="PlaceHolderMain">

  <h3>Page 2</h3>

  <% Response.Write("Hello world from server-side script!"); %>

</asp:Content>
```

Note that this page and the in-line script run just fine as long as the page remains uncustomized in a ghosted state. Remember that WSS compiles a ghosted page into an assembly DLL for processing. However, as soon as a user modifies any aspect of this page with the SharePoint Designer and moves the site page into an unghosted state, WSS then begins to use safe mode to process it. Because the page contains in-line script, WSS refuses to process it in safe mode and generates the error message shown in Figure 3-4.

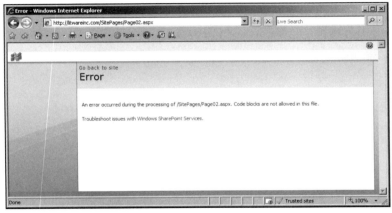

Figure 3-4 Customized pages run in safe mode and cannot contain in-line script.

You obviously don't want your users to experience error messages like the one shown in Figure 3-4. For this reason, you should avoid adding in-line script to page templates. Following this guideline helps to eliminate scenarios in which pages mysteriously stop working after they are edited by users with the SharePoint Designer.

In rare cases, you might decide to turn down or turn off the protection afforded by safe mode. In this situation, you can add an entry to the web.config file of the hosting Web application to instruct WSS to change the behavior of safe mode processing. For example, assume that you want to allow in-line scripts for site pages inside the SitePages folder in a site at the path of /sites/Sales. You can accomplish this by adding the following PageParserPath element within the SharePoint section of the web.config file.

```
<SharePoint>
  <SafeMode ... >
    <PageParserPaths>
      <PageParserPath
          VirtualPath="/sites/Sales/SitePages/*"
          IncludeSubFolders="true"
          CompilationMode="Always"
          AllowServerSideScript="true" />
    </PageParserPaths>
  </SafeMode>
</SharePoint>
```

If you examine the PageParserPath element, you see that the VirtualPath attribute has a Web application relative path followed by an asterisk, which includes every site page in that particular folder. Also note that the CompilationMode attribute has a value of Always and the AllowServerSideScript attribute has a value of true. This instructs the safe mode parser to compile all site pages into assembly DLLs and allow in-line script.

Note that a page must be compiled into an assembly DLL to support in-line script, which means that it is not valid to assign a value of Never to the CompilationMode attribute while assigning a value of true to the AllowServerSideScript attribute. Also note that you can assign a value of Auto instead of a value of Always to the CompilationMode attribute. This has the effect of compiling only pages that contain in-line script. When the CompilationMode attribute has a value of Auto, pages without in-line script are still run in no-compile mode.

It is possible to enable in-line script for all site pages within a Web application by configuring the VirtualPath attribute with a value of /* and then setting the CompilationMode attribute to a value of Always or Auto. However, two significant factors should motivate you not to do this.

The first factor is security. By enabling in-line script for all site pages within a Web application, you open the door to attacks on the Web server because any user who has the ability to customize a page can freely write managed code that executes on the Web server.

The second factor pertains to scalability. Earlier in this chapter, I discussed how no-compile pages are more scalable than compiled pages in a large Web application. WSS experiences scaling problems if your Web application attempts to compile and load thousands of assembly DLLs for all of your customized pages. At the very least, you should prefer a Compilation-Mode setting of Auto instead of Always so that only pages that actually contain script are compiled into assembly DLLs, whereas those pages that do not contain script continue to be parsed and processed in no-compile mode.

Safe Controls

Safe mode processing goes a step beyond protecting against in-line script by also considering what controls a user might place on a customized page. For example, imagine a scenario in which a site administrator tries to mount an attack by adding a server-side control to a site page and parameterizing it in a certain way. Safe mode allows the farm administrator to determine which controls can be used in pages that are processed in safe mode.

Customized pages can only contain server-side controls that are explicitly registered as safe controls. Registering a control as a safe control is accomplished by adding a SafeControl entry into the web.config file for the hosting Web application.

```
<SafeControls>
  <SafeControl
    Assembly="Microsoft.SharePoint, …"
    Namespace="Microsoft.SharePoint.WebControls"
    TypeName="*"
    AllowRemoteDesigner="True" />
</SafeControls>
```

Note that the standard web.config file for a Web application automatically includes Safe-Control entries for the standard server-side controls and Web Parts included with ASP.NET and WSS. In the next section, you will learn how to add a SafeControl entry that is required to place a custom server-side control on a customized page. In Chapter 4, "Web Parts," we will revisit the topic of safe controls and discuss how they pertain to custom Web Part deployment.

Note that a PageParserPath element, in addition to allowing in-line script, can also override the default safe mode behavior and allow for server-side controls that are explicitly registered as safe. For example, you can allow the users of a particular site to add any server-side controls to customized pages by using the following entry within the web.config file.

```
<SharePoint>
  <SafeMode ... >
    <PageParserPaths>
      <PageParserPath
          VirtualPath="/sites/Sales/*"
          AllowUnsafeControls="true" />
    </PageParserPaths>
  </SafeMode>
</SharePoint>
```

Note that using this option affects only which server-side controls can be added to a page when customizing a page with a tool, such as the SharePoint Designer. This configuration option does not extend to control instances when users are adding Web Parts to Web Part zones on a page through the browser. Assembly DLLs containing Web Parts must always be explicitly registered by using SafeControl elements for users to be able to place them inside Web Part zones.

Although you have just learned several ways to disable safe mode or lessen its effects, you should remember to proceed here with extreme caution. It's usually best to leave safe mode with its default behavior. WSS was engineered with safe mode processing to protect the farm from attacks and allow WSS to scale out the way it was designed in large farm environments.

Designing Site Pages by Using Controls

We have dealt with the nuts and bolts of site pages, page templates, and safe mode processing. It is now time to take a step back and discuss the development of page templates from a design perspective. In particular, we will discuss how to construct page templates by adding server-side controls to obtain the functionality and user interface components that you need.

In the ASP.NET programming model, two categories of server-side controls exist: custom controls and user controls, both of which are useful when designing page templates. Custom controls are more lightweight and must be compiled into an assembly DLL before being deployed to the front-end Web server. User controls are more productive because you can use the visual designer supplied by Visual Studio to create them.

After an overview of the use of custom controls and user controls, this section will address the creation of Web Part pages by creating a page template with one or more Web Part zones. During this discussion, we will explore the WSS infrastructure that makes browser-based user customization through Web Part possible.

Constructing Pages with Custom Controls

Let's begin with a simple example of a custom control. A server-side control in ASP.NET is defined as a class that inherits from the Control class. However, developers often choose to create custom controls by deriving from a richer class named WebControl, which inherits from the Control class. The following code example illustrates a custom control class that inherits from WebControl and implements "Hello World" functionality by overriding the RenderContents method and adding some simple code that programs against the WSS object model.

```
using System.Web.UI;
using System.Web.UI.WebControls;
using Microsoft.SharePoint;

namespace CustomSitePages {
  public class CustomControl1 : WebControl  {
    protected override void RenderContents(HtmlTextWriter output)  {
      SPWeb site = SPContext.Current.Web;
      output.Write("Current Site: " + site.Title);
```

```
        output.Write("<br/>");
        output.Write("Current Site ID: " + site.ID.ToString());
      }
    }
  }
}
```

You have two choices as to where to deploy an assembly DLL that contains a custom control when you want to use it in a site page. First, you can compile the assembly DLL with a strong name and install it in the Global Assembly Cache. Alternatively, you can deploy the assembly DLL by placing it inside the root directory of the hosting Web application inside a nested directory named bin. Note that when you plan to deploy the assembly DLL with custom controls in the bin directory, you have the option of compiling it with or without a strong name.

Once the assembly DLL with the custom control is properly deployed, you can then reference it within a page template by using the ASP.NET Register directive. The following code example displays a page template that uses the custom control shown previously.

```
<%@ Page MasterPageFile="~masterurl/default.master"
    meta:progid="SharePoint.WebPartPage.Document" %>

<%@ Register Assembly="CustomSitePages, ... "
    Namespace="CustomSitePages" TagPrefix="CustomSitePages" %>


<asp:Content ID="main"
    ContentPlaceHolderId="PlaceHolderMain"
    runat="server">

<h3>A custom control example</h3>

<CustomSitePages:CustomControl1 ID="cc1" runat="server" />

</asp:Content>
```

As you can see, adding a Register directive is just like adding an assembly reference to a project in Visual Studio because it makes the public components inside the target assembly available for use within the page. However, the Register directive also defines a TagPrefix attribute with a value of CustomSitePages. This TagPrefix value is then used to instantiate instances of the control within the page.

```
<CustomSitePages:CustomControl1 ID="cc1" runat="server" />
```

When you navigate to Page02.aspx, you should see that the page renders the output of the control so that it is visible to the user. However, this works only while the hosting page remains in a ghosted state. Remember that customized pages allow only for controls that are registered as safe controls. If a user customizes Page02.aspx with the SharePoint Designer, the page begins to execute in safe mode, and the presence of a control that is not registered as a safe control results in the error message shown in Figure 3-5.

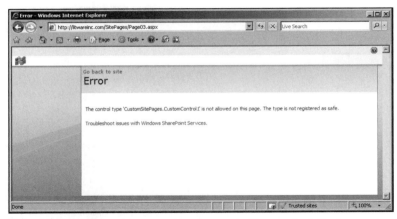

Figure 3-5 Safe mode processing does not allow controls that are not registered as safe controls.

To fix this problem, you must add a custom SafeControl entry to the hosting Web application's web.config file. You can accomplish this by adding a SafeControl entry that looks like the following:

```
<SafeControl
  Assembly="CustomSitePages, ..."
  Namespace="CustomSitePages"
  TypeName="CustomControl1"
/>
```

Note that when you add a SafeControl entry, you can define the type name for the control class explicitly as shown here, or you can alternatively use a TypeName value of * to register all of the server-side controls and Web Parts within the specific namespace that reside in the target assembly DLL.

Constructing Pages with User Controls

User controls provide a more productive alternative to custom controls. They are easier to develop because they are deployed on the front-end Web server as simple text files with an .ascx extension. The ASP.NET runtime provides the functionality to parse these .ascx files at run time and compile them into assembly DLLs just as it does for .aspx files.

Let's examine the source file for a simple user control. The following example of an .ascx file creates a simple user interface with a command button and a label and adds in an event handler to provide the classic "Hello World" functionality.

```
<%@ Control Language="C#" %>

<script runat="server">
  protected void cmdButton1_Click(object sender, EventArgs e) {
    lblStatus.Text = "Hello, World";
  }
</script>
```

```
<asp:Button ID="cmdAddCustomer" runat="server" Text="Add Customer"
            OnClick="cmdAddCustomer_Click" />
<br/>
<asp:Label ID="lblStatus" runat="server" Text="" />
```

As you can see, it's fairly easy to get started with user controls. You can even use notepad.exe to create and modify simple .ascx files. However, you will likely prefer using Visual Studio to develop .ascx files because it provides a user control editor. This visual editor provides significantly higher levels of productivity because you can use standard Visual Studio design tools, such as the control toolbox and property sheet shown in Figure 3-6.

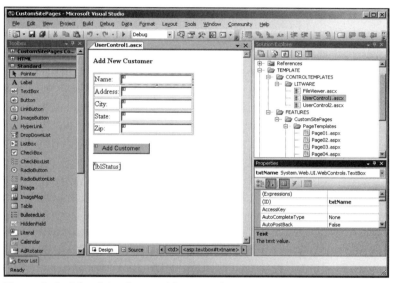

Figure 3-6   Visual Studio provides a productivity-oriented designer for developing user controls.

It is important to understand that WSS does not support user customization of user controls. User controls are always loaded from the file system of the front-end Web server and compiled into assembly DLLs. Furthermore, user controls can be copied to the front-end Web server only by someone with farm-level administrative privileges. For these reasons, you can assume that you can always write in-line code in an .ascx file.

Assume that you want to write in-line code in a user control that programs against the WSS object model. That's easy. All you have to do is add an assembly directive to the top of the .ascx file that references the four-part assembly name of Microsoft.SharePoint.dll. You can also add an Import directive to import one or more namespaces to make your code more concise.

```
<%@ Control Language="C#" %>
<%@ Assembly Name="Microsoft.SharePoint, ..." %>
<%@ Import Namespace="Microsoft.SharePoint" %>
```

```
<script runat="server">
  protected override void OnLoad(EventArgs e)  {
    SPWeb site = SPContext.Current.Web;
    lblDisplay.Text = "Current Site: " + site.Url;
  }
</script>

<asp:Label ID="lblDisplay" runat="server" />
```

In Chapter 2, you were introduced to the virtual _layouts directory and learned that this was the proper place to deploy application pages. WSS provides a similar virtual directory for deploying user controls. Inside the TEMPLATE directory resides a nested directory named CONTROLTEMPLATES. This directory contains many different user controls that are deployed as part of the standard WSS installation.

The CONTROLTEMPLATES directory is also a place where you should deploy custom user control files. However, it's a good practice to create your own nested directory inside the CONTROLTEMPLATES directory to avoid potential file name conflicts. The CustomSitePages project creates a company-specific inner directory named Litware and copies its user controls into that directory. Each custom user control is copied to a physical path that looks like the following:

```
TEMPLATES/CONTROLTEMPLATES/Litware/UserControl1.ascx
```

Each Web application is configured with a virtual directory named _controltemplates that points to the physical CONTROLTEMPLATES directory. This makes it possible to reference any user control file by using a standard path relative to the hosting Web application. For example, one of the user controls from the CustomSitePages project can be referenced by using a virtual path that looks like the following:

```
~/_controltemplates/Litware/UserControl1.ascx
```

When deploying user controls, it's important to remember that they follow the same rules with respect to safe mode processing. If you want to place a user control on a site page that might be customized, the .ascx file must be registered as a safe control in the web.config file of the hosting Web application. Fortunately, you don't have to worry about this if you deploy your custom user controls inside the virtual _controltemplates directory because the standard web.config file for a Web application already contains the following SafeControl entry:

```
<SafeControl
  Src="~/_controltemplates/*"
  IncludeSubFolders="True"
  Safe="True"
  AllowRemoteDesigner="True"
/>
```

Now that you have seen how to create and properly deploy a user control, the final step is constructing a page template that references the .ascx file and creates an instance. Similar to constructing pages with custom controls, this is accomplished by placing a Register directive on the page template. However, the process is different with user controls because the Register directive requires an src attribute that points to the virtual path of the target .ascx file.

```
<%@ Page MasterPageFile="~masterurl/default.master"
    meta:progid="SharePoint.WebPartPage.Document"  %>

<%@ Register TagPrefix="luc" TagName="UserControl1"
    src="~/_controltemplates/Litware/UserControl1.ascx" %>

<asp:Content runat="server" ContentPlaceHolderID="PlaceHolderMain">

  <luc:UserControl1 ID="id1" runat="server" />

</asp:Content>
```

You have now seen all of the steps involved with constructing site pages using custom controls and user controls. This provides you with a strategy to create components that are reusable and versionable, and also provides you with a technique for adding whatever custom code you want to pages that are running in safe mode.

Note that all techniques shown here for constructing pages with custom controls and user controls can be used within custom application pages in the same fashion as they are in site pages. The one major difference is that application pages do not support user customization and never run in safe mode. If you want to create a custom control or user control that is used only on application pages, you do not need to worry about registering controls as safe controls in the web.config file.

Designing Web Part Pages

Web Parts provide a valuable dimension to WSS. In particular, Web Parts make it possible for a site owner to customize a site page with changes that are seen by all users. Web Parts go even further to allow individual users to add personalization changes that are seen only by them. WSS provides the underlying mechanisms to track all of this customization and personalization inside the content database along with all of the other site-related data.

Before diving into the details of how Web Part pages work, two important aspects of their architecture must be noted. First, support for customizing and personalizing Web Parts is available in site pages but not in application pages, thus giving site pages a clear design advantage over application pages.

Second, adding and customizing Web Parts does not require customizing the Web Part pages that host them. A Web Part page defines Web Part zones but does not define what goes inside these zones. Instead, all of the data for tracking Web Part instances and their customization and personalization data are kept in separate tables inside the content database. This means that a Web Part page can remain in a ghosted state even though users are continually adding, customizing, and personalizing the Web Parts within its zone.

Web Part pages in a WSS 3.0 site are built on top of the new Web Part infrastructure introduced with ASP.NET 2.0. To create a Web Part page in an ASP.NET 2.0 application, you must create an .aspx page that contains exactly one instance of a control named WebPartManager and one or more WebPartZone controls. The WebPartManager is responsible for managing the lifetime of Web Part instances as well as serializing Web Part–related data so that they can be stored and retrieved from the tables in the ASP.NET services database.

The Web Part infrastructure of WSS 3.0 does not use the standard WebPartManager control from ASP.NET. Instead, WSS relies on a specialized control named SPWebPartManager that derives from the ASP.NET 2.0 WebPartManager control. The SPWebPartManager control overrides the standard behavior of the WebPartManager control to persist Web Part data inside the WSS content database instead of inside the ASP.NET services database.

In most cases, you don't have to worry about dealing with the SPWebPartManager control directly because the one and only required instance of the SPWebPartManager is already defined in the standard default.master page. When you create a site page that links to default.master, the SPWebPartManager control is automatically added to the page. Therefore, you simply need to add one or more WebPartZone controls.

Two things must be done when creating a page template for a Web Part page. The first is to inherit from the WebPartPage class that is defined inside the Microsoft.SharePoint.dll assembly. The second is to add one or more WebPartZone controls. Note that you must use the WebPartZone control defined by the WSS team and not the one of the same name defined by the ASP.NET team.

To add WebPartZone controls to a page template, you must add a Register directive that imports all of the controls from the Microsoft.SharePoint.dll assembly defined in the Microsoft.SharePoint.WebPartPages namespace as shown in the following page template definition.

```
<%@ Page MasterPageFile="~masterurl/default.master"
    Inherits="Microsoft.SharePoint.WebPartPages.WebPartPage,
            Microsoft.SharePoint, [full 4-part assembly name]"
    meta:progid="SharePoint.WebPartPage.Document"   %>

<%@ Register Tagprefix="WebPartPages"
    Namespace="Microsoft.SharePoint.WebPartPages"
    Assembly="Microsoft.SharePoint, ..." %>

<asp:Content ID="main" runat="server" ContentPlaceHolderID="PlaceHolderMain" >

<h3>Custom Web Part page</h3>

<table width="100%">
  <tr>
    <td valign="top" style="width:50%">
        <WebPartPages:WebPartZone ID="LeftZone" runat="server"
                                FrameType="TitleBarOnly"
```

```
                                Title="Left Web Part zone" />
        </td>
        <td valign="top" style="width:50%">
            <WebPartPages:WebPartZone ID="RightZone" runat="server"
                                      FrameType="TitleBarOnly"
                                      Title="Right Web Part zone" />
        </td>
    </tr>
</table>
</asp:Content>
```

It is easier to create pages that host Web Parts in the WSS framework than in the ASP.NET Framework. For example, when you design an ASP.NET application that involves Web Parts, you are required to add logic to each page that interacts with the WebPartManager control to manage the display mode. It is also necessary to explicitly add controls, such as Editor Zones and Catalog Zones, to the page so that users can customize existing Web Parts as well as add new Web Parts.

Fortunately, you don't need to worry about managing the display mode or adding Editor Zones and Catalog Zones when creating Web Part pages for WSS. When you create a Web Part page that inherits from the WebPartPage class, all of this work is done for you behind the scenes. The Site Actions menu automatically provides the Edit Page command that allows the user to enter a mode for adding and customizing Web Parts.

In the CustomSitePages project, three different site pages are provisioned from the page template named WebPartPage.aspx. If you navigate to the first site page named WebPartPage01.aspx and select the Edit Page command from the Site Actions menu, you will see that there are two empty zones, as shown in Figure 3-7. At this point, you can use basic WSS support to add a new Web Part instance as you would to any other Web Part page, such as default.aspx.

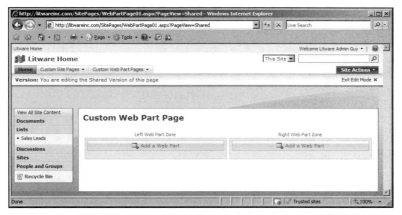

Figure 3-7   A Web Part page is designed with one or more Web Part zones.

When you provision a Web Part page from a page template, it initially contains no Web Parts in any of its Web Part zones. While you could rely on users manually adding Web Parts to your pages, it is more convenient and reliable for you to use a technique in which you pre-populate Web Part zones with whatever Web Parts your business solution requires.

There are two common techniques for adding a Web Part instance to a Web Part zone. The first technique involves a declarative approach used inside a feature in which you define an AllUsersWebPart element inside a File element. The following example demonstrates the File element that is used in the CustomSitePages project to provision the Web Part page named WebPartPage02.aspx.

```
<Elements xmlns="http://schemas.microsoft.com/sharepoint/">
  <Module Path="PageTemplates" Url="SitePages" >
    <File Url="WebPartPage.aspx" Name="WebPartPage02.aspx" Type="Ghostable" >
      <!-- Add a Web Part to left zone -->
      <AllUsersWebPart WebPartZoneID="LeftZone" WebPartOrder="0">
        <![CDATA[
          <WebPart xmlns="http://schemas.microsoft.com/WebPart/v2"
                   xmlns:iwp="http://schemas.microsoft.com/WebPart/v2/Image">
            <Assembly>Microsoft.SharePoint, ...</Assembly>
            <TypeName>Microsoft.SharePoint.WebPartPages.ImageWebPart</TypeName>
            <FrameType>None</FrameType>
            <Title>Watch My Gears Run</Title>
            <iwp:ImageLink>/_layouts/images/GEARS_AN.GIF</iwp:ImageLink>
          </WebPart>
        ]]>
      </AllUsersWebPart>
    </File>
  </Module>
</Elements>
```

As you can see, a File element can contain an inner AllUsersWebPart element that references a target Web Part zone and includes serialized data for the Web Part instance to be created. We will revisit the inner WebPart element in more detail in Chapter 4 when we discuss Web Part description files.

The second technique for adding a Web Part instance to a Web Part page involves writing code against the WSS object model. An example of this type of code is supplied in the FeatureActivated event handler for the CustomSitePages project. The code obtains a reference to the SPFile object associated with WebPartPage03.aspx and uses an SPLimitedWebPart-Manager object to add a new Web Part instance to a particular target zone.

```
public override void FeatureActivated(
                    SPFeatureReceiverProperties properties) {
  // acquire objects for site, page and limited Web Part Manager
  SPWeb site = (SPWeb)properties.Feature.Parent;
  SPFile page = site.GetFile("SitePages/WebPartPage03.aspx");
  SPLimitedWebPartManager mgr;
  mgr = page.GetLimitedWebPartManager(PersonalizationScope.Shared);
```

```
  // add Web Part to Right Zone
  ImageWebPart wp1 = new ImageWebPart();
  wp1.ChromeType = PartChromeType.None;
  wp1.ImageLink = @"/_layouts/images/IPVW.GIF";
  mgr.AddWebPart(wp1, "RightZone", 0);
}
```

The advantage to using the first technique is that Web Parts can be added to pages with declarative logic in the same place where the actual page is being provisioned. The advantage of using the second approach involving code is that it is more flexible. While you can execute code that adds a Web Part instance during feature activation, you can also execute the same code long after the feature is activated. For example, imagine a scenario in which you would like to write the code required to enumerate through every site within a farm to add a special Web Part to a target zone on every home page. The WSS object model makes it possible to automate this type of administrative task with Web Part pages.

Master Pages

One of the most tedious aspects of customizing and branding sites in WSS 2.0 has to do with creating a consistent look and feel across pages. The root of this problem is caused by the fact that ASP.NET 1.1 does not provide an effective page-templating technique that can be used to define a common layout across the pages within a WSS 2.0 site. As a result, many developers and designers working with WSS 2.0 and Microsoft SharePoint Portal Server 2003 have resorted to copying and pasting HTML layouts from page to page. As you can imagine, this makes it very hard to customize and maintain sites whose layout requirements differ from the out-of-the-box experience you get with a standard WSS 2.0 site.

When master pages were introduced with ASP.NET 2.0, they were embraced by developers because they provide a more elegant way to define the common layout for all pages within a site. The fact that WSS 3.0 was designed from the ground up around the concept of master pages is a very welcome change for those with experience branding sites with the previous version of WSS.

The last chapter reviewed the basic ASP.NET architecture for master pages. A master page is a template that allows you to define a standard page layout for an entire site with common elements, such as a banner and navigation controls. The pages that link to a master page are known as content pages. The key concept is that each content page that links to a master page benefits from the shared layout and then can extend that master page by using replaceable named placeholders to add unique content.

In this book, you have already seen several places where master pages have been used. In the previous chapter, you saw that the majority of standard WSS application pages link to a master page in the virtual _layouts directory named application.master. You have also seen that you can link to application.master when creating your own custom application pages.

In this chapter, you have seen how to create page templates for site pages that link to the standard master page named default.master. This makes it very simple to create site pages that have the same look and feel as the standard site pages that are provided out of the box with WSS.

As you begin to think through the bigger picture with respect to branding WSS sites with master pages, there is one critical factor to keep in mind. Site pages and application pages use separate master pages. In this chapter, we will examine how to provision and use a custom master page for the site pages within a site. This technique allows you to change the layout for every site page within any site to which you want to apply your own custom branding. However, the technique being covered in the next section cannot be applied to application pages because the majority of standard WSS application pages rely on a single master page named application.master that cannot be replaced or customized on a site-by-site basis.

Understanding default.master

Every WSS 3.0 site is provisioned with a special catalog known as the Master Page gallery containing a master page template named default.master. This standard master page is deployed during the standard WSS installation on the file system of the front-end Web server at the following path (there is a line break in the file path to make it more readable).

```
C:\Program Files\Common Files\Microsoft Shared
    \web server extensions\12\TEMPLATE\GLOBAL\default.master
```

Whenever you create a new site, WSS provides provisioning instructions to create the Master Page gallery and provision an instance of default.master within the site by using a standard site-relative path.

```
/_catalogs/masterpage/default.master
```

The default.master page is widely used in WSS. It defines a common layout for every site's home page (default.aspx) as well as all of the standard WSS form pages associated with lists and document libraries (e.g., AllItems.aspx or NewItem.aspx). The default.master page can also serve as the master page for your custom site pages, as has been demonstrated in all of the page templates used in the CustomSitePages project.

To understand the best practice for creating site pages that link to default.master, it's important that you have a basic understanding of what's defined inside this file. It's definitely worth your time to open up a copy of the default.master file within Visual Studio and try to absorb all that's there. While it might take some time to get to know everything inside, it's a worthwhile investment for any developer serious about mastering WSS development.

The default.master page contains the basic layout for a site page including elements such as HTML, HEAD, BODY, and FORM. Within these standard HTML elements, you will find three important types of components:

■ Controls for links, menus, icons, and navigation components

■ Named placeholders

■ Delegate controls

Many server-side controls that are used to construct the default.master page template represent encapsulated logic and user interface components that are compiled into the Microsoft.SharePoint assembly. Examples of these controls include the SPWebPartManager object and controls to provide navigation components, such as breadcrumb trails and menus for navigating around the site.

Named placeholders provide an extensibility mechanism used to add unique content to a page template or page instance that is linked to a master page. Delegate controls provide an elegant way to substitute elements into the layout of default.master that affects every site page that links to it. The following fragment of HTML is extracted from default.master and is simplified to demonstrate how each of these component types is used.

```
<%@Master language="C#"%>

<%@ Register Tagprefix="SharePoint"
    Namespace="Microsoft.SharePoint.WebControls" Assembly="Microsoft.SharePoint, …" %>

<HTML runat="server">

<HEAD runat="server">

    <!-- SharePoint Utility Controls -->
    <SharePoint:CssLink ID="CssLink1" runat="server"/>
    <SharePoint:Theme ID="Theme1" runat="server"/>

    <!-- Named Placeholders -->
    <Title ID=onetidTitle>
      <asp:ContentPlaceHolder id=PlaceHolderPageTitle runat="server"/>
    </Title>
    <asp:ContentPlaceHolder id="PlaceHolderAdditionalPageHead"
                        runat="server"/>

    <!-- Named Delegate Control -->
    <SharePoint:DelegateControl ID="DelegateControl1" runat="server"
                        ControlId="AdditionalPageHead"
                        AllowMultipleControls="true"/>
</HEAD>
```

The HEAD element of default.master shows the use of standard WSS server-side controls, such as CssLink and Theme. These controls contain the encapsulated logic to integrate the standard Cascading Style Sheet (CSS) files used by WSS and supply the support required for user-applied themes. Note that these same two controls are also present inside application.master so that the standard CSS files and themes continue to work as users navigate to application pages.

You can also see that the HEAD element defines two named placeholders with an ID of PlaceHolderPageTitle and PlaceHolderAdditionalPageHead. The placeholder named Place-HolderPageTitle makes it possible to substitute the page title when creating a page template or customizing a site page instance. The placeholder named PlaceHolderAdditionalPageHead makes it possible to add items such as extra meta tags into the HEAD section. The following example displays a page template that substitutes these two placeholders with unique content.

```
<%@ Page MasterPageFile="~masterurl/default.master" %>

<asp:Content ID="PageTitle" runat="server"
             ContentPlaceHolderID="PlaceHolderPageTitle">
  My Custom Page Title
</asp:Content>

<asp:Content ID="AdditionalPageHead" runat="server"
             ContentPlaceHolderID="PlaceHolderAdditionalPageHead">
  <META name="keywords" content="Software, Consulting, Money, Fame" />
</asp:Content>
```

WSS Navigation Components

Several standard controls are included with default.master that provide the basic infrastructure for navigation. For example, the ASP.NET SiteMapPath control that has been positioned at the very top of the page populates a breadcrumb navigation menu that allows users to navigate from the current site upward to the parent site and all the way to the top-level site of the current site collection.

Navigation in WSS is based on the navigation-provider infrastructure introduced in ASP.NET 2.0. In this model, a navigation provider is designed and created to provide a set of navigation nodes. In many cases, the nodes supplied by a navigation provider can be bound to a menu control or a treeview to give users a user interface component with which to navigate around the site.

WSS provides several standard navigation providers such as the SPNavigationProvider, SPSiteMapProvider, SPContentMapProvider, and SPXmlContentMapProvider classes. You can see where all the active navigation providers are defined by examining the siteMap section inside the system.web section of the standard WSS web.config file.

The top link bar and the Quick Launch menu represent the two main navigation components defined in default.master. The top link bar is defined by using a WSS-specific control of type AspMenu along with a SiteMapDataSource control that is configured to point to the standard SPNavigationProvider component. The Quick Launch menu is defined in the same way. The major difference between the two is that the SiteMapDataSource for the top link bar is configured with a StartingNodeUrl attribute with a value of sid:1002, whereas the Quick Launch menu is configured with a StartingNodeUrl attribute with a value of sid:1025.

The next question you should be asking is what the significance is between 1002 and 1025. It has to do with the data stored in the content database for tracking navigation nodes. The top node for the top link bar has an ID of 1002, and the top node to the Quick Launch menu has an ID of 1025.

WSS provides users with the flexibility to add navigation nodes to either the top link bar or the Quick Launch menu. You can access the application pages that allow users to perform these actions from the Site Settings page. What's nice about this scheme for developers is that you can customize the standard WSS navigation menus without making any changes to default.master. You simply need to find a way to add new navigation nodes to the content database.

While it's possible for users to add navigation nodes through site administration pages in the browser-based user interface, it's also possible and far more flexible to accomplish the same goal by using the WSS object model. The CustomSitePages feature provides code in the FeatureActivated event handler to add navigation nodes to construct a custom drop-down menu in a fashion that is not possible to replicate through the user interface. Examine the following code and observe how it creates SPNavigationNode objects and adds them to the collection of nodes that define the structure for the top link bar.

```
public override void FeatureActivated(SPFeatureReceiverProperties properties) {

  // get a hold of current site in context of feature activation
  SPWeb site = (SPWeb)properties.Feature.Parent;
  SPNavigationNodeCollection topNav = site.Navigation.TopNavigationBar;

  // create dropdown menu for custom site pages
  SPNavigationNode DropDownMenu1;
  DropDownMenu1 = new SPNavigationNode("Site Pages", "", false);
  topNav[0].Children.AddAsLast(DropDownMenu1);

  // add navigation nodes to create menu items
  DropDownMenu1.Children.AddAsLast(
      new SPNavigationNode( "Site Page 1",
                            "SitePages/Page01.aspx"));
  DropDownMenu1.Children.AddAsLast(
      new SPNavigationNode("Site Page 2",
                            "SitePages/Page02.aspx"));
}
```

Delegate Controls

WSS introduces a powerful new extensibility mechanism known as delegate controls. In some ways, a delegate control is similar to a named placeholder because it defines a region inside a master page that can be substituted with unique content to meet the needs of a particular business solution. Like a placeholder, a delegate control can optionally supply default content that is used until a substitution is performed.

One major difference when compared to placeholders is that the substitution mechanism for replacing the contents of a delegate control is driven through feature activation. Therefore, you can replace what's defined inside a delegate control in default.master without requiring any changes to default.master or the site pages that link to it. All you need to do is define a Control element within a feature and then activate that feature.

A significant aspect of using delegate controls involves the scope of the feature that is being used to drive substitution. When you design a feature to substitute the contents of a delegate control, your feature can be scoped at any of the four supported levels. These levels include site scope, site collection scope, Web application scope, and farm scope. This dimension of delegate controls provides a powerful mechanism for enabling and disabling functionality on a wide-scale basis.

Let's begin by looking at an example of a delegate control that is defined in default.master to create the region that defines the standard search area in site pages just above the Site Settings menu. The delegate control definition in default.master looks like the following:

```
<SharePoint:DelegateControl
  ID="DelegateControl5"
  runat="server"
  ControlId="SmallSearchInputBox"
/>
```

This is an example of a delegate control that defines no default content. Instead, the default content for this delegate control is supplied by a standard WSS feature named ContentLightup. The ContentLightup feature defines a Control element that substitutes content into the SmallSearchInputBox delegate control by referencing a built-in user control with the standard WSS search area content.

```
<Control
  Id="SmallSearchInputBox"
  Sequence="100"
  ControlSrc="~/_controltemplates/searcharea.ascx"
/>
```

Assume that you want to get rid of the standard search area content and replace it with your own custom content for a particular business solution. That's what delegate controls were designed for. If you want to follow along with the sample code that accompanies this chapter, you should open the Visual Studio project named CustomBranding. This project contains the definition for a feature named CustomBranding that is scoped to the level of a site collection.

If you want to replace a delegate control, such as the WSS search area, with your own customized version, you start by adding a Control element to a feature. The Control element should have an ID value of SmallSearchInputBox. The Control element should also have a Sequence number smaller than any other active Control element pointing to the same ID. The following code demonstrates how the Control element is defined inside the elements.xml file of the CustomBranding feature.

```
<Control
  Id="SmallSearchInputBox"
  Sequence="10"
  ControlSrc="~/_controltemplates/Litware/LitwareSearchArea.ascx"
/>
```

Note that this Control element has a sequence number of 10, which is smaller than the Control element defined in ContentLightup with a Sequence number of 100. Once the CustomBranding feature is activated within a site collection, all of the site pages that link to default.master replace the standard WSS search area with whatever content you have defined inside the custom user control named LitwareSearchArea.ascx. The following code defines a starting point for creating a custom user control that supplies custom search behavior.

```
<%@ Control Language="C#" %>

<script runat="server">
    protected void cmdRunSearch_Click(object sender, EventArgs e)    {
      // LEFT AS AN EXERCISE FOR THE READER
      // Step 1: add code here to perform custom search
      // Step 2: redirect user to custom search results page
    }
</script>

<table>
  <tr>
    <td>
      <asp:Button ID="cmdRunSearch" runat="server" Text="Search"
                  OnClick="cmdRunSearch_Click" />
    </td>
    <td>
      <asp:TextBox ID="txtSearchText" runat="server" Width="120" />
    </td>
  </tr>
</table>
```

While the CustomBranding feature is designed to activate at the level of a site collection, remember that delegate controls can be substituted at any scope supported by features. You can add the Control element that substitutes the delegate control named SmallSearchInputBox to a feature scoped at the Web application or farm level to replace the standard WSS search area on a larger scale.

If you have plans to replace the WSS search area by using a Control element, it's important for you to understand that Microsoft Office SharePoint Server (MOSS) uses the same approach. The Standard Edition of MOSS provides a feature that replaces the SmallSearchInputBox delegate control by using a Control element with a sequence number of 50. The Enterprise Edition of MOSS provides a feature that replaces the SmallSearchInputBox delegate control by using a Control element with a sequence number of 25.

The main point here is that you obtain a more enhanced version of the search area as you upgrade from WSS to MOSS Standard Edition and then to MOSS Enterprise Edition. You should assign the sequence number for your Control element accordingly depending on whether you want to override the enhanced versions of the search area supplied by MOSS.

In addition to substituting delegate controls by using .ascx files, WSS also supports delegate control substitution by using control classes that are compiled into assemblies installed in the Global Assembly Cache. As an example, let's examine a technique for replacing the SiteMapDataSource that is used to populate the Quick Launch menu. Examine the following fragment from the standard default.master page template that defines a delegate control named QuickLaunchDataSource.

```
<SharePoint:DelegateControl
    ID="DelegateControl8" runat="server"
    ControlId="QuickLaunchDataSource">
  <Template_Controls>
    <asp:SiteMapDataSource
      SiteMapProvider="SPNavigationProvider"
      ShowStartingNode="False"
      id="QuickLaunchSiteMap"
      StartingNodeUrl="sid:1025"
      runat="server" />
  </Template_Controls>
</SharePoint:DelegateControl>
```

Unlike the last example of a delegate control, this delegate control with a ControlId of QuickLaunchDataSource defines default content that is used until a substitution is performed. The default content includes a SiteMapDataSource control with an ID of QuickLaunchSiteMap. If you want to substitute this control with a different SiteMapData-Source control, you can add the following Control element to a custom feature.

```
<Control
 Id="QuickLaunchDataSource" Sequence="1"
 ControlAssembly="System.Web, ..."
 ControlClass="System.Web.UI.WebControls.SiteMapDataSource">
  <Property Name="ID">QuickLaunchSiteMap</Property>
  <Property Name="SiteMapProvider">SPSiteMapProvider</Property>
  <Property Name="ShowStartingNode">False</Property>
</Control>
```

As shown in the previous example, this Control element provides an ID that matches the ControlId of the target delegate on which the substitution should be performed. However, this example differs because it uses the ControlAssembly and ControlClass attributes to reference a specific control type within a target assembly.

You should also observe that the Control element contains several nested Property elements that define the initialization parameters for the control instance being used in the substitution. It is important in this example that the control instance being created is assigned an ID of QuickLaunchSiteMap because the hosting page expects to find a control of that name. The control instance is also initialized to use the SPSiteMapProvider class, which provides different behavior than the default that uses the SPNavigationProvider class instead.

Customizing default.master

The previous section of this chapter demonstrated several branding techniques involving placeholder and delegate controls that did not require making any changes to default.master. However, many developers and end users alike will come to the conclusion that they want to make changes to default.master. This is something that the SharePoint Designer makes very easy to accomplish. You can simply open default.master and make whatever changes you want. The SharePoint Designer makes it possible to work in either Code view or Design view when you are customizing a master page such as default.master.

From an architectural standpoint, it's important to acknowledge that the default.master page follows the same rules for ghosting and unghosting as the site pages that link to it. When a site is initially created, default.master is uncustomized. When site pages that link to default.master are requested, the master page template is loaded from the file system of the front-end Web server and processed like any other ghosted page. However, default.master becomes unghosted once a user customizes it with the SharePoint Designer. These customization changes are stored inside the content database just like customizations to site pages, such as default.aspx. From that point on, default.master is processed like any other customized page and must follow all of the rules of safe mode processing.

Note that it's possible to customize the master page for a site while leaving the site pages that link to it uncustomized. Likewise, it's possible to customize one or more site pages while leaving their underlying master page uncustomized. Furthermore, if you customize either the master page or site pages and later wish to undo your changes, both the browser-based UI of WSS and the SharePoint Designer provide simple menu commands to discard customization changes from the content database and revert back to the original page template.

Even though customizing a master page with the SharePoint Designer provides a quick and easy way to make changes, it's difficult to track these changes in a source code management system. It's also difficult to make such customization changes repeatable across site collections in a large-scale deployment. Instead of using this type of customization strategy, a better approach for a developer is to create a page template for a custom master page. This topic is covered in the next section of this chapter.

Creating a Custom Master Page Template

Creating a custom master page template involves several steps. First, you must create the master page template itself. Second, you must create a custom feature that provisions an instance of this master page template inside the Master Page gallery for a specific site. Finally, you need to add some code to redirect site pages to use your custom master page instead of using default.master. The Visual Studio project named CustomBranding provides a working sample that demonstrates how all of the pieces fit together.

Remember that the CustomBranding feature is scoped to the level of the site collection. While you can create a custom feature scoped at the site level to integrate a custom master page template, it's better to design such a feature at the site collection level because users typically want branding to occur at this level. It is less convenient if you force users to activate the feature separately for every site within a site collection.

You can create a custom template by using two different approaches. First, you can make a copy of default.master and then modify it according to taste. A second approach involves starting from scratch so that you can design the exact HTML layout you're looking for. If you start from scratch, be sure to think through which named placeholders you need to include. There are over 30 named placeholders defined inside default.master, and many of the standard site pages, such as default.aspx and AllItems.aspx, assume that whatever master page they link to will have these same named placeholders.

If you forget to include the same set of named placeholders found in default.master, you will likely experience problems. ASP.NET generates errors whenever it finds that a site page references a named placeholder that is not defined in the master page to which it is linked.

The custom master page template used in the CustomBranding project is named Litware.master. The Litware.master template is a variation on the default.master template with changes to allow for fly-out menus on both the top link bar and Quick Launch menu. The CustomBranding feature includes a Module element that has been designed to provision an instance of the Litware.master page template into the Master Page gallery of the top-level site.

```
<Module Name="MasterPages" List="116" Url="_catalogs/masterpage">
  <File Url="Litware.master" Type="GhostableInLibrary" />
</Module>
```

Note that this Module element has several differences compared with the Module element for provisioning site pages shown earlier in this chapter. While the previous Module was used to provision pages into a site, it did not target a document library. However, this Module targets the Master Page gallery, which is a special type of document library. Therefore, the Module is defined with a List attribute of 116, which is the list type identifier for the Master Page gallery. The Url attribute for this Module is defined with a value of _catalogs/masterpage, which is the standard site-relative path to the Master Page gallery.

If you examine the File element that provisions an instance of Litware.master, you notice that the Type attribute has a value of GhostableInLibrary as opposed to a value of Ghostable that was shown earlier when provisioning site pages inside a site but outside the scope of a document library. A value of GhostableInLibrary should be used whenever you are provisioning an instance of a file, such as a master page template, inside a target document library.

We have reviewed the steps involved in creating a master page template and provisioning an instance of it in the Master Page gallery of the top-level site. The next step involves redirecting all site pages within a site to link to this provisioned instance of our custom master page template. To understand the technique for accomplishing this, take a closer look at the MasterPageFile attribute defined within a Page directive. Examine the following page template, which is defined to link to a target master page by using a special syntax in the form of ~masterurl/default.master.

```
<%@ Page MasterPageFile="~masterurl/default.master" %>

<asp:Content ContentPlaceHolderId="PlaceHolderMain" runat="server">
  Custom content goes here
</asp:Content>
```

The value of ~masterurl/default.master represents a tokenized reference to a master page that can be changed programmatically on a site-wide basis. The support for tokenized master page references is provided by the SPVirtualPathProvider class. The way things work is that the SPVirtualPathProvider class reads the value of an SPWeb property named MasterUrl at run time and then parses this value into the MasterPageFile attribute of an .aspx file before sending it to the ASP.NET page parser. You can redirect any site page that uses this token by acquiring an SPWeb reference to the current site and then updating the MasterUrl property.

```
SPWeb site = SPContext.Current.Web;
string MasterUrlPath = site.ServerRelativeUrl;
if (!MasterUrlPath.EndsWith(@"/"))
  MasterUrlPath += @"/";
MasterUrlPath += @"_catalogs/masterpage/Litware.master";
site.MasterUrl = MasterUrlPath;
site.Update();
```

From this code, you can see that a MasterUrl property value should be parsed together using the ServerRelativeUrl property. You should also note that the ServerRelativeUrl property ends with a forward slash in some sites, but not all sites. Therefore, you should add conditional logic to append the forward slash onto the end of the ServerRelativeUrl property if it is not already there. Next, you should append a site-relative path to the master page instance where it exists inside the Master Page gallery. Once you parse together the complete server-relative path to the master page instance, you can assign that value to the MasterUrl property of the current SPWeb object and call the Update method to save your changes.

It's important to remember that the Master Page gallery is scoped at the site level and not the site collection level. Do not be confused into thinking that all sites inside a site collection automatically use the same master page instance. Each site has its own Master Page gallery with its own default.master instance as well as its own MasterUrl property. You must supply additional code if you want all child sites within a site collection to synchronize on a single master page instance in the Master Page gallery of the top-level site. With the use of recursion, it's not too difficult to write the code against the WSS object model to accomplish this task.

The CustomBranding project provides a custom application page named CustomBrand.aspx that provides code to redirect all site pages within a site collection to link to the instance of litware.master that is provisioned in the Master Page gallery of the top-level site. Once you activate the CustomBranding feature, you can navigate to the application page named CustomBrand.aspx by using a custom menu item that is added to the Site Settings menu. This application page provides a command button that allows the user to execute the following code.

```
protected void cmdApplyCustomBrand_Click(object sender, EventArgs e) {
  SPWeb site = SPContext.Current.Site.RootWeb
  string MasterUrlPath = site.ServerRelativeUrl;
  if (!MasterUrlPath.EndsWith(@"/"))
    MasterUrlPath += @"/";
  MasterUrlPath += @"_catalogs/masterpage/Litware.master";
  ApplyCustomBrand(MasterUrlPath, site);
}

protected void ApplyCustomBrand(string MasterUrlPath, SPWeb site) {
  site.MasterUrl = MasterUrlPath;
  site.Update();
  // use recusion to update all child sites in site collection
  foreach (SPWeb child in site.Webs) {
    ApplyCustomBrand(MasterUrlPath, child);
  }
}
```

The code in the event handler named cmdApplyCustomBrand_Click begins by parsing together the server-relative path to the instance of Litware.master in the Master Page gallery of the top-level site. The event handler then calls a method named ApplyCustomBrand to update the MasterUrl of the top-level site.

However, the ApplyCustomBrand method has also been written to enumerate through all child sites below the top-level site and recursively call itself to update them. This recursion continues to crawl the hierarchy of child sites until the MasterUrl property of every site within the site collection is updated to redirect all site pages so that they link to the instance of litware.master that is provisioned in the Master Page gallery of the top-level site.

This technique provides a quick and easy approach to redirect all site pages within a site collection to a custom master page. It works well because all standard WSS site pages, such as default.aspx and AllItems.aspx, are all defined by using the dynamic token

~masterurl/default.master. You can follow suit by defining site page templates using the same technique demonstrated in this chapter.

In addition to ~masterurl/default.master, there is another dynamic token for master pages in the form of ~masterurl/custom.master. This dynamic token works in conjunction with the CustomMasterUrl property of a site and provides a secondary target master page that can be switched out programmatically. This allows you to create designs in which you can switch the master page used by your custom page templates while leaving the standard WSS pages alone so they continue to link to default.master.

In addition to the two dynamic tokens presented in this chapter, WSS also supports two static master page tokens that start with either ~site or ~sitecollection. These static tokens allow you to hardcode a relative path to a master page from the root of either the current site or the current site collection. This allows you to create site page templates that point to a specific custom master page instance without requiring any code to perform redirection.

Branding WSS Sites by Using CSS Files

In the final section of this chapter, we will discuss a few additional topics that are relevant to branding sites. First, we will examine how WSS uses Cascading Style Sheets (CSS) and discuss how to extend this support in a custom branding solution. We will then examine how to replace the image used in the standard WSS page banner by using a custom graphics file.

Understanding core.css

The look and feel of every WSS site is controlled through a standard set of CSS files. The WSS team created a separate set of CSS files for each spoken language supported by WSS. You can find the standard CSS files that are localized for US English at the following path within the WSS TEMPLATE directory.

```
\TEMPLATE\LAYOUTS\1033\STYLES\
```

The file that defines the majority of the standard CSS classes used by pages in WSS is named core.css. WSS was designed so that every site page and every application page is automatically linked to core.css. The support for setting up these links is included in a WSS-specific control named CssLink shown earlier in this chapter. The CssLink control contains logic to link the current page to the most appropriate localized version of core.css. This decision is made by examining the regional settings for the current site and also determining what language packs are installed within the farm.

If you have never looked inside core.css, you should make a copy of this file and examine what's inside. This exercise is somewhat intimidating at first because core.css contains over 4,000 lines of CSS class definitions. However, understanding which CSS classes are defined by the WSS team and learning where they are used becomes an essential aspect of branding WSS sites.

It's important to understand that the core.css file is scoped at the farm level. Changes made to core.css affect every site in the farm; therefore, this is not a file that you should customize. Furthermore, the team at Microsoft responsible for creating updates to WSS reserves the right to install an updated version of core.css in future service packs, and such an action would overwrite any changes you make to core.css today.

WSS provides two recommended techniques for extending the CSS classes defined inside core.css. The first approach involves the use of WSS themes and is targeted at end users. The second approach is targeted at developers and involves creating a secondary CSS file to extend and override the CSS classes defined inside core.css.

WSS Themes

WSS allows users to quickly change the look and feel of a WSS site by changing its theme. The WSS support for changing themes is supplied by a standard application named themeweb.aspx that is accessible through a link on the Site Settings page.

Each theme is defined within its own directory on the front-end Web server. Themes are located in a THEMES directory within the TEMPLATE directory. For example, the built-in theme named Citrus is defined by a set of files residing in the following directory.

```
TEMPLATE\THEMES\CITRUS
```

If you examine the directory for a theme, you find that it includes CSS files and graphics files. When a user chooses a theme, WSS copies all of these files up into the site, including a primary CSS file. WSS also adds a link to the primary CSS file to each application page and each site page. Note that this link is always added after the link to core.css so that CSS classes inside the theme's CSS file override CSS classes defined inside core.css.

Once a user applies a theme to a site, the CSS files can be further customized by using the SharePoint Designer. For example, you can open a site that already has a theme applied in the SharePoint Designer and open the primary CSS file. Any changes you make to this CSS file are stored as ordinary customization with the content database.

From a design perspective, you should observe that themes are targeted more toward end users than developers. While you can create custom themes and deploy them in a WSS environment, the main idea is that themes are added to WSS to support the ability of users to enable or disable them on demand. If you want a site to have specific branding without giving the user control over enabling or disabling it, you should use a custom CSS file as shown in the next section.

AlternateCSS Property

It's fairly easy to integrate a custom CSS file into a custom branding solution. The Visual Studio project named CustomBranding that accompanies this chapter provides an example of how to accomplish this by copying a custom CSS file named LitwareBrand.css and some accompanying graphics files to the following directory.

```
TEMPLATE\LAYOUTS\1033\STYLES\Litware
```

You simply need to update an SPWeb property named AlternateCssUrl in each site where you want to apply your custom theme. Note that when you apply a custom CSS file, it's also a good idea to disable any theme applied by a user so that the CSS classes from a theme do not conflict with the ones defined in your custom CSS file. As shown in the following example, you can see that this step doesn't take much code to accomplish.

```
SPWeb site = SPContext.Current.Web;
site.ApplyTheme("");
site.AlternateCssUrl = "/_layouts/1033/STYLES/Litware/LitwareBrand.css";
site.Update();
```

Site Icon

In addition to supporting custom CSS files, WSS also provides a property so that you can substitute the standard WSS banner image with one more appropriate for your brand. The CustomBranding project contains a graphics file named LitwareFullLogo.png. This file is deployed inside the TEMPLATE\IMAGES directory in the following location.

TEMPLATE\LAYOUTS\Litware\LitwareFullLogo.png

It takes a few lines of code to replace the standard WSS site logo with your own.

```
SPWeb site = SPContext.Current.Web;
site.SiteLogoUrl = "/_layouts/images/Litware/LitwareFullLogo.png";
site.Update();
```

Best Practices for Site Branding

You have encountered several different techniques for adding custom branding to a site. The CustomBranding project provides a feature scoped to the site collection level that allows you to apply all of these branding techniques to all sites within a site collection. We will now examine all code behind the command button in the application page named CustomBrand.aspx. This example extends what was shown earlier by adding extra code so as to add a custom style sheet and custom site log, in addition to redirecting all of the site pages so that they link to Litware.master.

```
protected void cmdApplyCustomBrand_Click(object sender, EventArgs e) {
  SPWeb site = SPContext.Current.Web;
  string MasterUrlPath = site.ServerRelativeUrl;
  if (!MasterUrlPath.EndsWith(@"/"))
    MasterUrlPath += @"/";
  MasterUrlPath += @"_catalogs/masterpage/Litware.master";
  ApplyCustomBrand(MasterUrlPath, site);
  Response.Redirect(Request.RawUrl);
}
```

```
protected void ApplyCustomBrand(string MasterUrlPath, SPWeb site) {
  site.MasterUrl = MasterUrlPath;
  site.ApplyTheme("");
  site.AlternateCssUrl = "/_layouts/1033/STYLES/Litware/LitwareBrand.css";
  site.SiteLogoUrl = "/_layouts/images/Litware/LitwareFullLogo.png";
  site.Update();
  // use recursion to update all sites in site collection
  foreach (SPWeb child in site.Webs) {
    ApplyCustomBrand(MasterUrlPath, child);
  }
}
```

The CustomBranding project provides the code to enable and disable custom branding for a site collection through an application page with command buttons. However, you can extend this example and add the same code to the FeatureActivated event handler so that branding is applied whenever the CustomBranding feature is activated. You can even take this example one step further by writing code to enumerate every through site collection in a farm and activate the CustomBranding feature in each of these site collections along the way.

One final observation that we want you to make is that some branding techniques work across both site pages and application pages, which is the case for both the custom CSS file applied by using the AlternateCssUrl property as well as the site logo that can be replaced by using SiteLogoUrl. This occurs because support for these items is included in both the standard application.master template and the default.master template. However, the technique shown in this chapter for branding sites with a custom master page doesn't extend to application pages. Therefore, you might decide to do as much branding as possible by using CSS files and the replaceable site logo.

Summary

This chapter began with a detailed look into the architecture of site pages. You should now have a solid understanding of how WSS supports page customization as well as the how and why behind safe mode processing. The chapter also provided an introduction to considering how to create business solutions that leverage page templates constructed using controls and Web Part zones.

The second part of this chapter discussed master pages and offered recommendations on the best practices for creating a custom branding solution. You learned that many different techniques can be used including the creation of a custom master page template and custom CSS file as well as using a custom site logo. For WSS developers who worked with previous versions of WSS, it should be clear that the support offered by WSS 3.0 is significantly enhanced over the support offered in previous versions.

Chapter 4
Web Parts

- Understand the difference between traditional ASP.NET development and SharePoint development using Web Parts.
- Understand fundamental Web Part development, debugging, and deployment techniques for WSS.
- Understand and implement personalization and customization in Web Parts.
- Build connectable Web Parts.
- Work with Web Parts through the SharePoint Site Model.

Web Parts

The primary task of the SharePoint developer is to build reusable components for business users. Business users in turn will take these components and build applications, customizing the application for the particular business need and personalizing the application for their own working style. This development mindset is in contrast to typical Windows or Web software that is deployed as a complete unit. With WSS technologies, the application is always evolving as business users employ deployed components to build their own applications and workspaces. Web Parts are used within the site to enable further collaboration or integration within the site context.

Web Parts are the fundamental building blocks for SharePoint's user interface, and with them we can build and integrate many different types of applications. The built-in Web Parts serve as good design examples when writing your own. For example, the Data View Web Part can be configured to point at any data source and display the data in many different ways. In the same way, all of the Web Parts that ship with WSS are generic and built for reuse. Although you may build more specific applications with Web Parts, it is important to be as generic as possible to allow the greatest flexibility for your customer, the business user, who can then configure the Web Part for a specific use.

> ### Built-in Web Parts
>
> It's important to note that there are many Web Parts that might meet your business requirements out of the box with WSS, and there are even more available with Microsoft Office SharePoint Server. It's not always necessary to write code to integrate your application into SharePoint sites, especially for business data. There are many Microsoft Web Parts that can be customized and deployed using only Web Part Description XML

files, or used within your own Web Parts as WebControls. The following Web Parts are just a few of those included with WSS:

Content Editor Web Part   Use this to display static HTML content using a WYSIWYG editor or to link to a text file.

Data View Web Part   Use this to display database, XML, or SharePoint list data with rich design support through Microsoft SharePoint Designer.

List View Web Part   Use this to display view list content for any list in the SharePoint site.

Image Web Part   Use this to display an image.

Members Web Part   Use this to display members of the site.

Page Viewer Web Part   Use this to display an existing Web page in an IFrame.

Web Part Fundamentals

A *Web Part* is a class that inherits from the WebPart class defined in the System.Web.UI.Web-Controls.WebParts namespace inside the System.Web assembly. The Web Part is a special type of Web control that is deployable inside of a Web Part Zone control after the initial page has been created and deployed. A Web Part is loosely coupled with the page that it is deployed on, assuming the Web Part infrastructure is in place. (See Chapter 3, "Pages and Design," for more information on creating custom Web Part pages.) Web Parts interact with the Web Part Manager control, which itself adds and maintains the instances of Web Parts that are added to Web Part zones either at page design time or at run time. The Web Part Manager acts as a director for the page, adding Web Parts to the Web Part zones from the personalization database during the page's initialization. You can build Web Parts applications outside of SharePoint in traditional ASP.NET applications, but the Web Part framework built into WSS 3.0 contains a rich set of additional functionality including the dynamic SharePoint site model, templating framework, security framework, and Web Part management using the WSS Web Part Gallery. Figure 4-1 shows the inheritance model between SharePoint's Web Part Zone and Web Part Manager controls and the ASP.NET Web Part framework classes. Note that even though SharePoint contains specific implementations of the Web Part Zone and Web Part Manager, you will use the ASP.NET Web Part class as the base class for your Web Part applications.

The Web Part Manager class that SharePoint uses is SPWebPartManager, which is a bridge between the page's Web Part Zone objects and the content database. When you add a Web Part to the page, you are actually adding a serialized instance of the Web Part to the content database. You can also declare default Web Parts in pages added to Modules in Features, as shown in the previous chapter. To write the simplest Web Part, create a class that derives from System.Web.UI.WebControls.WebParts.WebPart. To render simple text or HTML to the page, simply override the RenderContents method by using the same syntax that is used when creating a simple WebControl for an ASP.NET application, as shown in Listing 4-1.

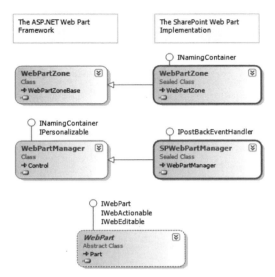

Figure 4-1   SharePoint's implementation of the Web Part framework

Listing 4-1   A very simple Web Part

```
namespace LitwareWebParts {
  // A very simple webpart
  public class HelloWebPart : System.Web.UI.WebControls.WebParts.WebPart {
    protected override void RenderContents(System.Web.UI.HtmlTextWriter writer) {
      writer.Write(string.Format("Hello, {0}!", this.Page.User.Identity.Name));
    }
  }
}
```

Web Parts render inside of *chrome*. Chrome refers to the common user interface elements, such as a formatted title bar and borders around the Web Part's body that the framework adds to controls. The chrome adds a bit of style to your Web Part in a way that is consistent with the user interface of the application. The rendering of chrome is handled by the application framework—when this Web Part is deployed in WSS, the resulting display includes the title of the Web Part as well as a drop-down menu with customization options. The Web Part chrome is responsible for rendering common properties and styles as well as menu and administration user interface elements. For an example of default chrome added to the HelloWebPart example, see Figure 4-2. Note that chrome is rendered by the Web Part framework only when Web Parts are deployed within Web Part zones, and it is not rendered when the Web Part is deployed declaratively as a Web control.

Because the chrome is rendered by the application framework (in our case WSS), applications built from multiple Web Parts are all easily maintained by users of the portal without additional training costs or learning curves. After users learn how to add or remove Web Parts and customize them using SharePoint's Tool Pane, they will be able to use your application deployed as a Web Part as well.

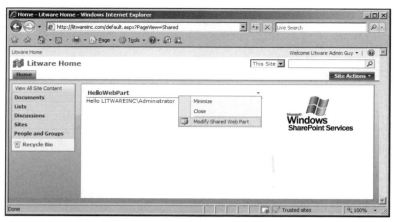

Figure 4-2   Even the simplest Web Part renders chrome.

Web Control Basics

Because Web Parts are WebControl classes, a basic understanding of the Web control is fundamental to programming Web Parts. Web controls are also the UI components that you will be using within your Web Part solutions, whether you write your own or use common ASP.NET or SharePoint Web controls such as the SPGridView control. Figure 4-3 displays the Web Part class model—the Web Part derives from the Panel Web control and implements the IWebEditable interface, which enables deployment and customization with the Web Part framework. You also can use Web Parts as controls, including using Microsoft's WSS Web Parts in your own custom Web Part.

> **Note**   Web Parts for SharePoint deployment derive from the System.Web.UI.WebParts.WebPart class. Although in ASP.NET 2.0 you can add a User Control (.ascx file) as a Web Part (using the GenericWebPart wrapper), the GenericWebPart is not deployable to SharePoint. Therefore, SharePoint is more restrictive than ASP.NET 2.0 in that you cannot directly use User Controls as Web Parts. Instead, you must use an indirect technique in which you write wrapper Web Parts to dynamically load and host User Controls. Read about the Smart Part (*http://www.SmartPart.info*) made famous by Jan Tielens if you want to see just how far you can take this idea.

There are a few methods that are crucial to understand in the control life cycle. OnLoad is used to initialize the control but is not intended for loading data or other processing functionality. OnPreRender is used to initiate any long-running processes such as database retrieval or Web service calls by initiating asynchronous calls. The Page class also fires a PreRender-Complete event after all of the page's prerender tasks are completed. If you are using controls for your display, the only method you'll need to implement for UI components is CreateChild-Controls. Controls added to the controls collection of the Web control will render from the framework, and so there is typically no need to override any render methods unless you need to directly use the HtmlTextWriter class. If you do need to render your own controls, you can do so in the RenderContents method, which will get rendered inside of the Web control chrome. You may want to render your own controls in order to display them in a table or other HTML layout. To receive postback data from an included control, you will need to create a private reference of your control and create it in the CreateChildControls method. Before accessing the control, you can ensure it is created by first calling the EnsureChildControls method. Table 4-1 lists the Web Part life cycle in general order of execution, including the standard methods and events to use when building Web Parts. There are some methods, however, that are not guaranteed to execute in order. These include CreateChildControls, EnsureChildControls, and methods marked with the ConnectionConsumer and ConnectionProvider attributes. Before accessing the properties of any composite controls, the EnsureChildControls method must be called to prevent null reference exceptions.

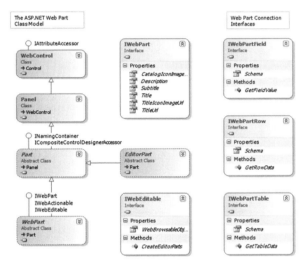

Figure 4-3   The ASP.NET Web Part class model

Table 4-1   The Web Part Life Cycle

Method/Event	Description
OnInit	Handles initialization of the control.
OnLoad	Handles the Load event.
CreateChildControls	Creates any child controls that are used as part of a composite control.
EnsureChildControls	Ensures that CreateChildControls has executed. Use this to ensure that a control you are referencing exists before accessing its data.
OnPreRender	Handles or initiates tasks such as data loading that must complete before the control can render. Asynchronous page tasks should be started from this method.
Page.PreRenderComplete	The page fires the PreRenderComplete event after all controls have completed their OnPreRender methods and the page has completed asynchronous tasks.
Render	Renders the entire control, including the outer tags and Web Part chrome.
RenderContents	Renders the contents of the control only, inside of the outer tags and style properties.

SharePoint Development Versus ASP.NET Development

Because SharePoint applications run in a virtualized site context using the content database, it is important to note several significant differences from traditional ASP.NET development, as well as some ASP.NET Framework requirements that may not be quite obvious. Web Parts that are added to pages within Web Part zones exist entirely in the content database, which means that they are processed through SharePoint's Safe Mode Parser (see below). Web Parts are also added to the page later in the page's life cycle than declarative controls. Web Part applications written for WSS should exist entirely in a compiled assembly, without additional dynamically compiled code files in the app_code directory as traditional ASP.NET 2.0 applications permit. Web Part applications should be as autonomous as possible, and they should contain all of the required resources such as images and scripts compiled into the assembly as resources and included through the Client Script Manager. Finally, Web Part applications for WSS will run under specific security settings and should be deployed through SharePoint Solution packages to correctly specify trust settings for deployment. While in development, you will most likely need to escalate the trust level in the site's web.config file to WSS_Medium or Full. We will talk about trust level and security policy in more detail in Chapter 9, "Solutions and Deployment."

Tip   Security Exceptions that result from running under a Code Access Security policy that is too restrictive are a common point of failure in Web Part applications.

The Safe Mode Parser

Code deployed through the Content Database is run through the *Safe Mode Parser*. SharePoint's Safe Mode Parser ensures that only code that has been configured as trusted can be dynamically deployed to the SharePoint server. Without the Safe Mode Parser, users could write and deploy malicious code in dynamic Web pages created as documents, posing a threat to the data integrity and security of the SharePoint site. To deploy code that does not run through the Safe Mode Parser requires physical access to the Web Server's file system, such as when one is deploying a custom application page, as described in Chapter 2. The Safe Mode Parser guarantees that code executed within the SharePoint application has been allowed by the server administrator.

Web Parts were first introduced in WSS 2.0 as the next version of Microsoft's Dashboard technology. ASP.NET 2.0 includes a new version of the Web Part framework that can run outside of WSS using standard ASP.NET components. The WSS 3.0 Web Part framework is built on this same Web Part framework. To write a Web Part for SharePoint, you will derive from the ASP.NET Web Part class System.Web.UI.WebControls.WebParts.WebPart. WSS 3.0 includes the Web Part class Microsoft.SharePoint.WebPartPages.WebPart for backward compatibility purposes, and this Web Part should be used only when migrating existing code from WSS 2.0. This Web Part derives from the ASP.NET WebPart class and includes multiple compatibility layers to simplify code migration. But it should not be used for new development. Table 4-2 lists the ASP.NET Web Part properties, methods, and components, along with the backward-compatible property, method, or component in the SharePoint.WebPartPages namespace. Another difference to note is that ASP.NET Web Parts and SharePoint backward-compatible Web Parts have different serialization formats, making a change in the base class a breaking change for deployed parts.

Table 4-2   WSS Backward-Compatibility Comparison Table

ASP.NET Web Parts	SharePoint Backward Compatibility
WebBrowsableAttribute	BrowsableAttribute
WebDisplayName	FriendlyName
WebDescription	Description
Personalizable	WebPartStorage
PersonalizationScope	Storage
EditorPart	ToolPart
EditorPartCollection	ToolPart[]
CreateEditorParts()	GetToolParts()
RenderContents()	RenderWebPart()
SetPersonalizationDirty()	SaveProperties

Developing Web Parts for WSS 3.0

To develop a Web Part application for WSS, create a new class library by using Visual Studio 2005 and add a reference to System.Web. To use the SharePoint site object model (including security and authorization), add a reference to the primary WSS assembly Microsoft .SharePoint.dll and Microsoft.SharePoint.Security.dll. To deploy your Web Part assembly with a strong name to the bin directory, you will also need to include the assembly attribute AllowPartiallyTrustedCallers. This attribute must be included once in the assembly and is typically included in the AssemblyInfo code file.

```
[assembly: System.Security.AllowPartiallyTrustedCallers]
```

To create your first Web Part, simply create a class that derives from WebPart and override the CreateChildControls method. Because the ASP.NET Framework will automatically render the controls in the collection, adding controls and handlers in this method is usually all you need to do to build your user interface. In the following examples, we will create a simple RSS Viewer Web Part along with an RSS feed picker Web Part and a custom Editor Part. The code in Listing 4-2 demonstrates the simplest "HelloWorld" Web Part, which we will eventually turn into our RSS Viewer Web Part. Even though your final Web Part will be complex, it is important to test your Web Part as it is developed, beginning with the simple shell.

Listing 4-2 The first steps in Web Part development

```
Starting Out: An RSS Web Part
using System;
using System.Web;
using System.Web.UI.WebControls;
using System.Web.UI.WebControls.WebParts;

namespace LitwareWebParts {
    public class RssViewWebPart : WebPart {
        protected override void CreateChildControls() {
            base.CreateChildControls();
            this.Controls.Add(new LiteralControl("Hello, world!"));
        }
    }
}
```

To deploy the Web Part to your WSS Site, you must then register the control as safe in web.config's SafeControls node, as described in Chapter 3. Assuming the project name LitwareWebParts, the following entry in the SafeControls node in web.config will register the assembly and namespace as safe.

```
<SafeControl Assembly="LitwareWebParts" Namespace="LitwareWebParts"
    TypeName="*" Safe="True" />
```

Note that for this example, we are not strong-naming the assembly, and therefore we can use the simple name of the assembly. When you strong-name the assembly, you should always register the SafeControl entry using the full four-part assembly name.

Next, you will need to compile the assembly dynamic-link library (DLL) and copy it to your SharePoint Web application's bin directory. Many developers like to do this as a post-build event in Visual Studio, or as a custom-build task using MSBuild, as in the following example.

```
xcopy /Y *.* C:\Inetpub\LitwareWebApp\bin\*.*
```

After adding the SafeControls entry, the next step is to test your Web Part by adding it to the gallery and a Web Part page. There are many ways to deploy a Web Part, but during development you will do this manually most of the time. To add your Web Part to the gallery, navigate to the following URL on your WSS site: *http://localhost/_catalogs/wp*. This gallery is also available from each top level site's Site Settings page. From this gallery, click the New button to get to the page *http://localhost/_layouts/NewDwp.aspx*. This page will list all Web Parts that are available either in the bin directory or global assembly cache and that are registered in this Web application's Safe Controls entries. If you don't see your Web Part on this page, take some time to troubleshoot. For example, ensure that your Web Part is public, derives from the WebPart class, is correctly registered as safe with the full namespace and proper assembly name, and is deployed to the right directory. If your Web Part assembly is signed, be sure that the correct strong name is referenced in the SafeControls entry. Figure 4-4 displays the new Web Part page where you can create Web Part Gallery entries using the Web interface.

> **Tip** The Web Part Gallery is a special type of document library that includes XML files that contain serialized Web Parts. Web Parts that are serialized using the new ASP.NET format have a .webpart extension, whereas backward-compatible Web Parts are serialized using the older WSS 2.0 format and have a .dwp extension.

Figure 4-4 The New Web Parts page enables you to discover Web Parts that have been marked as safe and to add these Web Parts to the Web Part Gallery for the current site collection.

When you select a Web Part on the New Web Parts page and click the Populate Gallery button, WSS generates a new entry in the site collection's Web Part Gallery. After this, the Web Part will be available to all pages, and you can access it with the Add A Web Part option from the Edit Page command. After the Web Part is added to the page, you can export it to a .webpart XML file. This is especially useful if you want to set default properties for deployment. It is this XML content that you can use when adding your Web Part to a site or feature definition's pages, as well as the XML that will be saved in the content database to serialize your Web Part. You also will want to add this XML file to your Visual Studio project and source control repository so that you can create a feature to automatically import these Web Part Gallery entries. Listing 4-3 displays an example Web Part file from our basic RSS View Web Part.

Listing 4-3 An example Web Part description file

```
An Example Web Part File
<webParts>
  <webPart xmlns="http://schemas.microsoft.com/WebPart/v3">
    <metaData>
      <type name="LitwareWebParts.RssViewWebPart" />
      <importErrorMessage>Cannot import this Web Part.</importErrorMessage>
    </metaData>
    <data>
```

```
        <properties>
          <!-- standard Web Part properties -->
          <property name="ChromeType" type="chrometype">Default</property>
          <property name="Title" type="string">Litware RSS View Web Part</property>
          <property name="Description" type="string">Use to ... </property>
          <property name="CatalogIconImageUrl" type="string">
            /_layouts/images/msxml1.gif
          </property>
          <property name="AllowConnect" type="bool">True</property>
          <property name="ExportMode" type="exportmode">All</property>

          <!-- custom Web Part properties -->
          <property name="XmlUrl" type="string">
            http://blogs.msdn.com/MainFeed.aspx?Type=AllBlogs
          </property>
        </properties>
      </data>
    </webPart>
  </webParts>
```

Creating a Feature for Importing Web Parts

When you develop Web Parts for distribution, we recommend that you create a feature designed to import your .webpart files into the Web Part Gallery. Because there is only one Web Part Gallery per site collection, a feature created to import .webpart files should be scoped at the site collection level instead of being scoped at the site level. Following is an example of the feature.xml file for a feature named LitwareWebParts that is part of the Visual Studio project that accompanies this chapter.

```
<Feature
  Id="FE016E00-8639-4839-925D-B40F659458A9"
  Title="Chapter 4: A demo feature to deploy Litware Web Parts"
  Description="Demo from Inside Windows SharePoint Services (Pattison/Larson)"
  Hidden="FALSE"
  Scope="Site"
  ImageUrl="actionssettings.gif"
  xmlns="http://schemas.microsoft.com/sharepoint/">
  <ElementManifests>
    <ElementManifest Location="elements.xml"/>
  </ElementManifests>
</Feature>
```

When it's time to deploy a feature for importing Web Parts, the actual .webpart files will need to be copied to the file system of the front end Web server. Therefore, you should copy your .webpart files inside the feature directory itself. In the LitwareWebParts feature, we have followed a common Microsoft convention and placed our .webpart files inside the feature directory in an inner directory named DWP.

After you have copied your .webpart files into the feature directory, update the elements.xml file by adding File elements within a Module element, as in the following example. This will copy the files into the Web Part Gallery of the current site collection during feature activation. Note that when targeting the Web Part Gallery, a Module element should be defined with a list type of 113, a Url value of "_catalogs/wp" and a RootWebOnly setting of true.

```
<Elements xmlns="http://schemas.microsoft.com/sharepoint/">
  <Module Name="LitwareWebParts" Path="dwp"
          List="113" Url="_catalogs/wp" RootWebOnly="true">

    <File Url="HelloWebPart.webpart" Type="GhostableInLibrary" >
      <Property Name="Group" Value="Litware Web Parts" />
    </File>

    <File Url="RssViewWebPart.webpart" Type="GhostableInLibrary" >
      <Property Name="Group" Value="Litware Web Parts" />
    </File>

    <File Url="FeedListWebPart.webpart" Type="GhostableInLibrary" >
      <Property Name="Group" Value="Litware Web Parts" />
    </File>

  </Module>
</Elements>
```

In the listing of the elements.xml file you have just seen, you should notice that the File element for each .webpart file contains an inner Property element that adds a Group property with a value of "Litware Web Parts." The Group property value must be set inside the File element in this fashion. This can be a bit confusing at first, because you cannot assign a Group property value inside the .webpart file itself as you can with other Web Part properties, such as Title and Description. However, adding a Group property value is helpful to users, because it enables your Web Parts to appear in custom groups in the standard WSS Add Web Parts dialog box, as shown in Figure 4-5.

You have just seen how to create a feature to import .webpart files into the Web Part Gallery, but this does not complete the story of how you deploy Web Parts into a production environment. You will have to wait until Chapter 9 to learn more, when we introduce solution packages and fill in the rest of the pieces. As you will see, a solution package can automatically deploy Web Part assembly DLLs and accompanying features to import their .webpart files. A solution package also can be used to deploy other related Web Part files, such as User Controls, and to add the required SafeControl entries to all the necessary web.config files on the various front-end Web servers in the farm. We also will use the Solution Package in Chapter 9 for deploying required Code Access Security policies and configurations required for our Web Parts to run in a partially trusted environment. Further changes to the web.config file can be made with Feature receivers deployed in the solution using the SPWebConfig-Modification class.

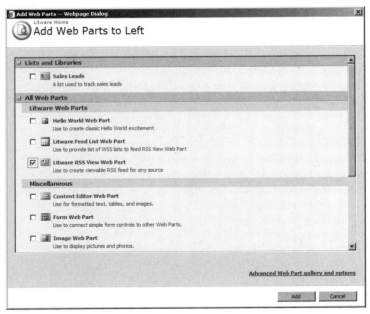

Figure 4-5 After you use a feature to import a Web Part to the Web Part Gallery, a user can add it easily to Web Part pages.

Debugging Web Parts

Debugging Web Parts is an essential skill, but fortunately, it is not too different from debugging traditional ASP.NET applications. The main difference is that you will use Visual Studio to attach to the w3wp.exe process running on Windows Server rather than pressing F5. To attach to the process using Visual Studio 2005, press Ctrl+Alt+P or choose Attach To Process from the Debug menu. When developing and debugging Web Parts for WSS, it is important to run Windows Server and have WSS running on your development machine with Visual Studio installed. A post-build event can be used to copy the .dll and .pdb files to the bin directory, after which you can attach the debugger. There are many things that can go wrong in a Web Part application for SharePoint, and stepping through the code as it runs is an everyday task.

Tip If a server environment is not available as your desktop operating system, Microsoft Virtual PC or Microsoft Virtual Server can be a viable alternative for development tasks, although you will notice a significant performance hit.

Customization and Personalization

Customization and personalization of Web Parts enable your Web Parts to be reused for multiple business applications. *Customization* refers to a change that is shared by all users of the Web Part instance, whereas *personalization* is specific to the individual user's Web Part instance. For example, the site owner may choose a specific news feed to display on a site's home page. This would be a customization, because the change would be shared by all users of the site. Individual users on the site may choose different rendering formats according to their preferences, which would be an example of personalization. Personalization applies to individual users and is persisted on a per-user basis.

> **Tip**   The performance cost of personalization in an application is higher than that of customization and should be planned for accordingly.

To add a new custom property, just add a public property and the Personalizable attribute. The WebBrowsable, WebDisplayName, WebDescription, and Category attributes also will be useful in administering the property from the Web Part's Editor Parts. These attributes are defined in the System.Web.UI.WebControls.WebParts and System.ComponentModel namespaces.

If you create a property and apply the WebBrowsable attribute, the Web Part framework will automatically display this property in a generic Editor Part when the user selects Modify Web Part. An *Editor Part* is a special type of control that is used only to edit Web Part properties that support customization and personalization. The following demonstration adds a persistent Web Part property named XmlUrl.

```
private string xmlUrl;
[ Personalizable(PersonalizationScope.Shared),
  WebBrowsable(true),
  WebDisplayName("Feed Url"),
  WebDescription("Set your RSS feed's XML URL here!"),
  Category("Configuration")]
public string XmlUrl {
    get { return xmlUrl; }
    set { xmlUrl = value; }
}
```

The Personalizable attribute is the one that instructs the Web Part Manager to persist the XmlUrl property value in the Web Part framework. In WSS, this will be persisted in the content database. Because the personalization scope is set to Shared, the XmlUrl property supports customization on a site-wide basis by the site owner, but it does not support per-user personalization. The other attributes applied to this property specify it should be shown in the generic Editor Part with a specific display name, a description for a tooltip, and a category group. Without any additional code, the XmlUrl property is exposed to the SharePoint tool pane through a default Editor Part.

Next, let's create a second property named HeadlineMode that supports per-user personalization. We will accomplish this by using a personalization scope of User instead of Shared. This is done so that our Web Part can enable each user to switch back and forth between two different supported rendering modes. The HeadlineMode property will be based on the following user-defined enumeration named RenderMode.

```
public enum RenderMode {
  Full,
  Titles
}
```

Once we have defined the RenderMode enumeration, we can define a new personalizable property along with a private field to track its value with the following code.

```
private RenderMode headlineMode = RenderMode.Full;
[Personalizable(PersonalizationScope.User),
  WebBrowsable(true),
  WebDisplayName("Headline Mode"),
  WebDescription("Do you want to only display headlines?"),
  Category("Configuration")]
public RenderMode HeadlineMode {
  get { return headlineMode; }
  set { headlineMode = value; }
}
```

Both the XmlUrl property and the HeadlineMode property have been defined with the WebBrowsable attribute. Using this approach, you will not be required to create a custom Editor Part, because WSS will display these properties automatically in the generic Web Part editor, enabling users to change their values. For example, when a site owner selects Modify Shared Web Part on this Web Part, the task pane will display these two properties in the generic Editor Part shown in Figure 4-6. Note that the property based on the RenderMode enumeration is rendered as a drop-down list.

Figure 4-6   Properties defined with the WebBrowsable attribute are exposed automatically in the standard WSS Editor Part.

One more thing to keep in mind is that the RenderMode property is defined with a personalization scope of User, whereas the XmlUrl property is defined with a personalization scope of Shared. When a user goes into personalization mode using the Personalize This Page menu item from the top-level welcome menu, the user will not be able to see or edit the XmlUrl property. It will only be displayed for editing in Shared Mode and not User Mode.

Creating Custom Editor Parts

For some Web Parts, you will find that it is sufficient to define persistent properties with the WebBrowsable attribute so that WSS automatically displays them for editing in the generic Editor Part. However, this will not be sufficient for all scenarios. There will be times when you will want to create your own custom Editor Parts for the tool pane. This section will step through what's required to accomplish this.

To create a custom Editor Part, you must create a new class that inherits from the EditorPart class defined inside the System.Web.UI.WebControls.WebParts namespace. In our example, we will create a new EditorPart-derived class named *RssViewEditorPart* to serve as a custom Editor Part of the RssViewWebPart class.

Note that in addition to creating the new RssViewEditorPart class, we must also make a few changes to the RssViewWebPart class. First, we will modify the Personalizable properties so that they do not appear in the generic Editor Part. This can be done by applying the WebBrowsable attribute with a value of false.

```
[Personalizable(PersonalizationScope.Shared),
  WebBrowsable(false)]
public string XmlUrl {
  get { return xmlUrl; }
  set { xmlUrl = value; }
}
```

Next, you must override the CreateEditorParts method within the Web Part class named RssViewWebPart to instruct WSS to load your custom Editor Part instead of or in addition to the standard Editor Parts that are normally displayed for Web Parts.

When you override CreateEditorParts, you must work with collection objects of type Editor-PartCollection. Once created, an EditorPartCollection object is immutable, but EditorPart-Collection has a constructor that takes an existing EditorPartCollection and an ICollection of EditorParts. Therefore, you use the approach of creating a new EditorPartCollection object that contains the standard Editor Parts in addition to your custom Editor Part.

When writing the code to create and initialize an EditorPart object, it is essential to set the ID property. If you forget to do this, you will get an ambiguous exception with very little debugging detail. The following example demonstrates the syntax for overriding the Create-EditorParts method and providing a custom Editor Part that gets loaded along with the standard Editor Parts that are normally displayed to the user.

```
public override EditorPartCollection CreateEditorParts() {
  List<EditorPart> editorParts = new List<EditorPart>(1);
  EditorPart part = new RssViewEditorPart();
  part.ID = this.ID + "_rssViewEditor";
  editorParts.Add(part);
  EditorPartCollection baseParts = base.CreateEditorParts();
  return new EditorPartCollection(baseParts, editorParts);
}
```

Now let's look at the details of creating the RssViewEditorPart class, which involves creating a new public class that derives from the EditorPart class. As in the case of creating a WebPart class, you add controls to an Editor Part by overriding the CreateChildControls method. When you intialize the controls in an Editor Part, it is common to use the current Web Part property values. The Web Part that is being edited by your Editor Part is available using a property named WebPartToEdit.

There are two important abstract methods to implement in the EditorPart class: they are named *ApplyChanges* and *SyncChanges*. These methods will set properties of the Web Part or set properties of the Editor Part from the Web Part. The ApplyChanges method will take input from the custom Editor Part and apply it to properties in the Web Part. The SyncChanges method will take settings from the Web Part and apply them to Editor Part input control values. When loading the Editor Part, it is the SyncChanges method (not OnLoad or Create-ChildControls) that will apply the initial values to the Editor Part. Listing 4-4 demonstrates a simple custom Editor Part for the RSS View Web Part. For larger applications, you will want to create Editor Parts based on interfaces for common Web Part properties. Note that within the Editor Part, you will need to check the personalization scope to enable or disable edits based on the current personalization scope. The user either will be editing shared Web Part custom-izations or Web Part personalizations, in which case the WebPartManager's Personalization-Scope will be set to PersonalizationScope.User.

Tip   When implementing a custom Editor Part for a property, you should also remove the WebBrowsable attribute from the property to remove the property from the default Editor Parts.

Listing 4-4   A custom Editor Part for updating RssViewWebPart property values

```
Example Editor Part: RssViewEditorPart
public class RssViewEditorPart : EditorPart {
  TextBox txtXmlUrl;
  RadioButtonList lstHeadlineMode;

  protected override void CreateChildControls() {
    Controls.Add(new LiteralControl("Feed Url:<br/>"));
    txtXmlUrl = new TextBox();
    txtXmlUrl.Width = new Unit("100%");
    txtXmlUrl.TextMode = TextBoxMode.MultiLine;
    txtXmlUrl.Rows = 3;
    // mark XmlUrl Textbox read-only in personalization mode
    if (WebPartManager.Personalization.Scope == PersonalizationScope.User)
      txtXmlUrl.Enabled = false;
    this.Controls.Add(txtXmlUrl);
    Controls.Add(new LiteralControl("Headline Model:<br/>"));
    lstHeadlineMode = new RadioButtonList();
    lstHeadlineMode.Items.Add(RenderMode.Full.ToString());
    lstHeadlineMode.Items.Add(RenderMode.Titles.ToString());
    this.Controls.Add(lstHeadlineMode);
  }
```

```
public override void SyncChanges() {
  this.EnsureChildControls();
  RssViewWebPart sourcePart = (RssViewWebPart)this.WebPartToEdit;
  string SelectedMode = sourcePart.HeadlineMode.ToString();
  lstHeadlineMode.Items.FindByText(SelectedMode).Selected = true;
  txtXmlUrl.Text = sourcePart.XmlUrl;
}

public override bool ApplyChanges() {
  this.EnsureChildControls();
  RssViewWebPart targetPart = (RssViewWebPart)this.WebPartToEdit;
  targetPart.XmlUrl = txtXmlUrl.Text;
  if(lstHeadlineMode.SelectedValue.Equals("Full"))
    targetPart.HeadlineMode = RenderMode.Full;
  else
    targetPart.HeadlineMode = RenderMode.Titles;
  return true;
}
}
```

Figure 4-7 shows the custom Editor Part that provides the user with a richer editing experience via a multiline TextBox and a RadioButtonList control. You should also take note that the implementation of the custom Editor Part has been written to distinguish between different modes in which the personalization scope is either Shared or User. When the Editor Part determines that the user is editing the Web Part with a personalization scope of User, it sets the Enabled property of the TextBox named txtXmlUrl to false so that the user cannot edit its value. The key observation is that when you create a custom Editor Part, you are responsible for knowing which properties support customization but not personalization and making sure you don't allow users to make edits to these properties while in User personalization mode.

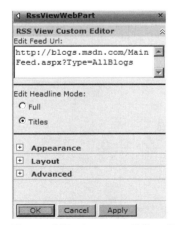

Figure 4-7   A custom Editor Part permits you to take over the user interface in the task pane that enables users to customize and personalize your persistent Web Part properties.

Asynchronous Web Part Processing

Web Part applications usually are deployed on pages with multiple Web Parts. Furthermore, you will not know how many and what type of Web Parts are running on the page, and in some cases several "expensive" Web Parts may coexist on the same page. Because of this, it is important that Web Parts process their data as efficiently as possible. For example, a database call, an LDAP call, and several Web Service calls in multiple Web Parts can add up to a slow page. Rather than having the page load at the combined processing time of all operations, asynchronous page processing lets the page load in the time of the longest operation (or the longest operation that has timed out). Although asynchronous page tasks are not exclusively a Web Part technology, they are perhaps most applicable in Web Part applications due to the composite nature of Web Part pages.

With ASP.NET 2.0, the Page class can register asynchronous tasks by using the RegisterAsync-Task method, in which multiple processes can occur at the same time. This not only decreases the page load time but also frees up the worker process threads of IIS, which are a limited resource on your server. Because they are limited resources, we don't want to tie them up while waiting on long-running operations, but instead we want to return them for other uses when we're not using them. With asynchronous page tasks, the IIS worker thread is returned to the thread pool (where it can serve other requests if needed) while the page is waiting for the asynchronous tasks to complete. In the example RSS View Web Part, an asynchronous task can be used to fetch the remote XML data, which will free the IIS worker thread while it is waiting for a response from the remote server. Before initiating the remote call, it is also a good idea to verify that the page is not in design mode, which can be done with a simple check of the Web Part Manager's Display Mode. Classes that implement the IAsyncResult design pattern work well with asynchronous tasks and are a good design pattern for your own middle tier code. Some examples of these classes include ADO.NET database classes, Web Requests, and Web Service Proxies. Listing 4-5 demonstrates the asynchronous task for retrieving remote data using the WebRequest class. Listing 4-6 is a simple XSLT file for an RSS Web Part application that will transform the output by using the XslCompiledTransform class. This file is compiled in as an embedded resource in this example, with the full name LitwareWebParts.Resources.RSS.xslt. (It is available as a resource stream by using the WebPartResources utility class in Listing 4-13.) You also will find an alternate XSLT file for transforming the feed into linked titles only when set to RenderMode.Titles in this chapter's code samples.

Listing 4-5   An Asynchronous RSS Web Part using Page.RegisterAsyncTask

```
RSS Viewer with Page.RegisterAsyncTask
using System;
using System.Collections.Generic;
using System.IO;
using System.Net;
using System.Web;
using System.Web.UI;
using System.Web.UI.WebControls;
using System.Web.UI.WebControls.WebParts;
using System.Xml;
```

```csharp
using System.Xml.XPath;
using System.Xml.Xsl;
using System.Reflection;

namespace LitwareWebParts {
  public class RssViewWebPart : WebPart, IWebEditable {
    // xmlUrl and RenderMode properties omitted for clarity

    private Stream xmlResponseStream = null;
    private WebRequest xmlReq;

    // Handle any prerender tasks including async operation initiation
    protected override void OnPreRender(EventArgs e) {
      base.OnPreRender(e);
      if (string.IsNullOrEmpty(this.xmlUrl))
        return;
      // Check to see if we're in design mode and if so skip request
      if (this.WebPartManager.DisplayMode.AllowPageDesign) {
        this.Controls.Add(new LiteralControl("No display while in design mode."));
        return;
      }

      try {
        Uri xmlUri = new Uri(this.xmlUrl);
        xmlReq = WebRequest.CreateDefault(xmlUri);
        xmlReq.Credentials = CredentialCache.DefaultCredentials;
        xmlReq.Timeout = 10000; // 10 seconds timeout
        this.Page.RegisterAsyncTask(
            new PageAsyncTask(new BeginEventHandler(BeginXmlRequest),
                              new EndEventHandler(EndXmlRequest),
                              new EndEventHandler(XmlRequestTimeout),
                              null, true)
          );
      } catch (System.Security.SecurityException) {
        this.Controls.Add(
          new LiteralControl("Permission denied - set trust level to WSS_Medium."));
      }
    }

    IAsyncResult BeginXmlRequest(object src, EventArgs args,
                                 AsyncCallback callback, object state) {
      return this.xmlReq.BeginGetResponse(callback, state);
    }

    void XmlRequestTimeout(IAsyncResult ar) {
      Label timeoutLabel = new Label();
      timeoutLabel.Text = string.Format(
          "The request timed out while waiting for {0}.", this.XmlUrl);
      this.Controls.Add(timeoutLabel);
    }

    void EndXmlRequest(IAsyncResult ar) {
      WebResponse response = this.xmlReq.EndGetResponse(ar);
      this.xmlResponseStream = response.GetResponseStream();
    }

    protected override void RenderContents(HtmlTextWriter writer) {
      base.RenderContents(writer);
```

```
    if (string.IsNullOrEmpty(this.xmlUrl) || this.xmlResponseStream == null)
      return;
    XslCompiledTransform transform = new XslCompiledTransform();
    string xslt;
    if (this.HeadlineMode == RenderMode.Full)
      xslt = @"Resources.RSS.xslt";
    else
      xslt = @"Resources.RssTitles.xslt";
    string resourceName = @"LitwareWebParts" + xslt;
    using (Stream res =
        Assembly.GetExecutingAssembly().GetManifestResourceStream(resourceName)) {
        using (XmlTextReader stylesheet = new XmlTextReader(res)) {
          transform.Load(stylesheet);
        }
    }

    try {
      using (XmlReader reader = new XmlTextReader(this.xmlResponseStream)) {
        XmlTextWriter results = new XmlTextWriter(writer.InnerWriter);
        transform.Transform(reader, results);
        reader.Close();
      }
    } catch (Exception ex) {
      writer.Write(ex.Message);
      if (this.xmlResponseStream != null) {
        this.xmlResponseStream.Close();
        this.xmlResponseStream.Dispose();
      }
    }
  }
 }
}
```

RSS and Syndicated Data

RSS (Really Simple Syndication) is a standard XML syndication format for news feeds, blogs, WSS lists, and enterprise data streams. Although it is a great way to incorporate external data into your portal, it is also a security risk that you should limit to trusted sites. Because the external HTML and script can be rendered in your portal page, which is a trusted site for most of your users, be careful what feeds you enable.

RSS is also a format that fits well with list data. Because SharePoint stores its data in lists, RSS is a natural fit, and it is a built-in component for WSS 3.0. The application page /_layouts/listfeed.aspx will serve any list as a security trimmed RSS feed when provided with the list's GUID as a parameter.

RSS can also be extended with common extensions such as Simple List Extensions and custom SharePoint extensions so that remote clients and aggregators can handle specific list types as strongly typed lists. For more information on the RSS specification, see *http://blogs.law.harvard.edu/tech/rss*.

Listing 4-6   A simple XSLT resource for transforming RSS XML

```
RSS XSLT Transform
<?xml version='1.0' encoding='UTF-8'?>
<xsl:stylesheet
  xmlns:xsl="http://www.w3.org/1999/XSL/Transform"
  xmlns:dc="http://purl.org/dc/elements/1.1/"
  version="1.0"
>
  <xsl:output omit-xml-declaration="yes" method="html" encoding="utf-16" />
  <xsl:template match='/rss'>
    <h3>
      <xsl:value-of select='channel/title'/>
    </h3>
    <xsl:apply-templates select='channel/item' />

  </xsl:template>

  <xsl:template match='item'>
    <div style='margin:6px;'>
      <strong>
        <a href='{link}'>
          <xsl:value-of select='title'/>
        </a>
      </strong><br/>

      <xsl:value-of select='description' disable-output-escaping='yes' />
      <xsl:text disable-output-escaping='yes'> </xsl:text>
      <a href='{link}'>Read the full item</a>.<br />
      <xsl:if test='dc:creator'>
        <strong>Author: </strong><xsl:value-of select='dc:creator' />
        <br/>
      </xsl:if>
      <strong>Published Date: </strong><xsl:value-of select='pubDate' /><br/>

      <font color='gray'>
        <xsl:for-each select='category'>
          <xsl:value-of select='.' /> |
        </xsl:for-each>
      </font>
      <br />


    </div>
  </xsl:template>
  <xsl:template match='category'>
    <xsl:value-of select='.'/> |
  </xsl:template>
</xsl:stylesheet>
```

Web Part Building Blocks

When creating your Web Parts, it's generally a good design principle to aggregate controls, resources, and business logic classes. You've already seen the use of resources using an XSLT file embedded as an assembly resource for the RSS Web Part. You also may want to use resources for static HTML, JavaScript, or images. In addition, you may want to use User Controls if you have existing applications, as well as using XML data sources such as RSS feeds or Web Service endpoints. In the next section, we will look at additional Web Part building blocks for composite Web Part applications.

Using User Controls in Web Parts

Sometimes you may have an existing Web page application that needs to be ported to Share-Point. It is relatively simple to do this by converting the pages to User Controls. Although User Controls aren't recommended for all Web Part applications, they can be a quick way to get an ASP.NET application deployed into your SharePoint Web sites. User Controls deployed in SharePoint either must inherit from the UserControl class or from a UserControl-derived class that is available to the Web application (through either the bin directory or the GAC) and must exist in the same IIS Web application. Web Part code then can load the control and add it to your Web Part using the method Page.LoadControl. Since your User Control will exist on the file system and not in the content database, it can contain inline code if needed, since it isn't processed through the Safe Mode Parser. Note that you cannot deploy User Controls through the content database. Listing 4-7 demonstrates a User Control Host Web Part. You only have to load the control and add it to the controls collection, and the Control framework will render it.

> **Tip**   Although User Controls can be deployed anywhere within the IIS Web application (on the physical file system), the preferred deployment path for WSS 3.0 is a subdirectory of the _ControlTemplates directory, located in %ProgramFiles%\Common Files\Microsoft Shared\web server extensions\12\TEMPLATE\CONTROLTEMPLATES. You could build a custom Editor Part to let users choose from available User Controls in a specific directory.

Listing 4-7   An example Web Part that loads a User Control

```
User Control Host Web Part
using System;
using System.Web;
using System.Web.UI;
using System.Web.UI.WebControls;
using System.Web.UI.WebControls.WebParts;

namespace LitwareWebParts {
  public class UserControlHost : WebPart {

    protected Control userControl;

    protected override void CreateChildControls() {
```

```
        this.Controls.Clear();
        string userControlPath =
                @"/_controltemplates/Litware/LitwareUserControl.ascx";
        this.userControl = this.Page.LoadControl(userControlPath);
        this.Controls.Add(this.userControl);
      }
    }
}
```

Using SharePoint's SPGridView Control

SharePoint has some very useful controls defined in the Microsoft.SharePoint.WebControls namespace that extend common ASP.NET controls with the SharePoint functionality and look and feel. Perhaps the most useful Web control is SPGridView. The SPGridView control extends the ASP.NET GridView class with SharePoint's style declarations and has additional support for WSS data sources such as Lists and Cross-Site Queries using the SPDataSource class. In our next example, we'll utilize the SharePoint site context to determine a list of feed URLs within the SharePoint site and its child sites. We'll expose the feed list through the SPGridView, from which we will later add a connection to our RSS View Web Part. The SPGridView control also can be bound to an SPDataSource object, which can wrap a list as a data source. For this example, we will use a DataTable object constructed of lists from aggregated SharePoint sites. Because this example lists available feeds, we will skip lists that are not news-based, such as the catalogs, galleries, and categories lists. Inspect the code in Listing 4-8 to see how the SPGridView control is populated using data about specific lists inside the current site.

Listing 4-8   A feed list Web Part using the SPGridView control

```
Feed List Web Part Using SPGridView
public class FeedListWebPart : WebPart {
  private SPGridView listsView;
  private DataTable dt;

  protected override void CreateChildControls() {
    List<SPList> lists = new List<SPList>();
    AddLists(lists, SPContext.Current.Web);
    listsView = new SPGridView();
    listsView.AutoGenerateColumns = false;
    this.Controls.Add(listsView);

    BoundField colTitle = new BoundField();
    colTitle.DataField = "Title";
    colTitle.HeaderText = "Title";
    listsView.Columns.Add(colTitle);

    BoundField colXml = new BoundField();
    colXml.DataField = "ItemCount";
    colXml.HeaderText = "Item Count";
    listsView.Columns.Add(colXml);

    CommandField colSelectButton = new CommandField();
    colSelectButton.HeaderText = "Action";
```

```
            colSelectButton.ControlStyle.Width = new Unit(75);
            colSelectButton.SelectText = "Show RSS";
            colSelectButton.ShowSelectButton = true;
            listsView.Columns.Add(colSelectButton);

            listsView.SelectedIndexChanged += new EventHandler(view_SelectedIndexChanged);

            if (!this.Page.IsPostBack) {
              dt = new DataTable();
              dt.Columns.Add("Title");
              dt.Columns.Add("ItemCount");
              dt.Columns.Add("XmlUrl");
              dt.Columns.Add("ID");
              foreach (SPList list in lists) {
                DataRow dr = dt.NewRow();
                dr["Title"] = list.Title;
                dr["ItemCount"] = list.ItemCount.ToString();
                dr["ID"] = list.ID;
                string url = this.Page.Request.Url.GetLeftPart(UriPartial.Authority)
                + SPUtility.MapWebURLToVirtualServerURL(
                    list.ParentWeb,
                    string.Format("{0}/_layouts/listfeed.aspx?List={1}",
                    list.ParentWebUrl, list.ID.ToString()));
                dr["XmlUrl"] = url;
                dt.Rows.Add(dr);
              }

              listsView.DataKeyNames = new string[] { "XmlUrl" };
              listsView.DataSource = dt;
              listsView.DataBind();
            }
        }

        void view_SelectedIndexChanged(object sender, EventArgs e) {
          GridViewRow row = listsView.SelectedRow;
          this.xmlUrl = listsView.SelectedValue.ToString();
        }

        private void AddLists(List<SPList> lists, SPWeb web) {
          foreach (SPList list in web.Lists)
            if (list.AllowRssFeeds && list.EnableSyndication &&
                    list.BaseTemplate != SPListTemplateType.Categories &&
                    list.BaseTemplate != SPListTemplateType.ListTemplateCatalog &&
                    list.BaseTemplate != SPListTemplateType.MasterPageCatalog &&
                    list.BaseTemplate != SPListTemplateType.WebPageLibrary &&
                    list.BaseTemplate != SPListTemplateType.WebPartCatalog &&
                    list.BaseTemplate != SPListTemplateType.WebTemplateCatalog &&
                    list.BaseTemplate != SPListTemplateType.UserInformation &&
                    list.DoesUserHavePermissions(SPBasePermissions.ViewListItems))
                lists.Add(list);
          foreach (SPWeb subweb in web.Webs) {
            if (web.DoesUserHavePermissions(SPBasePermissions.ViewListItems))
              AddLists(lists, subweb);
          }
        }
    }
```

Web Part Verbs

A Web Part Verb is an action that is rendered in the Web Part menu by the Web Part framework as part of the chrome that is rendered around the control. The action can call a client-side function or a server-side handler. To add Web Part Verbs as menu items, override the Verbs property of the Web Part. The Verbs property returns a read-only WebPartVerbCollection, so you will need to merge a collection of Verbs with the base.Verbs property to create a new WebPartVerbCollection. Listing 4-9 adds Verbs for both a server-side transfer and client-side JavaScript opener to the RSS View Web Part that enables the user to navigate to the source RSS feed. The resulting menu display is shown in Figure 4-8.

Listing 4-9   An example Web Part Verb implementation

```
Using Web Part Verbs for Custom Actions
namespace LitwareWebParts {

  public class RssViewWebPart : WebPart, IWebEditable {
    public override WebPartVerbCollection Verbs {
      get {
        List<WebPartVerb> verbs = new List<WebPartVerb>();
        if (!string.IsNullOrEmpty(this.XmlUrl)) {
          WebPartVerb verb1 = new WebPartVerb(this.ID + "_ClientSideRssOpenerVerb",
              string.Format("window.open('{0}','RSSXML')", this.XmlUrl));
          verb1.Description = "Open RSS Feed in an external window";
          verb1.Text = "Open RSS Feed";
          verbs.Add(verb1);

          WebPartVerb verb2 = new WebPartVerb(this.ID + "_ServerSideRssOpenerVerb",
              new WebPartEventHandler(ServerSideVerbHandler));
          verb2.Description = "Load the RSS Source Feed.";
          verb2.Text = "View RSS Source Feed";
          verbs.Add(verb2);
        }
        WebPartVerbCollection allverbs =
            new WebPartVerbCollection(base.Verbs, verbs);
        return allverbs;
      }
    }
    public void ServerSideVerbHandler(object sender, WebPartEventArgs e) {
      if (!string.IsNullOrEmpty(this.XmlUrl))
        Context.Response.Redirect(this.XmlUrl);
    }
    // (previous code omitted for clarity)
  }
}
```

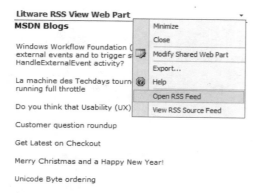

Figure 4-8   Web Parts support adding custom Verbs to provide extra menu items with either client-side or server-side event handlers.

Web Part Connections

Web Part connections are another Web Part technology that enables reuse among diverse applications. Connections are frequently used for master/detail records and are used in Web Parts for late-bound connections. As long as a Web Part provides data that your Web Part can consume, it can be connected using the Web Part framework.

> **Tip**   Web Part connections were first introduced with WSS 2.0. The implementation has changed considerably for version 3.0, which provides a much simpler interface using standard ASP.NET interfaces. As with the Microsoft.SharePoint.WebPartPages.WebPart class, the Microsoft.SharePoint.WebPartPages.Communication namespace and interfaces are only provided for backward compatibility and should be avoided for new development. Instead, use the attributes and interfaces defined in System.Web.UI.WebControls.WebParts.

Connections are enabled through the ConnectionProvider attribute. The simplest way to add a connection to your Web Part is by implementing a custom interface such as the ICustomerProvider interface in Listing 4-10 and specifying the data object with the ConnectionProvider attribute. The interface in this example simply defines the CustomerID property that will be provided to the connected Web Part. To connect to the provider Web Part, the consumer Web Part simply marks a connection method with the ConnectionConsumer attribute. Following are the required method signatures for the connection. Note that the ConnectionProvider and ConnectionConsumer attributes have multiple overloads for advanced connection types, although the simple connections demonstrated here will meet most development needs.

Listing 4-10   Example connection provider and consumer Web Parts

```
Example Connection Web Parts
using System;
using System.Web.UI;
using System.Web.UI.WebControls;
using System.Web.UI.WebControls.WebParts;
```

```
namespace LitwareWebParts {
  public interface ICustomerProvider {
    string CustomerID { get; }
  }
  public class SimpleProviderExample : WebPart, ICustomerProvider {
    private string customerID = "P1284";
    protected override void RenderContents(HtmlTextWriter writer) {
      writer.Write("Customer ID: " + this.CustomerID);
    }
    public string CustomerID {
      get { return this.customerID; }
    }
    [ConnectionProvider("Customer ID", AllowsMultipleConnections = true)]
    public ICustomerProvider GetCustomerProvider() {
      return this;
    }
  }
  public class SimpleConsumerExample : WebPart {
    private ICustomerProvider customerProvider;
    [ConnectionConsumer("Customer ID")]
    public void RegisterCustomerProvider(ICustomerProvider provider) {
      this.customerProvider = provider;
    }
    protected override void RenderContents(HtmlTextWriter writer) {
      if (this.customerProvider != null)
        writer.Write(this.customerProvider.CustomerID);
      else
        writer.Write("No connection");
    }
  }
}
```

Listing 4-10 demonstrates a connection that uses a known interface for business logic. There are also interfaces defined in the System.Web.UI.WebControls.WebParts namespace for generic connections, for cases in which you may want to pass a field of data between the Web Parts. To do so, you would use the IWebPartField interface. You also can pass a row of data by using the IWebPartRow interface, or you even can pass a table of data by using the IWebPartTable interface. These interfaces are useful for connecting very loosely coupled components and for enabling connections through third-party Web Parts. By implementing the IWebPartField interface in the RSS Web Part, we can receive connections from components we write as well as List View Web Parts for Links Lists.

Tip   The *IWebPartField* interface is implemented and connectable by many WSS Web Parts, including the List View Web Parts and the Image Web Part. For example, if your Web Part is connectable to an IWebPartField, you can consume the link from a Links List Web Part.

Listing 4-11 demonstrates a Web Part that implements the IWebPartField interface and provides a connection to the RSS View. This is a modification of the previous Feed List Web Part that will connect an XML URL to the RSS View Web Part. The IWebPartField interface defines the Schema property and the GetFieldValue method, where the Schema property returns reflection information about the parameter, and the GetFieldValue method will be used by a delegate in the consuming Web Part. To complete the connection implementation, a ConnectionProviderAttribute must be applied to a method that will return the provider reference to the consumer. Note that the method that provides the connection is not an interface or base class method, but is instead specified and made available by the Connection-Provider attribute.

Listing 4-11 Converting the Feed List Web Part to an IFieldProvider

```
The Feed List Web Part as IWebPartField
using System;
using System.ComponentModel;
using System.Web;
using System.Web.UI;
using System.Web.UI.WebControls.WebParts;
using System.Xml.Serialization;
using System.Web.UI.WebControls;

namespace LitwareWebParts {
    public class FeedListWebPart : WebPart, IWebPartField{
        /* Previous SPGridView code omitted for clarity */
        private string xmlUrl;
        [WebBrowsable(true),
            Category("Configuration"),
            Personalizable(PersonalizationScope.User),
            DefaultValue(""),
            WebDisplayName("Xml Url"),
            WebDescription("RSS Feed XML URL")]
        public string XmlUrl {
            get { return xmlUrl; }
            set {
                if (!string.IsNullOrEmpty(xmlUrl)) {
                    Uri xmlUri = new Uri(value);
                    xmlUrl = xmlUri.AbsolutePath;
                } else
                    xmlUrl = null;
            }
        }
        // Allows the consumer webpart to consume this data
        public void GetFieldValue(FieldCallback callback) {
            callback(Schema.GetValue(this));
        }


        // Gets a PropertyDescriptor for this connection
        public System.ComponentModel.PropertyDescriptor Schema {
            get {
                PropertyDescriptorCollection properties =
                    TypeDescriptor.GetProperties(this);
                return properties.Find("XmlUrl", false);
            }
        }
    }
```

```
        [ConnectionProvider("XmlUrl Provider")]
        public IWebPartField GetConnectionInterface() {
            return this;
        }
    }
}
```

Now you will be able to consume this connection in any Web Part by specifying the Connection-Consumer attribute on the SetConnectionInterface method. Note that the method is not in an interface or base class, but is specified by the attribute. We'll now add a connection point to the RSS Web Part so that it can receive the connection. The code for enabling the IWebPartField connection is provided in Listing 4-12. Note that there is additional code for handling the comma-separated field value that is provided by the Links List View Web Part, where the Links List provides the link and the description separated by a comma.

Listing 4-12   Enabling a connection to an IFieldProvider

```
Consuming the IWebPartField
namespace LitwareWebParts {
  public class RssViewWebPart: WebPart, IWebEditable {

    /* Previous code omitted for clarity */

    // Get the connection
    [ConnectionConsumer("Xml URL Consumer", AllowsMultipleConnections = false)]
    public void SetConnectionInterface(IWebPartField provider) {
      provider.GetFieldValue(new FieldCallback(GetXmlUrl));
    }

    // A callback method for the IWebPartField's delegate
    private void GetXmlUrl(object providedUrl) {
      if (providedUrl != null) {
        // A workaround for the Url field type
        string[] urls = ((string)providedUrl).Split(',');
        if (urls.Length > 0)
          this.XmlUrl = urls[0];
      }
    }
  }
}
```

With the connection code in place, our Web Parts now can be connected. Note that we didn't have to code them at the same time, and that they didn't have to know about each other before they were connected. Now our business user can connect the Web Parts at run time, and the user could even connect our Web Part to a third-party Web Part. Note that users must place a Web Part page into Edit Mode in order to create a Web Part connection. The connection can be established using the Connections menu item that appears in the standard Web Part menu, as shown in Figure 4-9.

Figure 4-9   You can establish a connection between two connectable Web Parts while the hosting Web Part page is in Edit Mode.

Using Resources

Resources are a great way to use static content in your Web Parts if control processing, with its associated overhead, is not needed. It is also a good technique for including static or localized resources without any deployment burdens. One technique for using resources is to load strings for use in the page layout. Another is to make script includes and images available through a URL that is accessible to your Web Part. To include a resource in your Web Part assembly, select the resource you want to include and choose the compile action "Embedded Resource" in the file's properties. You can access the resource from the assembly by using the resource's full namespace and file name. Listing 4-13 demonstrates a utility class that can be used to access a resource stream or resource as a string out of the assembly for use in a Literal Control.

Listing 4-13   A utility class for resource access

```
Getting Resources from the Assembly
using System;
using System.Reflection;
using System.IO;
internal static class WebPartResources {

  internal static string GetNamedResource(object reference, string fileName) {
    Assembly thisApp = Assembly.GetExecutingAssembly();
    string resource = null;
    string resourceName = string.Format(@"{0}.{1}.{2}",
                                thisApp.GetName().Name,
                                reference.GetType().Namespace,
                                fileName);
    using (Stream resStream = thisApp.GetManifestResourceStream(resourceName)) {
      using (StreamReader reader = new StreamReader(resStream)) {
        resource = reader.ReadToEnd();
      }
      resStream.Close();
    }
    return resource;
  }
}
```

```
internal static Stream GetNamedResourceStream(object reference, string fileName) {
  Assembly thisApp = Assembly.GetExecutingAssembly();
  string resourceName = string.Format(@"{0}.{1}",
                                      reference.GetType().Namespace,
                                      fileName);
  return thisApp.GetManifestResourceStream(resourceName);
  }
}
```

This technique is useful for HTML resources within your Web Parts, such as table layouts. For example, imagine you have a complex HTML toolbar that you want included in your control. Instead of coding it using HtmlControls in ASP.NET code, you could design the table in either an HTML file or an .ascx file that is compiled as Toolbar.ascx and then add it as a LiteralControl. When you are developing HTML resources, the .ascx extension provides a better design experience in Visual Studio, but note that you should not include any server code in a resource that is compiled in as an embedded resource. Use the following code to load the text of an embedded resource named Toolbar.ascx out of our assembly's Resource folder by using the GetNamed Resource method.

```
string controlText =
    WebPartResources.GetNamedResource("Resources", "Toolbar.ascx");
```

Another use of resources is to serve images or JavaScript files through the Assembly Resource Handler. The Assembly Resource Handler responds to Web requests mapped to webresource.axd, which is used by the ASP.NET AJAX Toolkit for script resources. With the Assembly Resource Handler, you can include any of the external resources, such as static HTML, JavaScript, or images that are referenced by your Web Part within the Web Part assembly. This enables you to attain the design goal of making the Web Part application as autonomous as possible without linking to external script resources or embedding JavaScript in the C# code.

The Web Resource Handler is an ASP.NET HTTP handler that is particularly useful in a Web Part application in which the Web Part is an independently deployable application. To make resources available through the handler, you will need to mark them with the WebResource attribute defined in the System.Web.UI namespace. You will also need to select the Build Action Embedded Resource in Visual Studio. The WebResource attribute ensures that only resources that are intended to be Web resources are served through the handler. The Web-Resource attribute will also let you specify a Content Type for the resource, the same way that you can specify a Content Type on a Response stream in any HTTP handler. When using the PerformSubstitution property, the Web resource will be served with replaced resource URLs so that you could specify the URL of another compiled Web resource by using the syntax <%=WebResource("*FullyQualifiedResourceName*")%>. The following attribute specifies the content type and fully qualified resource name for inclusion of the HTML file help.html as a Web resource, which could be used as online help for Litware Web Parts.

```
[assembly: WebResource(@"LitwareWebParts.Resources.help.html",
    @"text/html")]
```

When registering scripts through the System.Web.UI.ScriptManager class, the Web browser will access the resource through WebResource.axd or ScriptResource.axd. The generated URL will include a timestamp of the assembly's last build so that it will be cached appropriately by the browser. You also can include resources in satellite assemblies for culture specific localizations, including localizing JavaScript string resources that will enable you to localize your Web Part applications for international deployment. In the next chapter, as we look at creating ASP.NET AJAX–enabled Web Parts, we will make further use of compiled JavaScript resources.

Working with Web Parts Through the SharePoint Site Model

As with all data within SharePoint, the Web Part framework is exposed through Share-Point's object model. Web Part instances are exposed through Web Part collections that are available through the SPFile object. From the object model code, you can access the Web Part Manager by using an SPFile object's GetLimitedWebPartCollectionManager method. This is a different class from the Web Part Manager used by the Web page, which is a control, as seen in Figure 4-10. Instead, the SPLimitedWebPartManager is a resource manager that is used only to manage the site model's Web Parts. Whereas the SPWebPartManager derives from the WebPartManager class, which derives from Control, the SPLimitedWebPartManager derives from System.Object and contains no control functionality. This same pattern is applied to the SPLimitedWebPartCollection that it exposes as its WebParts property, which is a lightweight class similar to the SPWebPartCollection but is read-only and has limited functionality.

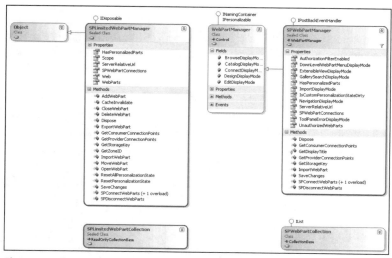

Figure 4-10   A comparison of the SPLimitedWebPartManager and the SPWebPartManager. For the sake of clarity, not all methods are shown.

Using the SPFile class with a specific URL, you can manipulate the Web Parts in the page's Web Part zones by using the SPLimitedWebPartManager. For example, on feature activation, you could edit properties of known Web Parts, add Web Parts, and remove other Web Parts.

You could also export Web Parts to their XML definitions and create file modules for use in features and site definitions with embedded Web Part descriptors from existing Web sites. The code in Listing 4-14 demonstrates adding an instance of RssViewWebPart to the default Web page. The SPLimitedWebPartManager can also be used to export Web Parts to XML with the ExportWebPart method. Listing 4-15 demonstrates how to export a Web Part to a file. This method is useful when you want to re-create a page definition in XML for inclusion in a feature definition.

Listing 4-14   Manipulating Web Parts using SharePoint's site model

```
Using the SPLimitedWebPartManager to Manipulate Web Parts
SPSite siteCollection = new SPSite("http://localhost");
SPWeb web = siteCollection.RootWeb;

SPFile file = web.Files["default.aspx"];
SPLimitedWebPartManager webPartManager =
file.GetLimitedWebPartManager(PersonalizationScope.Shared);

WebPart rssPart = new RssViewWebPart();
webPartManager.AddWebPart(rssPart, "Left", 0);
```

Listing 4-15   Exporting Web Parts using SharePoint's site model

```
Using the SPLimitedWebPartManager to Export Web Parts
SPSite siteCollection = new SPSite("http://localhost");
SPWeb web = siteCollection.RootWeb;

SPFile file = web.Files["default.aspx"];
SPLimitedWebPartManager webPartManager =
file.GetLimitedWebPartManager(PersonalizationScope.Shared);

XmlWriter xwriter = new XmlTextWriter("Example.webpart", Encoding.UTF8);
if (webPartManager.WebParts.Count > 0)
    webPartManager.ExportWebPart(webPartManager.WebParts[0], writer);
```

Summary

In this chapter, we learned the basics of Web Part development as well as advanced Web Part concepts including Editor Parts, Verbs, asynchronous tasks, and connections. We learned the difference in development patterns for WSS Web Parts versus the traditional ASP.NET programming model. At this point, you should be able to write your own Web Parts by using customizable and personalizable properties, connect them using the site context in your Web Parts, and use aggregated controls and asynchronous methods. You also should know how to manipulate Web Parts on Web Part Page instances using SharePoint's site object model. In the next chapter, we will take these fundamental techniques and learn how to create a rich Internet client interface by using the ASP.NET AJAX framework.

Chapter 5
AJAX Web Parts

- Understand the fundamentals of AJAX programming.

- Learn how to program with the ASP.NET AJAX Framework.

- Learn how to program and consume a service-oriented API by using XML data streams and Web services.

- Implement AJAX components within Web Parts.

- Use the SharePoint AJAX Toolkit to create rich Internet applications on the WSS platform.

Introduction

ASP.NET AJAX is the newest addition to ASP.NET 2.0 and is a supported Microsoft framework for next-generation Web development using AJAX technologies. AJAX is shorthand for "Asynchronous JavaScript + XML," an approach to Web applications that utilizes asynchronous data requests from the page with a client-side JavaScript engine. It is not one technology, but rather a combination of technologies that enables rich-client responsiveness in the browser when used together. It's also not a new technology, but rather a new trend that combines old technologies in a new way. The technologies include object-oriented JavaScript, asynchronous data requests utilizing the XMLHttpRequest object, XML data streams, Extensible Stylesheet Language Transformation (XSLT) transforms, and dynamic manipulation of the HTML Document Object Model (DOM). It more closely resembles a *recipe* for Web applications than a single architecture—it is an approach to Web applications based on rendering and manipulating data in smaller components during the page's life cycle in response to user actions on the client rather than the processing of the entire page as a whole. Because of this design pattern, Web Parts make an excellent deployment mechanism for AJAX components in Microsoft Windows SharePoint Services (WSS), and many of the built-in WSS APIs can be leveraged in JavaScript code from the browser.

The main benefit of using AJAX techniques in Web applications is an increased level of responsiveness once possible only in rich-client applications. Instead of waiting for a page reload or form post to update the user interface, the browser can send a discrete call to the server by using the XmlHttpRequest object while enabling the user to continue working.

A callback method on the client is then used to handle the Web request when it is completed. Compared to traditional applications, AJAX applications typically make smaller and more frequent data requests, loading data as needed rather than performing large data transfers up front. Figure 5-1 displays the traditional WSS page life cycle, in which the entire page is reprocessed as the user interacts with the data. In this traditional model, the page is requested and sent to the client as a whole. Upon page refresh, all required data must be reprocessed and resent, making data manipulations and navigation a disruptive activity. If multiple Web Parts exist on the page, each Web Part must be refreshed during the page request/response cycle. There is also significant overhead in the WSS page itself that would ideally be processed only once per user context rather than on each user interaction.

In contrast to the traditional processing model, the AJAX approach to WSS programming includes a client runtime based on the ASP.NET AJAX Library, custom controller components patterned after the Model View Controller design pattern, and service-oriented XML data sources. Figure 5-2 illustrates the dynamic nature of the AJAX approach. Instead of one fat data stream being processed in the main request/response, individual components are responsible for their processing and can be individually refreshed and updated in response to user actions, events, or timer components. The user interface and data streams could also evolve over the client life cycle of the page—new components can be spawned from additional data sources and loaded into new components, all without reloading or posting the Web page. The Web page life cycle is much longer in an AJAX application because the page is not refreshed after the initial page load.

Utilizing the ASP.NET AJAX Framework in WSS and Microsoft Office SharePoint Server allows you to take advantage of AJAX technologies and methods while using a tested and supported framework that is fully integrated with ASP.NET 2.0. Before we learn how to deploy AJAX components in Web Parts, we will first look at AJAX architecture patterns and examine an AJAX application outside of the WSS context.

Web Page Life Cycle (client browser)

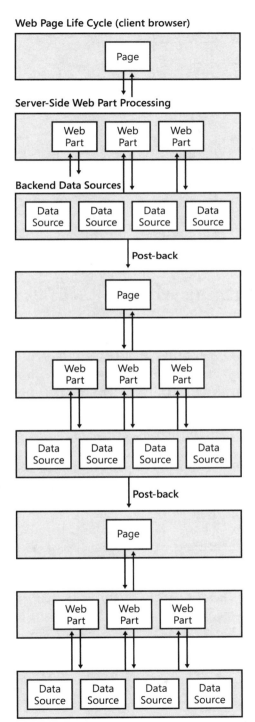

Server-Side Web Part Processing

Backend Data Sources

Post-back

Post-back

Figure 5-1   The traditional WSS Web page life cycle

Web Page Life Cycle (client browser)

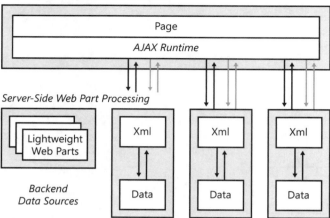

Figure 5-2 The AJAX WSS Web page life cycle

Building Rich Internet Applications with ASP.NET AJAX

To begin using ASP.NET AJAX, install the ASP.NET AJAX Framework from *http://ajax.asp.net*. The ASP.NET 2.0 AJAX SDK, server runtime, source code, and documentation can be installed from *http://ajax.asp.net* and is a prerequisite for the code samples in this chapter. ASP.NET AJAX installs System.Web.Extensions to the Global Assembly Cache as a Microsoft-supported extension to ASP.NET. Similar to other components in ASP.NET, objects within the ASP.NET AJAX Framework exist in the System.Web namespace.

To be an effective AJAX developer, you need a fundamental understanding of JavaScript. Microsoft extends JavaScript through the Microsoft AJAX Library, with which you can create rich Web interfaces and call backend data streams from the browser without writing a great deal of overly complicated JavaScript. You will write JavaScript, but you will use Microsoft's code library for the plumbing.

For AJAX code in WSS, we will use the SharePoint AJAX Toolkit that further abstracts Java-Script programming tasks for Web Parts. Although you will be writing more JavaScript in AJAX applications than in non-AJAX applications, the Microsoft AJAX Library adds a rich library of client-side API calls and adds enhancements to the object-oriented capabilities of JavaScript. Through libraries defined in the Microsoft AJAX Library and SharePoint AJAX Toolkit, the code you write will be greatly simplified. However, an understanding of the JavaScript language and Microsoft's client-side APIs is essential for developers.

Tip Script debugging tools used directly in the browser are essential for effective AJAX development. Essential debugging tools include Nikhil Kothari's *Web Development Helper* for Microsoft Internet Explorer 7.0, available from *http://projects.nikhilk.net/Projects/WebDevHelper.aspx* and *FireBug* for Mozilla Firefox 2.0, available from *http://www.getfirebug.com*.

The ASP.NET AJAX Update Panel is a popular choice for creating dynamic data grids in ASP.NET applications. However, it is only a minor part of ASP.NET AJAX and is used mainly to enable AJAX responsiveness in server-side controls. One drawback to the Update Panel is that it promotes a tightly coupled architecture in which the control is bound to a server-side data source that is not directly exposed to the client. With a pure AJAX architecture, the data sources are exposed to the client in the form of XML, JSON, or text data streams that can be consumed by multiple controls. AJAX pushes the presentation all the way down to the client and promotes server-side architectures based on services rather than controls. In the long run, the pure AJAX architecture is more flexible because it promotes reuse while exposing data sources to remote applications. Though the Update Panel has its place, we will not use the Update Panel in this book as it is a server-side technology that detracts from the AJAX programming model. To build truly dynamic rich Internet applications, you must embrace the client-side programming model of JavaScript components built against backend data services and dynamic manipulation of the DOM.

Object-Oriented JavaScript with ASP.NET AJAX

When creating JavaScript AJAX components, we will create classes just like we would build a class library in C#. We won't base them on a specific implementation, but we will program generic controls that a script runtime will initialize for the page. Though many programmers use JavaScript for pure procedural programming, JavaScript is, in fact, a rich object-oriented language. Because of its interpreted nature as a scripting language, it was misunderstood, misused, and neglected during the early 2000s as developers embraced pure server-oriented environments. But with advances in developer tools and AJAX development trends, JavaScript is an essential language to master for modern rich Internet applications. The Microsoft ASP.NET AJAX Script Library builds on the object-oriented nature of JavaScript and adds conventions similar to those found in .NET languages. The following conventions and techniques will help you write more robust script components and frameworks.

Namespaces

Namespaces can be used in script to differentiate your classes from other frameworks, just as namespaces within the .NET Framework prevent naming clashes between class libraries. To define a namespace, use the Type.registerNamespace method. To check whether a namespace is defined, simply check for its existence with the typeof function.

```
if (typeof(Litware) == 'undefined')
    Type.registerNamespace('Litware');
```

Functions as Objects

Functions are used to create objects when called with the *new* keyword. For example, the following code is used to define and instantiate an EditableControl object without a namespace.

```
function EditableControl(){}
var exampleControl = new EditableControl();
```

When defining a function within a namespace, you need to use the following syntax:

```
Litware.EditableControl = function(){}
var editControl = new Litware.EditableControl();
```

Note that you cannot create a function in a namespace by declaring the function. You need to assign the function to the namespace object as the previous example demonstrates.

Prototypes as Class Definitions

The prototype property of a function defines class properties and methods. Syntax within the prototype differs from function syntax—outside of functions, code in the prototype uses colons instead of equal signs, functions and fields must be separated by commas, and instance variables must be referred to with the "this" scope. The following code demonstrates a simple prototype for the EditableControl JavaScript class, which takes an element in the constructor and defines the initialize method.

```
Litware.EditableControl = function(element){
    element.editControl = this;
    this.element = element;
}
Litware.WikiControl.prototype = {
    element : null,
    editElement : null,
    initialize : function(text){
        this.editElement.innerHTML = text;
    }
}
```

Class Registration and Inheritance

The ASP.NET AJAX Framework extends the object type with the registerClass and inheritsFrom type system functions. These functions are used by the framework to manage type system and inheritance chains. Type registration is useful when creating JavaScript base classes and derived classes. The following method registers the Litware.EditableControl JavaScript class with Microsoft's JavaScript class framework so as to enable inheritance.

```
Litware.EditableControl.registerClass('Litware.EditableControl);
```

Likewise, the inheritsFrom function is used to manage inheritance of registered types. For example, the following WikiControl class inherits from EditableControl and therefore has all of the functionality of the EditableControl class, including the initialize method and any other methods we define in the EditableControl prototype.

```
Litware.WikiControl = function(element){
    Litware.WikiControl.initializeBase(this, [element]);
}
Litware.WikiControl.registerClass(
    'Litware.WikiControl', Litware.EditableControl);
Litware.WikiControl.inheritsFrom(Litware.EditableControl);
```

Global Namespace Functions

The ASP.NET AJAX Framework extends the global object and other primitives including String, Array, Boolean, Number, and Object. Additionally, the framework provides shortcuts to common functions, such as getElementById. The $get method can be used to obtain a reference to a named element. You might also want to use the $addHandler method to attach event handlers to objects. There are too many APIs to list here, but full reference to the client library is available as a local Microsoft Visual Studio Web site that you can download from *http://ajax.asp.net* or access online at *http://ajax.asp.net/docs/ClientReference*.

Creating a JavaScript Component with ASP.NET AJAX

To create your first application with ASP.NET AJAX, create a new ASP.NET AJAX–Enabled Web Site using Microsoft Visual Studio 2005. The ASP.NET AJAX-Enabled Web Site is a new Visual Studio project template installed with ASP.NET AJAX. In the following examples, we will create a simple wiki component. A *wiki* is a collaboration tool in which wiki users can freely edit text-based content and add links to new content. Our example wiki won't be as functional as the wiki library in WSS, but it will be a good example of a lightweight AJAX architecture. The following samples are part of the LitwareAjaxWebSite example code, available in the code downloads as a Visual Studio Web Site.

The base component for the wiki is an EditableControl component based on an HTML div element, providing rich text-editing capability. Remember that we are defining a JavaScript class for use in a deployable component, such as a Web page or even a Web Part control, so we should therefore strive to make the EditableControl as flexible as possible so that we can reuse it within different contexts. Listing 5-1 demonstrates a simple EditableControl class for use in an AJAX component. The EditableControl constructor takes an element as the parameter and defines an initialize method that creates the control with the specified text. Within the makeEditable method of the EditableControl, we will manipulate the DOM at runtime to make the content of the EditableControl editable. Note the use of $addHandler and $clear-Handlers to manage JavaScript event handlers. You will also notice that EditableControl isn't responsible for data persistence, which will be implemented in the control that will inherit from this class. We will also include some very simple wiki syntax parsing to the Editable-Control, which we will utilize within child classes. You can see that objects and inheritance in script can help you create reusable JavaScript components just as you're used to in C# code!

Listing 5-1   EditableControl.js—a simple component for an editable AJAX control

```
EditableControl JavaScript Class
// Defines the EditableControl Component
// A control-based component for a simple editable control
if (typeof(Litware) == 'undefined')
  Type.registerNamespace('Litware');
Litware.EditableControl = function(element){
  element.editControl = this;
  this.element = element;
}
```

```
Litware.EditableControl.prototype = {
  element : null,
  editElement : null,
  saveButton : null,
  toolbar : null,

  // initializes the control
  initialize : function(text){
    this.toolbar = document.createElement('DIV');
    this.toolbar.style.border = '1px solid silver';
    this.element.appendChild(this.toolbar);
    this.toolbar.style.visibility='hidden';

    this.saveButton = document.createElement('IMG');
    this.saveButton.src = '/_layouts/images/save.gif';
    this.saveButton.style.top='3px';
    this.saveButton.style.left='3px';
    this.saveButton.style.zIndex=100;
    this.toolbar.appendChild(this.saveButton);

    this.editElement = document.createElement('DIV');
    this.editElement.style.border = '1px solid';
    this.editElement.style.padding='3px';
    this.editElement.innerHTML = text;
    this.element.appendChild(this.editElement);
    $addHandler(this.editElement,'dblclick',Litware.EditableControl.MakeEditable);
    },
    // makes it editable
    makeEditable : function(){
      if (this.editElement.contentEditable == 'true'){
        this.saveContent();
        $addHandler(this.editElement,'dblclick',
        Litware.EditableControl.MakeEditable);
        $clearHandlers(this.saveButton);
        this.toolbar.style.visibility='hidden';
      }else{
        document.designMode = "On";
        this.editElement.contentEditable = 'true';
        this.editElement.style.backgroundColor='yellow';
        $clearHandlers(this.editElement);

        this.toolbar.style.visibility='visible';
        $addHandler(this.saveButton,'click',
        Litware.EditableControl.MakeEditable);
      }
    },

  // Saves the content
  saveContent : function() {
    document.designMode = "Off";
    this.editElement.contentEditable = 'false';
    this.editElement.style.backgroundColor='';
  },
```

```
  // converts the HTML format to WIKI text
  convertToWiki : function(element){
    var links = element.getElementsByTagName('span');
    var placeholders = new Array();
    for(var i=0;i<links.length;i++){
      if (links[i].className=='WIKILINK')
        Array.add(placeholders, links[i]);
    }
    for(var i=0;i<placeholders.length;i++){
      var wik = document.createTextNode(
        String.format('[[{0}]]', this.getText(placeholders[i])) );
      var old = placeholders[i].parentNode.replaceChild(
        wik, placeholders[i]);
      placeholders[i] = null;
    }
  },

  // Converts WIKI text to HTML format
  wikiToHtml : function(wikiText){
    var rex = new RegExp('\\[\\[([^\\]]+)\\]\\]',"mg");
    var match = rex.exec(wikiText);
    while (match){
      var linked = String.format(
      "<span class=\"WIKILINK\">{0}</span>",match[1]);
      wikiText = wikiText.replace(match[0],linked);
      match = rex.exec(wikiText);
    }
    return wikiText;
  },

  // Gets the text content of a DOM node
  getText : function(node){
    if (node == null)
      return '';
    if (node.innerText)
      return node.innerText;
    else if (node.textContent)
      return node.textContent;
    else return '';
  }
}

Litware.EditableControl.registerClass('Litware.EditableControl');

// anonymous method that calls into the Litware.editControl
Litware.EditableControl.MakeEditable = function(evt){
  var editControl = findParentEditElement(evt.target);
  if (editControl != null)
    editControl.makeEditable();
  else
    alert('Could not enable wiki!');
}
```

```
// Finds the parent editable element
function findParentEditElement(element){
  while (element.editControl == null || element == null){
    if (element.parentNode)
      element = element.parentNode;
    else if (element.parentElement)
      element = element.parentElement;
    else {
      var err = Error.invalidOperation();
      throw err;
    }
  }
  if (element != null)
    return element.editControl;
}
```

You see that the initialize function attaches the Litware.EditableControl.MakeEditable handler to the element's double-click event by using the $addHandler function, part of the Microsoft JavaScript library that attaches an event handler to an object. MakeEditable is called with an event, so you are not able to pass a direct object reference. However, you can find the parent EditableControl by looking up the control tree, as in the findParentEditElement function. Because you cannot attach an instance method of the EditableControl in the handler, you must look at the event target's parentElement (parentNode in Mozilla) to check for the editControl expando property (remembering that we set the element's editControl property to the instance of the EditableControl). An expando property is an arbitrary property set by script on an object. Because JavaScript objects are not constrained to predefined interfaces as they are with .NET objects, you can set expando properties on any object.

With the EditableControl component defined in the EditableControl.js file, we are now ready to add it to a Web page to test it out. Using the AJAX-enabled Web site project, all we need to do is add a ScriptReference to the ScriptManager control, add a placeholder control, and create a page load handler. The ScriptManager is used to register script references for the Microsoft AJAX Library and custom scripts (including scripts compiled as Web resources), and to manage JavaScript proxies to any registered Web services. To test the script we include the ScriptReference as a path. When working with the ScriptManager in code, you want to register a compiled script resource with the assembly and resource name. For now, the Script-Manager control is declared as follows:

```
<asp:ScriptManager ID="ScriptManager1" runat="server">
  <Scripts>
    <asp:ScriptReference Path="EditableControl.js" />
  </Scripts>
</asp:ScriptManager>
```

After creating the script reference, we can simply add a div placeholder and create a page load event handler. The page load event handler is similar to what we will later add to a Web Part—it is the code that creates the AJAX component based on the class we've defined. After defining a page load method named Litware.PageLoad, we can add that to the AJAX application's load event with the Sys.Application.add_load method. This is similar to handling the implementation of an ASP.NET page_load handler in C#, although this page load handler runs entirely on the client browser. The following code instantiates a new Edit-ableControl with the MainPlaceHolder div and initializes the EditableControl with the text "Hello, Litware Employees!" This code demonstrates the client-side load event, which happens after the JavaScript application runtime is loaded. Use this event to initialize your components and ensure that all required script resources are loaded.

```
<script type="text/javascript" language="javascript" >
if (typeof(Litware) == 'undefined')
  Type.registerNamespace('Litware');
Litware.PageLoad = function(){
  var control = $get('MainPlaceHolder');
  window.wiki = new Litware.WikiControl(control);
  window.wiki.initialize('Hello, Litware Employees!');
}
// Add the PageLoad to the AJAX Runtime load event
Sys.Application.add_load(Litware.PageLoad);
</script>
```

Now that we have a base control for notepad-like functionality, we can extend it with a persistence service to create a simple wiki (a micro-wiki). In traditional ASP.NET development, we might put code within a Page class to store control values such as the wiki text. In traditional WSS development, we might persist the wiki text within a Web Part. But in an AJAX development architecture, you define reusable services as an API framework that can be used in multiple components. In the following example, we will build a script-enabled Web service called *WikiService* that simply remembers the contents of the wikis. We will later tie this Web service to a simple WSS list instance, but for this prototype, we will define two methods and simply store the data in application memory.

To enable a JavaScript proxy, mark the Web service with the ScriptService attribute defined in the System.Web.Script.Services namespace. Web services that are marked with the Script-Service attribute can be referenced with Script References in the ScriptManager control. Listing 5-2 demonstrates a very simple persistence Web service for our very simple wiki.

Listing 5-2   AJAX-enabled Web services are marked with the ScriptService attribute.

A Script-Enabled Web Service for a Simple Wiki

```
<%@ WebService Language="C#" Class="Litware.WikiWebService" %>
using System;
using System.Web;
using System.Web.Services;
using System.Web.Services.Protocols;
using System.Web.Script.Services;

namespace Litware {

  [WebService(Namespace = "http://Litware.com/insideWSS/AJAX")]
```

```
[WebServiceBinding(ConformsTo = WsiProfiles.BasicProfile1_1)]
[ScriptService]
public class WikiWebService: System.Web.Services.WebService {

    private const string DefaultContent = "Welcome to the Simple Wiki!";
    private const string keyPrefix = @"litwiki_";

    [WebMethod]
    public string GetContent(string wikiID) {
        return ((string) Application[keyPrefix + wikiID] ?? DefaultContent);
    }

    [WebMethod]
    public void SetContent(string wikiID, string wikiContent) {
        Application[keyPrefix + wikiID] = wikiContent;
    }
}
```

With our Web service endpoint in place, we can create a reference to it in the Script Manager and reference it in our component. The Script Manager creates a client-side script reference to the component's generated JavaScript proxy, which is the path of the ASMX file with a "/js" switch appended. For example, the following Script Manager will create a reference to the script generated at the URL "*WikiWebService.asmx/js*":

```
<asp:ScriptManager ID="ScriptManager1" runat="server">
  <Services>
    <asp:ServiceReference Path="WikiWebService.asmx" />
  </Services>
</asp:ScriptManager>
```

If the application is run in debug mode (as defined by the web.config compilation attribute), the Script Manager's reference will point to "*WikiService.asmx/jsdebug*."

Tip   To examine the generated JavaScript proxy for script-enabled Web services, simply save the [*service*].asmx/jsdebug endpoint to a text file.

Adding to the EditableControl, we can create a WikiControl JavaScript class that inherits from the EditableControl but adds a layer of persistence. With this strategy, you can develop common base components and add custom functionality per your application needs. This simple example lays the foundation for real-world component inheritance later in this chapter. To provide persistence, we override the makeEditable method and add custom functionality to the base functionality. If the editElement is not editable after the base call, we know that we should save the element. This lets the base class take care of the rendering and user interface while letting the concrete WikiControl JavaScript class handle integration with our WikiService Web service API.

JavaScript proxies are generated with the same signature as the Web service signature, with the addition of a success callback handler, a failure callback handler, and a userContext object. For example, the signature public string GetContent(string) translates to the JavaScript signature GetContent(string,onSuccess,onFailed,userContext). The userContext parameter is an arbitrary object that is returned in the asynchronous callback. You could use it to pass a JavaScript object representing state, or you could simply pass a reference to the current object by using the keyword *this*. The value returned from the Web service is passed to the asynchronous callback handler and is a simple type, an XMLDOM object, or a JavaScript object. (If the Web service returns void, no value is returned on the callback other than the userContext object.) If you return a nonprimitive type from the Web service, ASP.NET AJAX automatically sends a JavaScript serialized object (formatted in JSON, the JavaScript object notation) that is passed to your callback handler unless you have specified the XML format with the ScriptMethod attribute.

With these concepts in mind, look at Listing 5-3, which demonstrates the full WikiControl containing the Web Service calls. This component is dependent on the WikiService Web service proxy and can be instantiated against different wikis as defined by the wiki ID passed in the control parameter and Web service calls. Note that this interface is designed for the MicroWiki list instance that we will create later in WSS.

Listing 5-3   The WikiControl uses script-enabled Web services for persistence.

```
WikiControl: An EditableControl with Persistence
// Defines the Micro Wiki Component tied to the WikiList
Litware.WikiControl = function(element,wikiID){
  Litware.WikiControl.initializeBase(this, [element]);
  this.wikiID = wikiID ;
  element.controlType='Litware.WikiControl';
  element.WikiControl = this;
}
Litware.WikiControl.prototype = {
  wikiID : null,
  makeEditable : function(){
    Litware.WikiControl.callBaseMethod(this, 'makeEditable');
    if (this.editElement.contentEditable == 'false'){
      this.editElement.innerHTML=this.wikiToHtml(this.editElement.innerHTML);
      this.addWikiHandlers(this.editElement);
      // Save the wiki in the wiki service
      // Required in WSS:
      // Litware.WikiWebService.set_path(window.spWebUrl+
      // '/_vti_bin/Litware/WikiWebService.asmx');
      Litware.WikiWebService.SetContent(
        this.wikiID,this.editElement.innerHTML);
    }
    else // Convert to wiki syntax
      this.convertToWiki(this.editElement);
  },
```

```
  initialize : function(){
    Litware.WikiControl.callBaseMethod(this, 'initialize',[ 'Loading...' ]);
    this.loadContent(this.wikiID);
  },

  loadContent : function(wikiID){
    this.wikiID = wikiID;
    // Required in WSS:
    // Litware.WikiWebService.set_path(window.spWebUrl+
    // '/_vti_bin/Litware/WikiWebService.asmx');
    Litware.WikiWebService.GetContent(wikiID,
      Litware.WikiControl.OnGetContent,
      Litware.WikiControl.OnGetFail, this);
  },

  setContent : function(html){
      this.editElement.innerHTML = html;
      this.addWikiHandlers(this.editElement);
  },

  // Adds click handlers to the WIKILINK spans
  addWikiHandlers : function(element){
    var links = element.getElementsByTagName('span');
    for(var i=0;i<links.length;i++){
      if (links[i].className=='WIKILINK')
        $addHandler(links[i],'click', Litware.wikiLink);
    }
  }
}

Litware.wikiLink = function(evt){
  var wiki = SharePoint.Ajax.FindParentControl(
    evt.target,'Litware.WikiControl');
  var link;
  if (evt.target.innerText)
    link = evt.target.innerText;
  else if (evt.target.textContent)
    link = evt.target.textContent;
  if (wiki != null && link != null && link != '')
    wiki.WikiControl.loadContent(link);
}

Litware.WikiControl.OnGetContent = function(contentResponse, WikiControl){
    WikiControl.setContent(contentResponse);
}

Litware.WikiControl.OnGetFail = function(error){
  alert(error.get_message() + '\n' + error.get_stackTrace());
}

Litware.WikiControl.registerClass('Litware.WikiControl',
  Litware.EditableControl);
Litware.WikiControl.inheritsFrom(Litware.EditableControl);
```

```
// WebPart initialization script:
Litware.WikiControl.Init = function(){
  if( window.WikiControlTemplates ){
    for(var i=0;i<window.WikiControlTemplates.length;i++){
      var o = window.WikiControlTemplates[i];
      if (o != null){
        var wiki = new Litware.WikiControl($get(o.Control), o.WikiID);
        wiki.initialize();
        o = null;
      }
    }
    window.WikiControlTemplates = null;
  }
}
Sys.Application.add_load(Litware.WikiControl.Init);
```

With the backend Web service in place and integrated with the WikiControl, we are ready to add it to our Web page. To add the Web service proxy and all of our JavaScript controls, the ScriptManager will be declared with the following references:

```
<asp:ScriptManager runat="server">
  <Scripts>
    <asp:ScriptReference Path="EditableControl.js" />
    <asp:ScriptReference Path="WikiControl.js" />
  </Scripts>
  <Services>
    <asp:ServiceReference Path="WikiService.asmx" />
  </Services>
</asp:ScriptManager>
```

To instantiate the WikiControl, we again add a handler to the load event with the method Sys.Application.add_load from within the Web page. To do this, we define a function and add it to the load as follows:

```
<script type="text/javascript" language="javascript" >
if (typeof(Litware) == 'undefined')
  Type.registerNamespace('Litware');
Litware.WikiPageLoad = function(){
  var control = $get('MainPlaceHolder');
  window.wiki = new Litware.WikiControl(
    control, '6614ed027597d4b6a9cfaa16f0bcd95e');
  window.wiki.initialize();
}
</script>
```

AJAX Architecture and WSS

The core architecture for AJAX applications consists of a library of XML APIs on the server and JavaScript components on the client that perform user interface implementation, XML data requests, and Web service calls. To apply this technique to Web Part development, we define JavaScript components that run in the context of a Web Part and program against XML data sources on the server. The server data sources utilize the WSS site context and object model as well as the WSS authorization and security framework. Some of these endpoints already exist for WSS, including RSS syndication for lists. Unfortunately, WSS 3.0 RTM Web Services are not script-enabled, so you may need to build your own API for AJAX components in the Microsoft Office 2007 timeframe. To develop AJAX components for WSS, you first define an API of service endpoints, including XML feeds and Web services. Because actual users are passing their credentials directly to the API, the API can utilize the caller's security context for authentication and impersonation within your server-side handlers.

Tip Within AJAX APIs, all endpoints must be secured and validated because we are directly exposing the API to the user.

Web Service Endpoints for WSS AJAX Components

Custom Web services utilizing the WSS site context can be used to create an API for WSS AJAX components as well as external applications. Building on the previous WikiWebService endpoint, we can modify the Web service to use a WSS list for persistence. By utilizing a flexible API, we are able to abstract the data store from the component so that we can later add a more robust user interface in script without modifying the back end. The WikiWebService, which is an adopted version of the WikiWebService with a WSS List as the persistence layer, is shown in Listing 5-4. Note that the Web service utilizes some advanced security concepts (discussed further in Chapter 10, "Application Security") and requires either full-trust or custom permissions (defined in the sample code solution manifest). This API defines one hidden wiki list per Web site, with a list of wiki items keyed by the title. By using this API, you could extend the wiki to a full-featured wiki application. Within the code samples, we include the Web services and Web Parts in a single assembly, but real application APIs should be developed independently and loosely coupled.

Tip To build a full-featured AJAX-wiki, you could add wiki text parsing to the EditableControl JavaScript component. (For more information on the full wiki syntax, refer to the built-in WSS wiki components.)

Listing 5-4 The WikiWebService with WSS list backing demonstrates a flexible API for WSS AJAX components.

```
WikiWebService for WSS
using System;
using System.Collections.Generic;
using System.Text;
using System.Web.Services;
using System.Web.Script.Services;
using Microsoft.SharePoint;
using System.Security.Permissions;
```

```
namespace Litware {

  // An example Web Service API for a Litware MicroWiki.
  [WebService(Namespace = "http://Litware.com/insideWSS/AJAX")]
  [WebServiceBinding(ConformsTo = WsiProfiles.BasicProfile1_1)]
  [ScriptService]
  public class WikiWebService : System.Web.Services.WebService {

    private const string wikiName = "litwareMicroWiki";
    private const string DefaultContent = " "

    [WebMethod]
    public string GetContent(string wikiID) {
      SPList wiki = this.GetWikiList(wikiID);
      if (wiki == null)
        return "Welcome to the MicroWiki!";
      SPQuery query = new SPQuery();
      query.ViewFields=@"<FieldRef Name='Content'/><FieldRef Name='Title'/>";
      query.Query = string.Format(
        @"<Where><Eq><FieldRef Name='Title'/>
          <Value Type='Text'>{0}</Value></Eq></Where>", wikiID);
      SPListItemCollection items = wiki.GetItems(query);
      if (items.Count > 0)
        return ((string)items[0]["Content"]);
      else
        return DefaultContent;
    }


    [WebMethod]
    public void SetContent(string wikiID, string wikiContent) {
      SPContext.Current.Web.AllowUnsafeUpdates = true;
      SPList wiki = this.GetWikiList(wikiID);
      SPQuery query = new SPQuery();
      query.ViewFields = @"<FieldRef Name='Content'/><FieldRef Name='Title'/>";
      query.Query = string.Format(
        @"<Where><Eq><FieldRef Name='Title'/>
          <Value Type='Text'>{0}</Value></Eq></Where>", wikiID);
      SPListItemCollection items = wiki.GetItems(query);
      if (items.Count > 0){
        // Queried items are read only.
        SPListItem item = wiki.Items[items[0].UniqueId];
        item["Content"] = wikiContent;
        item.Update();
      }
      else {
        SPListItem item = wiki.Items.Add();
        item["Content"] = wikiContent;
        item["Title"] = wikiID;
        item.Update();
      }
    }

    // Returns the wiki list for this site.
    [SecurityPermission(SecurityAction.Demand, UnmanagedCode = true)]
    private SPList GetWikiList(string wikiID) {
```

```
          SPWeb site = SPContext.Current.Web;
          SPList list = null;
          foreach (SPList alist in site.Lists) {
            if (alist.Title.Equals(wikiName,
                StringComparison.InvariantCultureIgnoreCase)) {
              list = alist;
              break;
            }
          }
          if (list != null)
            return list;
          else {
            // See chapter 10 for more details on RunWithElevatedPrivileges
            SPSecurity.RunWithElevatedPrivileges(
            delegate() {
              using (SPSite siteCollection=new SPSite(SPContext.Current.Site.ID)){
                using (SPWeb elevatedSite =
                    siteCollection.OpenWeb(SPContext.Current.Web.ID)) {
                  elevatedSite.AllowUnsafeUpdates = true;
                  Guid listID = elevatedSite.Lists.Add(wikiName,
                    "A microwiki", SPListTemplateType.GenericList);
                  SPList wikiList = elevatedSite.Lists[listID];
                  wikiList.WriteSecurity = 1; // All users
                  wikiList.ReadSecurity = 1; // All users
                  wikiList.Hidden = true;
                  wikiList.Fields.Add("Content", SPFieldType.Note, true);
                  wikiList.Update();
                  SPListItem homeWiki = wikiList.Items.Add();
                  homeWiki["Content"] = "Welcome to the MicroWiki!";
                  homeWiki["Title"] = wikiID;
                  homeWiki.Update();
                }
              }
            });
          }
          return null;
      }
    }
}
```

Before we build the wiki into a Web Part, we will look at the additional server-side services that are common in an AJAX architecture.

HTTP Handlers as Data Sources

HTTP handler endpoints are another preferred data source for AJAX applications in which data is returned in a simple XML, text, or JSON format representing the data query. This is a subset of the *REST* architecture pattern, or Representational State Transfer, in which the data served from a simple URL-based protocol is the representation of the current data's state. In a REST architecture, each URL endpoint defines the data for an item. For example, an Outline Processor Markup Language (OPML) endpoint for WSS would represent feeds for each site.

The site-relative endpoint opml.aspx would define the site feeds available in OPML format, and you would know by this convention that you can access the feed data for each site at this endpoint. This approach is taken in the following example. Because WSS applications are *virtualized*, we simply define one endpoint in web.config, and our handler picks up the WSS site context.

HTTP handlers are defined by the interface System.Web.IHttpHandler and provide a mechanism for working with the HTTP request and response. By using handlers, you can create a library of XML data sources that can be consumed by both JavaScript and .NET clients. The handler is similar to a Page object but does not have the control life cycle overhead of the Page class. In addition, it exists entirely in compiled code without interpreted markup. To implement a simple handler, merely implement the IHttpHandler interface's IsReusable read-only property and process the request within the ProcessRequest method. You generally want to set the Response's ContentType to "text/xml" and write XML by using the XmlTextWriter. The following handler demonstrates the use of the SharePoint site context, the IHttpHandler interface, and the XmlTextWriter.

```
using System;
using System.Web;
using Microsoft.SharePoint;
using System.Xml;

namespace LitwareAjaxWebParts {
  public class SimpleSiteHandler : IHttpHandler {

    public bool IsReusable { get { return false; } }

    public void ProcessRequest(HttpContext context) {
      SPWeb site = SPContext.Current.Web;
      XmlWriter writer = new XmlTextWriter(context.Response.Output);
      writer.WriteStartElement("site");
      writer.WriteAttributeString("url", site.Url);
      writer.WriteString(site.Title);
      writer.WriteEndElement();
      writer.Flush();
    }
  }
}
```

Tip   The IHttpAsyncHandler is the preferred interface for handlers that need to perform longer-running tasks, such as Web requests or database queries. For more information on the IHttpAsyncHandler interface, see the MSDN Library (*http://msdn.microsoft.com/library*).

Now that we've looked at a simple HTTP handler, let's look at an example of a real-life endpoint for an XML API. In the following Web Part examples, we will build a Feed List Web Part similar to the previous non-AJAX Feed List Web Part (see Listing 4-8 in Chapter 4, "Web Parts"). However, the Feed List will be built with an AJAX component that can navigate an entire site collection's hierarchy and send client-side connections to an AJAX List View Web Part, a specialized instance of an RSS Web Part. To build these components, we need a navigable XML data source of site feeds and an RSS data source for each WSS list instance. Fortunately, WSS already gives us RSS feeds for each list, so we need to build the data stream for the hierarchical list of feeds.

The format we used for the Feed List is OPML, an industry-standard XML format used to display outlines of RSS feeds in a hierarchical manner. The outline comprises outline nodes, in which a type can be specified in each node. We specify the type *site* for sites and the type *rss* for list feeds. Outline nodes typically include a title, htmlUrl, and/or an xmlUrl attribute that define either the "human readable" URL for an item or the XML URL for a feed or data source. Following is an example OPML document that we would generate for each site with our Feed List Handler. XML data sources, such as the Feed List Handler, are essential components in an AJAX architecture and enable rapid development of user interface components based on them. Because WSS applications run under site context, this same data source can be accessed through site-relative URLs to provide feed data from the current site context. To enable navigation, we include outline nodes for the direct children of the current site context and provide an attribute for the parent site if the site is not the root site. This scheme lets client code navigate up and down the site collection by using the URL of the site and the URL of the site-relative endpoint.

The following example XML stream is generated by the Feed List Handler and is used to build the user interface for the feed navigation:

```
<opml>
<head><title>Team Site: Site Feeds</title></head>
<body>
  <outline title="Team Site" type="site"
    htmlUrl="http://litwareserver" current="true">
    <outline title="Announcements" type="rss"
      xmlUrl="http://litwareserver/_layouts/listfeed.aspx?List=announcements"
      htmlUrl="http://litwareserver/Lists/Announcements/AllItems.aspx"
      listType="Announcements" />
    <outline title="Customers" type="rss"
      xmlUrl="http://litwareserver/_layouts/listfeed.aspx?List=customers"
      htmlUrl="http://litwareserver/Customers/AllItems.aspx"
      listType="10002" />
    <outline title="blog" type="site" htmlUrl="http://litwareserver/blog" />
    <outline title="litware" type="site" htmlUrl="http://litwareserver/litware" />
  </outline>
</body>
</opml>
```

To generate the OPML for the endpoint, we use a simple HTTP handler that just enumerates the child sites and lists of the current site. Because we are accessing the site by using the WSS site context, we have built-in security and only render lists that the user can access. We will discuss list security in more detail in Chapter 10 in our discussion of the ISecurableObject interface. For now, we can use the ISecurableObject interface to ensure that the requesting user can access the WSS list. To take this further, you can create a filter to serve only a particular type of list, such as the Posts list, to build a blog reader for a site collection. The FeedList-Handler class is listed in Listing 5-5.

Listing 5-5   The Feed List Handler provides an outline of XML feeds for the site.

```
The FeedListHandler XML Data Source
using System;
using System.Web;
using Microsoft.SharePoint;
using System.Xml;
using System.Security.Permissions;
using System.Globalization;
using System.Net;

namespace LitwareAjaxWebParts {
  [PermissionSet(SecurityAction.Demand)]
  public sealed class FeedListHandler : IHttpHandler {

    public bool IsReusable { get { return false; }}
    bool recursive = false;
    internal const string WssRssFeedFormat =
      @"{0}/_layouts/listfeed.aspx?List={{{1}}}";

    private SPWeb Site {get { return SPContext.Current.Web; }}

    public void ProcessRequest(HttpContext context) {
        if (!this.Site.AllowRssFeeds){
            context.Response.StatusCode = (int) HttpStatusCode.NoContent;
            return;
        }

        // Set the XML headers
        context.Response.ContentType = @"text/xml";
        context.Response.Expires = -1;
        XmlWriter xw = new XmlTextWriter(context.Response.Output);

        xw.WriteStartDocument();
        xw.WriteStartElement("opml");
        xw.WriteStartElement("head");
        xw.WriteElementString("title",
        SPContext.Current.Web.Title + ": " + @"Site Feeds");
        xw.WriteEndElement();
        xw.WriteStartElement("body");
        this.WriteSiteFeeds(SPContext.Current.Web, xw);
        xw.WriteEndElement();
        xw.WriteEndElement();
    }

    // Writes the site feed list
    private void WriteSiteFeeds(SPWeb site, XmlWriter xw) {
        if (!site.AllowRssFeeds) return;
        xw.WriteStartElement(@"outline");
        xw.WriteAttributeString(@"title", site.Title);
```

```
        xw.WriteAttributeString(@"type", @"site");
        xw.WriteAttributeString(@"htmlUrl", site.Url);
        if (site == SPContext.Current.Web)
            xw.WriteAttributeString(@"current", @"true");

        if (site.ParentWeb != null)
            xw.WriteAttributeString(@"parentWeb", site.ParentWeb.Url);

        foreach (SPList list in site.Lists) {
          if (!list.AllowRssFeeds) continue;
          if (HttpContext.Current.User.Identity.IsAuthenticated == false){
          if ((list.AnonymousPermMask64 & SPBasePermissions.ViewListItems)
                == SPBasePermissions.ViewListItems)
            WriteListReference(xw, list);
          } else {
           if (list.DoesUserHavePermissions(SPBasePermissions.ViewListItems))
            WriteListReference(xw, list);
          }
        }

        foreach (SPWeb childSite in site.Webs) {
            if (HttpContext.Current.User.Identity.IsAuthenticated==false){
                if ((childSite.AnonymousPermMask64 &
                        SPBasePermissions.ViewListItems) ==
                        SPBasePermissions.ViewListItems)
                    this.WriteSite(childSite, xw);
            } else if (childSite.DoesUserHavePermissions(
                    SPBasePermissions.ViewListItems))
                this.WriteSite(childSite, xw);
            }
            xw.WriteEndElement();
        }

private void WriteSite(SPWeb site, XmlWriter xw) {
  xw.WriteStartElement(@"outline");
  xw.WriteAttributeString(@"title", site.Title);
  xw.WriteAttributeString(@"type", @"site");
  xw.WriteAttributeString(@"htmlUrl", site.Url);
  xw.WriteEndElement();
}

private static void WriteListReference(XmlWriter xw, SPList list){
  if (!list.AllowRssFeeds || list.Hidden)
    continue;
  list.CheckPermissions(SPBasePermissions.ViewListItems);

  xw.WriteStartElement(@"outline");
  xw.WriteAttributeString(@"title", list.Title);
  string listFeed = string.Format(
    CultureInfo.InvariantCulture,
    WssRssFeedFormat,
    list.ParentWeb.Url,
    HttpContext.Current.Server.UrlEncode(list.ID.ToString()));
```

```
        xw.WriteAttributeString(@"xmlUrl", listFeed);
        xw.WriteAttributeString(@"type", @"rss");
        xw.WriteAttributeString(@"htmlUrl", list.ParentWeb.Site.Url +
          list.DefaultViewUrl);
        xw.WriteAttributeString(@"listType", list.BaseTemplate.ToString());
        xw.WriteEndElement(); // outline
      }
    }
  }
}
```

The Feed List Handler is registered in the web.config file through the following element in the httpHandlers node. In the code samples provided, this is registered through a Feature installer when deployed in the solution package or through the Visual Studio "Deploy" build.

```
<add verb="*" path="opml.ashx"
    type="LitwareAjaxWebParts.FeedListHandler, LitwareAjaxWebParts"/>
```

The HTTP handler defined in web.config is virtualized, meaning that this endpoint is exposed in each WSS site. When building your API, you want to program both virtualized endpoints that can expose data from within the site context and common nonvirtualized endpoints that provide application functionality outside of the site context. Oftentimes, you might want to implement custom endpoints that aggregate, filter, or manipulate external data, providing endpoints to external systems that also interact with the WSS site context.

Building AJAX Web Part Parts for WSS

Because we have built the server-side APIs for data sources, including XML feeds and Web service endpoints, the only components that go in the Web Part are JavaScript components and functions, HTML placeholders that get rendered within Web Part boundaries, and JavaScript runtime. The bulk of the server processing is moved from the Web Part to the services layer, exposed to the client runtime through XML feeds and Web services. We build JavaScript classes that can be instantiated on the client from within the Web Part and deploy these classes through the ScriptManager control. The System.Web.UI.ScriptManager class is an ASP.NET control that manages scripts within the framework. It is responsible for deploying our scripts, ensuring that the Microsoft ASP.NET AJAX Framework is included, and providing JavaScript proxy support for Web service references.

To use ASP.NET AJAX components in your Web Parts, you need to add an instance of the ScriptManager class to the page. Because there can be only one ScriptManager instance per page, be sure to obtain a reference to ScriptManager through its static GetCurrent method. To obtain a reference to ScriptManager, use a reference-safe property, such as the following property of the AjaxWebPart base class in the SharePoint AJAX Toolkit.

```
private ScriptManager scriptMan;
public ScriptManager AtlasScriptManager {
  get {
    if (scriptMan == null){
```

```
        scriptMan = ScriptManager.GetCurrent(this.Page);
        if (scriptMan == null) {
          scriptMan = new ScriptManager();
          this.Controls.Add(scriptMan);
        }
      }
      return scriptMan;
    }
}
```

WebConfig Requirements for ASP.NET AJAX

The ASP.NET AJAX runtime requires the following web.config modification to enable the client runtime. The following HTTP handler needs to be added in each IIS Web site's web.config. (When using the SharePoint AJAX Toolkit, the Feature Installer automatically adds this.)

```
<add verb="GET,HEAD" path="ScriptResource.axd" type="System.Web.Handlers.ScriptResourceHandl
er, System.Web.Extensions, Version=1.0.61025.0, Culture=neutral, PublicKeyToken=31bf3856ad36
4e35" validate="false" />
```

Within Web service application directories, typically deployed in subdirectories of 12\ISAPI (served through the virtualized path http://[serverroot]/[sitepath]/_vti_bin), you want to deploy a configuration file that enables JavaScript proxy generation. This configuration file removes the System.Web.Services.Protocols.WebServiceHandlerFactory handler for ASMX Web services and adds the System.Web.Script.Services.ScriptHandlerFactory handler. This handler builds the JavaScript proxies for endpoints marked with the ScriptService attribute defined in System.Web.Script.Services and passes control to the System.Web.Services.Protocols .WebServiceHandlerFactory for Web service methods. Following is a reference web.config for Web service applications. Note that you need to deploy only SOAP (ASMX) Web services in the ISAPI folder; REST Web services defined as HTTP handlers can be deployed within the root IIS application.

```
<?xml version="1.0"?>
<configuration>
  <system.web>
    <httpHandlers>
      <remove verb="*" path="*.asmx"/>
      <add verb="*" path="*.asmx" validate="false" type="System.Web.Script.Services.ScriptHandl
erFactory, System.Web.Extensions, Version=1.0.61025.0, Culture=neutral, PublicKeyToken=31bf3
856ad364e35"/>
    </httpHandlers>
  </system.web>
</configuration>
```

AJAX Web Parts

Because we have already defined a wiki Web service API and prototyped the WikiControl AJAX component, we are now ready for a wiki Web Part for WSS. In the following example, we will define the MicroWikiWebPart, which is a simple wrapper for the WikiControl AJAX component. Because Web Parts are deployed independently from the pages on which they run, AJAX components within Web Parts require using the Web Part Client Control Registration Pattern. With this design pattern, a placeholder is registered with the page and processed through a convention in the JavaScript application load event. The template is written to an array named by a convention based on the script component, such as the WikiControl-Templates array for the WikiControl JavaScript class. This script, along with a div element referenced in the component template, is written to the page by each Web Part within the RenderContents method. This enables multiple Web Parts based on the same AJAX component to be deployed on the same page with unique instances per control. For the MicroWiki Web Part, we want to generate the following HTML and JavaScript to process the template upon application load:

```
<div id="WikiComponentControlct100_m_g_95135f04" ></div>
<script type="text/javascript" language="javascript">
if (window.WikiControlTemplates == null)
    window.WikiControlTemplates = new Array();
var wikiTemplate = new Object();
wikiTemplate.Control = 'WikiComponentControlct100_m_g_95135f04';
wikiTemplate.WikiID = 'home';
window.WikiControlTemplates.push(wikiTemplate);
</script>
```

From the window.WikiControlTemplates array, the code within the WikiControl script component initializes components on application load. The control reference is passed by the control ID in the Control property, and other properties of the component, such as WikiID, are also set in the template object. The processing of this template array happens in the component's Init method that is added to the application load event, as demonstrated in the following addition to the WikiControl component:

```
// WebPart initialization script:
Litware.WikiControl.Init = function(){
  if( window.WikiControlTemplates ){
    for(var i=0;i<window.WikiControlTemplates.length;i++){
      var o =  window.WikiControlTemplates[i];
      if (o != null){
        var wiki = new Litware.WikiControl( $get(o.Control), o.WikiID );
        wiki.initialize();
        o = null;
      }
    }
    window.WikiControlTemplates = null;
  }
}
Sys.Application.add_load(Litware.WikiControl.Init);
```

When calling Web services in the SharePoint site context, the path of the Web service proxy needs to be set before it is called. Otherwise, you are accessing the Web service for the root site. To set the proxy's path, use the set_path method. You can set a window property of spWebUrl through your Web Part as follows:

```
this.Page.ClientScript.RegisterClientScriptBlock( this.GetType(),
  "spweburl", string.Format("window.spWebUrl='{0}';",
  SPContext.Current.Web.Url), true);
```

In the JavaScript component, you can then set the Web service proxy's path by using set_path. You should set the path before each call, as other components may set this to arbitrary site URLs based on their actions. The following JavaScript call sets the Litware.WikiWebService's path property to the current WSS site context:

```
Litware.WikiWebService.set_path(
  window.spWebUrl + '/_vti_bin/Litware/WikiWebService.asmx');
```

With the control initialization code in place, the MicroWiki Web Part only needs to render the initialization template and register the JavaScript resources and Web service proxy through the ScriptManager. The MicroWiki Web Part defined in Listing 5-6 demonstrates this principle—the AJAX Web Part simply registers script components and writes a placeholder control for the JavaScript component to initialize.

Warning   AJAX proxies to WSS Web services will not be created with the proper WSS site context. You must set the path before each call.

Listing 5-6   The MicroWiki WebPart demonstrates a simple AJAX implementation.

```
MicroWiki Web Part
using System;
using System.Web.UI;
using Microsoft.SharePoint;
using System.Web.UI.WebControls.WebParts;

namespace LitwareAjaxWebParts {
  public class MicroWikiWebPart : WebPart {

    private ScriptManager scriptMan;
    public ScriptManager AtlasScriptManager {
      get {
        if (scriptMan == null) {
          scriptMan = ScriptManager.GetCurrent(this.Page);
          if (scriptMan == null) {
            scriptMan = new ScriptManager();
            this.Controls.Add(scriptMan);
          }
        }
        return scriptMan;
      }
    }
```

```
private const string scriptFormat =
  @"if (window.WikiControlTemplates == null){{
  window.WikiControlTemplates = new Array();
  }}
  var xc = new Object();
  xc.Control = 'WikiComponentControl{0}';
  xc.WikiID = 'home';
  window.WikiControlTemplates.push(xc); ";

// Register controls and scripts
protected override void CreateChildControls() {
  base.CreateChildControls();

  ScriptReference editableControlScript = new ScriptReference(
    "LitwareAjaxWebParts.Resources.EditableControl.js",
    "LitwareAjaxWebParts");
  this.AtlasScriptManager.Scripts.Add(editableControlScript);

  ScriptReference wikiControlScript = new ScriptReference(
    "LitwareAjaxWebParts.Resources.WikiControl.js",
    "LitwareAjaxWebParts");
  this.AtlasScriptManager.Scripts.Add(wikiControlScript);

  ServiceReference serviceReference = new ServiceReference(
    SPContext.Current.Web.Url
    + "/_vti_bin/Litware/WikiWebService.asmx");
  this.AtlasScriptManager.Services.Add(serviceReference);
}

protected override void RenderContents(HtmlTextWriter writer) {
  base.RenderContents(writer);

  writer.Write(@"<div id=""WikiComponentControl{0}"" ></div>",
    this.ClientID);
  writer.Write(@"<script type=""text/javascript"" language=""javascript"">");
  writer.Write(scriptFormat, this.ClientID);
  writer.Write(@"</script>");
  }
 }
}
```

The MicroWiki Web Part demonstrates an AJAX Web Part that uses a simple Web service to persist the text content in a WSS list. In the following examples, we will look at more advanced Web Parts that utilize XML and XSLT transforms on the client. We'll also look at the SharePoint AJAX Toolkit, a framework for AJAX components that handles most of the heavy lifting for WSS AJAX components.

Introducing the SharePoint AJAX Toolkit

The SharePoint AJAX Toolkit is a developer framework for writing AJAX code for WSS and Microsoft Office SharePoint Server (MOSS) by using the ASP.NET AJAX Library. It includes a core script library for client-side data loading and XSLT transformations, base Web Part classes targeted for AJAX code, and a Solution Package installer that registers the required elements in web.config. The XML Web Part included in the Toolkit can be used for simple XML data loads and XSLT transforms and can be extended to add functionality. By default, the XML Web Part uses an XSLT style sheet for use with RSS data sources because WSS uses RSS for list syndication. The SharePoint AJAX Toolkit is available in both source code and binary distributions from *http://www.codeplex.com/sharepointajax* and is also included with the code samples for this book. Whether you use the SharePoint AJAX Toolkit or write your own AJAX implementation, the principles demonstrated in the Toolkit are central to AJAX programming.

The SharePoint AJAX Toolkit takes a purist approach to AJAX development and ASP.NET– HTML elements and JavaScript components are used to program against XML data sources by using XSLT transforms and Web service endpoints. This separates development projects into two categories: API-related components, including XML data streams and Web service endpoints; and user interface–related elements built with JavaScript and XSLT and deployed in Web Parts. Because much of the WSS framework is based on XML and already has XML APIs, you should find that this approach makes for an integrated architecture that is straight-forward and easily extended by lightweight user interface components. Common user interface code can be used to consume a library of rich data sources based on RSS, Collaborative Application Markup Language (CAML) queries, OPML, and other XML data sources.

The core Toolkit consists of two primary JavaScript files that form a library of WSS-friendly JavaScript functionality. The first file defines the SharePoint.Ajax JavaScript namespace and includes the utility functions used for everyday tasks. Primarily, these include data-loading functions and cross-browser XSLT transform code. Data loading in the Toolkit happens primarily with the SharePoint.Ajax.DataLoader method, which loads data from a given URL and performs a delegate callback upon completion by utilizing the Sys.Net.WebRequest object internally. For example, to call the static DataLoader method and call the set_Xml method of the current object instance, you could use the following method syntax, which would fire an asynchronous Web request and call the set_Xml method upon completion:

```
SharePoint.Ajax.DataLoader(url,'set_Xml',this)
```

When the LoadXml method is called, the instance reference is passed into the DataLoader, which calls the instance's set_Xml method in the callback, passing in the XML DOM object returned from the data source. Without the DataLoader function, you would need to create a static callback function and then call the instance method. By using the DataLoader function, the generic DataLoaderCallback function handles this for you.

The other technique that is central to AJAX programming is client-side XSLT. Making XML data requests and applying an XSLT transform on the client enables dynamic user interfaces that can evolve at runtime. The SharePoint AJAX Toolkit provides the XmlTransform method that takes an XML DOM parameter, an XSLT DOM parameter, and a Control parameter into which the content is transformed. Following is the source code for the cross-browser XSLT transform as well as the HtmlDecode method that is used for the Mozilla compatibility layer. The Internet Explorer method is simpler, using the transformNode function of the MSXML XMLDOM object, whereas Mozilla uses the browser's XSLTProcessor object and requires further decoding of HTML-encoded elements via the HtmlDecode method. Following is the source code for the XmlTransform method, a key component in the AJAX application architecture:

```
SharePoint.Ajax.XmlTransform = function (xml, xsl, control, decode){
  if(decode == null)decode = true;
  if (!window.XSLTProcessor){ // IE
    var content = xml.transformNode(xsl);
    control.innerHTML = content;
  }else{  // MOZILLA
  var processor = new XSLTProcessor();
  processor.importStylesheet(xsl);
  var content = processor.transformToFragment(xml, document);
    control.innerHTML = '';
    if(decode){
      var div = document.createElement('div');
      div.appendChild(content);
      control.innerHTML = SharePoint.Ajax.HtmlDecode(div.innerHTML);
    }else{
      control.appendChild(content);
    }
  }
}

// Client side version of the Server.HtmlDecode method
// for Mozilla RSS transform compatibility.
SharePoint.Ajax.HtmlDecode = function HtmlDecode(enc) {
  return enc.replace(/&quot;/gi,String.fromCharCode(0x0022))
.replace(/&amp;/gi,String.fromCharCode(0x0026))
.replace(/&lt;/gi,String.fromCharCode(0x003c))
.replace(/&gt;/gi,String.fromCharCode(0x003e));
}
```

Introducing the SharePoint.Ajax.XmlComponent

The main client component used in the SharePoint AJAX Toolkit is the XmlComponent, which is a simple JavaScript extension to an HTML element (such as a div) that adds XML data loading and transforming capabilities. The XmlComponent is a simple object to work with and provides the main building block of the AJAX user interface. By performing simple calls to the LoadXml and LoadXsl methods, you can build a dynamic AJAX user interface by using server data sources. These methods demonstrate the main principles of AJAX development—data loads happen asynchronously and must be handled in callbacks. The source code for the SharePoint.Ajax.XmlComponent is included in Listing 5-7.

Listing 5-7 The SharePoint.Ajax.XmlComponent demonstrates an AJAX component for client-side XML loading and transforms.

```
SharePoint.Ajax.XmlComponent
// XmlComponent Component
SharePoint.Ajax.XmlComponent = function(element){
  SharePoint.Ajax.XmlComponent.initializeBase(this);
  this.element = element;
  element.XmlComponent = this;
  element.controlType='XmlComponent';
}
SharePoint.Ajax.XmlComponent.prototype={
  initialize : function() {
    SharePoint.Ajax.XmlComponent.callBaseMethod(this, "initialize");
  },
  _rendered : false,
  _xml : null,
  _xsl : null,
  _visible : true,
  element : null,
  interval : null,
  timerID : null,
  xmlUrl : null,
  xslUrl : null,
  // defines a connection that can be used in custom code.
  Connection : null,

  set_Xml : function (xml){
    this._xml = xml;
    if (this._xml != null & this._xsl != null) this.Render();
  },
  set_Xsl : function (xml){
    this._xsl = xml;
    if (this._xml != null & this._xsl != null)
      this.Render();
  },

  set_Visible : function(visible){
    this._visible = visible;
    if (this.element == null) return;
    if (visible){
      this.element.style.display = 'block';
      if (this.parentElement != null)
        this.parentElement.style.display = 'block';
      }else {
      this.element.style.display = 'none';
      if (this.parentElement != null)
        this.parentElement.style.display = 'none';
    }
  },

  set_Refresh : function(int){
    if (this.timerID != null){
      window.clearInterval(this.timerID);
      this.timerID = null;
    }
```

```
    this.interval = int;
    if (int > 0){
      this.timerID = window.setInterval(
        String.format("SharePoint.Ajax.XmlComponent.Refresh('{0}')",
          this.element.id),int);
    }
},

set_Control : function(control){
  this.element = control;
  if (this._xml != null & this._xsl != null)
    this.Render();
},

parentElement : null,

set_Parent : function(control){
  this.parentElement = control;
},

Reload : function(){
  this.LoadXml(this.xmlUrl);
},

LoadXml : function(url){
  this.xmlUrl = url;
  SharePoint.Ajax.DataLoader(url,'set_Xml',this);
},

LoadXsl : function(url){
  this.xslUrl=url;
  SharePoint.Ajax.DataLoader(url,'set_Xsl',this);
},

Render : function(){
  if (this.element == null || this._xml == null || !this._visible)
    return;

  var control = this.element;
  SharePoint.Ajax.XmlTransform(this._xml, this._xsl, control);
  if (this.parentElement != null)
    this.parentElement.style.display = '';
  control.style.display = '';
  this._rendered = true;
},

// Dispose of any resources used by the component
dispose: function() {
  if (this.timerID != null)
    window.clearInterval(this.timerID);
  this._xml = null;
  if (this.element != null){
    this.element.innerHTML = '';
    this.element.parentNode.removeChild(this.element);
  }
```

```
        this.element = null;
        SharePoint.Ajax.XmlComponent.callBaseMethod(this, 'dispose');
    }
}

SharePoint.Ajax.XmlComponent.Refresh = function(arg){
    Sys.Debug.trace( String.format("XmlComponent.Refresh({0})", arg) );
    var element = $get(arg);
    var xmlComponent = element.XmlComponent;
    if (xmlComponent != null)
        xmlComponent.Reload();
    else
        Sys.Debug.trace( String.format("Component not found:{0}", arg) );
}
SharePoint.Ajax.XmlComponent.Init = function(){
    if( window.XmlComponentTemplates != 'undefined'
        && window.XmlComponentTemplates != null){
        for(var i=0;i<window.XmlComponentTemplates.length;i++){
            var o =  window.XmlComponentTemplates[i];
            if (o != null){
                var XmlControl =
                    new SharePoint.Ajax.XmlComponent( $get(o.Control) );
                XmlControl.LoadXml(o.XmlUrl);
                XmlControl.LoadXsl(o.XsltUrl);
                XmlControl.set_Refresh(o.Refresh);
                if( o.Connection != null && o.Connection.length > 0)
                    XmlControl.Connection = o.Connection;
                o = null;
            }
        }
    }
}
Sys.Application.add_load(SharePoint.Ajax.XmlComponent.Init);
```

You can create XmlComponent objects by passing in an element, such as a div, in the constructor and setting the XML and XSLT URLs, and the component then handles the processing. The LoadXml and LoadXsl functions use the DataLoader utility method to set the XML and XSL properties, in which the Render method is called when the data and transform are loaded. The following JavaScript code example creates an XmlComponent from the div element with the ID "Placeholder." This code could be executed in a page load script. Later in the chapter, we will build on this example to create arbitrary XmlComponent instances from Web Parts.

```
var formElement = $get('Placeholder');
var xmlControl = new SharePoint.Ajax.XmlComponent(formElement);
xmlControl.LoadXml('opml.aspx');
xmlControl.LoadXsl('opml.xslt);
```

The interface of the XmlComponent is described in Table 5-1. When using instances of Xml-Component, you work primarily with the methods listed in this table.

Table 5-1   SharePoint.Ajax.XmlComponent JavaScript Class

Name	Description
element	Defines the HTML element to which the behavior is added
LoadXml(xmlUrl)	Loads XML data specified by the xmlUrl parameter
LoadXsl(xmlUrl)	Loads XSL data specified by the xmlUrl parameter
set_Xml(XMLDOM)	Sets the manually loaded XMLDOM to the XML data source
set_Xsl(XMLDOM)	Sets the manually loaded XSLT style sheet
Render()	Redraws the component; automatically called when both the XML and XSL data sources are loaded
set_Refresh(Number)	Sets the refresh interval in milliseconds
Connection	Specifies the ID of the optionally connected component

Within a Web Part, we create the XmlComponent instance based on a placeholder that is rendered in the RenderContents method. The XML Web Part in the SharePoint AJAX Toolkit handles this for you in the Web Part's RenderContents method and serves as a pattern for custom AJAX Web Parts. Before looking at the XML Web Part, let's look first at the base Web Part class used for AJAX infrastructure.

AjaxWebPart in the SharePoint AJAX Toolkit

The AjaxWebPart class is part of the Toolkit that handles core framework requirements, such as ensuring that the Script Manager exists on the page and that the core Toolkit JavaScript libraries are included. The Script Manager is provided through the protected AtlasScriptManager property. The abstract class AjaxWebPart is included in Listing 5-8.

Tip   ASP.NET AJAX was code-named *Atlas* and is still referred to as Atlas in some code libraries.

Listing 5-8   The AjaxWebPart provides a common base class for AJAX Web Parts.

```
SharePoint.Ajax.AjaxWebPart Base Class
namespace SharePoint.Ajax.WebParts {
  // A base Web Part class for AJAX Web Part implementations.
  public abstract class AjaxWebPart :
      System.Web.UI.WebControls.WebParts.WebPart {

    private ScriptManager scriptMan;
    //Gets the ScriptManager for this page
    public ScriptManager AtlasScriptManager {
      get {
```

```
      if (scriptMan == null) {
        scriptMan = ScriptManager.GetCurrent(this.Page);
        if (scriptMan == null) {
          scriptMan = new ScriptManager();
          this.Controls.Add(scriptMan);
        }
      }
      return scriptMan;
    }
  }


  // Creates the required controls/script components
  // for the SharePoint.Ajax framework
  protected override void CreateChildControls() {
    base.CreateChildControls();

    ScriptReference framework =
        new ScriptReference("SharePoint.Ajax.Script.SharePoint.Ajax.js",
        "SharePoint.Ajax");
    ScriptReference xmlComponent = new
        ScriptReference("SharePoint.Ajax.Script.XmlComponent.js",
        "SharePoint.Ajax");

    this.AtlasScriptManager.Scripts.Add(framework);
    this.AtlasScriptManager.Scripts.Add(xmlComponent);
    }
  }
}
```

XmlWebPart in the SharePoint AJAX Toolkit

The toolkit's XmlWebPart class is a basic Web Part wrapper of a JavaScript XmlComponent that can serve as a base class for custom AJAX Web Parts using Xml data loads and transforms. This makes it easy to create a dynamic user interface by using SharePoint.Ajax.WebParts.Xml-WebPart, writing some simple JavaScript functions, and providing XSLT for rendering logic. The XmlWebPart has an XmlUrl property and XsltUrl property, along with an optional refresh timer property that is used to refresh the data of the XmlComponent at the specified interval. By using SharePoint.Ajax.WebParts.XmlWebPart as a base class, 90 percent of the functionality needed for AJAX Web Part implementations is already provided.

Building the Litware AJAX Web Part Library

After examining the plumbing of the SharePoint AJAX Toolkit, we are now ready to make use of it in the Litware AJAX Web Part library. For clarity, we will build a pure AJAX solution for the examples that follow. However, you might often wish to use a hybrid architecture by using a combination of "traditional" ASP.NET components for static content and AJAX components for dynamic content that can change in the life cycle of the page instance.

Because we are leveraging the SharePoint AJAX Toolkit, the implementation should be rather simple, thereby letting you focus on design elements using XSLT, data sources using the previously built XML API, and a small library of JavaScript objects and methods. Because the framework handles the plumbing, the amount of custom JavaScript code required is minimized.

In the following examples, we will build an AJAX List View Web Part (based on the Share-Point.Ajax.WebParts.XmlWebPart) for use with WSS lists as well as a Feed List Web Part that will be used to browse lists within the site collection and send a client-side connection to the AJAX List View Web Part by using standard Web Part connections. To begin, we will define an AjaxListViewWebPart class that derives from SharePoint.Ajax.XmlWebPart. Because the XmlWebPart provides all the initial implementation for an RSS view, there will be little code needed for our basic functionality. We will later extend this class to accept a connection from the AJAX Feed List Web Part. For now, the initial class declaration will be as follows:

```
namespace LitwareAjaxWebParts {
  // An AJAX version of the Litware RSS Web Part,
  // based on the SharePoint AJAX Toolkit
  public class AjaxListViewWebPart : XmlWebPart {
  }
}
```

To test the Web Part, compile and deploy the Web Part as previously explained in Chapter 4 and set the XML URL property to a list RSS feed from within the Editor Part. The Web Part is displayed in Figure 5-3.

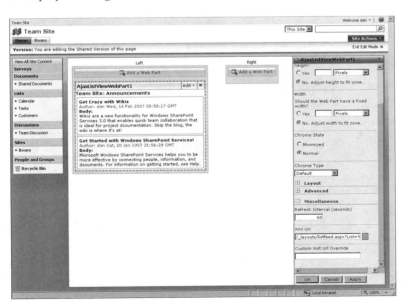

Figure 5-3   The AJAX List View Web Part renders the list's RSS feed using client-side XSLT.

Next, we will build a Feed List Web Part. The Feed List Web Part is also based on the SharePoint.Ajax.XmlWebPart and uses the previously defined FeedListHandler XML REST endpoint that renders security-trimmed OPML for the site. Within the Feed List Web Part, we will define an interface for the connection in the List View Web Part as well as register the XSLT and JavaScript components we will use in the client. These resources are compiled into the assembly as embedded resources and marked as WebResources within the assembly information file as discussed in Chapter 4. Because we are leveraging the XmlComponent JavaScript class and the XmlWebPart infrastructure, all we must do is create the additional script resources and XSLT transform used by our component. The Feed List Web Part is listed in Listing 5-9.

Within the CreateChildControls method, we will add the JavaScript components for our Web Part, as in previous examples. The base class framework registers the core script runtime, including the Microsoft AJAX Library, the SharePoint.Ajax namespace, and the SharePoint.Ajax.XmlComponent. Within the OnPreRender method, we will set the XML and XSLT URLs that let the base XmlWebPart create the specified XmlComponent instance.

Listing 5-9   The Feed List Web Part implements the XmlWebPart.

```
Feed List Web Part
using System;
using System.Collections.Generic;
using System.Text;
using SharePoint.Ajax.WebParts;
using System.Web.UI.WebControls.WebParts;
using Microsoft.SharePoint;
using System.Web.UI;
using System.Globalization;

namespace LitwareAjaxWebParts {

  // A WebPart for feed lists
  public class FeedListWebPart : XmlWebPart {

    protected override void CreateChildControls() {
      base.CreateChildControls();
      ScriptReference scriptReference =
        new ScriptReference(
          @"LitwareAjaxWebParts.Resources.FeedListWebPart.js",
          @"LitwareAjaxWebParts");
      this.AtlasScriptManager.Scripts.Add(scriptReference);
    }

    protected override void OnPreRender(EventArgs e) {
      base.OnPreRender(e);
      string xsl = this.Page.ClientScript.GetWebResourceUrl(
        typeof(FeedListWebPart),
        @"LitwareAjaxWebParts.Resources.OPML.xslt");
      this.XsltUrl = SPContext.Current.Web.Url + @"/" + xsl;
      this.XmlUrl = SPContext.Current.Web.Url + @"/opml.ashx";
    }
  }
}
```

The FeedListWebPart demonstrates the typical AJAX Web Part. It uses the XmlComponent from the base class framework, defines the initial data source URL, and adds a custom JavaScript component. Similar to the RSS view used in the List View Web Part, the Feed List Web Part builds its user interface from a transformed XML data source. It also embeds calls to JavaScript methods that reload the data so that the user can navigate through the site collection. For example, by clicking the node that represents a site, we call the Litware.FeedList.Load command to reload the site-relative OPML data source for the Feed List Web Part, as shown in the following XSLT example.

```
<span onclick="javascript:Litware.FeedList.Load(
    this, '{@htmlUrl}/opml.ashx');">
  <xsl:value-of select="@title" />
</span>
```

For List nodes, we will generate elements that call the Litware.FeedList.Navigate method used to send a Navigate command to the object to which the Feed List is connected:

```
<div onclick="javascript:Litware.FeedList.Navigate(this, '{@xmlUrl}');">
  <xsl:value-of select="@title" />
</div>
```

The full source of the OPML transform is shown in Listing 5-10. This architecture demonstrates the client-side XSLT pattern common in AJAX applications. The UI is rendered using XSLT with embedded script calls that perform data manipulation or navigational commands by calling methods defined in the Web Part's script component.

Tip   XSLT is a core technology for AJAX applications. For a primer on XSLT, we recommend the *XSLT: Programmer's Reference* by Michael Kay (Wiley Publishing, Inc.).

Listing 5-10   The OPML XSLT defines the user interface for the AJAX component.

```
Feed List OPML XSLT
<xsl:stylesheet version="1.0" xmlns:xsl="http://www.w3.org/1999/XSL/Transform">
    <xsl:output method="html" indent="yes" standalone="no"
        omit-xml-declaration="yes" />
    <xsl:template match="/">
        <xsl:apply-templates select="opml" />
    </xsl:template>

    <xsl:template match="opml">
        <xsl:apply-templates select="body" />
    </xsl:template>

    <xsl:template match="body">
        <xsl:if test="outline/@parentWeb">
            <div onclick="javascript:Litware.FeedList.Load(
                this, '{outline/@parentWeb}/opml.ashx');"
                style="cursor:hand;margin-top:3px;">
                <img src="/_layouts/images/DOCLINK.GIF"/>
```

```
                Up to parent site
            </div>
        </xsl:if>

        <ul  style="margin-left:15px; margin-top:0px;">
            <xsl:apply-templates select="outline" />
        </ul>
    </xsl:template>

    <xsl:template match="outline">
        <li>
            <xsl:choose>
                <xsl:when test="@type='rss'">
                    <xsl:attribute name="style">cursor:hand;
                    list-style-image:url(/_layouts/images/LIST.GIF);
                    padding-left:6px;margin:3px;</xsl:attribute>
                    <div onclick="javascript:Litware.FeedList.Navigate(
                            this, '{@xmlUrl}');">
                        <xsl:value-of select="@title" />
                    </div>
                </xsl:when>
                <xsl:when test="@type='site'">
                    <xsl:attribute name="style">cursor:hand;
                    list-style-image:url(/_layouts/images/sts_web16.gif);
                    padding-left:6px;margin:3px;</xsl:attribute>
                    <span onclick="javascript:Litware.FeedList.Load(
                            this, '{@htmlUrl}/opml.ashx');">
                        <xsl:value-of select="@title" />
                    </span>
                    <ul  style="margin-left:15px; margin-top:0px;">
                        <xsl:apply-templates select="outline" />
                    </ul>
                </xsl:when>
            </xsl:choose>
        </li>
    </xsl:template>
</xsl:stylesheet>
```

When creating AJAX interfaces based on the XmlComponent, you might need only simple utility functions and not need to create custom object-oriented classes. For the Feed List Web Part, we will simply define Navigate and Load utility functions. In these methods, we will use the function SharePoint.Ajax.FindParentControl that returns the first parent control of the element to which an XmlComponent is attached. This common pattern is one in which the user action inside an element needs to find its parent control. The FindParentControl function is listed in the following code:

```
// Looks up the control tree to find the parent control
// with the controlType expando property
SharePoint.Ajax.FindParentControl = function(child, controlType){
  var control = child;
  while (control != null && control.controlType != controlType){
```

```
      control = control.parentElement;
    }
    if (control.controlType == controlType){
      return control;
    }
    return null;
}
```

With the XmlComponent reference, we have the information needed to either reload the component's data from another URL in the case of the Load command or issue a LoadXml command to the connected object's XmlComponent. (We will look at client-side connections in the following section.) The Litware Feed List Component JavaScript Load and Navigate functions are simple methods that find the parent XmlComponent using SharePoint.Ajax.FindParentControl and call methods of the XmlComponent:

```
// Loads a new FeedList from the xmlUrl
Litware.FeedList.Load = function (ref, xmlUrl){
  var xmlControl = SharePoint.Ajax.FindParentControl(ref,'XmlComponent');
  if (xmlControl != null && xmlControl.XmlComponent != null)
    xmlControl.XmlComponent.LoadXml(xmlUrl);
}

// Issues a Navigate command to the feed at the xmlURL
Litware.FeedList.Navigate = function (ref, xmlUrl){
  var xmlControl = SharePoint.Ajax.FindParentControl(ref,'XmlComponent');
  if (xmlControl == null || xmlControl.XmlComponent == null) return;
  var id = xmlControl.XmlComponent.Connection;
  if (id != null){
    var control = $get(id);
    if (control != null && control.XmlComponent != null){
      control.XmlComponent.LoadXml(xmlUrl);
    }
  }
}
```

Client-Side Connections for AJAX Web Parts

AJAX Web Parts can be much more interesting when connected together. For example, a List Reader component can be connected to a List Browser, enabling the user to quickly browse through the site's feeds. The Web Parts connect together via the Web Part connection infrastructure and are then able to issue commands to each other on the client. To connect AJAX Web Parts, we will define a known interface and register the connection on the client. The XmlComponent defines a Connection property that is set when it is registered through the client component template.

The connection interface definition is simple and is the same technique used for non-AJAX Web Parts, as discussed in Chapter 4. Because the connection is specific to the client-side functionality, we will define an interface for use as a marker to identify the connectable components and provide the required server parameter. For this connection, we will define a simple IFeedProvider interface that specifies a component providing a feed to the XmlComponent of the XmlWebPart. The IFeedProvider interface simply defines a string that defines the connected Web Part's XmlComponent element, from which the client can obtain a reference to the object. In this model, it is the connection provider that maintains a reference to the connection consumer. Also note that the connection does not define the feed URL as does the connection defined in Chapter 4, but the connection defines components that interact on the client rather than on the server. The connection happens once on the server, and the client components can issue multiple arbitrary control commands in response to user actions on the client.

The following interface is implemented in server code by the FeedListWebPart, which provides a connection to the ListViewWebPart to send client-side commands to the client-side XmlComponent of the ListViewWebPart:

```
public interface IFeedProvider {
  string FeedConsumerID { get; set; }
}
```

Within the FeedListWebPart, the following property and GetFeedProvider connection method are used to provide the connection, which the consumer writes to just before the Render method is called. The connection provider attribute identifies the connection to the Web Part Manager to let the page designer set the connection in the page.

```
string feedConsumerID;
public string FeedConsumerID {
  get { return this.feedConsumerID; }
  set { this.feedConsumerID = value; }
}

[ConnectionProvider("Feed", AllowsMultipleConnections = false)]
public IFeedProvider GetFeedProvider() {
  return this;
}
```

Within the Feed List Web Part, we enable the connection by setting the connection provider's FeedConsumerID with the ID of the XMLComponent. The XmlComponent created on the client for the Feed List has a Connection property of the consumer's ID. This can then be used to get a reference of its XmlComponent and issue JavaScript commands against its interface. To complete the Connection, we need to implement the connection in the List View Web Part. In the connection code, it simply obtains a reference to the IFeedProvider custom interface that we will set in the OnPreRender method. Because the XmlUrl is now connection based and we don't want to allow customization of the RSS XSLT, we will also override the CreateEditorParts method. The final AjaxListViewWebPart is shown in Listing 5-11.

Listing 5-11   The AJAX List View Web Part accepts connections from the AJAX Feed List Web Part.

```
AJAX List View Web Part
using System;
using SharePoint.Ajax.WebParts;
using System.Web.UI.WebControls.WebParts;
using System.Web.UI;

namespace LitwareAjaxWebParts {

  // An AJAX version of the Litware RSS Web Part,
  // based on the SharePoint AJAX Toolkit
  public class AjaxListViewWebPart : XmlWebPart {

    private IFeedProvider feedProvider;

    [ConnectionConsumer("Feed")]
    public void RegisterCustomerProvider(IFeedProvider provider) {
      this.feedProvider = provider;
    }

    // Don't allow any editor parts
    public override EditorPartCollection CreateEditorParts() {
      return new EditorPartCollection();
    }

    protected override void OnPreRender(EventArgs e) {
      // Handle connection BEFORE base onprerender
      if (this.feedProvider != null)
      this.feedProvider.FeedConsumerID = this.XmlComponentID;
      this.XmlUrl = null;
      base.OnPreRender(e);
    }
  }
}
```

Summary

In this chapter, we learned the basics of AJAX development using the Microsoft ASP.NET AJAX Framework and discussed the performance, responsiveness, and architecture benefits of an AJAX application. We learned how to separate the server logic into a service-oriented API that can be shared between multiple components and how to build feeds within the site context. We learned how to build and deploy AJAX components within Web Parts as well as the design challenges associated with script components instantiated from Web Parts. Finally, we looked at the SharePoint AJAX Toolkit and how to leverage common architecture components to build and deploy lightweight AJAX controls. In the following chapters we will learn about lists and content in the WSS platform that can be further exposed to AJAX-enabled XML APIs.

Chapter 6
Lists and Content Types

- Understand the conceptual data model of WSS content storage.
- Program against lists, items, and fields with the WSS object model.
- Understand and create type definitions for site columns and content types.
- Develop features that contain custom list types.
- Write event handlers and bind them to WSS lists.

Lists and Content Types

The central component to collaborative applications is a flexible data model, with which users can store, manage, and collaborate on data. This data may represent people, things, or documents and can store a great amount of metadata about the actual pieces of data. For example, a document may have multiple keywords associated with it as well as approval status, author information, and tracking data. Another example of collaborative data may be represented by a customer who has associated industry-related data as well as people-related data and may link to data in additional lists.

Windows SharePoint Services List Data

Windows SharePoint Services (WSS) implements collaborative data with lists and content types, both of which are defined based on an XML-defined schema that is either created at runtime through user customization or predefined on the file system in XML-based files within features. These XML-based files are written in a WSS-specific language known as *Collaborative Application Markup Language (CAML)*. When you develop WSS type definitions with CAML—such as site columns, content types, and list templates—you are creating *provisioning components* that users can use in their own collaborative applications. When you create site columns, content types, and list templates through the WSS user interface, you are creating types of *customized content* that exist within the scope of a single site.

Although provisioning components are harder to create and test, they can be more easily reused across any site in a farm, and they can be packaged and deployed in WSS solution packages for remote deployment. Customized content within a live site, on the other hand, is not as reusable. The design and creation of provisioning components is the preferred approach when you want to reuse, repackage, or resell your components. However, customizing content through the WSS user interface is good for rapid prototyping or continuing to evolve a single site in production.

When developing provisioning components, you will find that it can be difficult, because there is little debugging support and often the error messages you get are cryptic. To be successful at developing provisioning components, you will want to use a variety of development techniques including automated testing and deployment scripts during the development process.

You will also want to refer to and dissect the built-in features and provisioning components that ship with WSS, as well as those that ship with Microsoft Office SharePoint Server 2007 (MOSS). Copying and editing these components will often get you very close to what you want, and adding custom functionality can be more stable than rewriting at times. However, as a rule of thumb, you should never modify the features and provisioning components that are included with the product. Instead, copy their files or their XML content into your own feature and provisioning components and then modify the copy.

Note   Although some of the C# code samples in this chapter will be written in console applications, you also could program similar code within feature event handlers. Note that the Console application code references *http://localhost*, because console applications in WSS can run against only the local server.

Working with WSS Lists

At the heart of the core WSS architecture is the infrastructure for defining list types and provisioning list instances to store content. Document libraries, which play a vital role in creating WSS business solutions, can be seen as hybrid lists that leverage and extend the same mechanisms and storage model that are used by standard lists.

WSS ships with a variety of built-in list types (shown in Table 6-1) that can solve many business needs without requiring custom development. These list types are visible on the standard WSS Create page, and they enable users to quickly create list instances on an ad hoc basis. Within the Create page, these built-in list types are broken out into sections including *Libraries*, *Communications*, *Tracking*, and *Custom Lists*.

Tip   WSS galleries such as Web Part galleries and master page galleries are all implemented based on specialized document libraries.

Table 6-1   WSS List Definitions

List Type	Description
Document library	Used for collaborating on documents with support for versioning, check-in and check-out, and workflow. Includes support for deep integration with Microsoft Office.
Form library	Used to store XML documents and forms for use with Microsoft Office InfoPath.
Wiki page library	Used for collaborative Web pages based on wiki pages, which are dynamically generated and collaboratively edited Web pages.

Table 6-1   WSS List Definitions

List Type	Description
Picture library	A specialized document library enhanced for use with pictures. Includes support for slide shows, thumbnails, and simple editing through Microsoft Office Picture Manager.
Announcements	Used for simple sharing of timely news with support for expiration.
Contacts	A list for tracking people and contact information, with support for integration into Microsoft Office Outlook and other WSS-compatible contacts applications.
Discussions	A simple list for threaded discussions with support for approval and managing discussion threads.
Links	A list for managing hyperlinks.
Calendar	A list for tracking upcoming events and deadlines. Includes support for integration and synchronization with Office Outlook.
Tasks	A list of activity-based items that can integrate with workflow.
Project tasks	An enhanced tasks list with support for Gannt chart rendering and integration with Microsoft Office Project.
Issue tracking	A list for tracking issues and resolution, with support for prioritization.
Custom list	An empty list definition for extending with custom columns, or created using Microsoft Office Excel spreadsheets.

At a lower level, WSS classifies list types using *base types*. Standard lists have a base type of 0, whereas document libraries have a base type of 1. There also are less frequently used base types for discussion forums (3), vote or survey lists (4), and issue lists (5). The base type defines a common set of columns, and all list types that are based on that base type automatically inherit those columns. For example, each of the built-in base types defines an ID field. This enables WSS to track each item in a list and to track each document in a document library behind the scenes with a unique integer identifier. WSS also adds several columns to the base type for document libraries that are not needed for standard list types.

List instances can be created either by users through the WSS user interface or by developers through the WSS object model. Later in the chapter, you also will see that you can create a list instance in a declarative fashion by adding a CAML element in a feature. Let's start with a basic code sample that demonstrates how to create a new list instance from one of the built-in list types.

Listing 6-1 provides the code to create a list instance. Before creating the list, the code checks to make sure a list of the same title doesn't already exist. You will notice that the code enumerates through the lists within the current site, checking each list to see if there is a matching title. If a list with a matching title does not exist, the code in this application then creates a new instance of the Announcements list type and adds a link to the Quick Launch menu for easy access.

Listing 6-1   Creating a new list instance using the WSS object model

```csharp
List Access Through the WSS Object Model
using System;
using Microsoft.SharePoint;

class Program {
  static void Main() {
    using (SPSite site = new SPSite("http://localhost")) {
      using (SPWeb web = site.OpenWeb()) {
        string listName = "Litware News";
        SPList list = null;
        foreach (SPList currentList in web.Lists) {
          if (currentList.Title.Equals(listName,
                              StringComparison.InvariantCultureIgnoreCase)) {
            list = currentList;
            break;
          }
        }

        if (list == null) {
          Guid listID = web.Lists.Add(listName,
                              "List for big news items",
                              SPListTemplateType.Announcements);
          list = web.Lists[listID];
          list.OnQuickLaunch = true;
          list.Update();
        }
      }
    }
  }
}
```

Note the required call to the Update method on the SPList object at the end of this listing. This is required to save any changes you have made to list properties, such as, in this case, assigning a value of "true" to the OnQuickLaunch property.

Lists can also be accessed by using the GetList methods of the SPWeb class:

```csharp
SPList announcementsList = web.GetList("/Lists/Announcements");
```

The GetList method takes a site-relative path to the list folder or a list form page as an argument. If the list instance is not found, the GetList method will throw an exception of type FileNotFoundException. The only way to check if a list exists without throwing an exception is to enumerate the site object's lists and check for its existence.

Tip   GetList is the preferred method to access a list by a URL. GetListFromUrl and GetList-FromWebPartPageUrl function the same way as GetList but throw a generic SPException on failure rather than the more descriptive FileNotFoundException.

After you have a reference to an SPList object for the list, you can create a new list item by adding an SPListItem to its Items collection. The SPListItem is a generic item with fields corresponding to the fields in the list. You can create and save a new list item by using the following code:

```
SPListItem newItem = list.Items.Add();
newItem ["Title"] = "Litware Goes Public!";
newItem ["Body"] = " We all live in exciting times.";
newItem["Expires"] = DateTime.Now + TimeSpan.FromDays(2);
newItem.Update();
```

The Update method of the SPListItem object commits the changes to the list. If you don't call the Update method, the list item data will not be saved. The fields (columns) of the list are specified using the display name. They can also be accessed by the GUID identifier of the field or the zero-based index in the Fields collection. If a field is specified that is not in the Fields collection for the list, an ArgumentException will be thrown. In some scenarios, you may want to enumerate through the fields in a list by using a foreach construct to ensure the field you are looking for really exists.

```
foreach (SPField field in list.Fields) {
  if (!field.Hidden && !field.ReadOnlyField)
    Console.WriteLine(field.Title);
}
```

Enumerating through the fields also can be useful when enumerating list items. You can use the Fields collection to access data from the list item. To limit the fields displayed, you may want to display only user editable fields as shown in the following code example:

```
foreach (SPListItem item in list.Items) {
  foreach (SPField field in list.Fields) {
    if (!field.Hidden && !field.ReadOnlyField)
      Console.WriteLine("{0} = {1}", field.Title, item[field.Id]);
  }
}
```

Using Queries for List Data

To get back specific results within a list, you can use the SPQuery object. When you use an SPQuery object, you will create CAML statements to select specific data within the target list. To select announcements that have expired, you may want to use a query built with CAML statements, as shown in the following example:

```
SPQuery query = new SPQuery();
query.ViewFields = @"<FieldRef Name='Title'/><FieldRef Name='Expires'/>";
query.Query =
@"<Where>
   <Lt>
     <FieldRef Name='Expires' />
     <Value Type='DateTime'>
```

```
      <Today /></Value>
    </Lt>
  </Where>";

SPList list = site.Lists["Litware News"];
SPListItemCollection items = list.GetItems(query);
foreach (SPListItem expiredItem in items) {
  Console.WriteLine(expiredItem["Title"]);
}
```

You must specify the fields you want returned in the query by using the ViewFields property. Also note that you must specify the fields in terms of the field Name, and not DisplayName. If you attempt to access fields without specifying them in ViewFields, you will experience an exception of type ArgumentException.

The basic syntax for the query is "<Where><*operator*><*operand* /><*operand* /></*operator*></Where>". Table 6-2, which appears later in this chapter, lists the basic CAML you will use with queries; for a more complete listing see the SDK.

SPQuery is a great way to get back items from a single list. Furthermore, using SPQuery can be significantly faster than enumerating through all the items within a particular list when you are looking only for items that match certain criteria. However, WSS 3.0 introduces a new query mechanism via the SPSiteDataQuery class. A query run with the SPSiteDataQuery class can return items from many different lists through an entire site collection. For this reason, queries run with the SPSiteDataQuery class are sometimes referred to as *cross-site queries*.

As you saw in the last example, queries run against an SPQuery object return an SPListItem-Collection. Queries run with an SPSiteDataQuery object are different, because they return an ADO.NET DataTable object. Just as with SPQuery, columns that are returned in the DataTable are specified as fields. For example, imagine a scenario in which you want to run a single query against every list in the current site collection that has been created from the Announcements list type and return all list items that were created today. The following code sample demonstrates how to do this by creating an SPSiteDataQuery object, initializing it with the necessary CAML statements, and then passing it to the current SPWeb object's GetSiteData method.

```
SPSiteDataQuery query = new SPSiteDataQuery();
query.Lists = @"<Lists ServerTemplate='104' />";
query.ViewFields = @"<FieldRef Name='Title'/><FieldRef Name='Created'/>";
query.Webs = "<Webs Scope='SiteCollection' />";

string queryText =
@"<Where>
    <Eq>
      <FieldRef Name='Created' />
      <Value Type=""DateTime"">
        <Today />
      </Value>
    </Eq>
```

```
  </Where>";

query.Query = queryText;

DataTable table = site.GetSiteData(query);

foreach (DataRow row in table.Rows) {
  Console.WriteLine(row["Title"].ToString());
}
```

This example assigns a CAML statement to the Lists property that specifies the ServerTemplate of 104, which is the list type identifier for the Announcements list. Even though GetSiteData is a method of the SPWeb reference, the query is performed against all sites in the current site collection. The scope of the query is controlled through a CAML statement in the SPSiteDataQuery's Webs property, which assigns a value of "SiteCollection" to the Scope attribute. You can limit the query to a scope of "Site" to just query the current site or to a scope of "Recursive" to query the current site and all the child sites beneath it.

If you need to get a reference to the actual list item, you can get it by using the columns WebId, ListId, and ID.

```
SPWeb parentWeb = web.Site.OpenWeb(new Guid(row["WebId"].ToString()));
SPList list = parentWeb.Lists[ new Guid(row["ListId"].ToString()) ];
SPListItem item = list.GetItemById((int.Parse(row["ID"].ToString())));
```

The SPSiteDataQuery class is perhaps most useful for creating data-aggregation Web Parts, or data-aggregation XML feeds, such as a recently published RSS feed. Listing 6-2 displays sample code for a recently published RSS feed. This same code could be used within a Web Part to create a rollup Web Part for any type of list, or you could use query parameters to vary the scope of the recently published items.

When using the SPSiteDataQuery class, you should note that only items that match the schema of the ViewFields parameter are returned. You also can filter the results by the ContentType field. In this case, we will filter on the Post content type. To use this handler, register it with the following element within the httpHandlers node of web.config:

```
<add verb="GET" path="recent.rss" type=
"LitwareHandlers.RecentPostsHandler, LitwareHandlers"/>
```

Tip   Because all SharePoint Requests are routed through the .NET Framework, you do not need to register special file extensions with IIS. This lets you use extensions such as .rss without additional configuration.

Listing 6-2   The site data query applied to recently published Items

A "Recently Published" Feed
```
using System;
using System.Web;
using Microsoft.SharePoint;
```

```csharp
using System.Data;
using System.Xml;
using Microsoft.SharePoint.Utilities;

namespace Litware.ContentWebParts.Handlers {
  public class RecentPostsHandler : IHttpHandler {

    public bool IsReusable {
      get { return true; }
    }

    public void ProcessRequest(HttpContext context) {
      SPWeb web = SPContext.Current.Web;
      SPSiteDataQuery query = new SPSiteDataQuery();

      query.ViewFields =
      @"<FieldRef Name=""Title""/><FieldRef Name=""PostCategory""/>
        <FieldRef Name=""PublishedDate""/><FieldRef Name=""Body""/>
        <FieldRef Name=""Author""/><FieldRef Name=""Permalink""/>
        <FieldRef Name=""ContentType""/>";

      string queryText =
      @"<Where>
          <And>
            <Eq>
              <FieldRef Name=""ContentType"" />
              <Value Type=""Text"">Post</Value>
            </Eq>
            <Eq>
              <FieldRef Name=""PublishedDate"" />
              <Value Type=""DateTime""><Today /></Value>
            </Eq>
          </And>
        </Where>";

      query.Query = queryText;
      query.Webs = @"<Webs Scope='Recursive' />";
      DataTable table = web.GetSiteData(query);

      context.Response.ContentType = "text/xml";

      XmlTextWriter xw = new XmlTextWriter(context.Response.Output);
      xw.WriteStartElement("rss");
      xw.WriteAttributeString("version", "2.0");
      xw.WriteStartElement("channel");
      xw.WriteElementString("title", "Recently Published: " + web.Title);
      xw.WriteElementString("description",
        "Recently published posts from " + web.Url);
      xw.WriteElementString("link", web.Url);

      foreach(DataRow row in table.Rows){
        xw.WriteStartElement("item");
        xw.WriteElementString("title", (string)row["Title"]);
        xw.WriteElementString("description", ((string)row["Body"]));
        xw.WriteElementString("pubDate", row["PublishedDate"].ToString("r"));

        string author =
```

```
            row["Author"].ToString().Split(new string[] { ";#" },
                                    StringSplitOptions.None)[1];
        xw.WriteElementString("author", author);

        string category =
        row["PostCategory"].ToString().Split(new string[] { ";#" },
                                    StringSplitOptions.None)[1];
        xw.WriteElementString("category", category);

        string link = string.Format(@"/Lists/Posts/Post.aspx?ID={0}",
                            row["Permalink"].ToString());
        xw.WriteElementString("link", link);

        xw.WriteEndElement(); //item
    }
    xw.WriteEndElement(); //channel
    xw.WriteEndElement(); //rss
    }
  }
}
```

Warning   In WSS 3.0, when working with posts from the blog site, the post "ContentType" is null. However, the ContentType field is set to "Post."

Table 6-2   Basic CAML Query Elements

Element	Description
And	Groups multiple conditions
BeginsWith	Searches for a string at the beginning of the text field
Contains	Searches for a string within the text field
Eq	Equal to
FieldRef	A reference to a field (useful for GroupBy elements)
Geq	Greater than or equal to
GroupBy	Groups results by these fields
Gt	Greater than
IsNotNull	Is not null (not empty)
IsNull	Is null (empty)
Leq	Less than or equal to
Lt	Less than
Neq	Not equal to
Now	The current date and time
Or	Boolean or operator
OrderBy	Orders the results of the query
Today	Today's date
TodayIso	Today's date in ISO format
Where	Used to specify the "Where" clause of the query

Tip For more information on the SPQuery syntax and a complete listing of CAML elements, consult the WSS SDK's "Query Syntax" topic under General Reference: Reference: Collaborative Application Markup Language: Query Schema.

Creating Custom List Elements

To create a list using the user interface, use the Site Actions menu to navigate to Create, Custom Lists, Custom List. The form on the resulting New page enables creation of an empty list by using the Custom List Type, which has no user editable columns (fields) except Title. After you create the list, you can then choose Create Column under the Settings menu to add new columns using standard WSS field types. A *field type* is a data type in WSS that can be used for content. It is similar to a SQL data type (and is defined with a SQL Data Type), although you can create your own field types as well. Table 6-3 displays the default WSS field (column) types available from the Create Column page.

Table 6-3 Basic WSS Built-in Field Types

Field Type	Description
Single Line Of Text	A single line of text. The maximum number of characters may be customized.
Multiple Lines Of Text	A text box with plain text, rich text (boldface, italics, text alignment), or enhanced rich text (pictures, tables, links). Rich text boxes are rendered in edit mode with a rich text toolbar.
Choice	A choice of several items you define.
Number	A numerical value. Options include minimum, maximum, decimal places, and so on.
Currency	A monetary value in a specific currency format.
Date And Time	Date information, or date and time information.
Lookup	A field that references a field value in another list on the site.
Yes/No	A Boolean field that is either true or false. Renders as a check box in the user interface.
Person Or Group	A user or member of the current site. This field can render with presence information, which ties into either Windows Live Messenger or Microsoft Office Live Communications Server.
Hyperlink Or Picture	A URL-formatted string.
Calculated	A value that is calculated from other fields.

Defining Custom List Elements with CAML

Now we are going to step through the process of defining site columns, content types, and list schemas. If you want to follow along with our sample code, you can open the Visual Studio project named LitwareTypes. This project contains several different examples of custom provisioning components. If you open and build this project, the install.bat file will copy all the required provisioning files into the TEMPLATES directory and will install a feature named LitwareTypes. Then you should be able to activate the LitwareTypes feature within the scope of any site collection in the farm so that you can begin to work with these sample provisioning components.

WSS provisioning components are created by using CAML to define data schemas and by rendering HTML. The structure of most CAML elements used in WSS is defined in the XML schema files in the TEMPLATE\XML directory. You can enable IntelliSense in Visual Studio 2005 using these schemas by copying these XSD files into %ProgramFiles%\Microsoft Visual Studio 8\Xml\Schemas. Note that CAML definitions can be tricky to program, and there is little debugging support, so testing is essential. For more advice on CAML Programming, see the sidebar "CAML Debugging Through Diagnostic Logging."

CAML Debugging Through Diagnostic Logging

CAML content definitions have no debugging support through Visual Studio. This can make it frustrating to develop custom content types, lists, and other provisioning components. You can, however, enable verbose logging through SharePoint Central Administration. From the Operations tab, under Logging and Reporting, select Diagnostic Logging. You can then set Event Throttling to report on all categories, to report on events of information criticality and above, and to report verbosely. For a personal development server, you can use just one log file for a period of ten minutes. The default path for the logs is C:\Program Files\Common Files\Microsoft Shared\Web Server Extensions\12\LOGS. You may want to import the log into Microsoft Office Excel 2007 or just use Visual Studio or Notepad to read the file.

Although the Web interface may only state a vague error message, such as "Exception from HRESULT: 0x81070201," the diagnostic log will give you the details needed to fix the XML, such as "Failed to retrieve the list schema for feature FBDECD96-62DC-48c8-8F0A-7B827A042FD9, list template 10001; expected to find it at: C:\Program Files\Common Files\Microsoft Shared\Web Server Extensions\12\Template\Features\LitwareTypes\VendorList."

Tip   Visual Studio 2005 extensions for Windows SharePoint Services 3.0 is a powerful toolkit for generating lightweight provisioning components. You may want to work with the extensions' output as a starting point for your handcrafted provisioning components, although they do not support some of the powerful new features introduced in WSS 3.0.

Defining Site Column Definitions

Lists store their data in *columns* (also referred to as *fields*), which can be defined in the context of a list. WSS 3.0 also introduces *site columns*, which make it possible to define a field in a reusable manner. Rather than defining a field such as FirstName multiple times, WSS defines a site column once and for all in a built-in WSS feature named *fields*. Listing 6-3 shows how the FirstName site column is defined in CAML using a Field element.

Listing 6-3   The standard FirstName site column definition

```
<Field ID="{4a722dd4-d406-4356-93f9-2550b8f50dd0}"
    Name="FirstName"
    SourceID="http://schemas.microsoft.com/sharepoint/v3"
    StaticName="FirstName"
    Group="$Resources:Person_Event_Columns"
    DisplayName="$Resources:core,First_Name;"
    Type="Text">
</Field>
```

Tip   The built-in columns are defined in the built-in "fields" feature, which can be a good reference when you are creating your own column definitions.

In Listing 6-3, you can observe that text-based aspects of the FirstName site column are defined using a special syntax with the "$" character, as in $Resources:core,First_Name. This syntax was introduced in ASP.NET 2.0 as a way to pull a localized string out of a resource file. The ability to localize such aspects of a site-column definition makes it possible for WSS to support localization of provisioning components for several different spoken languages. We will cover the topics of localization and globalization later in this book in Chapter 9.

As a simple example, in this chapter we will create a vendor list with the following columns: Company, Contact, Phone, Industry, Company Size, and Activity Notes. We will be able to use predefined WSS site columns for Company, Contact, and Phone. However, we will create two new site column definitions for the Industry column and the Activity Notes column. Later in the chapter, we also will create a custom field type for the Company Size column.

The LitwareTypes project contains a custom feature named LitwareTypes. As you can see from its Feature.xml file, shown in Listing 6-4, this feature is defined with a Scope attribute value of Site, which means it has been designed to be activated at the level of the site collection.

Listing 6-4   The LitwareTypes feature is scoped at the site collection level.

```
<?xml version="1.0" encoding="utf-8"?>
<Feature
  Id="FBDECD96-62DC-48c8-8F0A-7B827A042FD9"
  Title="Chapter 5: Litware Types"
  Description="Demo from Inside Windows SharePoint Services (Pattison/Larson)"
  Version="1.0.0.0"
  Hidden="false"
  Scope="Site"
  xmlns="http://schemas.microsoft.com/sharepoint/">
  <ElementManifests>
```

```
      <ElementManifest Location="LitwareSiteColumns.xml" />
      <ElementManifest Location="LitwareCustomFieldSiteColumns.xml" />
      <ElementManifest Location="LitwareContentTypes.xml" />
      <ElementManifest Location="VendorList.xml" />
   </ElementManifests>
 </Feature>
```

The first Element Manifest that is referenced in the LitwareTypes feature is LitwareSite-Columns.xml. Inside this CAML-based XML file, you will find the definitions for two site columns named Industry and ActivityNotes, as shown in Listing 6-5. As you can see, each of these site column definitions is defined using a Field element.

Listing 6-5   An example of creating custom column definitions

```
Custom Column Definitions
<?xml version="1.0" encoding="utf-8"?>
<!-- Litware Column Types -->
<Elements xmlns="http://schemas.microsoft.com/sharepoint/">
  <Field
      ID="{0C5BDEB7-0E0E-4c38-A2E5-F39941E61CE9}"
      Name="Industry"
      DisplayName="Industry"
      Type="Choice"
      Format="RadioButtons"
      Group="Litware Columns">
    <CHOICES>
      <CHOICE>High Tech</CHOICE>
      <CHOICE>Legal</CHOICE>
      <CHOICE>Medical</CHOICE>
    </CHOICES>
    <Default>High Tech</Default>
  </Field>

  <Field
      ID="{BED99611-EDE0-41cb-8C05-0FBD96A15D0F}"
      Type="Note"
      RichText="TRUE"
      AppendOnly="TRUE"
      Name="ActivityNotes"
      DisplayName="Activity Notes"
      Sortable="FALSE"
      SourceID="http://schemas.microsoft.com/sharepoint/v3"
      Group="Litware Columns">
  </Field>

</Elements>
```

The Industry site column definition is based on the underlying Choice field type, and it provides the user with three different industries from which to pick when assigning its value. The Industry site column definition also specifies that it should be rendered using Radio-Buttons, using the Format attribute.

The ActivityNotes site column definition is based on the underlying Notes field type, which enables the user to type in large text values that can span multiple lines. Also note that this site column definition has been defined to support rich text as well as the append-only behavior that was introduced in WSS 3.0. Note that any list that contains an append-only site column must have versioning enabled for the behavior to work as intended.

Now that you have seen how to create a site column definition, let's examine how they appear within a WSS site. Each site has a *Site Column Gallery*. After the LitwareTypes feature has been within a particular site collection, our custom site column definitions will appear in the Site Columns Gallery for the top-level site. You can see what's inside the Site Columns Gallery for a site by using the built-in application page named mngfield.aspx, which is accessible through a link in the Site Settings page. An example of inspecting the site columns that have been added by the LitwareTypes feature with this standard application page is shown in Figure 6-1.

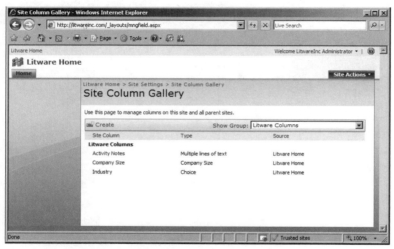

Figure 6-1 Each site contains a Site Column Gallery.

Note that after a site column has been added to the Site Column Gallery, it is available for use in the current site as well as all the child sites below that site in the site hierarchy. Therefore, adding a site column to the Site Column Gallery of a top-level site makes that column available for use in any list throughout the site collection. This provides a motivation for adding site column definitions mainly to features that are scoped at the site collection level as opposed to the site level.

After site column definitions have been added to a site, users can immediately use them when adding columns to a list. For example, a user can click the Add From Existing Site Columns link from the Settings page for a specific list (reached through Settings, List Settings). That makes it possible to add new columns from the available set of site column definitions, as shown in Figure 6-2.

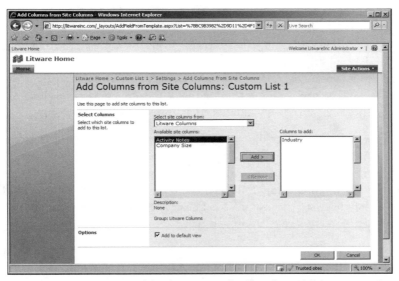

Figure 6-2   A user can add columns to a list based on visible custom site column definitions.

If you create a custom list and add two columns based on the site column definitions for Industry and ActivityNotes, you can test their behavior. For example, after you have added the Industry and ActivityNotes columns to a list, you should create a new item to see how these custom site columns appear to a typical user. As you can see from Figure 6-3, the Industry column renders as a set of radio buttons that enable the user to select one of its three possible values. The ActivityNotes column enables the user to type in notes or comments. When testing the ActivityNotes column, make sure versioning is enabled on the list itself. You should be able to observe that the user can add new notes without erasing the previous entries.

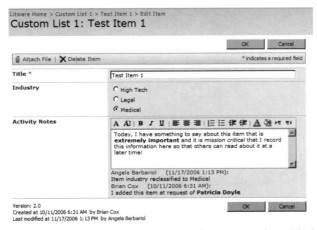

Figure 6-3   Custom site column definitions can be added as columns in lists.

Defining Custom Field Types

In the previous section, you saw examples of how to create custom site column definitions based on some of the built-in WSS field types such as Text, Choice, and Notes. However, WSS 3.0 introduces the ability to work at a lower level, where you can actually define your own custom field type. The motivation for doing this is to gain a greater level of control over the initialization, rendering, and data validation that goes on behind a column.

For example, imagine a scenario in which you need to create a column for a custom list that presents the user with a drop-down list that is populated with data from a backend database server or a Web service. Think about another scenario in which you need a column with values that must be constrained using domain-specific validation logic that you would like to write in a managed language such as C# or Visual Basic .NET. These are examples of scenarios in which it makes sense to create a custom field type.

A custom field type represents a new data type for columns. Custom field types are appealing to .NET developers because they are written in managed code and compiled into .NET assembly DLLs that must be installed in the Global Assembly Cache (GAC). Along with managed code to perform initialization and validation, a custom field type is also defined in terms of one or more ASP.NET server-side controls that give you extra control over rendering and enable you to leverage techniques that are popular in standard ASP.NET development.

In order to create a custom field type, you should create a new Class Library project in Visual Studio. The sample code for this chapter already contains a sample project named LitwareFieldTypes that provides all the pieces for implementing and deploying two custom field types. Note that the LitwareFieldTypes project is configured to compile its output Assembly DLL with a strong name so that it can be installed in the GAC, which is a requirement for deploying and testing a custom field type.

 Note Like many of the other Visual Studio projects shown in this book, the LitwareField-Types project includes an install.bat file that can be run simply by building the project. The batch file installs LitwareFieldTypes.dll in the GAC and copies a few important files into the TEMPLATES directory. After you build the project, you should be able to use its custom field types inside a WSS site.

Inside the source file named LitwareFieldTypes.cs there are two managed classes that are used to define a custom field type named CompanySize. The first class named CompanySizeField is used to define the custom field type itself. This class inherits from the SPFieldText class that is defined inside the core WSS assembly Microsoft.SharePoint.dll. The second class in this example is named CompanySizeFieldControl. This class is used to create and initialize an ASP.NET DropDownList control, which will give our custom field type a custom rendering behavior. Note that the CompanySizeFieldControl class inherits from another class defined inside Microsoft.SharePoint.dll named BaseFieldControl.

> **Tip**   For a full reference of custom field type base classes, refer to the SDK's "Custom Field Type Classes" topic. The Field Types all begin with *SPField*, and include Boolean, choice, currency, date, text, URL, and multiple column fields.

Listing 6-6 shows the code inside the CompanySizeField class. This class provides two standard constructors that are used on all custom field types. There is also a public read-only property named FieldRenderingControl that is used to create an instance of the Company-SizeFieldControl class. Lastly, there is an overridden implementation of a method named GetValidatedString. You override this method to add you own custom validation logic. In our example, we are simply checking to ensure the value is not left empty whenever the column is configured as required. However, you can add additional validation logic as complex as required to solve a particular business requirement.

Listing 6-6   A custom field type is created by creating a class that inherits from SPFieldText or one of the other built-in field type classes.

```
The CompanySizeField Class
public class CompanySizeField : SPFieldText {
  // each field type requires two standard constructors
  public CompanySizeField(SPFieldCollection fields, string fieldName)
    : base(fields, fieldName) { }
  public CompanySizeField(SPFieldCollection fields, string typeName,
                    string displayName)
    : base(fields, typeName, displayName) { }
  // public property used to instantiate control used for rendering
  public override BaseFieldControl FieldRenderingControl {
    get {
      BaseFieldControl control = new CompanySizeFieldControl();
      control.FieldName = this.InternalName;
      return control;
    }
  }
  // Standard method override used to add validation logic
  public override string GetValidatedString(object value) {
    if (this.Required || value.ToString().Equals(string.Empty)) {
      throw new SPFieldValidationException("Company size not assigned");
    }
    return base.GetValidatedString(value);
  }
}
```

Next, let's examine how the CompanySizeFieldControl class is written to work together with an ASP.NET User Control file named CompanySizeFieldControl.ascx. In particular, the CompanySizeFieldControl class uses the named RenderingTemplate control defined inside CompanySizeFieldControl.ascx. You should also note that the install.bat file in the Litware-FieldTypes project has been written to copy the CompanySizeFieldControl.ascx file where it needs to be deployed in the TEMPLATE\CONTROLTEMPLATES directory. As you can see, the RenderingTemplate control defined inside CompanySizeFieldControl.ascx is not very complicated.

```
<SharePoint:RenderingTemplate ID="CompanySizeFieldControl" runat="server">
  <Template>
    <asp:DropDownList ID="CompanySizeSelector" runat="server"  />
  </Template>
</SharePoint:RenderingTemplate>
```

Now examine the implementation of the CompanySizeFieldControl in Listing 6-7. This class contains a field named CompanySizeSelector that is based on the ASP.NET control type named DropDownList. There is also code inside the CreateChildControls method that binds this field to the instance of the DropDownList control defined in CompanySizeField-Control.ascx. This makes it possible for code inside this class to initialize the DropDownList control with a set of items.

Listing 6-7 Code to initialize the field control for the CompanySize field type

```
The CompanySizeFieldControl Class
public class CompanySizeFieldControl : BaseFieldControl {
  protected DropDownList CompanySizeSelector;
  protected override string DefaultTemplateName {
    get { return "CompanySizeFieldControl"; }
  }
  public override object Value {
    get {
      EnsureChildControls();
      return this.CompanySizeSelector.SelectedValue;
    }
    set {
      EnsureChildControls();
      this.CompanySizeSelector.SelectedValue = (string)this.ItemFieldValue;
    }
  }

  protected override void CreateChildControls() {
    if (this.Field == null || this.ControlMode == SPControlMode.Display)
      return;
    base.CreateChildControls();
    this.CompanySizeSelector =
        (DropDownList)TemplateContainer.FindControl("CompanySizeSelector");
    if (this.CompanySizeSelector == null)
      throw new ConfigurationErrorsException("Error: cannot load .ASCX file!");
    if (!this.Page.IsPostBack) {
      this.CompanySizeSelector.Items.AddRange(new ListItem[]
        { new ListItem(string.Empty, null),
          new ListItem("Mom and Pop Shop (1-20)", "1-20"),
          new ListItem("Small Business (21-100)", "21-100"),
          new ListItem("Medium-sized Business (101-1000)", "101-1000"),
          new ListItem("Big Business (1001-20,000)", "1001-20000"),
          new ListItem("Enterprise Business (over 20,000)", "20000+")});
    }
  }
}
```

The CompanySizeFieldControl class overrides a read-only property named DefaultTemplate-Name, which returns the string name of RenderingTemplate defined inside CompanySize-FieldControl.ascx. There is code in the base class of the CompanySizeFieldControl class that uses this string to load the RenderingTemplate from CompanySizeFieldControl.ascx at runtime.

You also should examine the overridden implementation of the Value property in the CompanySizeFieldControl class. The inner get method returns the value from the DropDown-List control. The inner set method takes the ItemFieldValue property defined by the base class and assigns this value to the DropDownList control.

Now you have seen how two classes and a RenderingTemplate inside an .ascx file work together to provide the implementation of a custom field type. The last piece of the puzzle is getting WSS to recognize that you have introduced a new custom field type into a farm by adding a *Field Schema* in a CAML-based file that is then copied into a well-known location.

Field types are defined in files named fldtypes*.xml that must be deployed in the TEMPLATE \XML directory. In our case, the field schema for our custom field type named CompanySize is defined using CAML in a file named *fldtypes_Litware.xml*. The CAML used to define the field schema is shown in Listing 6-8. Also note that the install.bat file for the LitwareFieldTypes project automatically copies this file to the TEMPLATE\XML directory when you compile the project along with installing the assembly file named LitwareFieldTypes.dll into the GAC. After you compile the project, you should then be able to use the CompanySize custom field type.

Listing 6-8   Implementing a custom field type requires writing a field schema using CAML.

```
A Custom Field Type Definition File
<?xml version="1.0" encoding="utf-8" ?>
<FieldTypes>
  <FieldType>
    <Field Name="TypeName">CompanySize</Field>
    <Field Name="ParentType">Text</Field>
    <Field Name="TypeDisplayName">Company Size</Field>
    <Field Name="TypeShortDescription">Company Size</Field>
    <Field Name="UserCreatable">TRUE</Field>
    <Field Name="ShowInListCreate">TRUE</Field>
    <Field Name="ShowInSurveyCreate">TRUE</Field>
    <Field Name="ShowInDocumentLibraryCreate">TRUE</Field>
    <Field Name="ShowInColumnTemplateCreate">TRUE</Field>
    <Field Name="FieldTypeClass">
      LitwareFieldTypes.CompanySizeField, LitwareFieldTypes, ...
    </Field>
    <RenderPattern Name="DisplayPattern">
      <Switch>
        <Expr><Column/></Expr>
        <Case Value=""></Case>
        <Default>
          <HTML><![CDATA[<span style="color:Red"><b>]]></HTML>
          <Column SubColumnNumber="0" HTMLEncode="TRUE"/>
          <HTML><![CDATA[</b></span>]]></HTML>
```

```
            </Default>
          </Switch>
        </RenderPattern>
      </FieldType>
    </FieldTypes>
```

After the custom field type is properly deployed within the farm, you can use it to add a new column to a list and to create a new site column through the browser-based interface of WSS. Figure 6-4 shows how the new custom field type CompanySize appears within the standard page that WSS presents to users for adding a new column to a list.

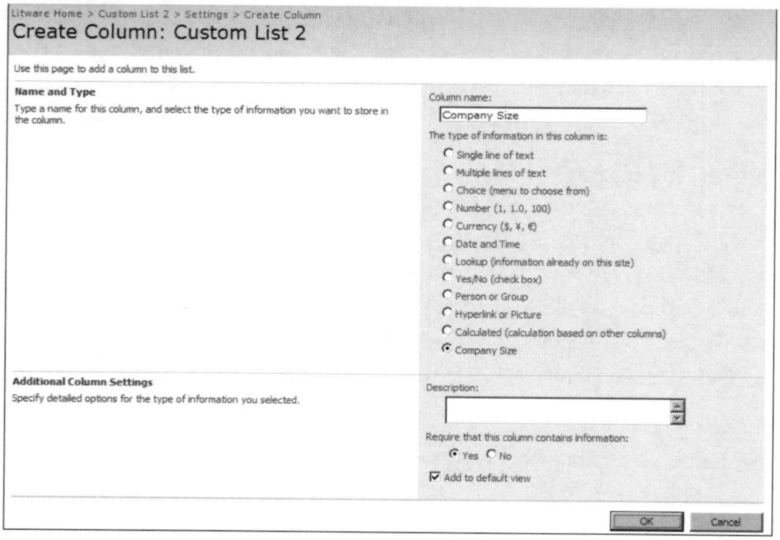

Figure 6-4   A custom field type can be used to add a new column to a list.

After you have created a new column within a list based on the CompanySize custom field type, you can test its appearance and behavior. Figure 6-5 shows an example assigning a value to column based on the CompanySize field type. Note that this custom field type renders a DropDownList control that presents the user with a predetermined set of values. Although this simple example has hard-coded the items into the DropDownList control, you can imagine it wouldn't be that difficult to extend this code to obtain item values for the DropDownList control from an external data source.

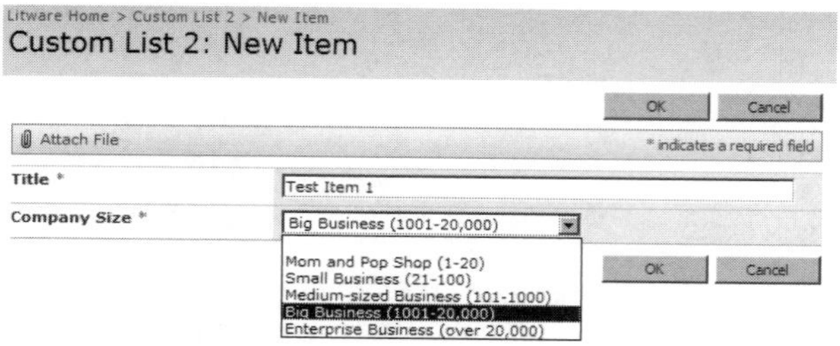

Figure 6-5   The CompanySize field type in use in a custom list.

Defining a Site Column for a Custom Field Type

Earlier in this chapter, we discussed creating custom site columns by using built-in field types such as Text, Notes, and Choice. Now that we have defined a custom field type, we would like to revisit that topic and create another site column by using CAML. However, the site column we will create here will be based on our custom CompanySize field type instead of one of the standard WSS field types.

Listing 6-9 shows the CAML for the Field element required to create a custom site column based on the CompanySize field type. The main point you should observe is that the Type attribute in the Field element is configured with the string name for the custom field type CompanySize. You should recall that the type name CompanySize was defined at the top of fldtypes_Litware.xml, which was shown in Listing 6-8. You can see that after you deploy a custom field type within a farm, its type name can be referenced in places where you would reference the standard WSS field type names, such as in this scenario in which we are creating a custom site column.

Listing 6-9   A site column feature manifest for a custom field type

```
Field in Site Columns Feature Definition
<Elements xmlns="http://schemas.microsoft.com/sharepoint/">
  <Field
    ID="{E2DE076E-1257-4457-9BBE-9331F7EAC46A}"
    SourceID="http://schemas.microsoft.com/sharepoint/v3"
    Name="CompanySize"
    StaticName="CompanySize"
    DisplayName="Company Size"
    Type="CompanySize"
    Group="Litware Columns">
  </Field>
</Elements>
```

Defining Items with Content Types

Content types are a powerful new enhancement introduced in WSS 3.0. The central idea is that a content type defines the underlying schema for either an item in a list or a document in a document library. However, it's important to understand that content types are defined independently outside the scope of any list or document library. After you have created a content type, you can use it across several different lists or several different document libraries.

For example, imagine you create a content type named Company that defines a set of columns for tracking information about a company. After creating this content type you could then create two different lists named Vendors and Customers and configure both of these lists to use the Company content type. This gives you something akin to polymorphism, because you have two different list types that contain homogeneous items that are defined by the same schema. With an application design such as this, you can write a Web Part by using the

SPSiteDataQuery that queries across lists and sites to find and display all the items that have content based on the Company content type.

Content types also provide you with the ability to maintain heterogeneous content inside a single list or document library. For example, you can configure a single list to support multiple content types. Imagine a business scenario in which you need to track customers, and those customers may be either companies or individuals. The problem you face is that customers that are companies and customers who are individuals require different columns to track their information. The solution is to create two different content types for each type of customer and then to create a Customers list and configure it to support both content types.

Content types are defined based upon the principles of inheritance. You will never create a content type from scratch. Instead, you always select an existing content type to serve as the base content type for the new content type you are creating. For example, you can create the most straightforward content type by inheriting from the built-in WSS content type named Item. This automatically provides your new content type with the standard columns and behavior that are common across all content types. Alternatively, you can elect to inherit from one of the more complex built-in content types that inherit from the Item content type, such as Announcement, Task, or Document.

Note that when you create a content type, you must decide whether you want it to be used inside document libraries. Only the Document content type and those content types that inherit from Document can be used inside of document libraries. However, these same content types that can be used in document libraries cannot be used in standard lists. For this reason, you can categorize content types as either *item-based* or *document-based*. Item-based content types are used exclusively in lists, and document-based content types are used exclusively in document libraries. You should observe that no content type can be used in a list and also in a document library.

In addition to supporting metadata columns, document-based content types also support document templates. For example, you could create a document-based content type named Litware Proposal for tracking a certain type of Word document used in a particular business scenario. When you create such a content type, you can define it with whatever metadata columns are required by the scenario. Furthermore, you can define this content type to use a preformatted document template created with Microsoft Office Word. After creating this document-based content type, you can then configure a document library to support it in such a way that the document library's New menu gives users the option to create new documents from the document template.

So far, we have discussed how creating a content type allows you to define the state for an item or a document by adding columns. However, it's important to understand that content types enable you to define the behavior as well. Content types can be used to bind event receivers and workflow associations to items and documents. For example, you can configure the Company content type with an event handler that executes code to perform column value validation. You can configure the Litware Proposal content type with a workflow association that initiates a managerial approval process that must be completed before a proposal document can be sent to a client. Event handlers will be discussed in depth later in this chapter, and a discussion of workflow associations will be deferred until Chapter 8.

> **Tip**   WSS includes several default content types that are defined in the "ctypes" Feature. These content types can be used as a reference when creating custom content types.

Creating a Content Type Definition in CAML

The LitwareTypes feature that accompanies this chapter defines two different content types in the file LitwareContentTypes.xml. The first content type is named Company, and the second one is named Individual. Listing 6-10 shows the CAML-based definition of the Company content type. As you examine this listing, you can see there is a ContentType element with attributes to define an ID and a Name. There is also an inner FieldRefs element used to define the columns. For each column you want to add, you must create a FieldRef element that references a site column by using its identifying GUID and its Name. You can optionally add a DisplayName attribute that is different than the Name.

Listing 6-10   The Company content type defines an ID and a Name along with a collection of site columns.

```
The Company Content Type Definition
<?xml version="1.0" encoding="utf-8" ?>
<Elements xmlns="http://schemas.microsoft.com/sharepoint/">
  <ContentType
    ID="0x0100E71A2716C18B4e96A9B0461156806FFA"
    Name="Company"
    Description="Create a new company"
    Version="0"
    Group="Litware Content Types" >

    <FieldRefs>
      <!-- add in and rename built-in WSS Title column-->
      <FieldRef ID="{fa564e0f-0c70-4ab9-b863-0177e6ddd247}"
                Name="Title" DisplayName="Company" Sealed="TRUE" />
      <FieldRef ID="{475c2610-c157-4b91-9e2d-6855031b3538}"
                Name="FullName" DisplayName="Contact" />
      <FieldRef ID="{fd630629-c165-4513-b43c-fdb16b86a14d}"
                Name="WorkPhone" DisplayName="Phone" />
      <FieldRef ID="{0C5BDEB7-0E0E-4c38-A2E5-F39941E61CE9}"
                Name="Industry" />
      <FieldRef ID="{E2DE076E-1257-4457-9BBE-9331F7EAC46A}"
                Name="CompanySize" DisplayName="Company Size" />
      <FieldRef ID="{BED99611-EDE0-41cb-8C05-0FBD96A15D0F}"
                Name="ActivityNotes" DisplayName="Activity Notes" />
    </FieldRefs>

  </ContentType>
</Elements>
```

Unlike a list, it is not possible to create a column in a content type directly based on an underlying field type. Columns within a content type must be defined in terms of existing site columns. Some of the columns in the Company content type shown in Listing 6-10 are based on site columns that are part of WSS, such as Title, FullName, and WorkPhone. Three other columns are based on the custom site columns named Industry, CompanySize, and Activity-Notes that we created earlier this chapter.

As you begin creating content types and lists, it is important to understand that the built-in site column named Title has special significance in WSS. That's because whatever column is based on the Title site column presents users with the drop-down ECB menu in the AllItems.aspx list view page. Although you should typically use the Title site column, you can change its caption by assigning a value to the DisplayName attribute. In the case of the Company content type, the Title site column has been used to define the first column, and it has been renamed Company. Keep in mind that this column will be used to present the ECB menu.

Tip   There is no error handling or debugging when deploying features. At best, you may get a cryptic error message such as "Value does not fall within the expected range." When developing features, it is important to test often and use source code management such as Visual Source Safe so that you can roll back breaking changes.

As you examine the Company content type definition in Listing 6-10, you will notice that the ID attribute used to identify the content type has a long and somewhat complicated format. This requires a little extra attention on your part because the IDs for content types have a very specific naming convention that must be followed. If you fail to properly format the ID for a new content type, you will experience an error when you attempt to activate the feature in which it is defined.

The first part of a content type ID is based on a hexadecimal number that identifies its base content type. The hexadecimal number for the base content type is followed by 00. The last part of a content type ID is a GUID that uniquely identifies the content type.

The hexadecimal number that identifies the System content type is 0x. The hexadecimal number that identifies the root Item Content Type ID is 0x01. To create a content type such as Company that inherits from the Item content type, append a GUID to **0x0100** as follows:

0x0100E71A2716C18B4e96A9B0461156806FFA

To create a content type that inherits from the Document content type, append a GUID to **0x010100** as follows:

0x010100A776D19644C04553982B8F1A503E2AA5

Note that content type IDs must be unique within a Site Collection. This should not be a problem as long as you generate a new GUID each time you create a content type. For more information, see the sidebar "Content Type IDs."

> **Tip**   To quickly reference the built-in Base Content Types and their IDs, browse to *http://localhost/_layouts/mngctype.aspx*, the Site Content Type Gallery, and mouse over the links of the Content Types.

Content Type IDs

Content IDs have a unique naming convention that must be unique within the site collection, and should be unique globally to avoid any conflicts in deployment. The ID is a string formatted with the complete genealogy of its inheritance chain.

Content Type Inheritance Table

Content Type	Hexadecimal ID
System	0x
Item	0x01
Document Content Types	
Document	0x0101
Form (XMLDocument, or InfoPath form)	0x010101
Picture	0x010102
WikiDocument	0x010108
BasicPage	0x010109
WebPartPage	0x01010901
List Content Types	
Event	0x0102
Issue	0x0103
Announcement	0x0104
Link	0x0105
Contact	0x0106
Message	0x0107
Task	0x0108
BlogPost	0x0110
BlogComment	0x0111
Folder Content Types	
Folder	0x0120
RootOfList	0x012001
Discussion	0x012002

Content Types in the Object Model

After activating a feature such as LitwareTypes in which you have defined content types, these content types will then be available for use through the browser-based user interface as well as through the WSS object model. Note that each site has its own *Content Type Gallery*. The Content Type Gallery for a site can be viewed and administered through an application page named mngctype.aspx that is accessible through a link in the Site Settings page.

Because each site has a Content Type Gallery, you could say that content types are scoped at the site level. However, when you add a content type to the Content Type Gallery within a particular site, that content type is not only available for use within that site but also in all the child sites below it in the site hierarchy. If you add a content type to the Content Type Gallery of a top-level site, it is available for use through the entire site collection. Because the Litware-Types feature has been designed to be activated within the scope of a site collection, its content types are added to the top-level site and are available for use throughout the site collection.

When programming against content types with the WSS object model, you can determine which content types are available within the current scope by acquiring the SPWeb object for the current site and accessing its AvailableContentTypes property. The AvailableContent-Types property returns a collection including the content types in the Content Type Gallery of the current site as well as the content types of all parent sites. Following is an example using a simple foreach loop to enumerate through and inspect all the available content types for a particular site.

```
SPSite siteCollection = new SPSite("http://localhost");
SPWeb site = siteCollection.OpenWeb();
foreach (SPContentType contentType in site.AvailableContentTypes) {
Console.WriteLine(contentType.Name);
}
```

If you want to access a particular content type through the WSS object model, you can use its string-based ID to create a ContentTypeId object. The ContentTypeId object then can be used as an index to the AvailableContentTypes property to obtain the SPContentType object you want, as shown in the following code:

```
SPWeb site = SPContext.Current.Web;
string id = @"0x0100E71A2716C18B4e96A9B0461156806FFA";
SPContentTypeId CompanyTypeID = new SPContentTypeId(id);
SPContentType CompanyType = site.AvailableContentTypes[CompanyTypeID];
```

One of the programmatic tasks you can perform using a content type is to add it to a list. For example, imagine a situation in which you'd like to automate the creation of a new list that supports the Company content type. You can start by creating a new list using the GenericList template and configuring the list with the property settings you require. In the case of a list in which you are adding content types, you probably will want to set the value of the Content-TypesEnabled property to true. After you have created the list and obtained a reference to an SPList object, you can add support for the new content type by calling the Add method on the SPList object's ContentTypes collection and passing an SPContentType object, as shown in the following code:

```
SPSite siteCollection = new SPSite("http://litwareinc.com");
SPWeb site = siteCollection.OpenWeb();
Guid listID = site.Lists.Add("Vendor List",
                             "A demo list created through code",
                             SPListTemplateType.GenericList);

// configure properties for new list
SPList list = site.Lists[listID];
list.ContentTypesEnabled = true;
list.OnQuickLaunch = true;
list.EnableAttachments = false;
list.EnableVersioning = true;
list.Update();

// add support for Company content type
string id = @"0x0100E71A2716C18B4e96A9B0461156806FFA";
SPContentTypeId CompanyTypeID = new SPContentTypeId(id);
SPContentType CompanyType = site.AvailableContentTypes[CompanyTypeID];
list.ContentTypes.Add(CompanyType);
list.Update();

// remove standard Item content type
foreach (SPContentType ContentType in list.ContentTypes) {
  if (ContentType.Name.Equals("Item")) {
    ContentType.Delete();
    break;
  }
}
```

Note that this code not only adds the Company content type, but it also removes the Item content type that is initially associated with the list after the list has been created. Removing this unneeded content type helps eliminate confusion on the part of the user by removing the "Item" menu command from the list's New menu and leaving only the "Company" menu command for creating new items in the list.

It is also important to note that when you add a content type to a list through the object model, WSS provisions columns for each content type field within the list. For example, when the Company content type is added to the new list, the Fields collection of the content type is copied locally to the list. As you might expect, changes made to fields within the list do not affect the Company content type. However, changes you make to the Company content type through the user interface can optionally be *pushed down* to all list instances where that content type is used.

In our example in which we added the Company content type to a generic list, there is one issue concerning the field named Title. Since the generic list already contained a field created from the Title site column, WSS did not add it. Therefore, the part of the Company content type definition that renamed this field with a DisplayName of "Company" does not have any effect. Therefore, we have added a few lines of code to rename the Title field to Company.

```
SPField TitleField = list.Fields["Title"];
TitleField.Title = "Company";
TitleField.Update();
```

Although WSS automatically adds the fields of the Company content type to the new list, it does not add any of these fields to the list's views. This all has to be done separately. For example, the All Items view of the generic list will show only the Title field until you obtain a reference to its SPView object and add the other fields through the view's ViewFields property. Note that when adding fields to the ViewFields collection, it is important to reference the field by its Name as opposed to its DisplayName.

```
SPView view = list.Views["All Items"];
view.ViewFields.Add("FullName");
view.ViewFields.Add("WorkPhone");
view.ViewFields.Add("Industry");
view.ViewFields.Add("CompanySize");
view.ViewFields.Add("ActivityNotes");
view.Update();
```

Now that we have created a new list and configured it to use the Company content type, let's take the next step and add an item through the object model. When creating a new item through the object model, it's possible to explicitly specify the content type, which is often required when dealing with lists that support multiple content types. This can be accomplished by creating and initializing an SPContentTypeId object and assigning that the new item's internal field named "Content Type ID", as shown in the following code:

```
// create SPContentType instance
string id = @"0x0100E71A2716C18B4e96A9B0461156806FFA";
SPContentTypeId CompanyTypeID = new SPContentTypeId(id);

// create new item using that content type
SPListItem item = list.Items.Add();
item["Content Type ID"] = CompanyTypeID;
item["Title"] = "Fabrikam";
item["FullName"] = "Mike Fitzmaurice";
item["WorkPhone"] = "(425)111-2222";
item["Industry"] = "High Tech";
item["CompanySize"] = "1-20";
item["ActivityNotes"] = "This Fitz guy has great widgets";
item.Update();
```

Additional Content Type Metadata

The CAML-based definition for a content type also can contain embedded XML documents that carry additional metadata about the content type. This metadata can be either custom data unique to your application or data within a WSS schema. You can include any XML content you like in the XmlDocument node as long as it is valid XML. The main use of the XmlDocument nodes within WSS itself is to specify custom data forms and event handlers. The following example shows a custom data form specification, in which the display, edit, and new forms are custom-defined. Notice that the *contenttype/forms* namespace URI defines the behavior.

```
<XmlDocuments>
  <XmlDocument
      NamespaceURI="http://schemas.microsoft.com/sharepoint/v3/contenttype/forms">
    <FormTemplates
        xmlns="http://schemas.microsoft.com/sharepoint/v3/contenttype/forms">
      <Display>CompanyData.aspx</Display>
      <Edit>EditCompanyData.aspx</Edit>
      <New>NewCompanyData.aspx</New>
    </FormTemplates>
  </XmlDocument>
</XmlDocuments>
```

Defining Content with List Schemas

Lists can be provisioned through the user interface, through the WSS object model as we just saw, or through provisioning components deployed in a feature. The provisioning component for defining a list type in WSS is the *List Schema*, which is created with CAML. Note that you also could package and deploy a list schema directly in a site definition, but this is not the recommended deployment strategy, because it eliminates the possibility of using the list schema within an existing site.

The LitwareTypes feature that we have used throughout this chapter contains an element manifest named VendorList.xml. This element manifest contains a ListTemplate element that provides the starting point for creating a list schema for a new list type named VendorList.

```
<ListTemplate
  Name="VendorList"
  Type="10001"
  BaseType="0"
  VersioningEnabled="True"
  Hidden="false"
  Sequence="2000"
  DisplayName="Litware Vendors"
  Description="Create a custom vendor list to track companies."
  Image="/_layouts/images/itcontct.gif"
/>
```

As you can see, this ListTemplate element has a Name attribute that has a value of VendorList. The Name within a ListTemplate element is important because there must be a directory inside the feature directory with the same name that contains a file with the well-known name schema.xml. Within the LitwareTypes feature directory, you should be able to locate a directory named VendorList that contains the required schema.xml file. The heart of the list schema for the VendorList type is defined inside this schema.xml file.

In addition to the Name, the ListTemplate element also defines attributes such as Type, Base-Type, VersioningEnabled, Hidden, Sequence, DisplayName, Description, and Image. Note that the Type attribute defines a list type identifier and by convention should be given a value of 10,000 or higher for custom list types. The BaseType attribute value 0 is used to indicate that this is a list type for standard lists. The Hidden attribute is given a value of false so that this list type shows up on the standard Create page, enabling users to create instances of this list type through the standard user interface. The Sequence attribute value is used to position the new list type's link on the Create page.

Note that developing list schemas is much more complicated than developing content types. Although the content type defines only the data schema and behavior, the list schema inside a schema.xml file must define content type references and its own separate data schema as well as views and forms. The section of the schema.xml file that defines the views is typically several thousand lines in length because of all the required CAML rendering instructions. Therefore, the entire schema.xml file used to define the VendorList type is far too long to display as a listing in a book such as this. Listing 6-11 shows the skeleton of the schema.xml file used to define the VendorList type.

Listing 6-11   The skeleton of the schema.xml file for the VendorList type

```
Vendors List Schema Skeleton
<List
    Title="Vendors"
    Url="Lists/Vendors"
    BaseType="0"
    DisableAttachments="True"
    VersioningEnabled="True"
    xmlns="http://schemas.microsoft.com/sharepoint/" >

  <MetaData>
    <ContentTypes> <!-- add content types --> </ContentTypes>
    <Fields> <!-- add fields --> </Fields>
    <Views> <!-- define views here -->   </Views>
    <Forms> <!-- add support for forms here --> </Forms>
  </MetaData>

</List>
```

Now let's examine individual sections of the schema.xml file in more detail. We will begin with the section named ContentTypes. This section is used to add references to the content types that will be used for the list. In our case, we will add a reference to the Vendors content type, and we'll also add a reference to the standard content type for Folders, which has an ID of 0x0120.

```
<ContentTypes>
  <ContentTypeRef ID="0x0100E71A2716C18B4e96A9B0461156806FFA">
    <Folder TargetName="Vendors" />
  </ContentTypeRef>
  <ContentTypeRef ID="0x0120" />
</ContentTypes>
```

Next, we will examine the Fields section. Dealing with fields from one or more content types in a list schema is more complicated than the example shown earlier, when we added a content type to a list through the object model. When you add a content type through the object model, WSS automatically adds the fields of the content type into the Fields collection of the list. This doesn't happen automatically when you add a content type reference in schema.xml. You still must explicitly add each field by using its ID and include other attributes such as its Name and Type. Listing 6-12 shows what the Fields element looks like inside the schema.xml file for the VendorList type.

Listing 6-12   The list schema within the schema.xml file defines a Fields collection.

```
<Fields>

  <Field ID="{fa564e0f-0c70-4ab9-b863-0177e6ddd247}"
         Name="Title" Type="Text" Sealed="TRUE" DisplayName="Company"
         SourceID="http://schemas.microsoft.com/sharepoint/v3" />

  <Field ID="{82642ec8-ef9b-478f-acf9-31f7d45fbc31}"
         Name="LinkTitle" DisplayName="Company" Sealed="TRUE"
         SourceID="http://schemas.microsoft.com/sharepoint/v3" />

  <Field ID="{bc91a437-52e7-49e1-8c4e-4698904b2b6d}"
         Name="LinkTitleNoMenu" DisplayName="Company" Sealed="TRUE"
         SourceID="http://schemas.microsoft.com/sharepoint/v3" />

  <Field ID="{475c2610-c157-4b91-9e2d-6855031b3538}"
         Name="FullName" Type="Text" DisplayName="Contact"
         SourceID="http://schemas.microsoft.com/sharepoint/v3" />

  <Field ID="{fd630629-c165-4513-b43c-fdb16b86a14d}"
         Name="WorkPhone" Type="Text" DisplayName="Phone"
         SourceID="http://schemas.microsoft.com/sharepoint/v3" />

  <Field ID="{0C5BDEB7-0E0E-4c38-A2E5-F39941E61CE9}"
         Name="Industry" DisplayName="Industry"
         Type="Choice" Format="RadioButtons"
         SourceID="http://schemas.microsoft.com/sharepoint/v3" >
    <CHOICES>
      <CHOICE>High Tech</CHOICE>
      <CHOICE>Legal</CHOICE>
      <CHOICE>Medical</CHOICE>
```

```
        </CHOICES>
        <Default>High Tech</Default>
    </Field>

    <Field ID="{E2DE076E-1257-4457-9BBE-9331F7EAC46A}"
           Name="CompanySize" Type="CompanySize" DisplayName="Company Size"
           SourceID="http://schemas.microsoft.com/sharepoint/v3" />

    <Field ID="{BED99611-EDE0-41cb-8C05-0FBD96A15D0F}"
           Name="ActivityNotes" DisplayName="Activity Notes"
           Type="Note" RichText="TRUE" AppendOnly="TRUE" Sortable="FALSE"
           SourceID="http://schemas.microsoft.com/sharepoint/v3" />

</Fields>
```

When developers first work with schema.xml files, the requirement to add redundant field definitions into the list schema doesn't seem too intuitive. After all, we've already defined the fields once in the Company content type, so why should we be forced to define them a second time in the list schema? WSS, however, doesn't supply any mechanism to copy the fields from content types that are referenced from inside the schema.xml file.

If you are creating a list schema that references one or more content types, you should include all fields from all the referenced content types. You can think about a list schema as a data store that provides storage for one or more well-defined item schemas, each of which may or may not use each field defined in the list schema's Fields collection.

For large sets of data, the list schema can define indexes on fields that can significantly improve data access and querying list content. This makes lists a viable storage mechanism for external business applications with the added value of the collaborative interface of WSS. Indexed fields can be defined in the list schema, or they can be specified after creation through the Web interface or the object model. List indexes are similar to the concept of a SQL index, although the index is defined in a SQL-indexed name-value table that contains a reference to the list as well as the indexed column values.

After adding fields, you also will want to specify the fields used in the various views supported by the list, such as the standard All Items view. The view section itself defines one or more views and is fairly cumbersome to work with due to all the required CAML rendering instructions. One of the easiest ways to create the views for a new schema.xml file is to copy the Views node from the Custom List feature (12\TEMPLATE\FEATURES\Custom-List\CustList\Schema.xml) and insert it into your custom list schema.

After copying the Views node from an existing list schema such as the one for custom lists, you can then search for the ViewFields node for each View node and insert your custom field references. The following code listing displays the ViewFields node that is used in each of the View elements defined inside the schema.xml file of the list schema:

```
<ViewFields>
    <FieldRef ID="{82642ec8-ef9b-478f-acf9-31f7d45fbc31}"
              Name="LinkTitle" />
```

```
       <FieldRef ID="{475c2610-c157-4b91-9e2d-6855031b3538}"
                 Name="FullName" DisplayName="Contact" />
       <FieldRef ID="{fd630629-c165-4513-b43c-fdb16b86a14d}"
                 Name="WorkPhone" DisplayName="Phone" />
       <FieldRef ID="{0C5BDEB7-0E0E-4c38-A2E5-F39941E61CE9}"
                 Name="Industry" DisplayName="Industry" />
       <FieldRef ID="{E2DE076E-1257-4457-9BBE-9331F7EAC46A}"
                 Name="CompanySize" DisplayName="Company Size" />
       <FieldRef ID="{BED99611-EDE0-41cb-8C05-0FBD96A15D0F}"
                 Name="ActivityNotes" DisplayName="Activity Notes" />
    </ViewFields>
```

A list schema can optionally be written to use custom forms for viewing and editing content. The default list schemas use standard form pages defined in 12\TEMPLATE\Pages. These forms display content using CAML rendering instructions maintained in the Views node. This is what we have done with the custom list schemas defined inside the LitwareTypes feature. However, you also can specify custom form pages, or you can use custom form pages defined by a content type. If a custom form is not specified, the form page "form.aspx" is instantiated into three Web Part pages in the WSS site. It has one WebPartZone that is populated with an instance of the ListFormWebPart, which uses the appropriate list view defined in schema.xml.

Creating a List Instance

Now that we have created the VendorList type and its associated list schema, it's time to create an instance of this list. Earlier in this chapter, you saw how to do this using the object model. This time we will create a new list instance by adding a CAML element to the LitwareTypes feature. In particular, you can accomplish this by adding a ListInstance element with the following attribute settings:

```
<ListInstance
    TemplateType="10001"
    Id="Vendors"
    Title="Vendors"
    Url="Vendors"
    Description="Litware Vendors"
    OnQuickLaunch="True" >
  <Data>
    <Rows>
      <Row>
        <Field Name="ContentType">Company</Field>
        <Field Name="Title">Acme Corp, Inc</Field>
        <Field Name="FullName">Bob Jones</Field>
        <Field Name="WorkPhone">(813)345-5432</Field>
        <Field Name="Industry">High Tech</Field>
        <Field Name="CompanySize">101-1000</Field>
        <Field Name="ActivityNotes">These folks have some super fine gadgets</Field>
      </Row>
    </Rows>
  </Data>
</ListInstance>
```

This example also demonstrates how you can use CAML to add new items to a list declaratively. A Data node can be created with one or more Row nodes. Within each Row node, you can add Field elements to assign a value to each column including the content type.

Configuring Lists with RSS Feeds

Really Simple Syndication (RSS) is an XML specification for content distribution that is simple to generate, easy to consume, and an open format for integration. Although there are several specifications for content syndication, RSS is the simplest and most widely used. Listing 6-13 displays XML from an announcements list RSS feed. The RSS XML stream defines a list of recurring items, where each item has a title, description, link, and author. The RSS document contains an RSS channel as well that defines information about the feed. This data specification makes RSS a natural fit for WSS Lists and list items, which also have the same corresponding information. Each list item has a link that points to the item's display page, unique identifier, and title. The description RSS field is the only field that SharePoint has to make assumptions on, and this is configured through List Settings.

Listing 6-13   An announcements RSS feed, autogenerated by Windows SharePoint Services

```
An Announcements RSS Feed
<?xml version="1.0" encoding="UTF-8"?>
<rss version="2.0">
  <channel>
    <title>Litware Teams: Announcements</title>
    <link>http://litwareinc.com/Announcements/AllItems.aspx</link>
    <description>RSS feed for the Announcements list.</description>
    <lastBuildDate>Mon, 20 Nov 2006 06:53:29 GMT</lastBuildDate>
    <generator>Windows SharePoint Services V3 RSS Generator</generator>
    <ttl>60</ttl>
    <image>
      <title>Litware Teams: Announcements</title>
      <url>/_layouts/images/homepage.gif</url>
      <link>http://litwareinc.com/Announcements/AllItems.aspx</link>
    </image>
    <item>
      <title>Stay connected with Windows SharePoint Services!</title>
      <link>http://litwareinc.com/Announcements/DispForm.aspx?ID=1</link>
      <description><![CDATA[Microsoft Windows SharePoint Services helps you to be more
                  effective by connecting people, information, and documents with
                  the syndication power of RSS!]]>
      </description>
      <author>Mike Fitzmaurice</author>
      <pubDate>Sun, 19 Nov 2006 23:18:27 GMT</pubDate>
      <guid isPermaLink="true">
        http://litwareinc.com/Announcements/DispForm.aspx?ID=1
      </guid>
    </item>
  </channel>
</rss>
```

The RSS feed for a WSS list is security trimmed; this means that if a list item has security applied to it that prevents a user from seeing the item from the list view, the user will not be able to see it from the RSS view either. The RSS feed also can be accessed from code using the object model, where the list has a method called WriteRssFeed that generates the XML based on list settings and the credentials of the current thread's security context.

> **Tip**   To ensure the integrity of security and authorization, WSS code uses the security context of the user that is making the Web request or executing the current code. As long as your code impersonates the user and doesn't run with escalated credentials, you can be sure that data in SharePoint is secure!

The RSS feed is not meant to be an authoritative list of the content of a given list or document library. Rather, it is intended for timely updates through loosely coupled integration so that users can keep up with content without directly viewing the list. Often the feed consumer is an enterprise news aggregator such as NewsGator Enterprise Server, Feed Demon, Microsoft Office Outlook, or another SharePoint site.

Event Receivers

Event Receivers represent a developer-extensibility mechanism that can be used to add behaviors to various elements such as lists and list items. An event receiver is a class that contains one or more methods known as *event handlers* that are executed automatically by WSS in response to events such as a user adding a column to a list or a user deleting a list item. The event handlers are typically written to perform data validation, to ensure data integrity, or to kick off custom business processing.

Events supported by WSS can be separated into two categories: *before events* and *after events*. A before event fires before an action has been completed. For example, WSS fires a Field-Adding event when a user attempts to add a new column to a list. It is referred to as a "before" event because it fires before the field is added to the list, and the event gives the developer an opportunity to supply an event handler, which cancels the action. Before events are executed synchronously in a blocking manner on the same thread that handles the request. For this reason, before events are sometimes referred to as *synchronous events*.

An after event is different because it fires after an action has been completed, and it does not provide the developer with an opportunity to cancel the action. For example, WSS fires an ItemAdded event after an item has been added to a list. An after event such as this provides the developer with the opportunity to write an event handler to kick off custom business processing such as reformatting a field value inside the item that has just been added or sending out a notification e-mail message. Note that after events are nonblocking, because they are executed asynchronously on a secondary thread. For this reason, after events are sometimes referred to as *asynchronous events*.

> **Tip** Event Receivers are equivalent to the Event Sink concept from WSS 2.0, although event receivers can be applied to any list type, whereas Event Sinks in WSS 2.0 can only be applied to Document Library–based lists.

To create an event receiver, you must create a class that inherits from one of the special event receiver base classes provided by the WSS object model. It is also important to note that event receiver classes must be compiled into strong-named assemblies and deployed in the GAC before they can be used or tested.

The LitwareTypes project contains three different examples of event receiver classes. The first one we will examine is the event receiver class named VendorListEventReceiver from the source file VendorListEventReceiver.cs, which is shown in Listing 6-14. This class has been written to inherit from the SPListEventReceiver class so that it can handle list-based events. As in the case of all event receiver classes, you create event handler method implementations by overriding methods defined in the base class.

Listing 6-14   An example list event receiver

```
The VendorListEventReceiver Class
using System;
using Microsoft.SharePoint;

namespace LitwareTypes {
  public class VendorListEventReceiver : SPListEventReceiver {

    public override void FieldAdding(SPListEventProperties properties) {
      properties.ErrorMessage = "You cannot change this list schema!";
      properties.Cancel = true;
    }

    public override void FieldUpdating(SPListEventProperties properties) {
      properties.ErrorMessage = "You cannot change this list schema!";
      properties.Cancel = true;
    }

    public override void FieldDeleting(SPListEventProperties properties) {
      properties.ErrorMessage = "You cannot change this list schema!";
      properties.Cancel = true;
    }
  }
}
```

The VendorListEventReceiver class provides three event handlers by overriding the methods named FieldAdding, FieldUpdating, and FieldDeleting. Because all three of the events being handled are before events, the event handlers can cancel whatever action caused the event to fire. In this case, the three event handlers use the SPListEventProperties parameter to assign an error message and cancel the event. After these event handlers have been properly bound to a list, they will prevent the users (even those users with administrator privileges) from being able to add, rename, or delete any of its fields.

Now it's time to discuss how to bind the event handlers within this event receiver class to a list type. You can accomplish this by adding a Receivers element within a feature like the one shown in Listing 6-15. The Receivers element in this example has a ListTemplateId attribute with a value of 10001 that will bind its inner receivers to all instances of our custom Vendor-List type. Note that inside the Receivers element there is an individual Receivers element for each event handler. You should observe that each event handler method must be bound by its own Receiver element because there is no way to bind multiple event handlers at once.

Listing 6-15   You can use a feature to bind event handlers to a specific list type.

```
<Elements xmlns="http://schemas.microsoft.com/sharepoint/">
  <!-- Receivers element can only be used in feature where Scope=Web -->
  <Receivers ListTemplateId="10001" >
    <Receiver>
      <Name>Field Adding Event</Name>
      <Type>FieldAdding</Type>
      <Assembly>LitwareTypes, [full 4-part assembly name goes here] </Assembly>
      <Class>LitwareTypes.VendorListEventReceiver</Class>
      <SequenceNumber>1000</SequenceNumber>
    </Receiver>
    <Receiver>
      <Name>Field Updating Event</Name>
      <Type>FieldUpdating</Type>
      <Assembly>LitwareTypes, [full 4-part assembly name goes here] </Assembly>
      <Class>LitwareTypes.VendorListEventReceiver</Class>
      <SequenceNumber>1000</SequenceNumber>
    </Receiver>
    <Receiver>
      <Name>Field Deleting Event</Name>
      <Type>FieldDeleting</Type>
      <Assembly>LitwareTypes, [full 4-part assembly name goes here] </Assembly>
      <Class>LitwareTypes.VendorListEventReceiver</Class>
      <SequenceNumber>1000</SequenceNumber>
    </Receiver>
  </Receivers>
</Elements>
```

The technique shown in Listing 6-15 for binding event handlers by using a Receivers element has a few noteworthy limitations. First, a Receivers element can be used only in features scoped at the site level. It cannot be used in features scoped at other levels including the site collection level, which means we cannot use this event binding technique in the LitwareTypes feature. Secondly, the Receivers element allows you to bind event handlers only to a list type. It does not provide the flexibility to bind event handlers to list instances or to a content type. In many cases, you will want to use the WSS object model to bind your event handlers, because this approach provides much more flexibility.

Now let's discuss how to bind event handlers to a list instance instead of a list type. Listing 6-16 shows code using the WSS object model to bind the event handlers of the VendorListEventReceiver class to the list instance named Vendors. This code has been written inside the FeatureActivated method, which executes as the final part of the activation sequence for the LitwareTypes feature. If you examine this code, you can see it acquires a reference to the SPList object for the Vendors list and then calls the Add method on the Event-Receivers property. When you add an event handler in this fashion, the event binding information is persisted in the content database just like any other customization that is recorded for the target list.

Listing 6-16 Event handlers can be bound to list events through the WSS object model.

```
public override void FeatureActivated(SPFeatureReceiverProperties properties) {
  SPSite siteCollection = (SPSite)properties.Feature.Parent;
  SPWeb site = siteCollection.RootWeb;
  SPList lstVendors = site.Lists["Vendors"];
  string asmName = "LitwareTypes, [full 4-part assembly name goes here] ";
  string listReceiverName = "LitwareTypes.VendorListEventReceiver";
  // add event receiver to fire before new column is added
  lstVendors.EventReceivers.Add(SPEventReceiverType.FieldAdding,
                                asmName, listReceiverName);
  // add event receiver to fire before existing column is updated
  lstVendors.EventReceivers.Add(SPEventReceiverType.FieldUpdating,
                                asmName, listReceiverName);
  // add event receiver to fire before existing column is updated
  lstVendors.EventReceivers.Add(SPEventReceiverType.FieldDeleting,
                                asmName, listReceiverName);
}
```

Writing Event Handlers

It is common to write event handlers that allow an action to occur only if a certain condition is met. For example, you can write an ItemDeleting handler that cancels the action whenever the current user is not a site administrator.

```
public class VendorItemEventReceiver : SPItemEventReceiver {
  public override void ItemDeleting(SPItemEventProperties properties) {
    if (!properties.OpenWeb().CurrentUser.IsSiteAdmin) {
      properties.Status = SPEventReceiverStatus.CancelWithError;
      properties.ErrorMessage = "Vendor can only be deleted by site administrator";
      properties.Cancel = true;
    }
  }
}
```

It is also common to write event handlers for before events that contain validation logic. For example, imagine a scenario in which you want to require that any item added to the Vendors list contain a phone number that is at least seven characters in length. Therefore, you must supply an ItemAdding event handler as well as an ItemUpdating event handler to perform the validation logic. Listing 6-17 shown an example of how to create such an event receiver class with a helper method named PhoneIsValid so that you can maintain all the validation logic in one place.

Listing 6-17   An example of how to structure event validation logic

```
public class VendorItemEventReceiver : SPItemEventReceiver {
  // provide method with validation logic
  private bool PhoneIsValid(string Phone) {
    if ((Phone == null) || (Phone.Length < 7))
      return false;
    else
      return true;
  }

  // provide error message
  const string PhoneInvalidErrorMessage =
      "VALIDATION ERROR: Phone must be at least 7 digits.";

  public override void ItemAdding(SPItemEventProperties properties) {
    // validate Phone column for new vendor item
    string Phone = properties.AfterProperties["WorkPhone"].ToString();
    if (!PhoneIsValid(Phone)) {
      properties.Status = SPEventReceiverStatus.CancelWithError;
      properties.ErrorMessage = PhoneInvalidErrorMessage;
      properties.Cancel = true;
    }
  }

  public override void ItemUpdating(SPItemEventProperties properties) {
    // validate Phone column for update to vendor item
    string Phone = properties.AfterProperties["WorkPhone"].ToString();
    if (!PhoneIsValid(Phone)) {
      properties.Status = SPEventReceiverStatus.CancelWithError;
      properties.ErrorMessage = PhoneInvalidErrorMessage;
      properties.Cancel = true;
    }
  }
}
```

Note that the ItemAdding event handler and the ItemUpdating event handler shown in Listing 6-17 must each obtain the WorkPhone column value that the user is attempting to save. These event handler methods accomplish this by using the AfterProperties property of the SPItemEventProperties parameter. The AfterProperties property allows you to gain access to column values of the item being modified using the underlying Name of the field (not the DisplayName). Likewise, the SPItemEventProperties parameter also exposes a BeforeProperties property so that you can determine the initial value of a column before it was changed by the user in scenarios that require you to perform change-based validation.

Although before events are typically used for validation, after events can be used to maintain data integrity or to kick off custom processing. Imagine a scenario in which the Company names must all be maintained with uppercase characters. In this case, we will write event handlers for after events that reformat a column value any time it is changed. Listing 6-18 shows a receiver class named CompanyItemEventReceiver that provides an ItemAdded event handler and an ItemUpdated event handler. As you can see, these event handlers simply take the updated column value, modify it to the required format, and then save it back to the same column in the current list item.

Listing 6-18   Event handlers for after events can be used to maintain data integrity.

```
public class CompanyItemEventReceiver : SPItemEventReceiver {
  // custom logic to format a field value
  private string FormatCompanyName(string value) {
    return value.ToUpper();
  }

  public override void ItemAdded(SPItemEventProperties properties) {
    DisableEventFiring();
    string CompanyName = properties.ListItem["Company"].ToString();
    properties.ListItem["Company"] = FormatCompanyName(CompanyName);
    properties.ListItem.Update();
    EnableEventFiring();
  }

  public override void ItemUpdated(SPItemEventProperties properties) {
    DisableEventFiring();
    string CompanyName = properties.ListItem["Company"].ToString();
    properties.ListItem["Company"] = FormatCompanyName(CompanyName);
    properties.ListItem.Update();
    EnableEventFiring();
  }
}
```

You should observe the calls to DisableEventFiring and EnableEventFiring in the event handlers in the CompanyItemEventReceiver class in Listing 6-18. By disabling event handling inside an event handler, you can update columns within a list without causing additional events to fire. This is necessary to prevent recursive behavior that could cause the code inside an event handler to fire itself repeatedly.

Binding Event Handlers to a Content Type

In the previous section, we created the CompanyItemEventReceiver class to maintain data integrity on Company names that must all be formatted using uppercase characters. As the final topic of this chapter, we now want to show how to bind the event handlers within this event receiver class to the Company content type. This is accomplished inside the content type definition by using an inner XmlDocument node, which is shown in Listing 6-19. As you can see, each event handler must be bound separately using the same information that is used to bind event handlers with the object model or with a Receivers element in a feature.

Listing 6-19 An XmlDocument element can be used to bind an event handler to a content type.

```
<ContentType ID="0x0100E71A2716C18B4e96A9B0461156806FFA" Name="Company" >
  <!-- FieldRefs element omitted for clarity -->
  <!-- event handlers added to content type using XmlDocument element -->
  <XmlDocuments>
    <XmlDocument NamespaceURI="http://schemas.microsoft.com/sharepoint/events">
      <spe:Receivers xmlns:spe="http://schemas.microsoft.com/sharepoint/events">
        <spe:Receiver>
          <spe:Name>ItemAddedReceiver</spe:Name>
          <spe:Type>ItemAdded</spe:Type>
          <spe:Assembly>LitwareTypes, [full 4-part assembly name] </spe:Assembly>
          <spe:Class>LitwareTypes.CompanyItemEventReceiver</spe:Class>
        </spe:Receiver>
        <spe:Receiver>
          <spe:Name>ItemUpdatedReceiver</spe:Name>
          <spe:Type>ItemUpdated</spe:Type>
          <spe:Assembly>LitwareTypes, [full 4-part assembly name] </spe:Assembly>
          <spe:Class>LitwareTypes.CompanyItemEventReceiver</spe:Class>
        </spe:Receiver>
      </spe:Receivers>
    </XmlDocument>
  </XmlDocuments>
</ContentType>
```

Summary

This chapter has introduced you to the basic architecture of lists and the WSS type system. You have seen how to create and query lists by using the WSS object model. You also have learned about the fundamentals of WSS type definitions that include site columns, custom field types, content types, and list templates.

Much of this chapter was dedicated to developing custom provisioning components. Although there is extra work involved with using CAML to create features containing custom definitions for site columns, content types, and list templates, it is often well worth the effort required. CAML provides the most reliable approach for creating storage mechanisms that can be reused across sites, farms, and various business solutions.

Chapter 7
Document Libraries

- Program with the SPDocumentLibrary class.
- Access documents as SPListItem and SPFile objects.
- Configure document libraries with custom document templates.
- Work with InfoPath and forms libraries.
- Generate documents with the Office Open XML file formats.

Working with Document Libraries

This book has already touched on several examples of developing and programming with documents and document libraries. At the end of Chapter 2, "SharePoint Architecture," we showed you an example of adding a custom ECB menu item for documents in a document library that redirects the user to a custom application page that examines various properties of the current document. Chapter 3, "Pages and Design," provided examples of programming against SPFile and SPFolder objects. Although the Chapter 3 examples dealt with .aspx pages that are not actually stored within document libraries, the programming techniques involving the SPFile and SPFolder classes are also valuable when working with documents stored within document libraries.

This chapter begins with an exploration of programming techniques involving the SPDocumentLibrary class, which gives you a better feel for designing and implementing document management solutions by using Microsoft Windows SharePoint Services (WSS). The chapter then examines the use of forms libraries and Windows SharePoint Services integration with Microsoft Office InfoPath 2007. At the end of this chapter, we will introduce the Office Open XML file formats, which provide techniques for generating, reading, and manipulating documents with server-side code in applications such as Microsoft Office Word 2007, Microsoft Office Excel 2007, and Microsoft Office PowerPoint 2007.

Note The majority of code samples in this chapter are based on a sample Microsoft Visual Studio project named DocumentManager that includes a feature named DocumentManager plus several custom application pages. If you want to follow along with the code examples here, you can open the DocumentManager project and build it, which copies all the relevant files to their proper locations in the TEMPLATES directory and installs the DocumentManager feature. You can then activate the feature in any site you want to test the code. And you can activate this feature from the Site Features page of any site.

217

SPDocumentLibrary Class

In terms of general WSS architecture, it's important to observe that a document library is really just a specialized type of list. Similar to any standard list, you can add additional columns to a document library. This is a common practice in custom SharePoint solutions because it makes it possible to track metadata for documents. It is also important to note that each document library instance is included within the Lists collection of the current site.

```
SPWeb site = SPContext.Current.Web;
foreach (SPList list in site.Lists) {
    // steps through all lists including document libraries
}
```

The main difference between a document library and a standard WSS list is that a document library is designed to store documents instead of merely list items. The SPDocumentLibrary class is included in the WSS object model to provide programmatic control over the additional functionality that document libraries have over standard lists. Note that the SPDocumentLibrary class inherits from the SPList class. Once you obtain a reference to an SPList object, you can determine whether the list is also a document library by testing to see whether the SPList object is compatible with the SPDocumentLibrary type.

```
public bool IsListAlsoDocumentLibrary(SPList list) {
  if (list is SPDocumentLibrary)
    return true;
  else
    return false;
}
```

Assume that you want to write the code for a custom application page or a Web Part to populate a DropDownList control named lstTargetLibrary with the Title of the document library instances inside the current site. Keep in mind that there are many hidden document libraries that you might not want to display to users, such as the Web Part gallery, Site Template gallery, List Template gallery, and Master Page gallery. Therefore, you want to write your code to discover all of the document library instances for the current site that are not hidden.

```
SPWeb site = SPContext.Current.Web;
foreach (SPList list in site.Lists) {
  if (list is SPDocumentLibrary && !list.Hidden) {
    SPDocumentLibrary docLib = (SPDocumentLibrary)list;
    // Add document library to DropDownList control
    lstTargetLibrary.Items.Add(
      new ListItem(docLib.Title, docLib.ID.ToString()));
  }
}
```

Note that the code shown here adds ListItem entries to the DropDownList control that includes the Title as the ListItem Text and the GUID-based ID as the ListItem Value. When a user selects a particular document library title from the DropDownList control, you can quickly access the target document library from the current site's Lists collection by using its identifying GUID and converting it to an SPDocumentLibrary class.

```
SPWeb site = SPContext.Current.Web;
Guid libraryID = new Guid(lstTargetLibrary.SelectedValue);
SPDocumentLibrary library = (SPDocumentLibrary)site.Lists[libraryID];
```

Programming Against Documents

There is a dual aspect to working with documents within a document library. Because every document library is represented in the WSS object model with an SPList object, every document in a document library has an associated SPListItem object. However, each document in a document library is also represented with an SPFile object, which means that you can program against a document in a document library as either an SPListItem or SPFile object. The following code presents an example of enumerating through a document library and creating both an SPList and SPFile object to program against each document.

```
void ProcessDocuments(SPDocumentLibrary docLib) {
  foreach (SPListItem item in docLib.Items) {
    // program against item variable as SPListItem object
    SPFile file = item.File;
    // program against file as SPFile object
  }
}
```

As you can see, once you have the SPListItem object for a document, you can then retrieve the associated SPFile object by accessing the File property. The SPListItem object can be used to track a document's ID and read or write metadata columns.

```
foreach (SPListItem item in docLib.Items) {
  // get document ID
  int itemID = item.ID;
  // read metadata column
  string clientColumnValue = item["Client"].ToString();
  // write metadata column
  item["Client"] = "AdventureWorks";
  item.Update();
}
```

The SPFile object, on the other hand, can be used to control other aspects of the document and to read or write the document's content. Examine the following code fragment:

```
foreach (SPListItem item in docLib.Items) {
  if (item.FileSystemObjectType == SPFileSystemObjectType.File) {
    SPFile file = item.File;
    // check on number of versions
    int versionCount = file.Versions.Count;
    // determine when document was checked out
    DateTime checkedOutDate = file.CheckedOutDate;
    // open document for stream-based access
    using(Stream fileContents = file.OpenBinaryStream()) {
      // program against stream to access document content
    }
  }
}
```

One thing you must watch for is the scenario in which a document library contains folders in addition to documents. Note that folders, like files, are stored as items within a document library and show up as SPListItem objects in the Items collection. This is why the previous code checks the FileSystemObjectType property of the current SPListItem object before attempting to process it as an SPFile object.

Discovering documents by enumerating through the Items collection of a document library finds all documents without regard for whether they exist within the root folder or within folders nested below the root folder. If you would rather enumerate through only the documents within the root folder of a document library, you can use a different approach, similar to what was demonstrated in Chapter 3 when using the SPFolder and SPFile classes.

```
void ProcessDocumentsAtRoot(SPDocumentLibrary docLib) {
  foreach (SPFile file in docLib.RootFolder.Files) {
    // program against file using SPFile class
  }
}
```

If you want to write code in this fashion that continues to discover documents in nested folders, you can write code that involves recursion. In the DocumentManager project, a custom application page named DocumentManager1.aspx, which is accessible through the Site Settings menu, contains code to discover all documents in a site that exist within document libraries that are not hidden. The code populates a TreeView control displaying the document libraries as well as the hierarchy of the folder structure within each document library, as shown in Figure 7-1.

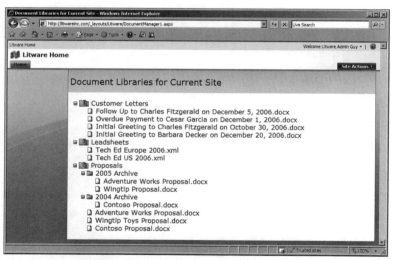

Figure 7-1   DocumentManager1.aspx contains code to populate an ASP.NET TreeView control with nodes for all documents within the current site.

The code used to populate the TreeView control in DocumentManager1.aspx is not overly complex. It contains an OnLoad event handler that enumerates through all of the lists and discovers which are document libraries that are not hidden. For each of these document libraries, it creates a TreeNode control and then calls a helper method named Load-FolderNodes to create child TreeNode controls for each document. The LoadFolderNodes method calls itself to move recursively through all folders that might be nested below the root folder.

```
const string DOCLIB_IMG = @"\_layouts\images\ITDLSM.GIF";
const string FOLDER_IMG = @"\_layouts\images\FOLDER.GIF";
const string FILE_IMG = @"\_layouts\images\ICGEN.GIF";

protected override void OnLoad(EventArgs e) {
  SPWeb site = SPContext.Current.Web;
  foreach (SPList list in site.Lists) {
    if (list is SPDocumentLibrary && !list.Hidden) {
      SPDocumentLibrary docLib = (SPDocumentLibrary)list;
      SPFolder folder = docLib.RootFolder;
      TreeNode docLibNode = new TreeNode(docLib.Title,
                                        docLib.DefaultViewUrl,
                                        DOCLIB_IMG);
      LoadFolderNodes(folder, docLibNode);
      treeSitesFiles.Nodes.Add(docLibNode);
    }
  }
  treeSitesFiles.ExpandDepth = 1;
}

protected void LoadFolderNodes(SPFolder folder, TreeNode folderNode) {
  foreach (SPFolder childFolder in folder.SubFolders) {
    if (childFolder.Name != "Forms") {
      TreeNode childFolderNode = new TreeNode(childFolder.Name,
                                              childFolder.Name,
                                              FOLDER_IMG);
      LoadFolderNodes(childFolder, childFolderNode);
      folderNode.ChildNodes.Add(childFolderNode);
    }
  }
  foreach (SPFile file in folder.Files) {
    TreeNode fileNode;
    fileNode = new TreeNode(file.Name, file.Name, FILE_IMG);
    folderNode.ChildNodes.Add(fileNode);
  }
}
```

Adding a New File to a Document Library

It is now time to write the code required to create a new document within a document library. If you want to follow along in the DocumentManager project, use Microsoft Visual Studio to open the custom application page named DocumentManager2.aspx and examine the code in the OnLoad event handler that populates a DropDownList control named lstTargetLibrary with all of the available document libraries in the current site. The page definition for DocumentManager2.aspx also contains a check box named chkShowHiddenLibraries that enables the user to determine whether the hidden libraries should be shown to users.

```
SPWeb site = SPContext.Current.Web;
if (!IsPostBack) {
  lstTargetLibrary.Items.Clear();
  foreach (SPList list in site.Lists) {
    if ( (list is SPDocumentLibrary) &&
       ( !list.Hidden || chkShowHiddenLibraries.Checked) ) {
      SPDocumentLibrary docLib = (SPDocumentLibrary)list;
      lstTargetLibrary.Items.Add(
               new ListItem(docLib.Title, docLib.ID.ToString()));
    }
  }
}
```

Figure 7-2 displays the basic page layout for the custom application page named DocumentManager2.aspx. The user interface enables the user to select a target document library and type in a file name. It also provides a multiline TextBox control that enables the user to type in the content to be written into the new file. Although this example is fairly simple, it steps through what's required to programmatically create a new document and save it within a document library.

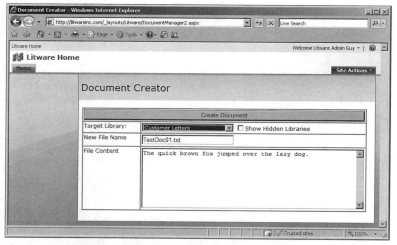

Figure 7-2 DocumentManager2.aspx demonstrates a programmatic technique for creating new documents through the WSS object model.

When the user clicks the button with the caption Create Document, an event handler executes the code required to create a simple text file and store it within the target document library. The first issue you must deal with is parsing together the path for the new document. Examine the following code, which uses the ServerRelativeUrl property of a document library's

RootFolder object together with the MakeFullUrl method of the current SPSite object to construct the full path for a new document.

```
SPSite siteCollection = SPContext.Current.Site;
SPWeb site = SPContext.Current.Web;
Guid libraryID = new Guid(lstTargetLibrary.SelectedValue);
SPDocumentLibrary library = (SPDocumentLibrary)site.Lists[libraryID];
// parse together name of new document inside target library
string documentName = txtFileName.Text;
string libraryRelativePath = library.RootFolder.ServerRelativeUrl;
string libraryPath = siteCollection.MakeFullUrl(libraryRelativePath);
string documentPath = libraryPath + "/" + documentName;
```

As you can see, the document path is parsed together using the file name as well as a full path to the target document library. Once you have parsed together the path, it's necessary to use a stream-based programming technique to write the contents of the new file. There are many possible ways to accomplish this by using various classes within the System.IO namespace. One efficient way to accomplish this task for a simple text file is by creating a MemoryStream object and writing into it by using a StreamWriter object.

```
// create a memory stream and add document content
Stream documentStream = new MemoryStream();
StreamWriter writer = new StreamWriter(documentStream);
writer.Write(txtDocumentBody.Text);
writer.Flush();
```

Once you have parsed together the path for the new document and written the new document's content into a MemoryStream, you can then simply save the new document into the target document library by calling the Add method on the Files collection on the SPWeb object for the current site.

```
// add document into document library
site.Files.Add(documentPath, documentStream, true);
```

At first you might think this code to store a document in a document library is a bit counter-intuitive because you are not calling an Add method on an object that represents the document library itself. The Add method is called on the Files collection of the current site, and nothing except the document path that you parsed together tells WSS which document library to target when storing the new document.

Now, consider a scenario in which you are adding a document to a document library that has custom metadata columns. For example, imagine that you are dealing with a document library with a custom column named Client that is used to associate each document with a particular client. What should you do if you want to assign a value to this column when you store the document?

An overloaded version of the Add method exists for scenarios when you are adding new documents to a document library that has custom metadata columns. Before calling this over-loaded implementation of the Add method, you should create a new Hashtable object and add a name-value pair for each custom metadata column. For example, imagine that you want to save a document into a document library and assign a value to a custom metadata column named Client as well as the built-in Title column. You can accomplish this by using the following code:

```
Hashtable docProperties = new Hashtable();
docProperties["Client"] = "AdventureWorks";
docProperties["vti_title"] = "AdventureWorks Sales Proposal";
site.Files.Add(documentPath, documentStream, docProperties, true);
```

Note that the property name of the Title column is vti_title and not Title, as you might expect. Many of the built-in columns used in WSS lists and document libraries have similar names that are not intuitive. You can discover these file property names by enumerating through the Properties collection of an SPFile object created from an object in the target document library.

```
SPList list = site.Lists["Proposals"];
foreach (SPListItem item in list.Items) {
  SPFile file = item.File;
  foreach (DictionaryEntry entry in file.Properties) {
    Console.WriteLine(entry.Key + ": " + entry.Value);
  }
  break;
}
```

Using a Feature to Provision a New Document Library Instance

When you need to create a document library instance within a site for a business solution, you have several different options. You can create a custom document library type following the same steps that were outlined in Chapter 6, "Lists and Content Types," for creating a custom list type. You can also create custom content types designed specifically for the types of documents with which you are dealing and then define a document library type that is based on those content types.

However, in a situation in which you just need to provision an instance of a standard document library, you can take a much simpler approach. For example, the DocumentManager feature contains a ListInstance element that automatically provisions an instance of the standard WSS document library type named Proposals on activation.

```
<ListInstance
  FeatureId="00BFEA71-E717-4E80-AA17-D0C71B360101"
  TemplateType="101"
  Id="Proposals"
  Description="Document Library for proposals"
  OnQuickLaunch="True"
  Title="Proposals"
  Url="Proposals" >
</ListInstance>
```

When you use the ListInstance element to create an instance of the standard WSS document library type, the FeatureId attribute value must be assigned the GUID that identifies the standard WSS feature named DocumentLibrary, and the TemplateType attribute value must be assigned the type identifier for the standard document library type, which is 101. All other attributes are used to configure the new document library instance.

If you would like to preload some documents into this document library instance, you can place the physical document files into the feature directory and provision them into the document library by adding a Module element after the ListInstance element. For example, if your feature directory contains an inner directory named TestData containing standard documents, you can provision those documents into the document library instance on feature activation by adding the following Module element:

```
<Module Name="TestData" List="101" Path="TestData" Url="Proposals" >
  <File Url="Adventure Works Proposal.docx" Type="GhostableInLibrary" />
  <File Url="Contoso Proposal.docx" Type="GhostableInLibrary" />
</Module>
```

Now that you have seen how to provision a document library instance within a feature, you likely want to replace the standard document template with one of your own. Quite a bit of work is involved if you want to add support for a custom document template using only Collaborative Application Markup Language (CAML) because CAML only enables you to define document templates in a site definition, something that involves far more work then necessary for this scenario. A much easier approach involves mixing declarative CAML logic with some WSS object model code in the Feature_Activated event.

You should start by using CAML to provision the custom document template file into the target site by using a Module element. When doing this, it is recommended that you place the document template within the Forms folder of the target document library.

```
<Module Name="WordTemplate" List="101" Url="Proposals/Forms">
  <File Url="ProposalTemplate.dotx" Type="GhostableInLibrary" />
</Module>
```

Next, you can create a FeatureActivated event handler and add the code required to create an SPDocumentLibrary object associated with the target document library. You can then assign a path to the document template to the DocumentTemplateUrl property. Make sure you remember to call the Update method to save your changes.

```
public override void FeatureActivated(
                       SPFeatureReceiverProperties properties) {
  SPWeb site = (SPWeb)properties.Feature.Parent;
  SPDocumentLibrary libProposals;
  libProposals = (SPDocumentLibrary)site.Lists["Proposals"];
  string templateUrl = @"Proposals/Forms/ProposalTemplate.dotx";
  libProposals.DocumentTemplateUrl = templateUrl;
  libProposals.Update();
}
```

When you obtain an SPDocumentLibrary reference to the newly created document library, you can do far more than simply assign a custom document template. You can also configure many other aspects of the document library's behavior, such as disabling folder creation, enabling versioning, and enabling forced document checkout.

```
libProposals.EnableFolderCreation = false;
libProposals.EnableVersioning = true;
libProposals.ForceCheckout = true;
libProposals.Update();
```

Creating a Custom Application Page for Document Management

As you are designing and implementing document libraries for a custom business solution, you might want to give users the ability to perform custom operations on the documents inside them. By creating CustomAction elements within a feature, it's easy to add custom menu items to the ECB menu for documents within a document library. In Chapter 2, you viewed an example of the addition of a CustomAction based on the list type for Document Libraries, which is 101.

```
<CustomAction Id="Example1.ECBItemMenu"
  RegistrationType="List"
  RegistrationId="101"
  <!-other attributes omitted for clarity -->
/>
```

While this action adds an ECB menu item for each document in a standard document library, it is not guaranteed to add this ECB menu for all documents. For example, there could be specialized types of document libraries, such as forms libraries (shown later in this chapter) that have a different list type ID.

A second option when creating a CustomAction is to specify the target item in terms of its file extension. This provides the ability to supply a custom ECB menu item for a special type of file, for example, those with .doc, .docx, and .pdf extensions.

```
<CustomAction Id="Example2.ECBItemMenu"
  RegistrationType="FileType"
  RegistrationId="docx"
  <!-other attributes omitted for clarity -->
/>
```

A third option when creating a CustomAction is to specify the target item in terms of its content type, which provides more flexibility because content types support inheritance. When you specify a content type, it automatically includes all of the other content types that inherit from it. For example, if you wanted to add an ECB menu item for every type of item, including documents, you can use the generic Item content type with a RegistrationId of 0x01.

```
<CustomAction Id="Example3.ECBItemMenu"
  RegistrationType="ContentType"
  RegistrationId="0x01"
  <!-other attributes omitted for clarity -->
/>
```

In the DocumentManager feature, a CustomAction element is provided to create a custom ECB menu item for any type of document. Therefore, it has been created in terms of the generic Document content type. The full CustomAction element looks like this:

```
<CustomAction Id="DocumentManager.ECBItemMenu"
  RegistrationType="ContentType"
  RegistrationId="0x0101"
  ImageUrl="/_layouts/images/GORTL.GIF"
  Location="EditControlBlock"
  Sequence="120"
  Title="Document Manager Assistance" >
  <UrlAction Url="~site/_layouts/Litware/
              DocumentManager3.aspx?ItemId={ItemId}&amp;ListId={ListId}"/>
</CustomAction>
```

Note that in this book the string value of the Url attribute of the inner UrlAction element is broken into two lines for readability. However, when you create a CustomAction element in an actual source file, make sure the string value for the Url attribute does not include line breaks.

Once you activate the DocumentManager feature within a site, every document within any document library receives a new ECB menu item with a title of Document Manager Assistance, as shown in Figure 7-3. When a user selects this ECB menu item for a specific document, WSS responds by redirecting the user to the URL specified in the UrlAction element. As discussed in Chapter 2, WSS dynamically replaces the tokens ~site, {ItemId}, and {ListId} when it generates this URL at run time. This resulting URL is site specific and redirects the user to the custom application page named DocumentManager3.aspx with a QueryString indentifying the document and its document library.

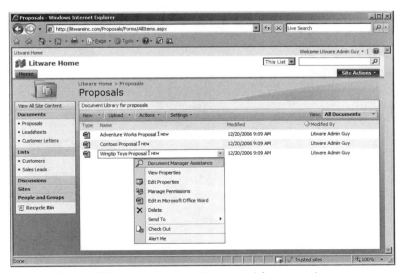

Figure 7-3   An ECB menu item can be created for every document.

Code in the OnLoad event for DocumentManager3.aspx assumes that it can retrieve both the item ID for the document as well as the GUID for its document library from inside the QueryString of the incoming request. By using these pieces of information, the code inside DocumentManager3.aspx can create an SPList object for the document library as well as an SPListItem object for the document. It can also create an SPDocumentLibrary and SPFile object to display the information shown in Figure 7-4.

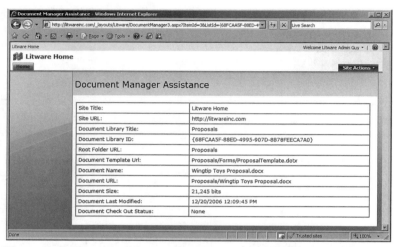

Figure 7-4 DocumentManager3.aspx uses the WSS object model to inspect document properties.

Keep in mind that it's important in some scenarios to perform a test on an SPList object to ensure that it is compatible with the SPDocumentLibrary class before performing a conversion. However, in this particular scenario, this test is unnecessary because the ECB menu item used to redirect users to DocumentManger3.aspx is based on the Document content type. Therefore, this custom menu item appears only in the ECB menu of documents within document libraries. The following is a listing of the code in DocumentManager3.aspx that programs against the document from which the ECB menu item was selected:

```
protected override void OnLoad(EventArgs e) {
  // display information about current site
  SPWeb site = SPContext.Current.Web;
  lblSiteTile.Text = site.Title;
  lblSiteUrl.Text = site.Url.ToLower();

  // display document library information using SPList object
  string ListId = Request.QueryString["ListId"];
  lblListID.Text = ListId;
  SPList list = site.Lists[new Guid(ListId)];
  lblListTile.Text = list.Title;
  lblRootFolderUrl.Text = list.RootFolder.Url;
```

```
    // display document library information using SPDocumentLibrary object
    SPDocumentLibrary documentLibrary = (SPDocumentLibrary)list;
    lblDocumentTemplateUrl.Text = documentLibrary.DocumentTemplateUrl;

    // display document information using SPListItem object
    string ItemId = Request.QueryString["ItemId"];
    SPListItem item = list.Items.GetItemById(Convert.ToInt32(ItemId));
    lblDocumentName.Text = item.Name;
    lblDocumentUrl.Text = item.Url;

    // display document information using SPFile object
    SPFile file = item.File;
    lblFileSize.Text = file.TotalLength.ToString("0,###") + " bits";
    lblFileLastModified.Text = file.TimeLastModified.ToLocalTime().ToString();
    lblFileCheckOutStatus.Text = file.CheckOutStatus.ToString();
}
```

The previous example demonstrates a familiar pattern in a custom solution in which you extend an ECB menu with a menu item that allows the user to navigate to a custom application page that provides information or other options on a specific item or document. Though the custom application page shown here merely displays information, we leave it to your imagination as to how to extend this technique to create custom application pages that assist users by automating document management tasks.

Forms Libraries and Microsoft Office InfoPath

Since Microsoft Windows SharePoint Services 2.0, WSS has provided integration with Office InfoPath through forms libraries. A *forms library* is a specialized type of document library designed to store XML documents created from InfoPath forms. The main difference is that standard document libraries are based on a built-in WSS content type named Document, whereas forms libraries are based on a built-in content type named Form that inherits from Document.

InfoPath and WSS provide a good deal of synergy when used together because users can employ InfoPath to produce XML documents that are then stored in WSS forms libraries. When stored in WSS, these XML documents are afforded all of the benefits of standard document libraries, such as metadata columns, versioning, check-in/checkout, event handlers, and workflows. The fact that InfoPath documents are stored as schema-validated XML documents makes their content very easy to access programmatically.

Although it is not the intention of this book to teach you how to design forms with InfoPath, we do want to provide a quick look at provisioning a forms library and configuring it with a custom InfoPath form template. An InfoPath form template is saved as a CAB file with an .xsn extension. Inside the form template is an .xsd file that defines the XML schema associated with the form template and with all XML documents created from the form template. The DocumentManager sample contains an InfoPath form template named Leadsheet.xsn that provides users with the input form, as shown in Figure 7-5.

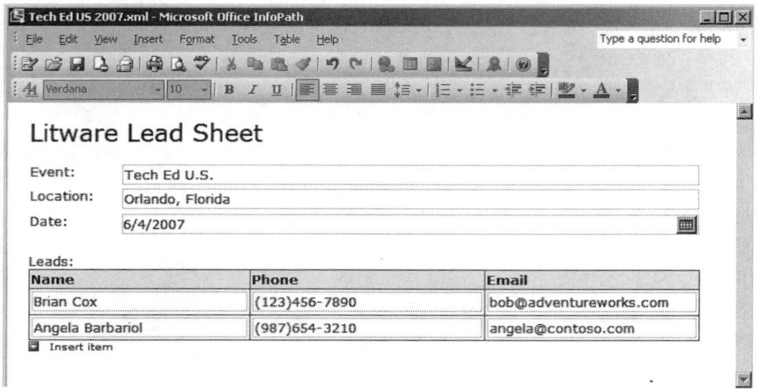

Figure 7-5 A WSS forms library with a custom form template can serve up InfoPath forms.

As you can see from Figure 7-5, the Leadsheet form is used to track sales leads gathered at industry events, such as conferences and trade shows. Each Leadsheet form is designed to track information about a specific event, including its location and date. The Leadsheet form also makes it possible to track many different sales leads. Note that the XML schema behind the Leadsheet form requires at least one sales lead but allows the user to enter as many sales leads as needed.

The DocumentManager feature provisions an instance of a forms library and configures it to use Leadsheet.xsn as its document template by using the same technique shown earlier in this chapter with the Proposals document library. The DocumentManager features contains a ListInstance element to provision the forms library instance as well as a Module element to provision an instance of Leadsheet.xsn into the site so that it can be used as the document template.

```
<ListInstance
 FeatureId="00BFEA71-1E1D-4562-B56A-F05371BB0115"
 TemplateType="115"
 Id="Leadsheets"
 Description="Leadsheets for tracking sales leads"
 OnQuickLaunch="True"
 Title="Leadsheets"
 Url="Leadsheets" >
</ListInstance>

<Module Name="LeadsheetTemplate" List="115" Url="Leadsheets/Forms">
  <File Url="Leadsheet.xsn" Type="GhostableInLibrary" />
</Module>
```

The FeatureId and TemplateType are different than those shown earlier because the forms library type is defined with a type ID of 115 inside another feature named XmlDocument. However, all other aspects of provisioning the forms library instance are the same, including the code in the FeatureActivated event for configuring the document template and other properties of the new forms library. Because a forms library is a specialized type of document library, you can program against it in the FeatureActivated event by using the SPDocument-Library class.

```
SPWeb site = (SPWeb)properties.Feature.Parent;
SPDocumentLibrary libLeadsheets;
libLeadsheets = (SPDocumentLibrary)site.Lists["Leadsheets"];
libLeadsheets.DocumentTemplateUrl = @"Leadsheets/Forms/Leadsheet.xsn";
libLeadsheets.EnableVersioning = true;
libLeadsheets.EnableFolderCreation = false;
libLeadsheets.ForceCheckout = true;
libLeadsheets.Update();
```

You've now seen how to provision the Leadsheets forms library and configure some of its properties. Next, we will bind an event handler to the ItemAdded event that fires whenever a user uploads a new Leadsheet document. This gives us an opportunity to see how to access the content of a document from an event handler that is bound to a document library.

You can bind an event handler to a document library by using a Receivers element in a feature or by using the WSS object model, as demonstrated in Chapter 6. Using a Receivers element in a feature isn't very flexible because you can bind an event handler only by using a list type ID such as 101, which binds the event handler to all standard document libraries, or 115, which binds the event handler to all forms libraries. However, in our case, we simply want to bind an event handler to a single instance of the forms library type, which can be accomplished by calling the Add method on the EventReceivers collection.

```
string asmName = "DocumentManager, [full 4-part name]";
string className = "DocumentManager.ItemEventHandler";
libLeadsheets.EventReceivers.Add(SPEventReceiverType.ItemAdded,
                                 asmName, className);
```

Now that you have seen the code to bind the event handler, let's look at the event handler itself. Just like the event handler for a standard list type, an event handler for a document library is created by using a class that inherits from SPItemEventReceiver. In the following example, we are simply going to handle the ItemAdded event that fires asynchronously after a new InfoPath form is added to the Leadsheets Forms library. The basic structure of the event handler class looks like the following:

```
namespace DocumentManager {
  public class ItemEventHandler : SPItemEventReceiver {
    public override void ItemAdded(SPItemEventProperties properties) {
      SPFile documentFile = properties.ListItem.File;
      using (Stream documentStream = documentFile.OpenBinaryStream()) {
        // program against document stream
      }
    }
  }
}
```

As you can see, the SPItemEventProperties parameter of the ItemAdded method makes it easy to access the SPFile object associated with the InfoPath form that has just been uploaded. Once you have a reference to this SPFile object, you can access the form's content as a byte array by calling the OpenBinary method or as a stream by calling the OpenBinaryStream method. You should observe that the preceding example uses the best practice of opening the stream within a using statement so that the stream object is properly disposed of after it is used.

Once you open a stream to access the InfoPath form's content, you have several options. For example, you can read the XML content inside the form by using a class from the System.Xml namespace, such as XmlReader or XmlDocument. However, there's an easier method. Because every InfoPath form has an associated XML schema, you can use the XSD.EXE utility to generate a schema-derived class, which is the technique used by the DocumentManager solution.

The DocumentManager project contains a source file named Leadsheet.cs that is generated with XSD.EXE from the XML schema associated with the InfoPath form Leadsheet.xsn. Inside Leadsheet.cs are two schema-generated classes named Leadsheet and Lead. You can use the XmlSerializer class to deserialize the XML content in the InfoPath form into strongly typed objects. For example, you can write the code inside the ItemAdded event handler to deserialize the content of the form into a Leadsheet object. You can then access the leads by using a foreach loop to enumerate through Lead objects.

```
XmlSerializer serializer = new XmlSerializer(typeof(LeadSheet));
SPFile docFile = properties.ListItem.File;
using (Stream documentStream = docFile.OpenBinaryStream()) {
  LeadSheet leadsheet = (LeadSheet)serializer.Deserialize(documentStream);
  foreach (Lead lead in leadsheet.Lead) {
    string leadName = lead.Name;
    string phone = lead.Phone;
    string email = lead.Email;
  }
}
```

The DocumentManager demonstrates this technique by deserializing the Leadsheet data and writing information about each of the leads into a WSS list in the current site named Sales Leads. Each time that a new InfoPath form is uploaded, this event handler automates the task of taking the data inside it and writing it into a list. The following code is a complete listing of the ItemAdded event handler from the DocumentManager solution.

```
public override void ItemAdded(SPItemEventProperties properties) {
  XmlSerializer serializer = new XmlSerializer(typeof(LeadSheet));
  SPWeb site = properties.OpenWeb();
  SPList targetList = site.Lists["Sales Leads"];
  SPFile docFile = properties.ListItem.File;
  using (Stream documentStream = docFile.OpenBinaryStream()) {
    LeadSheet sheet = (LeadSheet)serializer.Deserialize(documentStream);
    foreach (Lead lead in sheet.Lead) {
      SPListItem newItem = targetList.Items.Add();
      newItem["Lead Name"] = lead.Name;
      newItem["Phone"] = lead.Phone;
      newItem["Email"] = lead.Email;
      newItem.Update();
    }
  }
}
```

It's important to note that after-the-fact events, such as ItemAdded, fire asynchronously, which means that the event handler might continue to run even after control is returned back to the user. Asynchronous event handlers run under the identity of the user that triggers them. For example, imagine that the user Brian Cox uploads a new InfoPath form that causes this event handler to run. When the ItemAdded event handler adds new items to the Sales Leads list, it does so with Brian's permissions and with Brian's identity. We will discuss how you can change this default behavior of an event handler when we discuss security in Chapter 10, "Application Security."

> **Tip**   If you are using only WSS and not Microsoft Office SharePoint Server (MOSS), the use of InfoPath forms requires the installation of Microsoft InfoPath on the desktop of each user who requires access to these forms. However, MOSS provides new technology involving server-side components that can render InfoPath forms within a browser, thus eliminating a user's dependency on InfoPath as well as eliminating dependencies on the Microsoft Internet Explorer Web browser and the Microsoft Windows operating system. This technology is included with Office Forms Services, which is part of the MOSS Enterprise Edition and also in a standalone product named Office Forms Server.

Office Open XML File Formats

The remainder of this chapter discusses how to generate documents by using the new Office Open XML file formats that are being introduced with the 2007 Microsoft Office System. As you will see, these new file formats make it possible to generate Office Word 2007 documents and Office Excel 2007 workbooks on the server without running a desktop version of Word or Excel. Along the way, we will describe what makes using the Office Open XML file formats especially attractive when creating custom solutions for WSS and MOSS.

The Office Open XML file format specification was approved in 2006 by Ecma International as the Ecma 376 standard and was under review by the ISO international standards body at press time. You can download the Office Open XML specification as well as other great online resources at *http://openxmldeveloper.com*. Our goal in this chapter is to get you up and running with the programming techniques required to create simple Word documents within a WSS solution.

Motivation for the Office Open XML File Format

It used to be challenging to write and deploy server-side applications that could read, modify, and generate documents used by the Microsoft Office suite of applications. The older binary file format used by Word, Excel, and Office PowerPoint was introduced in 1997 and remained the default file format up through the Microsoft Office 2003 editions. Experience has shown that this binary file format has proven to be too tricky for most companies to work with directly because one little mistake in the code that generates or modifies an Office document typically corrupts the entire file. The vast majority of production applications that read and write documents using the Microsoft Office 2003 editions (or earlier) do so by going through the object model of the hosting application.

Custom applications and components that use the application object model, such as Word or Excel, run much better on the desktop than they do in server-side scenarios. Anyone who has spent time writing the extra infrastructure code required to make a desktop application behave reliably on the server will tell you it's a hack because desktop applications, such as Word and Excel, were never designed to run on the server. They require a custom utility program to terminate and restart them whenever they encounter a modal dialog box that requires human intervention.

What is far more desirable in a server-side scenario is the ability to read and write documents without going through the object model of the hosting application. The Microsoft Office 2000 and Microsoft Office 2003 editions introduced some modest capabilities for using XML to create the content for Excel workbooks and Word documents. This advancement introduced the possibility of writing portions of a document by using an XML parser, such as the one contained in the .NET Framework provided through the *System.XML* namespace.

With the 2007 Microsoft Office System, Microsoft has taken this idea much further by adopting the Office Open XML file formats for documents used by Word, Excel, and PowerPoint. Office Open XML file formats are an exciting advancement for WSS and MOSS developers because these formats provide the ability to read, write, and generate a Word document, Excel workbook, or PowerPoint presentation on the server without requiring the hosting Web server to run a desktop application.

Word 2007 Document Internals

Let's begin by examining the structure of a simple Word document based on the Office Open XML file formats. Office Open XML file formats are based on standard ZIP file technology. Each top-level file is saved as a ZIP archive, which means you are able to open a Word document just as you would any other ZIP file and snoop around inside by using the ZIP file support built into Windows Explorer.

You should note that the 2007 Microsoft Office suite of applications, such as Word and Excel, introduced new file extensions for documents that use the new formats. For example, the .docx extension is used for Word documents stored in the Office Open XML file format, whereas the older and more familiar .doc extension continues to be used for Word documents stored in the older binary format.

Once Word 2007 is installed, you can start by creating a new Word document and adding the text "Hello World." Save the document using the default format to a new file named Hello.docx and close Word. Next, locate Hello.docx in the file system by using Windows Explorer. Rename it Hello.zip. This enables Windows Explorer to recognize the file as a ZIP archive. You can now open the Hello.zip archive and see the structure of folders and files that Word created, as shown in Figure 7-6.

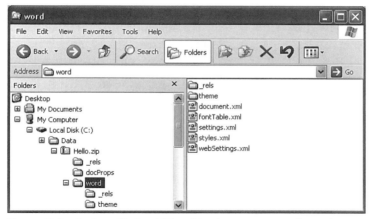

Figure 7-6 A .docx file is a ZIP archive known as a package that contains parts and items.

After this quick look inside a .docx file, it's time to introduce some basic concepts and terminology involved with documents conforming to the Office Open XML file formats. The top-level file (such as Hello.docx) is known as a *package*. Because a package is implemented as a standard ZIP archive, it automatically provides compression and makes its contents instantly accessible to many existing utilities and APIs on Windows platforms and non-Windows platforms alike.

Inside a package are two kinds of internal components: *parts* and *items*. In general, parts contain content and items contain metadata describing the parts. Items can be further subdivided into *relationship items* and *content-type items*. We will now dive into a bit more detail on each type of component.

A *part* is an internal component containing content that is persisted inside the package. The majority of parts are simple text files serialized as XML with an associated XML schema. However, parts can also be serialized as binary data when necessary, such as when a Word document contains a graphic image or media file.

A part is named by using a uniform resource identifier (URI) that contains its relative path within the package file combined with the part file name. For example, the main part within the package for a Word document is named /word/document.xml. The following list presents examples of typical part names that you will find inside the package for a simple Word document.

```
/docProps/app.xml
/docProps/core.xml
/word/document.xml
/word/fontTable.xml
/word/settings.xml
/word/styles.xml
/word/theme/theme1.xml
```

Office Open XML file formats use *relationships* to define associations between a source and a target part. A *package relationship* defines an association between the top-level package and a part. A *part relationship* defines an association between a parent part and a child part.

Relationships are important because they make these associations discoverable without examining the content within the parts in question. Relationships are independent of content-specific schemas and are, therefore, faster to resolve. An additional benefit is that you can establish a relationship between two parts without modifying either of them.

Relationships are defined in internal components known as relationship items. A *relationship item* is stored inside the package just like a part, although a relationship item is not actually considered a part. For consistency, relationship items are always created inside folders named _rels.

For example, a package contains exactly one package relationship item named /_rels/.rels. The package relationship item contains XML elements to define package relationships, such as the one between the top-level package for a .docx file and the internal part /word/document.xml.

```xml
<?xml version="1.0" encoding="UTF-8" standalone="yes"?>
<Relationships xmlns="../package/2006/relationships ">
  <Relationship Id="rId1"
                Type="../officeDocument/2006/relationships/officeDocument"
                Target="word/document.xml"/>
</Relationships>
```

As you can see, a Relationship element defines a name, type, and target part. You should also observe that the type name for a relationship is defined by using the same conventions used to create XML namespaces.

In addition to a single package relationship item, a package can also contain one or more part relationship items. For example, you define relationships between /word/document.xml and child parts inside a package relationship item located at the URI /word/_rels/document.xml.rels. Note that the Target attribute for a relationship in a part relationship item is a URI relative to the parent part and not the top-level package.

Every part inside a package is defined in terms of a specific content type. Don't confuse these content types with a content type in WSS because the two are distinct. A content type within a package is metadata that defines a part's media type, a subtype, and a set of optional parameters. Any content type used within a package must be explicitly defined inside a component known as a *content type item*. Each package has exactly one content type item named /[Content_Types].xml. The following is an example of content type definitions inside the /[Content_Types].xml item of a typical Word document.

```xml
<?xml version="1.0" encoding="UTF-8" standalone="yes"?>
<Types xmlns="http://schemas.openxmlformats.org/package/2006/content-types">
  <Default
     Extension="rels"
     ContentType="application/vnd.openxmlformats-
                  package.relationships+xml"/>
  <Default
     Extension="xml"
     ContentType="application/xml"/>
```

```
    <Override
     PartName="/word/document.xml"
     ContentType="application/vnd.openxmlformats-
                  officedocument.wordprocessingml.document.main+xml "/>
   </Types>
```

Content types are used by the consumer of a package to interpret how to read and render the content within its parts. As you can see in the previous listing, a default content type is typically associated with a file extension, such as .rels or .xml. Override content types are used to define a specific part in terms of a content type that differs from the default content type associated with its file extension. For example, /word/document.xml is associated with an Override content type that differs from the default content type used for files with an .xml extension.

Generating Your First .docx File

Although there are several existing libraries that you can use to read and write to ZIP archives, you should prefer using the new packaging API that is part of the WindowsBase.dll assembly that ships with the .NET 3.0 Framework because the packaging API is aware of the Office Open XML file formats. For example, certain convenience methods make it easy to add relationship elements to a relationship item and add content type elements to a content type item. The packaging API makes things easier because you never have to touch relationship or content type items directly.

One of the nice things about developing for WSS 3.0 is that it has dependency on the .NET 3.0 Framework. You can be certain that the WindowsBase assembly and packaging API will always be available on any Web server running WSS 3.0 or MOSS.

To begin programming against the packaging API in a Microsoft Visual Studio 2005 project, you should add a reference to the WindowsBase assembly, as shown in Figure 7-7.

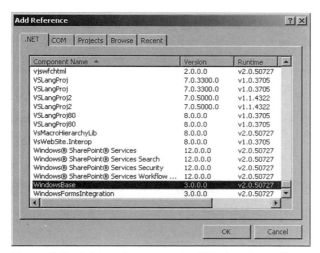

Figure 7-7   Add a reference to the WindowsBase.dll assembly to begin programming against the new packaging API.

Let's begin by creating a simple console application that generates a .docx file using the Office Open XML file formats. We will then modify the code to generate a .docx file on the server from a custom application page in the DocumentManager solution in response to a client request from the browser.

The classes that make up the packaging API are contained inside the System.IO.Package namespace. When working with packages, you are also frequently programming against older (and hopefully familiar) classes in the System.IO and System.Xml namespaces. Examine the following code that shows the skeleton for creating a new package:

```
using System;
using System.IO;
using System.IO.Packaging;
using System.Xml;

namespace HelloDocx {
  class Program {
    static void Main() {
      // (1) create a new package
      Package package = Package.Open(@"c:\Data\Hello.docx",
                         FileMode.Create,
                         FileAccess.ReadWrite);
      // (2) WRITE CODE HERE TO CREATE PARTS AND ADD CONTENT
      // (3) close package
      package.Close();
    }
  }
}
```

The System.IO.Packaging namespace contains the Package class that exposes a shared method named Open that can be used to create new packages as well as to open existing packages. As with many other classes that deal with file IO, a call to Open should always be complemented with a call to Close.

Once you create the new package, the next step is to create one or more parts and serialize content into them. In our next example, we follow the official guidelines for a "hello world" application that requires the creation of a single part named /word/document.xml. You can create a part by calling the CreatePart method on an open Package object and passing parameters for a URI and a string-based content type.

```
// create main document part (document.xml) ...
Uri uri = new Uri("/word/document.xml", UriKind.Relative);
string partContentType;
partContentType = "application/vnd.openxmlformats" +
                  "-officedocument.wordprocessingml.document.main+xml";
PackagePart part = package.CreatePart(uri, partContentType);

// get stream for document.xml
StreamWriter streamPart;
streamPart = new StreamWriter(part.GetStream(FileMode.Create,
                                             FileAccess.Write));
```

The call to CreatePart passes a URI based on the path /word/document.xml and the content type that's required by the Office Open XML file formats for the part in a word processing document containing the main story. Once you create a part, you must serialize your content into it by using standard stream-based programming techniques. The previous code opens a stream on the part by calling the GetStream method and uses this stream object to initialize a StreamWriter object.

The StreamWriter object is used to serialize the "hello world" XML document into document.xml. However, it's important that you understand what the resulting XML is going to look like. Examine the following XML that represents the simplest of XML documents that can be serialized into document.xml.

```
<?xml version="1.0" encoding="utf-8"?>
<w:document xmlns:w="http://schemas.openxmlformats.org/wordprocessingml/2006/main">
  <w:body>
    <w:p>
      <w:r>
        <w:t>Hello Open XML</w:t>
      </w:r>
    </w:p>
  </w:body>
</w:document>
```

Note that all elements within this XML document are defined within the *http://schemas.openxmlformats.org/wordprocessingml/2006/main* namespace as required by the Office Open XML file formats. The XML document contains a high-level document element, and within the document element is a body element that contains the main story of the Word document itself.

Within the body element is a <p> element for each paragraph. Within the <p> element is an <r> element that defines a run. A *run* is a region of elements that share the same set of characteristics. Within the run is a <t> element that defines a range of text.

It is now time to generate this XML document with code by using the XmlWriter class from the System.Xml namespace. Examine how the following code creates these elements within the proper structure and by using the appropriate namespace.

```
// define string variable for Open XML namespace for nsWP:
string nsWP = "http://schemas.openxmlformats.org" +
              "/wordprocessingml/2006/main";

// write elements into XML document...
XmlWriter writer = XmlWriter.Create(streamPart);
writer.WriteStartDocument();
writer.WriteStartElement("w", "document", nsWP);
writer.WriteStartElement("body", nsWP);
writer.WriteStartElement("p", nsWP);
writer.WriteStartElement("r", nsWP);
writer.WriteStartElement("t", nsWP);
// write hello world text into Word Text element
```

```
writer.WriteValue("Hello Open XML");
// close all elements
writer.WriteEndElement();
writer.WriteEndElement();
writer.WriteEndElement();
writer.WriteEndElement();
writer.WriteEndElement();
writer.WriteEndDocument();
// close XmlWriter object
writer.Close();
```

We are through writing the XML content into document.xml. The final step is to create a relationship between the package and document.xml by calling the CreateRelationship method of the Package object. This is an easy process as long as you know the correct string value for the relationship type and can come up with a unique name (such as "rId1") for the relationship being created.

```
// create the relationship part
string relationshipType;
relationshipType = "http://schemas.openxmlformats.org" +
                   "/officeDocument/2006/relationships/officeDocument";
package.CreateRelationship(uri,
                           TargetMode.Internal,
                           relationshipType,
                           "rId1");
package.Flush();
```

You should observe the call to Flush after the call to CreateRelationship. This call forces the packaging API to update the package relationship item with the proper Relationship element. The final call to the Close method of the Package object completes the package serialization and releases the file handle on Hello.docx.

You have viewed all of the necessary steps to generate a simple .docx file from a console application written in C#. If you want to step through this console application, it is available on the companion Web site in the project named HelloDocx.

Generating .docx Files on the Server

The first thing to consider when modifying code from the console application to run on a Web server is that you probably want to avoid saving the package as a physical file on the host computer. Instead, it is faster to write the contents of the package file into a MemoryStream object created within the hosting IIS worker process. Once you write the package file contents into memory, you can then write the file back to the client by using the OutputStream object of the ASP.NET Response object.

Let's start by changing the code to use a MemoryStream object instead of a physical file. Examine the following code that has been added to a server-side event handler inside an ASP.NET 2.0 page in the Visual Studio Web site project named HelloDocxfromASPNET.

```
// create in-memory stream as buffer
MemoryStream bufferStream = new MemoryStream();
// create new package in memory stream
Package package = Package.Open(bufferStream,
                               FileMode.Create,
                               FileAccess.ReadWrite);
// this calls same code shown in previous HelloDocx example
WriteContentToPackage(package);
// save/close package object leaving DOCX file in MemoryStream
package.Close();
// (1) TODO - SET UP HTTP HEADERS FOR RESPONSE
// (2) TODO - WRITE PACKAGE CONTENT INTO RESPONSE BODY
```

Note that the first parameter to Package.Open has changed from the string-based file path to a MemoryStream object. This approach enables you to reuse the same code for generating the package file and its parts that was shown in the previous console application example. However, you need not worry about creating and naming an OS-level file. This approach also provides faster response times and better throughput in high-traffic scenarios because it eliminates any need for disk I/O.

The previous code in this section creates a MemoryStream object and then serializes a .docx file into it just as you would serialize a .docx file into a physical file. The code inside the custom WriteContentToPackage method was taken directly from the HelloDocx console application project shown earlier, but it's now creating a package and serializing it into a buffer in memory instead of into a physical file.

Once you write the package into the MemoryStream object and call Close on the package object, you are done with the packaging API. Let's assume that we don't want to store the newly created package file on the server in this case. Instead, we simply want to send it back to the client for viewing and editing. This also gives the user the option to save the package file locally or back into a WSS document library. All that's left to do is set up the appropriate HTTP headers and write the package content into the body of the response that is being sent back to the client.

Let's start with the HTTP headers. You should call methods on the ASP.NET Response object to clear any existing headers and add a content disposition header specifying that the response contains an attachment with the file name Hello.docx.

```
Response.ClearHeaders();
Response.AddHeader("content-disposition",
                   "attachment; filename=Hello.docx");
```

Next, you must set up the encoding and Multipurpose Internet Mail Extensions (MIME) content type for the HTTP response and then write the binary content for the package into the body of the HTTP response. This can be accomplished with the following code:

```
Response.ClearContent();
Response.ContentEncoding = System.Text.Encoding.UTF8;
Response.ContentType = "application/vnd.ms-word.document.12";
```

```
// write package to response stream
bufferStream.Position = 0;
BinaryWriter writer = new BinaryWriter(Response.OutputStream);
BinaryReader reader = new BinaryReader(bufferStream);
writer.Write(reader.ReadBytes((int)bufferStream.Length));
reader.Close();
writer.Close();
bufferStream.Close();
// flush and close the response object
Response.Flush();
Response.Close();
```

Note that the last two calls to Response.Flush and Response.Close are required to make sure the entire package is completely written into the HTTP response before it is transmitted back to the caller. If you would like to test the code you have just seen, the sample code for this chapter contains a directory named HelloDocxFromASPNET that contains an ASP.NET 2.0 Web site with a functioning version. Using Visual Studio, you can use the Open Web Site command and open the directory for this project through the file system.

When you run the code behind the default.aspx to generate the .docx file, it executes all of the code you have just seen and transmits the file back to the user. As long as the client machine is configured to understand the MIME content type associated with a .docx file, the user is presented with the dialog box shown in Figure 7-8, which provides the option to open the document immediately within Word or to save it to a location on the local hard drive. The correct MIME type is configured whenever you install Word 2007, and it is also configured to work correctly with earlier versions of Word as long as you install the converter for .docx files that can be downloaded for free from the Microsoft public Web site.

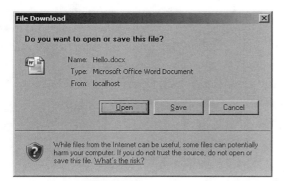

Figure 7-8 When you set up the appropriate MIME content type, the user is given a chance to open a server-side–generated .docx file directly in Word.

If the user clicks the Open button, the .docx file opens automatically in Word. It is interesting to note that, up to this point, the package file has never been saved as a physical file to the file system, but has only been stored in memory both on the Web server and on the client desktop computer. If the user closes the document without saving it, it is as if it never existed at all. This approach of generating documents on the server is ideal for creating letters, memos, customer lists, and other types of documents based on data in WSS lists and databases.

Although the Word document we just created was perhaps a little boring, the concepts and possibilities of what you can do with the Office Open XML file formats are far more exciting. With a little imagination, you can start pulling data from WSS lists as well as backend databases and Web services to create Word documents that make your users and their managers happy. Once again, we encourage you to frequent the community site at *http://openxmldeveloper.com* to view some great examples and expand your horizons even further.

Saving a .docx File in a Document Library

The last two examples demonstrated how to generate a .docx file from both a console application and a standard ASP.NET 2.0 page. Now that you know the basic concepts, we will move ahead and provide some examples in a custom application page that's part of the Document-Manager solution.

The DocumentManager4.aspx application page, which is accessible through the Site Actions menu, enables a user to select a customer and a letter template, as shown in Figure 7-9. Note that the DocumentManager feature adds a Customers list and a Letter Templates list and populates each of them with some sample data during feature activation. Once the user selects a customer and letter template, two command buttons with event handlers demonstrate two different methods to create a .docx file. Although the two event handlers use different techniques to create a customer letter, both save the resulting .docx file to a document library named Customer Letters.

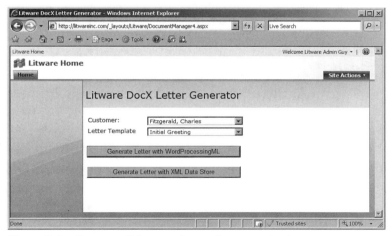

Figure 7-9   DocumentManager4.aspx demonstrates two ways to generate a .docx file from WSS list data.

Open the DocumentManager4.aspx application page in Visual Studio and look at the event handler named cmdGenerateLetter1_Click, which provides the code to determine the selected customer and letter templates. It then uses this data to retrieve the required information to generate a customer letter from the Customers and Letter Templates lists. It accomplishes this task by creating a package file in a MemoryStream object and dynamically generating the document.xml part as you saw in the last example.

This example differs from the previous one because it saves the generated .docx file into a document library named Customer Letters. To accomplish this, the code must determine the path to the document library as well as the path to be used to save the .docx file.

```
SPDocumentLibrary targetLibrary;
targetLibrary = (SPDocumentLibrary)site.Lists["Customer Letters"];
string libraryRelativePath = targetLibrary.RootFolder.ServerRelativeUrl;
string libraryPath = siteCollection.MakeFullUrl(libraryRelativePath);
string documentName = "CustomerLetter01.docx";
string documentPath = libraryPath + "/" + documentName;
```

Once you determine the document path and write the package for the .docx file into a memory stream, you can call the Add method of the current site's Files collection.

```
MemoryStream documentStream = new MemoryStream();
// create new package in memory stream
Package package = Package.Open(documentStream,
                               FileMode.Create,
                               FileAccess.ReadWrite);
// Code to write package for .docx file omitted for clarity
package.Close();
site.Files.Add(documentPath, documentStream, true);
Response.Redirect(libraryPath);
```

If you examine the code inside the cmdGenerateLetter1_Click event handler that generates the WordProcessingML content for document.xml, you see that it is more involved than the Hello World example shown earlier. The code demonstrates the creation of multiple paragraphs in a document as well as using line breaks and paragraph formatting.

A Closer Look at Relationships

The structure of a package in the Office Open XML file formats is heavily dependent on relationships. If you create parts but fail to associate them to the package through relationships, then consumer applications (such as Word) are not able to recognize them because every part must have a relationship or a chain of relationships that associate it with its containing package.

As discussed earlier in this chapter, package relationships define an association between a package and its top-level parts. Figure 7-10 shows that the typical top-level parts in a .docx file created with Word 2007 are /docProps/app.xml, /docProps/core.xml, and /word/document.xml. Part relationships define a parent-child relationship between two parts within the same package. The part /word/document.xml typically has relationships to several different child parts, such as /word/settings.xml and /word/styles.xml.

Figure 7-10 A package defines a hierarchy of relationships in which the package is always the root.

The Office Open XML file format specification states that every part inside a package must be associated either directly or indirectly with the package itself. A part, such as /word/document.xml, is directly associated with the package through a package relationship. Another part, such as /word/styles.xml, is associated with the package indirectly because it is associated with the top-level part /word/document.xml that is, in turn, associated with the package.

A very important concept to understand is that a consumer application must be able to discover any part within a package by enumerating through its relationships. In fact, when you are writing your own applications that read packages created by other applications, such as Word 2007 and Excel 2007, you are also encouraged to discover the existing parts by enumerating relationships.

Package Viewer Sample Application

As mentioned earlier, the specification for the Office Open XML file format states that all parts within a package must be discoverable through relationships. Therefore, it's possible to write an application that inspects a package and displays all of the parts inside it.

This chapter is accompanied by a sample Windows Forms application named the Package Viewer, which is available on the companion Web site. You can open this project in Visual Studio and run it to test out the code. The Package Viewer application enables the user to open a file structured using the Office Open XML file formats. When the user opens a package file, the Package Viewer populates a TreeView control with nodes that show a package and all of its parts nested within a hierarchy of relationships, as shown in Figure 7-11. The application also provides more information about the package and specific parts when you click a node in the tree view. For each part, you can see its content type, its parent, and the relationship type that associates it with its parent.

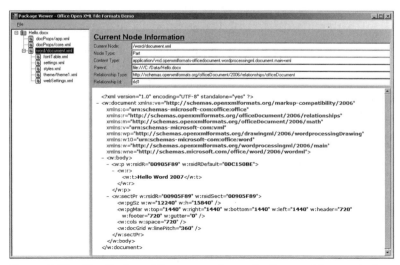

Figure 7-11 The Package Viewer sample application enables you to inspect the parts within a package.

The Package Viewer application enables the user to select a package file by using the standard Open File dialog box. Once the user selects a file, the application enumerates through all of the package relationships to discover the top-level parts.

The Package Viewer also provides the functionality to display the contents of any XML-based parts within the package by reopening the package and acquiring stream-based access to the target part. The XML-based content of the part is then written to a temporary file. Finally, the file is loaded into the Windows Forms WebBrowser control, which displays the XML content with color coding and collapsible sections. Hopefully, you will find this sample application useful as you begin learning about the parts and the XML required to work with Office Open XML file format documents.

From our discussion so far, you should have a better idea concerning what's required to generate documents for Word, Excel, and PowerPoint using the Office Open XML file formats. In theory, it's quite simple. All that you must do is create a new package file, add the required parts, and fill them up with XML content structured in accordance with the appropriate XML schemas. Yet though the theory is simple, the learning curve for getting up to speed on the practical details takes some time. It also requires that you read through the relevant sections of the Office Open XML file formats that can be downloaded from *http://openxmldeveloper.org*.

If you are going to work with Word documents, you must learn what types of parts go inside a package and how they must be structured in terms of content types and relationships. You also must learn how to generate the WordProcessingML that goes inside each of these parts. If you want to work with Excel spreadsheets, the content types and relationships are different. Instead of using WordProcessingML, you need to learn SpreadsheetML. It takes an investment on your part if you want to generate the XML required to create documents from scratch that contain things such as tables, graphics, and fancy formatting. However, the value of programmatically generating rich documents directly from backend data is often well worth the investment.

Data Binding to Word Content Controls

We conclude this chapter by showing you one more technique for creating professional-looking Word 2007 documents. However, this technique does not require you to write any code to generate WordProcessingML at run time.

We start by introducing two new features of Word 2007 that can be used when working with documents stored in the new Office Open XML file formats. The first feature is the *XML Data Store*, which enables you to embed one or more user-defined XML documents as parts inside a .docx file. The second feature is *Content Controls*, which are user interface components defined inside the /word/document.xml part that support data entry and data binding.

If you want to experiment with using Content Controls, you should first go to the Word Options dialog box in Word 2007 and enable the Show Developer Tab In The Ribbon option.

Enable and navigate to the Developer tab to find the set of controls that can be added to a Word document, as shown in Figure 7-12.

Figure 7-12   The Developer tab in Word 2007 provides a set of Content Controls.

Note that you can add Content Controls to only Word documents that are stored in the new .docx format. Content Controls are not supported in .doc files because they cannot be defined by using the older binary format. However, when working in the new format, Content Controls can be added to provide user input elements into a Word document. For example, you can construct a Word document that solicits the user for certain pieces of information to complete a business document, as shown in Figure 7-13.

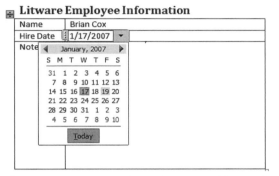

Figure 7-13   Content Controls can provide user input capabilities to a Word document.

Keep in mind that Content Controls have two different modes: edit mode and display mode. Edit mode enables the user to do things such as type text, pick a date from a date picker, or select an item from a drop-down list. Display mode is optimized for displaying and printing. In other words, the editing aspects of Content Controls are invisible to a user who is no longer in edit mode.

Separating Data from Presentation in Word 2007

Although the XML Data Store and Content Controls are two separate features of Word 2007 that can be used independently of one another, they provide a powerful level of synergy when used together. For example, you can embed an XML document customer data or an invoice inside a Word document. You can then bind Content Controls to data inside this XML document by using XPath expressions. This effectively enables you to separate your data from the formatting instructions that tell Word how to display it.

The second example of generating a .docx file in the DocumentManager4.aspx custom application page doesn't involve writing code to generate WordProcessingML. Instead, it works with a standard XML document that holds the data required to create a customer letter. The following example demonstrates what one of these XML document instances looks like.

```xml
<?xml version="1.0" encoding="UTF-8" standalone="yes"?>
<LitwareLetter xmlns:xsi="http://www.w3.org/2001/XMLSchema-instance"
               xmlns:xsd="http://www.w3.org/2001/XMLSchema"
               xmlns="http://litware.com/2006/letters">

  <Customer>
    <FirstName>Brian</FirstName>
    <LastName>Cox</LastName>
    <Company>Litware</Company>
    <Address>1000 Madison Ave</Address>
    <City>Las Vegas</City>
    <State>NV</State>
    <Zip>32145</Zip>
  </Customer>

  <Date>December 25, 2006</Date>

  <Body>We miss you. Please give us a call.</Body>

  <Employee>
    <Name>Angela Barbariol</Name>
  </Employee>

</LitwareLetter>
```

Using the technique discussed here usually involves manually manipulating the contents of the .docx file that you intend to use as the template. When you begin building a template from a new .docx file, you should change its file extension to .zip so that you can open the package file directly and add parts by dragging them into the package by using Windows Explorer.

Inside the sample code for this chapter is a directory named LitwareLetterTemplate. Inside this directory is a sample template file named LetterTemplate.docx that contains all of the necessary parts and relationships for binding Content Controls to an XML document in the XML Data Store. We encourage you to inspect LetterTemplate.docx with the Package Viewer application because this allows you to see quickly how all of the pieces fit together.

The XML document shown in this section is embedded as a part inside the LetterTemplate.docx file using the URI /customXml/item1.xml. Note that you can name this part something other than item1.xml. However, in this example, we wanted to be consistent with the names that Word 2007 uses when it creates and renames parts in the XML Data Store.

The next thing you must do is create a way to identify the content within the customer XML document. You do this by defining a datastoreItem with an identifying GUID, which is accomplished by creating a part named /customXml/itemProps1.xml and establishing a relation between it and its parent part /customXml/item1.xml. The following example displays what the contents of /customXml/itemProps1.xml should look like.

```xml
<?xml version="1.0" encoding="UTF-8" standalone="no" ?>
<ds:datastoreItem ds:itemID="{00295134-23AA-4F2E-B2D5-494BBA5D5434}"
 xmlns:ds="http://schemas.openxmlformats.org/officeDocument/2006/customXml">
  <ds:schemaRefs>
    <ds:schemaRef ds:uri="http://www.w3.org/2001/XMLSchema" />
    <ds:schemaRef ds:uri="http://litware.com/2006/letters" />
  </ds:schemaRefs>
</ds:datastoreItem>
```

The next step is to create a part relationship between /word/document.xml and /customXml/item1.xml. The relationship should define the parent part as /word/document.xml and the child part as /customXml/item1.xml, and the relationship type should be established using the following string.

```
http://schemas.openxmlformats.org/officeDocument/2006/relationships/customXml
```

After you have completed these steps to set up a user-defined XML document as an identifiable datastoreItem, you can now access its data from /word/document.xml. For example, you can write VBA code behind a macro-enabled Word 2007 document that retrieves a CustomXmlPart object from the ActiveDocument object and pulls the required customer data out of the embedded XML document. In our case, we are going to create Content Controls in /word/document.xml and bind them to particular elements within the XML document with the customer data.

Unfortunately, Word 2007 provides no way through its user interface to bind Content Controls to elements within the XML Data Store. Therefore, you are required to make direct edits to a /word/document.xml part by using an XML editor, such as Visual Studio 2005. In the following example of the WordprocessingML element, you can add to the /word/document.xml part to create a binding to the FirstName element within the Customer element of the user-defined XML document.

```xml
<w:sdtPr>
  <w:dataBinding
  w:prefixMappings="xmlns:ns0='http://litware.com/2006/letters'"
  w:xpath="/ns0:LitwareLetter[1]/ns0:Customer[1]/ns0:FirstName"
  w:storeItemID="{00295134-23AA-4F2E-B2D5-494BBA5D5434}" />
</w:sdtPr>
```

The data-binding element contains a storeItemID attribute that references the GUID of the datastoreItem that holds the customer data. The data-binding element also contains an xpath attribute that defines an XPath expression to bind the Content Control to a specific element within the user-defined XML file. Once you have updated the /word/document.xml file to contain all of the data-binding elements you need to display the relevant data from the user-defined XML file, you can construct a Word document with bound controls that can read from and write back to the item1.xml part.

Although it might take some time to become fluent with the technique of manually constructing Word documents that contain user-defined XML files and bound Content Controls, it is often well worth the effort. The design approach provides an elegant solution to separating your data from the presentation of that data. Once you have created a minimal Word document with bound Content Controls, you can do the rest of the work in making the document look professional directly within Word. For example, you can add literal text and a logo just like any other Word user. You can create new tables and sections and simply drag the Content Controls where you would like them to appear.

It's also important to keep in mind that bound Content Controls can provide two-way synchronization with data in a user-defined XML file. Although users can see whatever data you have added to the user-defined XML file, they can also update this data. When a user updates the data in a Content Control and saves the document, those changes are written back to the user-defined XML file. This makes it very easy to extract the updated data in an XML format that can conform to any XML schema that you would like to work with.

Updating the XML Data Store Programmatically

You have seen how to bind Content Controls to a user-defined XML document in the XML Data Store. The final step is to write code that generates a new instance of that XML document with the data for a particular customer letter and to overwrite the XML document inside an existing Word document template that is set up with the proper bound Content Controls.

Now let's return to the custom application page named DocumentManager4.aspx and discuss the code behind the second command button's OnClick event handler. This code loads the pre-defined document template named LetterTemplate.docx into a MemoryStream object and then opens it with the .NET 3.0 packaging API.

```
Stream documentStream = new MemoryStream();
SPFile DocumentTemplate =
        site.GetFile(libraryPath + "/Forms/LetterTemplate.docx");
Stream documentTemplateStream = DocumentTemplate.OpenBinaryStream();
BinaryReader DocumentTemplateReader;
DocumentTemplateReader = new BinaryReader(documentTemplateStream);
BinaryWriter DocumentWriter = new BinaryWriter(documentStream);
DocumentWriter.Write(
    DocumentTemplateReader.ReadBytes((int)documentTemplateStream.Length));
DocumentWriter.Flush();
DocumentTemplateReader.Close();
documentTemplateStream.Dispose();
```

```
// open .docx file in memory stream as package file
Package package = Package.Open(documentStream,
                               FileMode.Open,
                               FileAccess.ReadWrite);


// retrieve package part with XML data
Uri uriData = new Uri("/customXML/item1.xml", UriKind.Relative);
PackagePart LetterXmlPart = package.GetPart(uriData);


// get stream for item1.xml and delete any content that's inside it
Stream LetterXmlPartStream = LetterXmlPart.GetStream();
LetterXmlPartStream.SetLength(0);
```

Once LetterTemplate.docx is loaded into a MemoryStream object, the code in this listing obtains stream-based access to the /customXML/item1.xml part and deletes any existing content inside. All that is now required is to write a new XML document with content for a new customer letter into this part. In our example, we create the new XML document instance by using a schema-generated class named LitwareLetter that is defined in the source file LitwareLetter.cs. Once the code creates an instance of the LitwareLetter class and initializes it with data for a specific customer letter, it then serializes the XML document into item1.xml by using an XmlSerialization object.

```
// create objects from schema-generated types
LitwareLetter letter = new LitwareLetter();
// code to populate LitwareLetter object omitted for clarity
XmlSerializer serializer = new XmlSerializer(typeof(LitwareLetter));
serializer.Serialize(LetterXmlPartStream, letter);
//close package file to finalize writing to memory buffer
LetterXmlPartStream.Close();
package.Close();
// add new .docx file into target library
site.Files.Add(documentPath, documentStream, true);
```

As you can see, there is also code to close the stream used to access item1.xml and close the package file itself. Finally, a call to the Add method of the current SPWeb object's Files collection is used to actually save the new .docx file into the document library named Customer Letters. The resulting Word document produced by this code is shown in Figure 7-14. The resulting document is richly formatted, but our code does not need to deal with that aspect because the formatting is part of the document template and is separated from the letter content.

This concludes our introduction to generating documents in the 2007 Microsoft Office System by using the Office Open XML file formats. Although the examples shown here are solely presented as an introduction, you can see that quite a bit of potential exists for creating rich business solutions and that you can pack quite a punch by using the Office Open XML file formats together with WSS and MOSS. Once you create your documents, you have a place to store and manage them while utilizing all of the valuable aspects of document management in SharePoint Technologies such as collaboration, search, and archiving.

Figure 7-14   The DocumentManager4.aspx custom application page demonstrates the power of using Content Controls together with the XML Data Store to generate formatted Word documents.

Summary

In this chapter, we discussed many different aspects of handling documents and document libraries in a custom WSS solution. You have seen various options for programming documents and storing them in document libraries. You have also seen how to create a feature that provisions a document library and configures it to use a custom document template. By gaining an understanding of these techniques, you can use these skills to put together the basic building blocks to construct document management solutions with WSS and MOSS.

The second half of this chapter explored several possibilities when integrating WSS and its document libraries with other applications such as InfoPath, Word, and Excel. You have seen how to use Forms libraries to capture and process information entered into InfoPath forms. You have also seen how to build rich documents for Word, Excel, and PowerPoint from within server-side components running within a custom WSS solution.

Chapter 8
SharePoint Workflows

- Learn the fundamental concepts of the Windows Workflow Foundation (WF).
- Learn to create WF programs using the Microsoft Visual Studio workflow designer.
- Understand what value WSS provides on top of the WF.
- Learn how to develop workflow templates for WSS.
- Learn how to integrate workflow input forms with WSS workflow templates.

Windows Workflow Foundation

What you are about to read is the longest chapter of this book. Our goal is to get you up to speed so that you can start creating custom workflow programs with Microsoft Visual Studio and deploy these programs within Microsoft Windows SharePoint Services (WSS) sites. However, there is quite a bit of ground to cover along the way.

The chapter begins with a motivation for the Windows Workflow Foundation (WF). We feel it's essential for you to gain an understanding of why this platform and its unique new development paradigm help you to create programs that automate business processes. After providing this motivation, we then take you on a brief tour through WF development before we begin discussing how it integrates with WSS.

After discussing the WF as it stands alone, this chapter then dives into a discussion of how WSS integrates with and extends the WF. We first explain *why* the SharePoint team felt the need to extend the WF by adding a human dimension. We then move on to explain *how* you actually build workflow programs with the WF that target WSS sites. Any readers who want to start immediately building workflow programs inside Visual Studio should feel free to skip ahead to the section titled "Developing Custom Workflow Templates" later in this chapter.

Reactive Programs

The Windows Workflow Foundation is a new programming framework introduced in .NET 3.0 for creating reactive programs. We begin this chapter by explaining exactly what a reactive program is to motivate you to understand why the WF is helpful in building certain types of applications.

A *reactive program* typically represents a set of instructions used to capture and automate a specific business process. Examples of real-world problems that are best solved by reactive programs include the processing of an insurance claim or the approval of a document, such as a print advertisement or a quarterly report.

Reactive programs often have a common characteristic. Once they start, they cannot immediately run to completion. Instead, reactive programs run up until a point at which they are forced to pause in the middle of their execution and wait. They must wait for additional input from a human being or for some other external event to occur. For example, a reactive program written to capture an approval process must wait on a business user with managerial responsibilities to review and then approve an item or document. When a reactive program pauses and patiently waits for this critical human interaction, it could be a matter of days or even months until it is able to resume its work.

Reactive programs are often referred to as *episodic*. This means that they run in episodes— short little bursts of activity that are followed by longer periods of inactivity in which they are waiting for additional input. Reactive programs must also be written so that they are *resumable*. The reactive program must provide some sort of listening mechanism so that it can wake up and continue its execution at the point where it left off when the desired input arrives.

When a reactive program wakes up and resumes its execution, it experiences another episodic short burst of activity until either the program completes or it reaches another point at which it must go back to sleep and await more input. The life cycle for a reactive program that automates a very simple document approval process might involve two or three episodes and one or two places in its logic where it might need to sleep and then resume its execution. The life cycle for a more complicated reactive program could involve 10 to 20 episodes.

At a high level, developing a reactive program to capture a business process involves managing the state for whatever data are involved and writing the control-of-flow logic. For example, a reactive program for document approval might need to track the document name, approver, approval status, due date, and other pieces of data, such as approver comments. When a user initiates an approval process, the reactive program must somehow send a notification to inform the approver that a document needs to be approved or rejected. Finally, the reactive program needs to provide some sort of mechanism so that it can react to the event when the approver either approves or rejects the document.

If you decide that you want to develop a Windows Forms application to model a reactive program for document approval, you can design your application to track the necessary data each time a user initiates an approval process. Your application can be designed to send an e-mail notification to the approver saying that it is time to review a document for approval. The approver can launch your application, and you can display a form with all of the pending documents awaiting approval or rejection from that user. The code you write for this sort of application requires control-of-flow logic to move each document approval process through its life cycle from one episode to the next.

Due to the episodic nature of a reactive program that automates long-running tasks, such as document approval, it is impractical to merely track its data in memory. Instead, it is necessary to write the data associated with document approvals into some persistent store, such as a database. This is a critical aspect of reactive programs because, without persistence, the approval data would be lost in the face of an application crash or machine reboot.

Let's now change the scenario from the client to the server. Instead of developing a reactive program as a desktop application, imagine that you need to develop it as a server-side application using the ASP.NET Framework. In one sense, the ASP.NET Framework is ideal for building large applications because it provides features that promote scalability, such as built-in thread pooling and the ability to run in a Web farm environment.

However, there are several downsides to building a reactive program from scratch using the ASP.NET Framework. First, much of the scalability afforded to ASP.NET applications is based on the fact that they don't maintain state in the Internet Information Services (IIS) worker process from one request to the next. Therefore, the development of a reactive program in ASP.NET requires a design and implementation that constantly writes data for a specific approval process into a persistent store, such as a database, and then pulls these data back into memory on the Web server on a per-request basis.

Also consider what is involved when writing the logic for managing the episodes in an ASP.NET application that automates document approval. You must somehow assign tasks to users and then supply some sort of listener to react to their responses. For example, how would you interact with a human when it is time to approve a document?

One approach to solving this problem is to develop a series of ASP.NET pages to model a reactive program. The first page you write is one that allows a user to initiate the approval process on a specific document. You can design this page so that the user can select a document as well as select the user who can be the approver. After selecting a document and an approver, the user can then click a Start button that sends an e-mail notification to the approver. This e-mail notification can provide a link to a second page that enables the approver to add some comments and then click an Approve or Reject button.

The exercise we are going through here is attempting to design a reactive program that coordinates control-of-flow logic through a series of episodes. Clicking the Start button on the first page takes the approval process through the first episode up until a point of waiting. When the approver clicks the Approve or Reject button on the second page, the approval process runs through another episode until completion or up to another point of waiting. As you might imagine, the control-of-flow logic is going to become more difficult to write and much harder to understand and maintain as it spreads out across more pages. Consider trying to write a reactive program for a complex business process in such a fashion that your logic ends up being spread out across hundreds of ASP.NET pages.

At this point, we can make a general observation: ASP.NET and other similar server-side frameworks achieve scalability and robustness through a stateless and connectionless model. However, this scalability and robustness come at a price because they significantly compromise a developer's ability to manage state and to express the control-of-flow logic in a natural and maintainable fashion. If we changed our design to create the server-side reactive program as a Web service instead of a Web application, the problem only becomes worse because part of the control-of-flow logic must then be written in the client applications that called this Web service.

Wouldn't it be great if you could develop a single class definition that could manage the state and provide the control-of-flow logic required for a complete reactive program involving many different episodes and lots of branching? That would make it significantly easier for a developer to write the logic required to automate a real-world business process as well as to review a reactive program written by another developer and be able to understand what's going on.

It would be even more appealing if you can find a runtime environment that fires event handlers in your reactive program whenever it is time to start the next episode so that you don't have to design and implement your own listener mechanism. To put the icing on the cake, it would be particularly valuable if this runtime environment could deal with the plumbing details such as persistence, multithreading, asynchronous execution, and request queuing that are required to achieve scalability in server-side applications. The lofty goals described here were the motivation for Microsoft to create the Windows Workflow Foundation.

Windows Framework Foundation Architecture

Microsoft created the Windows Workflow Foundation to provide a development platform and set of developer tools specifically for building reactive programs. In WF terminology, these reactive programs are known as *WF programs*. It is important to note that WF programs must be created in accordance with a programming model that is mandated by the WF. It is also required that these WF programs run in a special environment known as the *WF runtime*, which is included as part of the .NET 3.0 Framework.

A WF program is a class definition that is usually designed and implemented to automate a business process, such as online purchasing or document approval. Each time you initiate a WF program, you create a *workflow instance*. You add fields to the class that represents your WF program to manage the state that must be tracked within each workflow instance. You add control-of-flow logic to your WF program to move each workflow instance through its life cycle from episode to episode until it completes or is terminated.

Throughout the life cycle of a workflow instance are periods of inactivity in which its state must be serialized and persisted out into some form of durable storage, such as a database. As another episode begins, this state must be retrieved so that a workflow instance can be deserialized back to its previous form. A significant benefit of the WF is that the WF runtime deals with the persistence and reloading of workflow instances in a manner that is transparent to your WF program. It's basically one of the services that you get for free when you use the WF.

Take a moment and consider the value that the WF provides on top of the Common Language Runtime (CLR). The CLR provides the plumbing needed to create objects in memory. However, these CLR objects are bound to the lifetime of the hosting process and disappear once the process has been shut down or recycled. The WF extends the CLR by adding support to persist and rehydrate CLR objects across process boundaries and even across machine boundaries as required within Web farm environments.

Tip   The version numbers associated with the Microsoft .NET Framework can be fairly confusing. You might assume that the Microsoft .NET 3.0 Framework is an update that replaces the Microsoft .NET 2.0 Framework; however, this is not the case. Instead, the .NET 3.0 Framework is a new layer that sits on top of and extends the .NET 2.0 Framework. The .NET 2.0 Framework provides the CLR and ASP.NET 2.0. The .NET 3.0 Framework provides the WF that is built on top of the CLR. WSS 3.0 depends on the CLR and ASP.NET from the .NET 2.0 Framework as well as the WF from the .NET 3.0 Framework.

It's also important to keep in mind that the WF does more than just save and reload the state associated with workflow instances. The WF must also provide a way to remember how far each workflow instance progresses within its life cycle. When a certain action occurs that triggers the start of a new episode, the WF runtime must determine not only which workflow instance to load, but also where to resume execution within the control-of-flow logic defined inside the WF program. The WF deals with these scheduling requirements by using atomic executable statements known as activities and the concept of bookmarking.

Activities

Activities are the building blocks that developers use to construct WF programs. You can think of each activity as an atomic and reusable set of instructions that represents a single unit of work. As a developer building WF programs, you can reuse many of the activities from within the *Base Activity Library (BAL)* included with the WF. As a developer building WF programs that target WSS and Microsoft Office SharePoint Server (MOSS), you can also reuse SharePoint-specific activities that are part of the *WSS Activity Library*.

An activity is a class that inherits from the Activity class defined within the *System.Workflow. ComponentModel* assembly inside a namespace of the same name. The Activity class contains an overridable method named Execute. The Execute method is overridden by activity authors to give their activities the behavior they require. Note that the Execute method of an activity is always called by the WF runtime and never by programmers directly.

It's helpful if you regard activities in the same fashion as you think about server-side controls in ASP.NET. Like controls, activities are black boxes of reusable code that expose properties and events. As with controls, the consumer of an activity can simply drag and drop it on a design surface within Visual Studio. The activity consumer then initializes the properties for the activity by using a standard property sheet. The activity consumer also generates event handlers for activities and writes code behind these event handlers. This development paradigm makes it relatively simple to add and maintain custom logic within a WF program.

The one aspect of an activity that makes it fundamentally different from an ASP.NET control is that it is resumable. The WF programming model builds the capability of resuming execution into each activity through an internal bookmarking scheme that involves delegates and callback methods. When the WF runtime loads a workflow instance into memory to begin another episode, certain activities within the WF program provide possible points of re-entry into the flow of executable logic.

Another very important aspect of the WF programming model is that certain types of activities can have child activities, which are known as *composite activities*. The WF programming model includes a class named CompositeActivity that inherits from Activity. The CompositeActivity class extends the Activity base class by including an Activities property that exposes a collection used to add and track child activities. Many of the activities you reuse from the BAL inherit from CompositeActivity and can contain child activities.

Each composite activity manages the execution of its child activities, which allows composite activities to provide control-of-flow constructs within a WF program. For example, the BAL provides a composite activity named While that repeatedly executes a child activity as long as some condition within the WF program remains true. There is another composite activity named IfThen that conditionally executes child activities contained in two possible paths depending on whether a certain condition in the WF program is met.

Your ability to express control-of-flow constructs within a WF program using composite activities results in creating application logic that is natural and easy to understand. It also makes it possible to encapsulate and reuse complex control-of-flow constructs in a fashion that isn't possible in programming languages, such as C# and Visual Basic .NET. For example, the BAL provides a composite activity named Parallel that executes two different groups of child activities in parallel. As a consumer of the Parallel activity, you don't have to worry about starting two different paths of execution at the same time, nor do you have to worry about the details of synchronizing the completion of these two paths before moving on to the next activity. These details of managing the control of flow are handled by the logic encapsulated within the Parallel activity.

Let us give you one more example. The purpose of a very powerful composite activity named Replicator is to take a flow of one or more child activities and replicate this flow so that it can be executed multiple times with different parameters. For example, imagine that you have created a flow of activities to assign a task to a user who needs to approve a document and then to wait on that user to either approve or reject the document. However, what should you do if you need three different users to approve a document in a particular business scenario? You can add the flow of approval-related activities within the Replicator activity and configure it to execute the flow three different times. You can even use the property sheet to switch the behavior of this replication by changing the ExecutionType property back and forth between Sequence and Parallel.

Creating WF Programs

A WF program is a composite activity that contains child activities. The WF program's child activities can also be composite activities with children of their own and so on. Therefore, a WF program is really nothing more than a composition of activities with a hierarchical tree-like structure.

Every activity within a WF program has a Name property that is assigned by the activity consumer at design time. The Name property for an activity represents important metadata that the WF runtime uses to identify continuation points in the WF program's logic. Note that the Name property cannot be changed at run time.

Every activity has a Parent property that references the composite activity in which it is contained. The only activity that should have a Parent property value equal to null is the root activity that represents the WF program itself. When it is time to start a workflow instance, the WF runtime calls the Execute method on this root activity of the WF program. The lifetime of the workflow instance is then controlled by however the WF program manages the execution flow from one activity to the next.

The WF programming model provides support for creating two different styles of WF programs. The first style is a *sequential WF program* that typically has several predicable paths of execution that can be modeled in the form of a flowchart, as shown on the left side of Figure 8-1. When you create a sequential WF program to model a business process, you can commonly use composite activities such as While, IfElse, and Replicator to design the control of flow and achieve the conditional branching required.

In real-world scenarios, certain types of business processes are difficult to model using a flowchart when a business process has many possible paths of execution, as shown on the right side of Figure 8-1. A *state machine WF program* models the different states that a business process goes through on its way toward completion.

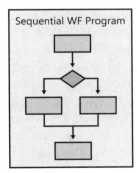
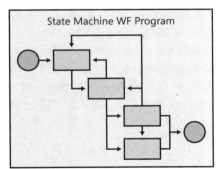

Figure 8-1   In the WF, programs can model sequential workflows or state machine workflows.

For example, think about modeling the business process used to automate online credit card purchases. This model could define states such as OrderCreated, CreditCardAuthenticated, OrderFullfilled, AwaitingBackorder, and OrderShipped. Once you have designed a state machine WF program as a finite set of states, you then add the required logic by defining the *transitions* between these states in terms of *actions* and *events*. This makes it possible to evolve the logic for a complex business process without having to worry about the linear flow from the beginning to the end.

The WF programming model provides a base class of each type of WF program. The SequentialWorkflowActivity class is used to create sequential WF programs, while the StateMachineWorkflowActivity class is used to create state machine WF programs. Both of these classes inherit from CompositeActivity and enable you to create a derived class that serves as the root activity in a WF program.

Given the scope of this chapter, we're presenting examples of only sequential WF programs, which will suffice for creating WF programs that automate a business process, such as document approval in a WSS or MOSS environment. However, you should note that both styles of WF program are useful for automating business processes within WSS and MOSS. As you learn more about WF development, you will see that some business processes are easier to model with sequential WF programs, while others are more manageable and easier to model using state machine WF programs.

Visual Studio Workflow Designer

After discussing the concepts of composing a WF program by using activities, let's see how it's actually done. The first thing you need to do is install the .NET 3.0 Framework on your development workstation so that the WF runtime and WF assembly libraries are present. Remember that WSS 3.0 depends on the WF. Therefore, if you have already successfully installed WSS 3.0, you know the WF is already present on the machine.

After installing the .NET 3.0 Framework, you must then install *Visual Studio Extensions for Windows Workflow Foundation*. This is the add-in created by the WF team, and it installs the workflow designer into Visual Studio. Once the Visual Studio add-in has been installed, you should see several new Visual Studio project types, such as Sequential Workflow Library and State Machine Workflow Library, for creating new WF programs. When you begin working with the workflow designer, it is helpful to create small test projects by using the Visual Studio project template named Sequential Workflow Console Application. Doing so makes it possible for you to create a WF program and experience using the workflow designer, as shown in Figure 8-2. The project types also create a Console application that acts as a client test harness. To get a "Hello World" WF program up and going, you can drag a Code activity from the Toolkit onto the WF program designer, add an event handler with a call to Console.WriteLine, and press F5. There's nothing like instant gratification.

We introduce one last concept about activities in this section. The WF programming model allows for activities with *data-bound properties*. The main idea behind data-bound properties is that they facilitate the declarative flow of data across activities. The implementation involves assigning an expression to an activity's property value that is evaluated at run time. We will revisit this topic later in the chapter in the section titled "Developing Custom Workflow Templates" when we begin to build WF programs for a document approval process in WSS. You'll see that data binding is required yet is also very easy to set up inside Visual Studio by using dialog boxes supplied by the workflow designer.

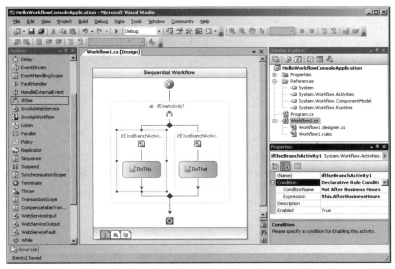

Figure 8-2   WF programs are created by dragging and dropping activities onto the workflow designer.

WF Runtime

It's important to remember that the WF does not supply an application server or any type of hosting process in and of itself. Instead, the WF is a general-purpose runtime environment that can be loaded into the process for any application you would like. Let's take a look at the code for a simple console application that fires up the WF runtime and then uses a custom .NET class named Workflow1, which represents a WF program, to start a workflow instance.

```
using System;
using System.Workflow.Runtime;
using System.Workflow.Runtime.Hosting;

namespace HelloWorkflowConsoleApplication {
  class Program {
    static void Main() {

      // start WF runtime
      WorkflowRuntime wfRuntime = new WorkflowRuntime();
      wfRuntime.StartRuntime();

      // create and start workflow instance
      WorkflowInstance workflowInstance1;
      workflowInstance1 = wfRuntime.CreateWorkflow(typeof(Workflow1));
      workflowInstance1.Start();

      // pause until test workflow instance completes
      Console.ReadLine();
```

```
        // stop WF runtime
        wfRuntime.StopRuntime();
        wfRuntime.Dispose();
      }
    }
  }
```

The preceding code is fairly easy to understand. A hosting application simply needs to start the runtime, and it can then create and start workflow instances from any WF program. Though this process makes it relatively simple to write and test simple WF programs, this console application doesn't provide support for one of the most valuable aspects of the WF—the capability to persist the workflow instance into durable storage so that it's not tied to the lifetime of the hosting process. To add that support, the hosting application needs to initialize the WF runtime with one or more WF runtime services.

An application or service written to use the WF must often interact with an external entity, such as a backend database server, to persist the serialized data for its workflow instances. The WF was designed so that all such interaction with external entities is delegated to the *WF runtime services*. A key aspect of this design is that each WF runtime service is modeled using an abstract class such that various developers and companies can create their own pluggable versions when required.

Consider a workflow instance that needs to be serialized and written out to a database several times within its lifetime. What type of database should be used? Should the WF force every-one to use the same type of database? Fortunately, the answer is no; any developer or company can create a pluggable component that persists workflow instance state to whatever type of database they would like. They can then create a hosting application that starts up the WF runtime and initializes it to load their component as the WF runtime service that manages workflow instance persistence.

Let's now discuss a workflow instance that is created to automate a document approval process for a document within a WSS site. When it's time to persist the serialized data for the workflow instance, where should the data be saved? The obvious answer is to save it right inside the WSS content database. Fortunately, the high-level design of the WF enabled the WSS team members to write their own persistence service to make this possible.

The WF programming model defines an abstract base class named WorkflowPersistenceService that defines a set of abstract methods called by the WF runtime when it's time to load or save workflow instance state. The WSS team created a class named SPWinOePersistenceService that inherits from WorkflowPersistenceService and implements the methods required to load and save workflow instances from the content database. The WSS runtime also provides the initialization logic required within the IIS worker process (W3WP.EXE) to load and start up the WF runtime and initialize it by using the SPWinOePersistenceService class as a WF runtime service. The big picture of how all of the pieces fit together is shown in Figure 8-3.

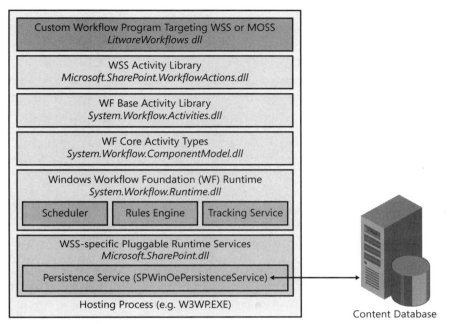

Figure 8-3   The WSS runtime loads the WF runtime environment and initializes it with a custom runtime service to save and load workflow instances from the content database.

In this section, we discussed the architecture of WF runtime services to demonstrate two points. First, WF runtime services provide a flexible, pluggable architecture that makes it possible to store workflow instance data anywhere you choose. Second, the WSS team has taken advantage of this flexible architecture to persist workflow instance data to the content database.

Now that you have a high-level understanding of how these pieces fit together, there really isn't a need for you to learn more about the details of how WF runtime services work. This is a key reason why the WSS development platform provides value over the ASP.NET development platform. If you are writing an ASP.NET application to host WF programs, you might be required to develop your own WF runtime services and also to worry about the details of starting and initializing the WF runtime with whatever WF runtime services you needed.

This concludes our brief introduction to the WF. We are ready to move ahead and begin discussing the layers that WSS and MOSS add on top of the WF. If you are looking for a good how-to guide as you get started using the Visual Studio workflow designer and learning how to use the Base Activity Library provided by the WF, we recommend you read *Microsoft Windows Workflow Foundation Step By Step* by Kenn Scribner. If you want to continue building your understanding of how the WF works internally, we recommend that you read *Essential Windows Workflow Foundation* by Dharma Shukla and Bob Schmidt. This book does a great job of providing a bottom-up view of the WF from the perspective of a software architect and an advanced developer. It also delves into many topics that we do not cover in this book, such as writing your own custom activities and developing state machine WF programs.

SharePoint Workflows

For nearly 20 years, desktop applications of the Microsoft Office applications—such as Microsoft Office Word, Microsoft Office Excel, and Microsoft Office PowerPoint—have grown in popularity to the point that they are now ubiquitous in business environments. These applications have built a reputation in the software industry as reliable tools for creating, editing, and reviewing the documents that are critical to running a business. The introduction of Microsoft Windows SharePoint Services 2.0 into the Microsoft Office 2003 System extended the capabilities of applications even further by enabling the creation, editing, and reviewing of documents across teams in a collaborative environment.

Though tools such as Office Word and Office Excel that were designed to create, edit, and review documents are important to a business, these applications clearly do not offer the capabilities to manage the entire document life cycle. Many documents in a business environment must go through one or more approval processes. Other documents need to be published or archived. Some companies must follow regulations that mandate their documents be kept on record for a certain length of time before disposal.

When the Microsoft Office team members first began to consider what features they wanted to include with WSS 3.0 and MOSS, they knew they could improve their support for managing the full document life cyle. In particular, they began to consider how to add automation support for the tasks required later in the document life cycle such as approval, publishing, archiving, and disposition. It became evident that they needed to add support for developing reactive programs and integrating them into WSS and MOSS to automate workflow-style tasks on documents and list items.

The timing was fortuitous between the development schedules of the team at Microsoft building the WF and the teams within the Microsoft Office group building WSS 3.0 and MOSS. The design and development of the WF was far enough along that the Microsoft Office team was able to use it as the underlying platform to build workflow support into WSS 3.0.

The teams building WSS 3.0 and MOSS benefited from having a platform supplying much of the necessary infrastructure for developing and managing WF programs. The WF team benefited from having a large number of developers from the Microsoft Office team kicking the tires of the WF runtime and development tools long before the WF was released to the outside world. This enabled them to find bugs and design flaws and fix them very early in the product life cycle so that the WF could be adapted to the needs of large-scale, Web-based applications running in a Web-farm environment.

SharePoint Workflow Design Goals

When the Microsoft Office team began to integrate WF support into WSS and MOSS, their primary design goal was to attach business logic to documents and list items using WF programs. The WF and its ability to create reactive programs that run in episodes is exactly what is needed for capturing business processes to automate tasks throughout the entire document life cycle.

Another critical design goal was to add a human dimension of responsibility and accountability because, after all, many business processes are reliant on humans and their actions. Humans are required, for example, to provide input in the form of an approval, a signature, or feedback. The Microsoft Office team felt that it was important to add support so that WF programs could assign *tasks* to users who were responsible for driving (or holding up) the business processes being automated.

In addition to assigning tasks, the Microsoft Office team felt it was important for users and their organizations to have access to information about the status of a business process that was being automated by a workflow instance. They came up with the idea that each workflow instance should be able to log entries into a workflow history list that would keep users up to date on workflow status. For example, a user should be able to navigate to a special page within a WSS site that displays the status of a workflow instance, including the steps it has gone through and the tasks (if any) that have been assigned to it.

When the Microsoft Office team began integrating WF support into WSS, they knew that it was important for site owners and users to be able to administrate and run WF programs without involvement from the IT department. WSS had made many other aspects of administration within a site collection accessible to users, and it was essential for the Microsoft Office team to make the administration of WF programs equally accessible.

While the Microsoft Office team spent a good deal of energy making their workflow story accessible to users and information workers, they did not want to forget about developers and their need to build custom WF programs. It was important to the Microsoft Office team that they extend the WF in such a way that SharePoint developers could create SharePoint-targeted workflows by using Visual Studio and the WF workflow designer with the same levels of convenience and productivity as developers experience when building WF programs for standard WF components and applications.

The final design goal might have been the biggest one. The Microsoft Office team wanted to provide several valuable out-of-the-box WF programs to automate common business processes, such as document approval and signature collection. This design goal was aimed at providing value to customers who either could not or did not want to spend money on custom development. However, the vast majority of out-of-the-box workflows created by the Microsoft Office team are included with MOSS but not with WSS.

SharePoint Workflow Fundamentals

WSS extends the WF by introducing the concept of a *workflow template*. At the heart of each workflow template is a single WF program that you create in Visual Studio by using the standard WF workflow designer. The main purpose of the workflow template is to integrate WF programs into WSS so that they can be installed, configured, and parameterized for use.

A workflow template is created by adding a Workflow element to a feature that is scoped to the level of the site collection. The definition for a Workflow element must point to a specific

WF program and can optionally contain references to one or more input forms that solicit additional information from users. The types of input forms that can be included as part of a workflow template will be discussed in the next section, titled "Workflow Input Forms."

When it's time to deploy a workflow template, you must first install the assembly DLL containing the WF program in the Global Assembly Cache (GAC). Next, you must install the feature that defines the workflow template as you would install any other feature with WSS. Finally, you activate the feature within any site collection in which you want to use the workflow template.

WSS does not let you run workflow templates directly on documents or list items. Instead, you must create an intermediate layer known as a workflow association. A *workflow association* is a named set of parameterization data that is used to bind a workflow template to a specific list or document library.

Once the feature with a workflow template is activated within the current site collection, a privileged user, such as the site or list owner, creates a new workflow association on any list or document library. This can be done by clicking the *Workflow settings* link on the List Settings page to navigate to a standard application page named AddWrkfl.aspx that's used to create a workflow association, as shown in Figure 8-4. Although the page title says "Add a Workflow," you now know that it really means to add a workflow association.

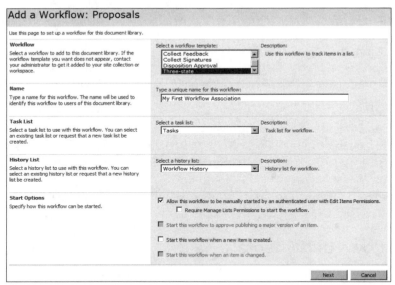

Figure 8-4   WSS provides a standard application page named AddWrkfl.aspx to assist users with the creation of workflow associations.

A primary function of the workflow association is to hold parameterization data for the workflow template that is used to initialize workflow instances. Keep in mind that for one particular list or document library in a WSS site, you can create two different workflow associations from the same workflow template and parameterize them in different ways.

For example, imagine that you have a workflow template that automates an approval process. You could create one workflow association to automate approvals that go through the Litware art department and another workflow association to automate approvals that go through the Litware legal department. Each of two different workflow associations would then be parameterized to use an approver from their respective departments.

As discussed in the previous section, WSS extends the WF with a human dimension by providing every workflow instance with access to a workflow task list and workflow history list. The *workflow task list* allows workflow instances to assign tasks to users involved in various business processes. The *workflow history list* allows workflow instances to log their actions so that users can keep apprised of their status. Yet, how does WSS know which task list and which history list should be associated with a particular workflow instance? That's a job for the workflow association.

When a user creates a new workflow association through the standard WSS user interface, that user is given a choice of selecting an existing task list or creating a new task list. The user is also given a choice of selecting an existing history list or creating a new history list. The key point is that any valid workflow association must have a task list and a history list that are accessible to WF programs and visible to users.

While workflow associations are often created directly on lists and document libraries, WSS provides even more flexibility. A workflow association can also be created on a content type that exists within the Content Type Gallery for the current site. For example, you could create a workflow association on the built-in Document content type within the Content Type Gallery of a top-level site, thus making it possible to create and configure a single workflow association that is available to run on any document within any document library throughout the entire site collection.

You already learned that it is possible to create a workflow association on a list, document library, or content type within the Content Type Gallery for a site. However, a third and final option exists for creating a new workflow association. Instead of creating the workflow association for a content type within the site, you can also create a workflow association for one of the content types defined within a list.

For example, if you navigate from the List Settings page to the Advanced Settings page for a list or document library, you can enable the option to allow management of content types. Once you do this, you can add additional content types to the list as well as drill down into the settings for a content type that has been added to the list and create a new workflow association. Therefore, you can configure a list so that different items within it have different available workflow associations depending on their content type. In summary, there are three different levels at which you can create a workflow summary:

- At the level of a list (or document library)
- At the level of a content type defined at site scope
- At the level of a content type defined at list scope

Initiating Workflow Instances on Items and Documents

Once you create one or more workflow associations, you can then begin to create a workflow instance that represents a running instance of a WF program. Within WSS, each workflow instance must be associated with one specific list item or document. Because a workflow instance is started from a specific workflow association, it is also associated with one specific workflow template.

When a privileged user creates a workflow association, this user configures how workflow instances should be started. For example, you can create a workflow association that automatically starts a workflow instance anytime a new item or document is created. You can alternatively create a workflow association that gives users the ability to create workflow instances on demand through the standard WSS user interface.

WSS provides standard elements within the user interface to give users the ability to initiate and manage workflow instances as well as to see their status. The workflow menu item shown in Figure 8-5 appears in the standard ECB menu for list items and documents. The workflow menu item provides users with the ability to navigate to an application page named workflow.aspx that allows a user to see, initiate, and manage workflow instances for a specific list item or document.

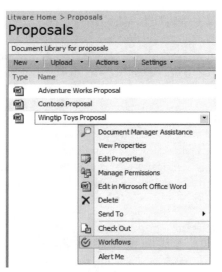

Figure 8-5　A workflow association can be configured to allow users to launch workflow instances manually.

A typical view of workflow.aspx is shown in Figure 8-6. As you can see, this page provides a built-in facility in WSS that displays the workflow associations available to initiate new workflow instances. This page lists an aggregation of the workflow associations that are created on the list (or document library) as well as on the content type associations with that current item (or document). In addition to available workflow associations, the page also displays a list of workflow instances that are still running as well as those that have completed. Both lists of workflow instances let the user click on links to drill down the history of a particular workflow instance.

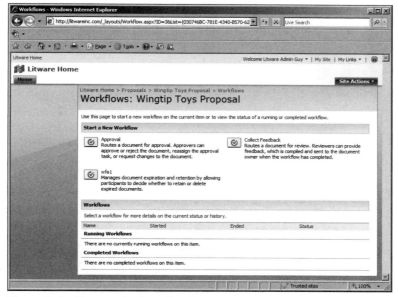

Figure 8-6   The standard application page named workflow.aspx provides workflow management over items and documents.

WSS displays the Workflow Status page named WrkStat.aspx when users want to drill down and examine the history of a particular workflow instance. This page (shown in Figure 8-7) displays standard information about the workflow instance, as well as a list of tasks created by the workflow instance and a history list showing activity that occurred on the workflow since it was initiated.

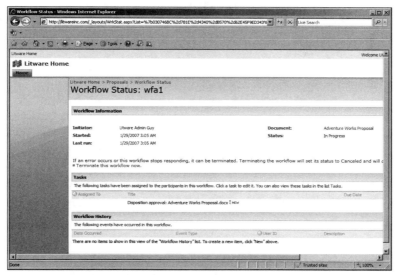

Figure 8-7   The Workflow Status page provides information on the status of one specific workflow instance.

Workflow Input Forms

Now that we have covered the high-level concepts involved with workflow templates, workflow associations, and workflow instances, we can revisit the topic of *workflow input forms*. These forms make it possible for a developer to design and implement a custom workflow template that interacts with users to solicit data to parameterize workflow associations and workflow instances.

When you design a workflow template, you can create four different types of input forms including an association form, an initiation form, a modification form, and a task edit form. Note that these forms are optional when you create a workflow template. You can add any one of these form types to a workflow template and omit the other three. You can also supply all four types of workflow input forms if you have a scenario that calls for it.

A custom *workflow association form* allows the developer to prompt the user for parameterization data when a new workflow association is created. A workflow association form is presented to the user as a final step when creating a workflow association. Note that the workflow association form can also be used by those who want to make modifications to parameterization data within an existing workflow association.

A custom *workflow initiation form* allows the developer to prompt the user for parameterization data when a new workflow instance is created from a workflow association. Note that workflow initiation forms can be used only when the workflow association allows users to start the workflow instance manually. When a workflow association is configured to start workflows automatically, it is not possible to prompt the user with a workflow initiation form.

Once a workflow instance has been started, there might be a need for the user to change some of its properties on the fly, such as who should approve the item or document in question. The *workflow modification form* is intended for this purpose. A developer can add a link to the Workflow Status page, making it possible for the user to navigate to the modification form for a particular workflow instance. Using the modification form, the developer can allow the user to perform whatever types of modifications make sense.

As you know, each workflow association is configured with a task list that makes it possible for workflow instances to create tasks and assign them to the users. WSS supplies a special content type named WorkflowTask with an ID of 0x010801. When you design a WF program to create tasks, you can choose the standard WorkflowTask content type or create your own custom content type. If you create your own custom content type, you must create it so that it inherits from the standard WorkflowTask content type.

One advantage to creating a custom content type for workflow tasks is that you can add extra fields beyond those defined in the standard WorkflowTask content type. A second advantage is that you can create a custom *Task Edit Form*. This allows you to take over the user experience when a user needs to edit a task. For example, you can supply a task edit form containing only the necessary controls, such as an Approve and Reject button.

Tip   Two different approaches can be used to develop custom input forms for a WSS workflow template. You can create your forms by using custom application pages, which are standard .aspx pages deployed to run out of the _layouts directory. We will discuss these workflow input forms in this chapter. If you can assume that your custom workflow templates will always run in an environment in which MOSS is installed, you also have the option of creating custom workflow forms using Microsoft Office InfoPath 2007.

There are many benefits to using Office InfoPath 2007 to create the forms for a custom workflow template. First, the integration of InfoPath Forms into a WSS workflow template significantly reduces the amount of code that you need to supply. Secondly, InfoPath forms provide a level of integration with the 2007 Microsoft Office suite client applications such as Word, Excel, Office PowerPoint, and Microsoft Office Outlook. While InfoPath forms can be presented to the user through the browser, they can also be hosted directly from within the 2007 Microsoft Office suite application, providing a more seamless user experience.

The obvious drawback to creating a workflow template that uses InfoPath forms is that it picks up a dependency on MOSS and cannot be used within environments running on WSS. For this reason, this chapter focuses on creating workflow input forms using .aspx files so that they can be deployed within any WSS 3.0 environment regardless of whether MOSS is also installed.

Developing Custom Workflow Templates

The primary goal of this chapter is to teach you how to create a custom workflow template for WSS and MOSS by using Visual Studio 2005. As you will see, you can use the workflow designer within Visual Studio to develop a WF program for each workflow template you want to produce. However, the Visual Studio project for a custom workflow template contains other source files, such as Collaborative Application Markup Language (CAML)-based XML files, to define the feature that will be used to deploy the workflow template. The project can optionally contain a set of .aspx pages used to create custom workflow input forms.

Once you successfully install WSS 3.0 on your development workstation, you already have all of the runtime support required to run workflows within WSS sites because installation of the .NET 3.0 framework is a prerequisite to installing WSS 3.0. Also note that the basic installation of WSS 3.0 adds several assemblies critical to the WSS workflow architecture, such as Microsoft.SharePoint.Workflows.dll and Microsoft.SharePoint.WorkflowActions.dll.

As mentioned earlier in this chapter, you need to install the Visual Studio Extensions for Windows Workflow Foundation before you begin to develop custom WF programs. This is the add-in created by the WF team, and it installs the workflow designer to Visual Studio. You can use this workflow designer to create WF programs whether your development efforts are targeting WSS or not.

Once you install the Visual Studio Extensions for Windows Workflow Foundation, your next step is to install one of the workflow starter kits created by the Microsoft Office team to assist with creating SharePoint-targeted workflow templates. Which SDK and workflow starter kit you download depends on whether you are developing workflow templates for WSS or for MOSS. The following items are what you need to consider.

If you want to develop custom workflow templates that run in a WSS environment whether MOSS is installed or not, you should download the Windows SharePoint Services 3.0: Software Development Kit (SDK), which includes the Workflow Developer Starter Kit. This SDK contains two Visual Studio Project Templates for WSS-targeted WF programs titled Sequential Workflow Library and State Machine Workflow Library. In addition to these two project templates, the SDK also includes a single sample project named ASPXCollectFeedback, which demonstrates how to build a custom workflow template that includes workflow input forms built using .aspx pages.

If you want to develop custom workflow templates that run exclusively in a MOSS environment, you should download the Microsoft Office SharePoint Server 2007 Software Development Kit (SDK), which includes the Enterprise Content Management Starter Kit. This includes the same two Visual Studio project templates that come with the WSS SDK, but also adds support for integrating InfoPath forms into your workflow templates. Instead of including only one sample project to demonstrate the creation of a custom workflow template such as the WSS SDK, the Enterprise Content Management Starter Kit provides over one dozen sample projects that all involve using InfoPath forms instead of .aspx pages for creating workflow input forms.

The obvious caveat to using the Enterprise Content Management Starter Kit to build custom workflow templates is that they can pick up a dependency on MOSS that prevents them from working correctly within an environment in which WSS (but not MOSS) is installed. In this book, we focus on developing custom workflow templates with the WSS SDK and the Workflow Developer Starter Kit to ensure that the templates run in a WSS environment even when MOSS is not installed.

Create Ad-hoc Workflow Associations with the SharePoint Designer

Note that the SharePoint Designer makes it possible to create custom workflow associations directly on a list or document library. This support for creating ad hoc custom workflow associations is not actually intended for professional developers as much as it is for sophisticated users in the role of a business analyst or Web designer.

The advantage of creating ad hoc workflows is that they eliminate the need for custom development of WF programs and workflow input forms. They also remove the need to create a solution package to deploy and install all of the pieces required by a workflow template on each front-end Web server.

The limitations of creating ad hoc workflow associations involve a lack of flexibility and an inability to effectively reuse custom workflow logic. Once a user creates an ad hoc workflow association on a particular list with the SharePoint Designer, there is no supported technique that allows the user to reuse that ad hoc customization on another pre-existing list. However, it is possible to create an ad hoc workflow association on a list and then create a list template from the list. Any workflow association created on a list that is used to create a list template is automatically created on lists that are created from the list template.

Although creating ad hoc custom workflow associations with the SharePoint Designer is an interesting and valuable topic that might warrant your attention, it is not developer focused and, therefore, is not covered in this book.

Creating the "Hello World" Workflow Template

At this point, we assume that you have already installed the Visual Studio Extensions for Windows Workflow Foundation as well as the WSS SDK that includes the Workflow Developer Starter Kit. Having these pieces of software installed on your development workstation allows you to create and test your first custom workflow template. During this initial walk-through, we will follow the guidelines for creating a classic Hello World sample.

When you create a new project in Visual Studio, you should notice that the New Project dialog box contains a SharePoint folder of project templates for both Microsoft Visual Basic and C#, as shown in Figure 8-8. Within the SharePoint folder, you should see two Visual Studio project templates named Sequential Workflow Library and State Machine Workflow Library. In this walk-through, we are going to create a new C# project named HelloWorkflow by using the Sequential Workflow Library project template.

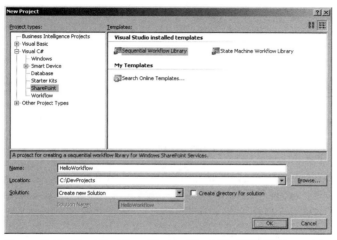

Figure 8-8   The Workflow Starter Kit of the WSS SDK provides Visual Studio project templates for creating new custom workflow templates that target WSS.

Once you create a new Visual Studio project based on the SharePoint Sequential Workflow Library project template, you are provided with several different source files as a starting point. These source files include feature.xml, workflow.xml, install.bat, Workflow1.cs, and Workflow1.designer.cs, as shown in Figure 8-9.

The two files named feature.xml and workflow.xml are important when it's time to deploy your workflow template. These two files are used to define a feature that makes it possible to install the workflow template so that it is recognized by WSS. The provided install.bat file contains command-line instructions to copy the required source files into the TEMPLATE directory of WSS and install the feature containing the workflow template by using the stsadm.exe utility. We will revisit these three files at the end of this section because they are an essential part of installing the workflow template, which is a required step before you can conduct any testing or debugging.

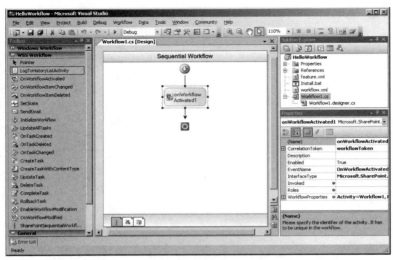

Figure 8-9   New projects created with the Workflow Starter Kit templates provide a WF program as well as the starting files used to create features.

We now turn our attention to the two source files named Workflow1.cs and Workflow1. designer.cs. These two files are used together to define the WF program that is at the heart of your workflow template. This WF program is defined as a class named *Workflow1*. You can observe that Workflow1 inherits from the standard base class named SequentialWorkflow-Activity from the WF programming model. Note that *Workflow1* is defined as a partial class that is spread out across both Workflow1.cs and Workflow1.designer.cs.

As the author of a custom workflow template, you are required to work with WF program files, such as Workflow1.cs, in both *Designer view* and *Code view*. When you are working in Designer view, the WF workflow designer provides you with the convenience of dragging and dropping activities from the Toolbox onto the design surface of Workflow1.cs, which is how you compose the flow of activities for your WF program. Designer view also makes it possible to modify an activity by selecting it and then modifying its properties using a standard property sheet.

Tip   Figure 8-9 demonstrates what the Visual Studio Toolbox should look like when you are working with a WF program in Designer view with all WSS-specific activities. However, it's possible that you might not see these WSS-specific activities in the Visual Studio Toolbox even after installing the WSS SDK and the Workflow Starter Kit. To get these WSS-specific activities to show up, you have two choices. First, you can modify the class for your workflow program to inherit from SharePointSequentialWorkflowActivity instead of SequentialWorkflowActivity. This will be described in the next section of this chapter titled "Working with Activities."

The second approach is to manually add the WSS-specific activities to your toolbox. You can accomplish this by right-clicking the Toolbox and selecting the Choose Items command, which brings up a dialog box that makes it possible for you to choose the components you would like to add. From the tab labeled .NET Framework Components, sort the components by namespace and select all components that have the Microsoft.SharePoint.WorkflowActions namespace. This adds the WSS-specific activities to the Toolbox so that you can drag and drop them onto your WF programs.

Let's take a moment and describe the relationship between the two source files named Workflow1.cs and Workflow1.designer.cs. Although you can work directly with Workflow1.cs, it is unnecessary to make direct edits to Workflow1.designer.cs. Instead, the code generator built into the workflow designer makes the necessary changes to Workflow1.designer.cs for you behind the scenes as you work on Workflow1.cs in Designer view.

For example, when you drag and drop a new activity onto the design surface of Workflow1.cs, the code generator that's part of the workflow designer automatically adds code to Workflow1. designer.cs to create a new activity instance. It also adds the code required to initialize the properties of the new activity instance and add it to the Activities collection of Workflow1. Furthermore, when you select an activity in Designer view and modify it by using the property sheet, the code generator makes the necessary updates to Workflow1.designer.cs to track your changes.

> **Warning**   It is recommended that you avoid making direct edits to Workflow1.designer.cs unless you truly know what you are doing. If you add code that isn't formatted correctly, you can prevent the code generator from working properly as well as prevent the designer from opening.

Let's begin working on Workflow1.cs to start development of a WF program. You should start by double-clicking Workflow1.cs within the project explorer, which opens Workflow1.cs in Designer view, as shown earlier in Figure 8-9. The next thing you must do is become comfortable switching Workflow1.cs back and forth between Designer view and Code view, which is something you will do on a regular basis as you develop WF programs with the workflow designer.

If you right-click the window of the workflow designer, you see context menu items that allow you to toggle back and forth between Designer view and Code view. When in Designer view, there is a context menu item titled View Code. When in Code view, there is a context menu item titled View Designer. Practice moving back and forth between these two views.

You should observe that the context menu in the workflow designer window provides several other important options, as shown in Figure 8-10. A Generate Handlers menu item is used to quickly create event handlers for the WF program as well as for child activities. Other menu items make it possible to navigate between the main SequentialWorkflow view and two other views, Cancel Handler and Fault Handler.

Working with Activities

When you open Workflow1.cs in Designer view, you notice that it already contains an existing activity named onWorkflowActivated1 that was created using the onWorkflowActivated activity type. This is an important requirement for any WF program targeting WSS or MOSS. More specifically, the first activity within the WF program running in WSS must be of the OnWorkflowActivated activity type. For this reason, you should never remove the activity instance named onWorkflowActivated1, nor should you add any other activities in front of it.

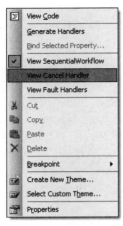

Figure 8-10 Right-clicking the workflow designer window provides several important context menu items.

Before we make any modifications to Workflow1.cs, let's switch over to Code view and examine the code that is provided as a starting point. The code you see should be roughly the equivalent of the following code:

```
// using statements omitted for clarity
namespace HelloWorkflow {
  public sealed partial class Workflow1 : SequentialWorkflowActivity {
    public Workflow1() {
      InitializeComponent();
    }
    public Guid workflowId = default(System.Guid);
    public SPWorkflowActivationProperties workflowProperties;
    workflowProperties = new SPWorkflowActivationProperties();
  }
}
```

Tip When you create a new sequential workflow project by using the Visual Studio templates installed by the WSS SDK, it creates the class for your workflow program by inheriting from the standard SequentialWorkflowActivity class defined by the WF base activity library. However, if you use the Visual Studio templates installed by the Office SharePoint Server SDK, you will notice that it creates a class that inherits from a different base class created by the Office Server team named SharePointSequentialWorkflowActivity. Note that the SharePoint-SequentialWorkflowActivity class inherits from the SequentialWorkflowActivity class.

You should understand that there is no real difference in the behavior between these two classes. The only difference is that the SharePointSequentialWorkflowActivity class has been created with attributes that tell Visual Studio to display the WSS-specific activities on the toolbox when a class of type SharePointSequentialWorkflowActivity is displayed in Design View. If you find it more convenient, you can substitute the SharePointSequentialWorkflow-Activity class for the SequentialWorkflowActivity immediately after creating a new sequential workflow project with the WSS SDK.

The class named Workflow1 is defined as a partial class because the other half of the class definition for Workflow1 exists within Workflow1.designer.cs. You can also see that the preprovided constructor for the Workflow1 class calls a method from Workflow1.designer.cs named InitializeComponent. The InitializeComponent method contains the code created by the code generator of the workflow designer that creates and initializes the activities added to the WF program while in Designer view.

We now turn our attention to the two public fields that have already been defined in the Workflow1 class: workflowId and workflowProperties. These fields need to be initialized by the OnWorkflowActivated activity whenever a new workflow instance is created from the WF program named Workflow1. As it turns out, the Visual Studio project template that you used to create the current project has already added what is needed to initialize the workflowProperties field.

Initialization of the workflowProperties field is accomplished through data binding. The activity named onWorkflowActivated1 contains a data-binding–enabled property named WorkflowProperties. While in Designer view, select onWorkflowActivated1 and inspect the property named WorkflowProperties in the Visual Studio property sheet. You should be able to verify that the value of this property is preconfigured with the following property value, which constitutes a data-binding expression that is evaluated at run time.

```
Activity=Workflow1, Path=workflowProperties
```

As mentioned earlier in the chapter, the entire idea behind data binding within a WF program is to facilitate the declarative flow of data across activities. In this case, the WorkflowProperties property of the activity named onWorkflowActivated1 is data bound to the workflowProperties field of Workflow1. When the WF runtime creates the activity instance named onWorkflowActivated1, this child activity initializes the new workflow instance. After onWorkflowActivated1 completes its work, the workflowProperties field in Workflow1 references a fully initialized SPWorkflowActivationProperties object that can then be used in any event handler to retrieve information about the current workflow instance.

Now that you have seen an example of data binding with an activity property, it's time to create an event handler for an activity. In particular, let's create an event handler for the activity named onWorkflowActivated1 to initialize the other field in the Workflow1 class named workflowId.

Switch Workflow1.cs back to Designer view and then right-click the activity named onWorkflowActivated1. Select the Generate Handlers menu item, which creates an event handler method inside Workflow1.cs named onWorkflowActivated1_Invoked. Note that this event handler executes as part of the initialization sequence for any workflow instance created from this WF program.

It's important to understand that the event handler for an activity of type onWorkflowActivated runs after the activity has completed its work, which means that the event handler runs after the data binding has initialized the workflowProperties field in Workflow1. Therefore, you can initialize the workflowId field by using the workflowProperties field.

```
private void onWorkflowActivated1_Invoked(...) {
  workflowId = this.workflowProperties.WorkflowId;
}
```

To complete the first phase of our Hello World sample, let's add a second activity to Workflow1 that writes a message into the workflow history table. Navigate to Designer view. In the Toolbox, locate the activity type LogToHistoryListActivity. Drag this activity type onto the designer surface to create a new activity instance immediately after onWorkflowActivated1. After you create this activity, select it and examine its properties in the Visual Studio property sheet.

The new activity is named logToHistoryListActivity1. You can leave the name of this activity as is or change it to something more descriptive, such as logActivated. You should also note that two other properties are visible within the property sheet named HistoryDescription and HistoryOutcome. Whenever an activity of type LogToHistoryListActivity writes an entry into the workflow history table, it writes the values of these two properties so that users can see them.

While it is possible to assign static values for the HistoryDescription and HistoryOutcome properties directly inside the property sheet, it is more flexible if you create two new string fields inside the Workflow1 class and then data-bind them to the HistoryDescription and HistoryOutcome properties. Start by adding two fields to the Workflow1 class named HistoryDescription and HistoryOutcome.

```
public sealed partial class Workflow1 : SequentialWorkflowActivity {
  // other members removed for clarity
  public String HistoryDescription;
  public String HistoryOutcome;
}
```

Once you add these two public string fields to Workflow1, you can bind them to any data-binding–enabled properties of child activities as long as these properties are based on the string type. Switch Workflow1.cs back into Designer view and select the activity you created from the LogToHistoryListActivity activity type. You can now data-bind the History-Description and HistoryOutcome properties from this activity to the two fields you just added to Workflow1.

To configure data binding for a property, click the little blue circle to the right of its name, which causes the workflow designer to invoke a special dialog box that makes it possible to data-bind property value to public fields or public properties exposed by another activity, such as Workflow1. Once you have data-bound the HistoryDescription and HistoryOutcome properties to the two fields in Workflow1, your property sheet should look like the one shown in Figure 8-11.

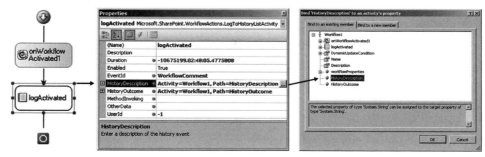

Figure 8-11   The properties of activities can be bound to fields within the WF program.

> **Tip**   As you have just seen, the dialog box shown on the far right of Figure 8-11 makes it possible to data-bind an activity property to an existing public field or property such as the HistoryDescription field defined within the workflow class named Workflow1. You should also note that there is a tab in this dialog box with the caption Bind To A New Member that provides the means to quickly create new public fields or properties inside the workflow program class. When you create a new public field or property by using this dialog box, it is automatically data-bound to the current activity property. Once you become comfortable with this dialog box, you will likely favor using this technique as opposed to manually adding public fields and properties to the workflow class.

Once you successfully add the LogToHistoryListActivity activity and data-bind its properties, it's time to add another event handler. Right-click the LogToHistoryListActivity activity and click Generate Handlers. This creates an event handler that fires just before the LogTo-HistoryListActivity activity writes its entry into the workflow history table. Therefore, you can write code in this event handler to assign a value to each of the two fields before data binding takes place. Write the event handler using the following code:

```
private void logActivated_MethodInvoking(object sender, EventArgs e) {
  // Generate message using information of current item
  SPListItem item = workflowProperties.Item;
  // determine whether workflow is running on a standard item or a document
  if (item.File == null) {
    HistoryDescription = "Workflow started on item " + item.Title;
  }
  else {
    HistoryDescription = "Workflow started on document " + item.File.Name;
  }
  HistoryOutcome = "Workflow activation complete";
}
```

The previous example demonstrates a few important things about writing code within the event handler for a WF program targeting WSS. First, you see it's very simple to program against the item or the document on which the workflow is running because the workflowProperties field exposes an Item property that, in turn, exposes a File property. The code in this example checks to see whether the File property is null to determine whether the workflow instance started on a standard list item or on a document.

> **Tip** Note that the WF programs run under the security context of the SHAREPOINT\system account. If you want to log history list activity under the name of the current user, you must assign a value to the UserId property of the LogToHistoryListActivity with a value other than –1. For example, you can log the history list entries by using the account name of the user that initiated the current workflow instance by binding the UserId property of the LogToHistory-ListActivity to workflowProperties.OriginatorUser.ID.

The second important observation about this example is that the event handler assigns values to fields that are data bound to properties within the LogToHistoryListActivity activity. The timing is important here because the LogToHistoryListActivity activity does its work of evaluating its data-bound expressions and writing its entry into the workflow history after the event handler fires. This is the opposite of the timing involved with the onWorkflowActivated activity, which fires its event handler after completing its work of initializing the new workflow instance and assigning values back to the workflowProperties field in the Workflow1 class as a result of a data-bound property setting.

In the previous simple example, you saw the declarative data flow controlled through data binding that worked in both directions. The first example shows how data-binding the WorkflowProperties property of the onWorkflowActivated activity enables the flow of data from a child activity to the top-level activity named Workflow1. The second example shows you how to assign values to fields within Workflow1 that flow to a child activity.

Deploying a Workflow Template for Testing

At this point, the WF program named Workflow1 with the HelloWorkflow project has enough functionality that we can move through the steps of deployment to test our work. This section walks you through the details of installing the workflow template, creating an association, and initiating a workflow instance.

Note that WSS requires that an assembly DLL containing WF programs associated with a workflow template be installed in the GAC prior to use. That means that you must add a signing key to your assembly project so that its output assembly DLL is built with a strong name. Go ahead and add a strong name key file to the HelloWorkflow project so that the output assembly HelloWorkflow.dll is built with a strong name that makes it possible to deploy it in the GAC.

Next, you need to modify the two files named feature.xml and workflow.xml to define an installable feature that contains a Workflow element used to define a workflow template. After you complete this step, you should be able to install the feature with WSS by using stsadm.exe. Begin by opening the file named feature.xml, which is initially empty of content. Add the following CAML-based content to define the high-level feature attributes.

```
<Feature
  Id="0CEED7AE-D327-41ad-BC33-B3F3F8A4DAD2"
  Title="Hello World Workflow Template Feature"
  Description="This feature installs our Hello World Workflow Template"
  Version="12.0.0.0"
  Scope="Site"
  xmlns="http://schemas.microsoft.com/sharepoint/">

  <ElementManifests>
    <ElementManifest Location="workflow.xml" />
  </ElementManifests>

</Feature>
```

Within the Feature element, you can see it has typical attribute settings, such as a new unique GUID for its Id attribute along with a Title and Description. You should take note that the Scope attribute has a value of Site, which means that this feature is scoped at the site collection level as opposed to the site level. This is important because workflow templates can be defined only within features that are defined at Site Collection scope.

> **Tip** The Workflow Starter Kit of the SDK provides code snippets that enable you to generate the starting XML-based content for feature.xml and workflow.xml.

Next, open the workflow.xml file. You can see that this file is also initially empty of content. You need to add a Workflow element that defines a workflow template. Add the following XML-based content into workflow.xml:

```
<Elements xmlns="http://schemas.microsoft.com/sharepoint/">

  <Workflow
    Id="1EE1C818-DB7A-4a55-B21B-959D413C6A9C"
    Name="Hello World Workflow Template"
    Description="This workflow templates has Hello World functionality"
    CodeBesideClass="HelloWorkflow.Workflow1"
    CodeBesideAssembly="HelloWorkflow, [four-part assembly name]" >

    <Categories/> <!-- no catagories needed -->
    <MetaData />  <!-- no metadata needed -->

  </Workflow>
</Elements>
```

As you add this Workflow element into workflow.xml to define a workflow template, you must create a new GUID and assign it the Id attribute. Note that this GUID is different from the GUID used to identify the feature itself. You should also note that you are not limited to one workflow template per feature.

For example, assume that you want to add three WF programs to your Visual Studio project. Each one of these WF programs must be defined as a separate workflow template and requires its own Workflow element within the workflow.xml file. Of course, each of these workflow templates needs its own unique GUID to serve as its Id.

In addition to the Id, the Workflow element used to define a workflow template requires a Name, a Description, and two other attributes named CodeBesideClass and CodeBeside-Assembly that should be configured to point to a class name of a WF program that has been compiled into an assembly DLL and installed in the GAC. At this point, we have done enough within workflow.xml to install our Hello World workflow template. Later in the chapter, in the section titled "Integrating Workflow Input Forms," we will revisit the topic of working with the Workflow element when it's time to integrate workflow input forms with our workflow template.

Now that we are finished editing feature.xml and workflow.xml, you should open the install.bat file and examine what's inside. You need to make some edits to the install.bat file so that it contains the proper command-line instructions required to copy the feature files to the correct location and install the feature with the stsadm.exe utility. The install.bat file should also be written to install HelloWorkflow.dll into the GAC. Comments found inside install.bat provide instructions on what needs to be done. In most cases, all you really need to do is find and replace the text "MyFeature" with the name of your feature. This find and replace operation will take place about 14 different times. You'll need to do more only if you change the default file names for your XML files or deploy to a non-root site collection.

> **Tip**   The install.bat file generated by the Visual Studio project templates from the WSS Workflow Starter kit does not include a fully qualified path to the STSADM.EXE command-line utility. When you try to run install.bat, you might get an error saying it cannot find STSADM.EXE. To fix this problem, you can either add a System path to your development workstation or update install.bat as discussed in the sidebar in Chapter 1 titled "The STSADM.EXE Command Line Utility."

After editing install.bat, you are now ready to deploy the workflow template for testing. First, build the HelloWorkflow project to ensure that the assembly DLL is up to date. Next, run install.bat from the command line or by double-clicking it within Windows Explorer. Note that installation of the assembly DLL in the GAC fails if you have not compiled HelloWorkflow.dll with a strong name. However, if install.bat runs successfully, you can then move to the next step of the workflow template test.

Testing the Hello World Workflow Template

Once you have installed the feature that contains the Hello World workflow template, you should be able to activate it with a site collection for testing. Create or navigate to a test site collection that you can use to test your work. Once you get to the top-level site of the site collection, go to the Site Settings page and click the Site Collection Features link. At the Site Collection Features page, you should see the feature that defines your workflow template. Activating the feature makes your workflow template available to create workflow associations on lists, document libraries, and other content types throughout the site collection.

It's now time to create a workflow association. Create or navigate to a list. Go to the List Settings page for the list and click the Workflow Settings link. If there are no existing workflow associations on the list, clicking the Workflow Settings link should take you to a page named AddWrkfl.aspx, which allows you to create new workflow associations. If there are already existing workflow associations on the list, clicking the Workflow Settings link should take you to the standard Workflow Settings page named WrkSetng.aspx. The WrkSetng. aspx.page displays existing workflow associations and provides a link that redirects you to a page that allows you to create a new workflow association.

Click the Add A Workflow link, which takes you to the Add A Workflow page named AddWrkfl.aspx. On this page, you can see all of the workflow templates that are activated with the current site collection, including your Hello World workflow template. Select the Hello World workflow template and use it to create a new workflow association named Hello World Workflow Association. When you click the OK button, it creates the new association and returns you to the Workflow Settings page.

Now that the workflow association is created, it's time to create a workflow instance on an item within the list. Return to the main page for the list named AllItems.aspx so that you can create a new list item. Once you create the new item, drop down the ECB menu for that list item and click the ECB menu item titled Workflows. Clicking the Workflow ECB menu item should take you to the Workflow.aspx page, where you should have the option of starting a new workflow instance by using your Hello World workflow association. Start a new workflow instance by clicking Hello World Workflow Association.

After starting the workflow instance, return to the AllItems.aspx page for the list and look at the item for which you just started the new workflow instance. There should be a new column for the workflow association and a Completed link indicating that the workflow ran and was able to complete. Click this link so that you can drill down into the workflow status page named WrkStat.aspx. You should see information about the workflow instance, including the entry written to the workflow history table by the LogToHistoryListActivity activity that you added to your workflow. If you followed all of the steps correctly, the workflow status page should look like the page shown in Figure 8-12.

We have now walked through the steps for creating, deploying, and testing a very simple workflow template. However, a typical workflow template in the real world does not run to completion as soon as it is initiated. Instead, it performs one or more tasks and then uses events to go to sleep until the user(s) responsible for modifying those tasks performs additional work, which is the topic of our next section.

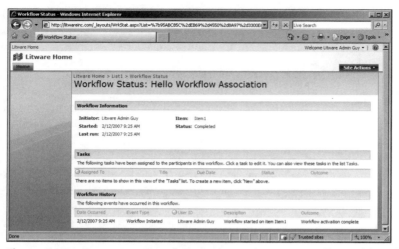

Figure 8-12   Once you successfully deploy and test your Hello World workflow template, you should see your message in the workflow history table for a specific workflow instance.

Creating and Waiting On Tasks

Earlier in this chapter, we explained at a high level how WSS adds a human dimension on top of the WF for task-driven activities. However, to take advantage of this dimension, you must learn how to develop WF programs that create WSS tasks associated with workflow instances. It is equally important for you to learn how to put a workflow instance to sleep in a way that allows it to wake up and resume its execution when a user updates one of the tasks associated with it.

When you create a task that's associated with a workflow instance, you don't do it by calling the Items.Add method on an SPList object as you would when creating new list items in other WSS development scenarios. Instead, you must go through the *WSS Workflow Services API* so that each new task is created with a subscription. The subscription is something that associates a new task with a workflow instance by wiring up event handlers that react to users who modify or delete the task.

Fortunately, it is not necessary for you to program against the WSS Workflow Services API directly. Instead, you can create WF programs using activities based on activity types such as CreateTask, OnTaskCreated, UpdateTask, OnTaskChanged, and CompleteTask. These activity types contain the code that encapsulates the necessary calls into the WSS Workflow Services API. When you use these activity types, you can create a WF program that creates a task and then puts the current workflow instance to sleep. At a later time when the task is updated by a user, an event handler that has been registered by the WSS Workflow Services API fires and brings the workflow instance back to life to continue its execution.

It is important that you begin to distinguish between method activities and event activities. The activities created from method activity types, such as CreateTask, UpdateTask, CompleteTask, and DeleteTask, are represented with blue shapes in the workflow designer, whereas activities created from event activity types, such as OnTaskCreated, OnTaskChanged, and OnTask-Deleted, are represented with green shapes.

A *method activity* is one that performs an action, such as creating or updating a task. An *event activity* is one that runs in response to an action occurring. Event activities are particularly important in creating episodic WF programs because they can provide the blocking behavior required when a workflow instance needs to wait for some external event before continuing with its execution.

Let's continue working with the WF program named Workflow1 from the HelloWorkflow project that we began developing earlier in this chapter. We are now going to extend Workflow1 to create and wait on a task, and we begin by adding two new activities. First, we create a new activity by using the CreateTask method activity type. Next, we create a second new activity after it by using the OnTaskCreated event activity type. After creating these two activities, the Designer view window of Workflow1.cs should look like the image in Figure 8-13.

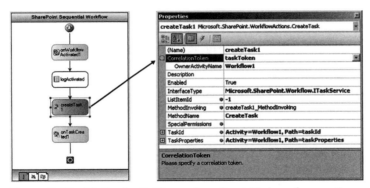

Figure 8-13   Method activities such as CreateTask perform actions, whereas event activities such as OnTaskCreated respond to actions.

When several different method activities and event activities within a WF program work on the same task, it's important for all of these activities to be able to identify this task. The WSS workflow infrastructure relies on *correlators* to accomplish this. A correlator involves the use of both a GUID and a *correlation token*. The following text explains what's required to properly set up the correlator that allows several different activities to all work on the same task.

We begin by creating a new correlation token for the task. Navigate to the property sheet for the CreateTask activity and take a look at the CorrelationToken property. The value for this property is initially empty, yet it needs to be assigned a valid value before the CreateTask activity can function correctly. If you look at the drop-down list for this property value, you see an existing CorrelationToken value of workflowToken that you can select. However, you don't want to select workflowToken because it identifies the workflow instance and not the task that is being created. Instead, you must create a new CorrelationToken object.

It's actually fairly simple to create the new CorrelationToken object for the new task being created. Simply place your cursor into the property sheet and type in a new string value for the CorrelationToken, such as "taskToken," and then hit the ENTER key. The code generator of the workflow designer responds by adding the code into Workflow1.designer.cs to create a new CorrelationToken object named taskToken. The code generator also does the work to initialize the taskToken object and bind it to the CorrelationToken property of the CreateTask activity.

Note that after you create the new CorrelationToken object named taskToken and assign it to the CorrelationToken property of the CreateTask activity, you must still assign its Owner-ActivityName property value as shown in Figure 8-13. The OwnerActivityName property value can point back to the parent activity, which in this case is the top-level WF program itself named Workflow1.

Once you create the CorrelationToken named taskToken within the property sheet for the CreateTask activity, you can use it as the CorrelationToken property value for other task-related activities within the same WF program. For example, you can select the other activity named OnTaskCreated and, from its property sheet, assign taskToken to its CorrelationToken property by selecting it from the drop-down menu.

After creating the correlation token for the task, the next thing you must do is add two new fields to the Workflow1 class that will be data bound to properties of the CreateTask activity. The first field is used to track a new GUID that passes to the CreateTask activity so that it can properly initialize its correlation token. The second field should be defined by using the SPWorkflowTaskProperties class. You use this field to pass a reference to the CreateTask activity that points to an SPWorkflowTaskProperties object that holds the initial values for the task to be created. Add the following two fields to the Workflow1 class:

```
public Guid taskId = default(System.Guid);
public SPWorkflowTaskProperties taskProperties = new SPWorkflowTaskProperties();
```

Next, you must create an event handler for the CreateTask activity. Note that CreateTask is a method activity, which means that its event handler fires before it calls the WSS Workflow Services API to perform its work. This gives you a chance to initialize fields within the WF program that can then be passed to the CreateTask activity through data binding.

Switch back to Designer view, right-click the CreateTask activity, and select the Generate Handlers command. This generates an event handler with a name such as createTask1_MethodInvoking. Add the following code to this event handler to initialize the taskId field with a new GUID and initialize the SPWorkflowTaskProperties object referenced by the taskProperties field.

```
private void createTask1_MethodInvoking(object sender, EventArgs e) {
  // generate new GUID used to initialize task correlation token
  taskId = Guid.NewGuid();
  // assign initial properties prior to task creation
  taskProperties.Title = "Task for " + workflowProperties.Item.Title;
  taskProperties.Description = "Please review and approve this item.";
  taskProperties.AssignedTo = @"LITWAREINC\BrianC";
  taskProperties.PercentComplete = 0;
  taskProperties.StartDate = DateTime.Today;
  taskProperties.DueDate = DateTime.Today.AddDays(2);
}
```

As you can see, this code is simply initializing the data that the CreateTask activity uses to perform its work when it calls the WSS Workflow Services API. The final step is to data-bind the taskId and taskProperties fields to properties in the CreateTask activity. Navigate back to Designer view and select the CreateTask activity. Proceed to the property sheet and configure data binding so that the TaskId property of the CreateTask activity is initialized with the taskId field in Workflow1. Configure data binding so that the TaskProperties property of the CreateTask activity is initialized with the taskProperties field in Workflow1.

You should now be through working with the CreateTask activity. Select the event activity named OnTaskCreated and look at its property sheet. If you haven't already done so, assign the CorrelationToken object named taskToken to its CorrelationToken property. Next, data-bind the same two fields from the Workflow1 class to the OnTaskCreated activity that you already data-bound to the CreateTask activity. In particular, data-bind the TaskId property of the OnTaskCreated activity to the taskId field in Workflow1, and data-bind the TaskProperties property of the OnTaskCreated activity to the taskProperties field in Workflow1.

One subtle yet important point must be understand concerning how method activities and event activities work. WSS batches all modifications made by a sequence of method activities into a single transaction and writes them all to the content database at once. This means that the work for a method activity is not committed when the activity finishes its work. If you don't understand when the transaction for one or more method activities is committed, it is possible to get into trouble.

For example, what would happen if you added a Code activity in between the CreateTask and OnTaskCreated activities? This Code activity would not be able to see the just-created task in a committed state because WSS has not yet written the task to the content database. WSS does not write the task to the database until the workflow instance is put to sleep by encountering an event activity, such as OnTaskCreated. However, if you add a Code activity after the OnTaskCreated activity, things will be different because you are at a point where WSS has already saved the task to the content database.

If you look at the property sheet for the OnTaskCreated activity, you notice that it has a data-binding–enabled property named TaskAfterProperties. You can use this property to get hold of an object that allows you to see the state of the new task after it is committed to the content database. Start by adding a new field to Workflow1 named taskAfterProperties based on the SPWorkflowTaskProperties type. Initialize this field with a new instance by using the following code:

```
public SPWorkflowTaskProperties taskAfterProperties =
                        new SPWorkflowTaskProperties();
```

Once you add this new field to the Code view of Workflow1.cs, navigate back to Designer view and go to the property sheet for the OnTaskCreated activity. Now data-bind the field you just created to the AfterProperties property of the OnTaskCreated activity. Next, create an event handler for this activity and add the following code:

```
void onTaskCreated1_Invoked(object sender, ExternalDataEventArgs e) {
   HistoryDescription = "Task created and assigned to " +
                        taskAfterProperties.AssignedTo;
   Guid TaskStatusFieldId = new Guid("c15b34c3-ce7d-490a-b133-3f4de8801b76");
   string TaskStatus =
          taskAfterProperties.ExtendedProperties[TaskStatusFieldId].ToString();
   HistoryOutcome = "Task status: " + TaskStatus;
}
```

This code displays an example of inspecting the after properties of a task during the event handler for an OnTaskCreated activity. Note that the taskAfterProperties field of type SPWorkflowTaskProperties makes it possible to access standard task item fields, such as AssignedTo, through strong-typed properties. Also note that some task fields, such as TaskStatus, are not available through a strong-typed property and must be accessed by using the ExtendedProperties property that exposes a collection of name/value pairs. The previous code listing demonstrates how to access the TaskStatus field by using the GUID used to define its underlying site column.

Now that you have created a task, it's time to employ the OnTaskChanged activity type to put the workflow instance to sleep. Whenever the WF program encounters an OnTaskChanged event activity, it puts the current workflow instance to sleep and registers an event handler to wake it up and resume execution whenever it is changed. In our simple Hello World example, we want our WF program to examine the TaskStatus field and determine whether it has been updated to a value of Completed. If the TaskStatus field is updated to a value of Completed, we want the workflow instance to complete its life cycle. If the TaskStatus field is not updated with a value of Completed, we want to put the workflow instance back to sleep and have it wake up the next time a user updates the task.

We can use a While activity in this example to get the proper control of flow. If the user who updates the task assigns a value of Completed to the TaskStatus field, we want to break out of the While activities loop behavior and end the life cycle of the workflow instance. However, when a user updates the task and does not assign a value of Completed to the TaskStatus field, we want to put the workflow instance back to sleep until the task is updated again in the future.

Add a While activity just after the OnTaskCreated activity, and then add an OnTaskChanged activity as a child activity inside of it, as shown in Figure 8-14. Once you add these two activities, you must then create the logic so that the While activity loops around when it should and then breaks out when a user assigns the TaskStatus field with a value of Completed.

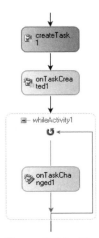

Figure 8-14   Placing an OnTaskChanged activity inside a While activity makes it possible to achieve the correct control-of-flow logic to ensure that a task is properly updated before continuing.

> **Tip**   Note that a While activity can contain only a single child activity. In our example, we are using the OnTaskChanged activity. However, in situations in which you want a sequence of several child activities inside a While activity, you must use a slightly different approach. You can add an activity by using the Sequence activity type as a child activity to the While activity. You can then add multiple child activities to the Sequence activity so that you can have several child activities execute inside the scope of a While activity.

You should start by adding a new field to the Workflow1 class that is used to control the looping behavior of the While activity. In particular, add a public field named TaskNotCompleted that is based on a Boolean type and initialized to a value of true.

```
public bool TaskNotCompleted = true;
```

Now that you have created the TaskNotCompleted field in Workflow1, you can use it to control looping behavior of the While activity. Switch back to Designer view, select the While activity, and inspect its property sheet. Locate the property named Condition and drop down its combo box to view the available values. You should see two possible values named Declarative Rule Condition and Code Condition. Select a value of Declarative Rule Condition, and then put your cursor into the property field of the Condition name. If you then click the ellipsis, you should see the Rule Condition Editor as shown in Figure 8-15, where you can simply add the field name of TaskNotCompleted. You might notice that the Rule Condition Editor provides IntelliSense just as if you were typing C# code inside a code editor window.

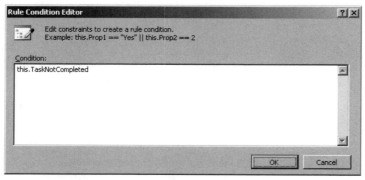

Figure 8-15 You can use the Rule Condition Editor to add a Declarative Rule Condition that controls the looping behavior of a While activity.

Once you add the code condition to control the While activity, the final step is to properly configure the OnTaskChanged activity. Make sure to assign the taskToken to its correlation token property and bind its properties to the fields in Workflow1 just as you bound the properties of the other task-related activities. Finally, add an event handler to the OnTaskChanged activity by clicking the Generate Handlers command. Once you generate the event handler, add the following code:

```
private void onTaskChanged1_Invoked(object sender, ExternalDataEventArgs e)
{
  TaskStatus = taskAfterProperties.ExtendedProperties[TaskStatusFieldId].ToString();
  if (TaskStatus.Equals("Completed")) {
    // update variable to break out of while loop
    TaskNotCompleted = false;
  }
  // generate info for history list entry
  HistoryDescription = "Task updated";
  HistoryOutcome = "Task status: " + TaskStatus;
}
```

At this point, you should be able to test your work. Recompile your WF program and then run the install.bat file to install the new version in the GAC, refresh the feature installation, and reset IIS. After doing this, you should be able to test the new version of your workflow template. If you are successful, you should be able to initiate new workflow instances that create tasks and then go to sleep while they are still in progress. Once you initiate a workflow instance, you should drill down to the workflow status page to see whether the task has been created. If a task is created, the workflow status page makes it possible to open this task for editing. Try editing the task to see whether changing the Task Status column value to Completed advances the workflow instance to the end of its life cycle.

This completes our walk-through of the creation of a simple workflow template that interacts with users by using workflow tasks. While this sample does not deal with many of the scenarios you might deal with in the development of real-world WF programs, it should give you an appreciation for what is required to work with tasks. You create tasks with the CreateTask method activity and then use event activities, such as OnTaskCreated and OnTaskChanged, to inspect the task after it is saved. You will typically also be required to manage the execution of WF programs that create tasks by using control-of-flow activities, such as the While activity.

Integrating Workflow Input Forms

This chapter concludes with a discussion of integrating workflow input forms into a workflow template. Our discussion focuses on a sample Visual Studio project named Litware-Workflows that accompanies this chapter. The LitwareWorkflows project contains a single WF program named LitwareApproval, along with a feature that defines a workflow template. The workflow template integrates each of the four different types of workflow input forms. By becoming familiar with the LitwareWorkflows sample project, you can learn the basic techniques that enable you to develop and integrate custom workflow input forms into the workflow templates that you create.

Open the project named LitwareWorkflows and take a moment to become familiar with all of the source files inside. As you can see from Figure 8-16, a file named LitwareApproval.cs contains the definition for the WF program itself. Next, three XML files are used to define the feature named LitwareWorkflows that installs the workflow template within a WSS farm. At this point in the chapter, you should already have a general understanding about how to create a WF program and the feature used to install it as a workflow template. We will now focus on how the other source files inside the LitwareWorkflows project are used to integrate workflow input forms.

The LitwareWorkflows project contains four different .aspx files to supply each of the four available types of input forms: an association form, an initiation form, a modification form, and a task edit form. Note that all of these forms are implemented as custom application pages that are deployed within the LAYOUTS directory. As you remember, the fundamental concepts of developing and deploying custom application pages were covered in Chapter 2, "SharePoint Architecture."

It is recommended that you do not deploy your custom application pages directly inside the LAYOUTS directory. Instead, you should create a company-specific directory inside the LAYOUTS directory to deploy your custom application pages. The LitwareWorkflows project is structured to deploy its four custom application pages within a custom Litware directory that is nested inside the LAYOUTS directory.

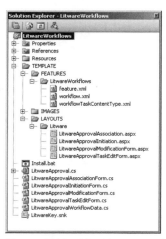

Figure 8-16 The LitwareWorkflows project demonstrates how to implement the four different types of workflow input forms.

Open the file named workflow.xml and inspect the definition of the Workflow element that defines the workflow template. You should see the attributes named AssociationUrl, InstantiationUrl, and ModificationUrl that contain references to three of the workflow input forms.

```
<Workflow
  Id="4797A6A6-4F31-40ca-9814-746402C2DB56"
  Name="Litware Approval"
  Description="Sample workflow template demonstrating workflow input forms"
  CodeBesideClass="LitwareWorkflows.LitwareApproval"
  CodeBesideAssembly="LitwareWorkflows, [full 4-part assembly name]"
  AssociationUrl="_layouts/Litware/LitwareApprovalAssociation.aspx"
  InstantiationUrl="_layouts/Litware/LitwareApprovalInitiation.aspx"
  ModificationUrl="_layouts/Litware/LitwareApprovalModificationForm.aspx"
  TaskListContentTypeId="0x0108010084565D92BEFE4a75A28C2F658B7BECCA"   >
  <MetaData>
    <Modification_c7a53c4e-ab25-450f-a595-ae2b380d7c3e_Name>
      Modify workflow instance with a custom Litware form
    </Modification_c7a53c4e-ab25-450f-a595-ae2b380d7c3e_Name>
  </MetaData>
  <Categories/>
</Workflow>
```

While there are attributes containing references to three of four of the workflow input forms, there is no reference to the task edit form because you do not integrate a task edit form in the same fashion as the other three types of workflow input forms. Instead, if you want a custom form as opposed to the standard WSS task edit form, you must create a custom content type that inherits from the standard workflow task content type. When you create a custom content type for a custom workflow task, you can define it to use its own custom edit form, which is the approach used in the LitwareWorkflows project. Note that within the

Workflow element inside workflow.xml is a TaskListContentTypeId attribute that is configured with the ID content type, which identifies the custom content type defined inside workflowTaskContentType.xml.

Walk Through Using the Litware Approval Workflow Input Forms

To test the workflow template and workflow input forms defined by the LitwareWorkflows project, you must do three things. First, you must install the assembly named LitwareWorkflow.dll into the GAC. Second, you must copy all of the files that need to be deployed inside the TEMPLATES directory. Third, you must install the feature that defines the workflow template. The LitwareWorkflows project contains an install.bat file that automates all three steps. You can run this batch file simply by building the LitwareWorkflows project.

Once you build the LitwareWorkflow project, you should then be able to activate the feature with the Litware Approval workflow template within any site collection within the farm. Next, create a new site collection or navigate to an existing site collection so that you can test this workflow template. Once you navigate to a top-level site within this site collection, go to the standard application page that allows you to activate site collection features. You should see the feature titled *A Sample Feature: Litware Workflows*. Activate this feature to make its workflow template available within the site collection. At this point, you should be able to use the workflow template to create a new workflow association.

Custom Association Forms

It's now time to create a new list (or document library) so that you have a place to create a new workflow association from the Litware Approval workflow template. Once you create the new list, go to the List Settings page and click the Workflow Settings link to the page on which you can view the existing workflow associations. Click the Add A Workflow link to navigate to the standard application page named AddWrkfl.aspx, which allows you to create a new workflow association for the list. You should see Litware Approval as an available workflow template, as shown in Figure 8-17.

The AddWrkfl.aspx page allows the user to select a workflow template, provide a unique name, and parameterize other standard aspects of a workflow association. For example, the user can parameterize the workflow association to use an existing task list and history list. The user can alternatively choose to create a new task list and/or new history list. Continue the walk-through by selecting the Litware Approval workflow template, giving the new workflow association the name Legal Approval, and then clicking Next.

Here's an important question. What happens when a user clicks the Next button on the AddWrkfl.aspx page? The answer depends on whether your workflow template is configured with an association form. If your workflow template is not configured with an association form, the code behind the Next button executes all of the logic required to create the workflow association and create a new task list and new history list if necessary.

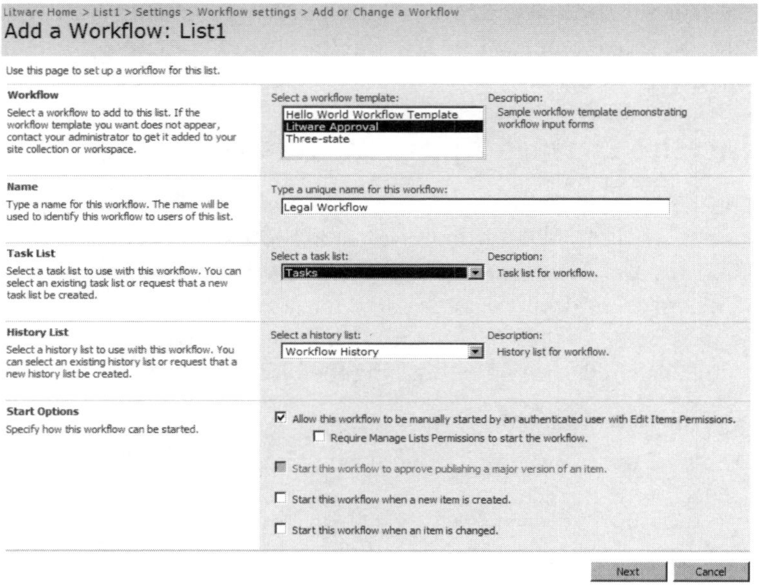

Figure 8-17 The standard application AddWrkfl.aspx page is always shown before a custom association form.

However, if your workflow template is configured with an association form, clicking Next simply redirects the user to that association form. When you click Next to create the Legal Approval workflow association in the walk-through, you should be redirected to the custom association form named LitwareApprovalAssociation.aspx, as shown in Figure 8-18.

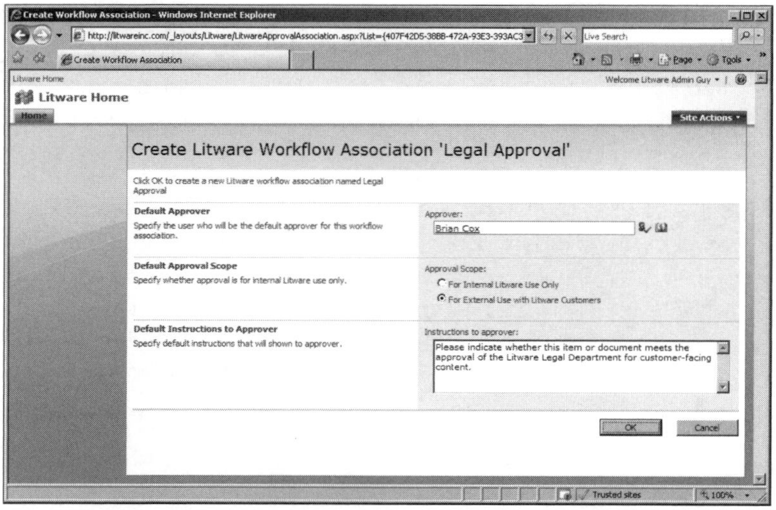

Figure 8-18 A custom workflow association form is used to gather parameterization information for a new workflow association.

An important observation is that when you configure a workflow template with a custom association form, you then take on the responsibility of supplying the code to create the new workflow association. You must also supply the code to create a new task list and/or new history list if that is what the user requests.

Take a moment and consider the primary purpose of a custom association form. It's used to prompt users for extra parameterization data whenever they create a new workflow association. In the case of the Litware Approval workflow template, the association form is used to obtain default values for the approver, the approval scope (internal versus external), and instructions to the approver. When a user enters data into this association form and clicks OK, your code must serialize the user input values into a string that is saved as *association data*. The association data are then used by the initiation form each time a user starts a new workflow instance from the workflow association.

Implementing a Custom Association Form

We will now walk through some implementation details of the association form. Open Litware-ApprovalAssociation.aspx and inspect what's inside. You should notice that this source file does not contain any code inside. Instead, it simply contains input controls, two command buttons, and layout details. The actual code for the association form is written into a class named LitwareApprovalAssociationForm that is compiled into the same assembly DLL as the WF program itself, LitwareWorkflows.dll. If you look at the Page directive within Litware-ApprovalAssociationForm.aspx, you can see that it is defined to inherit from the code-behind class named LitwareApprovalAssociationForm.

Open the source file named LitwareApprovalAssociationForm.cs and examine the class inside that defines the behavior for LitwareApprovalAssociationForm.aspx. You can see that the LitwareApprovalAssociationForm class inherits from the LayoutsPageBase, which follows the best practice for developing custom application pages. You might also notice that this class contains over 300 lines of code even though this is a fairly simple example about creating a custom association form. The high-level structure for this class definition looks like the following code:

```
public class LitwareApprovalAssociationForm : LayoutsPageBase {
  // control fields
  // form-level variables
  protected override void OnLoad(EventArgs e) {...}
  protected void PopulateFormDataFromString(string AssociationData){...}
  protected string SerializeFormDataToString(){...}
  protected void UpdateAssociation(SPWorkflowAssociation wfa,
                                    SPList TaskList, SPList HistoryList) {...}
  public void cmdCancel_OnClick(object sender, EventArgs e) {...}
  public void cmdSubmit_OnClick(object sender, EventArgs e) {...}
  protected override void OnPreRender(EventArgs e) {...}
}
```

LitwareApprovalAssociationForm.aspx defines several input controls to gather input data from the user. For example, it defines an instance of the WSS PeopleEditor control that provides a handy technique when you need a user to select another user, such as the approver. The following example demonstrates what the control tag looks like inside LitwareApproval-AssociationForm.aspx.

```
<SharePoint:PeopleEditor
  id="pickerApprover"
  AllowEmpty="false"
  ValidatorEnabled="true"
  MultiSelect="false"
  runat="server"
  SelectionSet="User"
  width='300px'
  />
```

When you have an .aspx file and a code-behind class, there is a handy technique in ASP.NET programming in which the code-behind class defines a control field by using the same name as a control instance in the .aspx page. When the ASP.NET runtime compiles the .aspx file, it adds support to create the control instance and assign a reference to the control field in the code-behind class. This makes it possible for methods within the code-behind class to access the control instances defined inside the .aspx file. All of the workflow input forms in the LitwareWorkflows project rely on this technique. For example, the LitwareApprovalAssociation-Form class defines a control field named pickerApprover to match the control instance defined in LitwareApprovalAssociationForm.aspx.

```
public class LitwareApprovalAssociationForm : LayoutsPageBase {
  // define control field with name that matches .aspx file
  protected PeopleEditor pickerApprover;
}
```

The benefit to using this technique is that now all of the methods within the LitwareApproval-AssociationForm class have direct access to all of the control instances defined inside LitwareApprovalAssociationForm.aspx. This is important because the code-behind class must provide the code to initialize input controls with default values and retrieve the input values that are entered by users.

Now, examine the form-level variables (that is, fields) in the LitwareApprovalAssociationForm class and then walk through the code inside the OnLoad method. You can see that the code in this event handler retrieves parameter values that are passed by WSS and uses them to initialize strings, GUIDs, and various objects from the WSS object model. You can also see that the code in the OnLoad event must determine whether the workflow association is being created on a list, a site-level content type, or a list-level content type. If the new workflow association is being created on a list, conditional code behind the OK button executes this code:

```
WorkflowAssociation =
   SPWorkflowAssociation.CreateListAssociation(WorkflowTemplate,
                                               WorkflowAssociationName,
                                               TaskList,
                                               HistoryList);
```

However, when the workflow association is being created on a content type in the two other possible scenarios, the code behind the OK button must be conditionally programmed to call either CreateSiteContentTypeAssociation or CreateListContentTypeAssociation instead of CreateListAssociation. The code must also deal with the scenario in which the user is updating an existing workflow association instead of creating a new one. In this scenario, the code must call the UpdateWorkflowAssociation method on either an SPList object or SPContentType object.

A utility method named UpdateAssociation accepts an SPWorkflowAssociation object and makes the necessary changes to prepare the object to be saved. As you can see, your code must deal with whatever options are selected by the user, such as whether the workflow association should be configured to automatically start new workflow instances or whether to allow users to start workflow instances manually.

```
protected void UpdateAssociation(SPWorkflowAssociation wfa,
                                 SPList TaskList, SPList HistoryList) {
  wfa.Name = WorkflowAssociationName;
  wfa.AutoStartCreate = (Request.Params["AutoStartCreate"] == "ON");
  wfa.AutoStartChange = (Request.Params["AutoStartChange"] == "ON");
  wfa.AllowManual = (Request.Params["AllowManual"] == "ON");
  wfa.AssociationData = SerializeFormDataToString();
  if (wfa.TaskListTitle != TaskList.Title) {
    wfa.SetTaskList(TaskList);
  }
  if (wfa.HistoryListTitle != HistoryList.Title) {
    wfa.SetHistoryList(HistoryList);
  }
}
```

The other important aspect of implementing an association form is how to manage user input values. The values that a user enters into the form's input controls must be serialized as a string and then saved to the AssociationData property of the SPWorkflowAssociation object. When a user chooses to modify an existing workflow association, the current value of the AssociationData property must be deserialized and then used to populate the form's input controls during initialization.

Note that the examples of serializing and deserializing data used in the LitwareWorkflows project involve the use of a schema-generated class named LitwareApprovalWorkflowData. This class can be used together with the XmlSerializer class to create strong-typed .NET objects that can be converted back and forth with XML documents that adhere to the following XML format:

```
<LitwareApproval>
  <Approver>LITWAREINC\BrianC</Approver>
  <ApprovalScope>Internal</ApprovalScope>
  <Instructions>This is a sample instruction</Instructions>
  <Comments>This is a sample comment</Comments>
</LitwareApproval>
```

The LitwareApprovalAssociationForm class supplies two methods, named SerializeForm-DataToString and PopulateFormDataFromString. These methods are used to move input data back and forth between the form's input controls and a serialized string that is saved back to the AssociationData property prior to creating or updating the workflow association. The following example displays the implementation of the SerializeFormDataToString method.

```
protected string SerializeFormDataToString() {
  LitwareApprovalWorkflowData FormData = new LitwareApprovalWorkflowData();
  PickerEntity ApproverEntity = (PickerEntity)pickerApprover.Entities[0];
  FormData.Approver = ApproverEntity.Key;
  if (radInternalApproval.Checked) {
    FormData.ApprovalScope = "Internal";
  }
  else {
    FormData.ApprovalScope = "External";
  }
  FormData.Instructions = txtInstructions.Text;
  using (MemoryStream stream = new MemoryStream()) {
    XmlSerializer serializer =
                new XmlSerializer(typeof(LitwareApprovalWorkflowData));
    serializer.Serialize(stream, FormData);
    stream.Position = 0;
    byte[] bytes = new byte[stream.Length];
    stream.Read(bytes, 0, bytes.Length);
    return Encoding.UTF8.GetString(bytes);
  }
}
```

You can see how most of the pieces fit together when it's time to create and parameterize a new workflow association. You can now understand the following code behind the association form's OK button, which is written to create and parameterize a new workflow association and then to append it to the collection of workflow associations for the target list.

```
WorkflowAssociation =
  SPWorkflowAssociation.CreateListAssociation(WorkflowTemplate,
                                              WorkflowAssociationName,
                                              TaskList,
                                              HistoryList);

UpdateAssociation(WorkflowAssociation, TaskList, HistoryList);
List.AddWorkflowAssociation(WorkflowAssociation);
```

The final implementation detail that warrants your attention is the logic in the association form that's responsible for creating a new task list and new history list when required. It's a bit peculiar, but WSS places a z character at the beginning of the incoming list name to indicate that it is the name for a new list that needs to be created. There is logic in the OnLoad method to initialize Boolean variables named NewTaskListRequired and NewHistoryListRequired with a value of true or false. The first few lines of code behind the OK button then execute the following code:

```
if (NewTaskListRequired) {
  Guid TaskListId = Web.Lists.Add(NewTaskListName,
                                  "Workflow Tasks",
                                  SPListTemplateType.Tasks);
  // obtain reference to SPList item
  TaskList = Web.Lists[TaskListId];
}

if (NewHistoryListRequired) {
  Guid HistoryListId = Web.Lists.Add(NewHistoryListName,
                                     "Workflow History",
                                     SPListTemplateType.WorkflowHistory);
  // obtain reference to SPList item
  HistoryList = Web.Lists[HistoryListId];
}
```

As you can see, association forms require a good deal of code. However, you can also see that much of this code is boilerplate in nature and, once written, it can be generically reused across association forms for many different workflow templates.

Custom Initiation Forms

It is now time to discuss the creation of a custom initiation form. Let's start the discussion by conducting a walk-through of the user experience. Once the user creates the Legal Approval workflow association from the Litware Approval workflow template, the user should then be able to see the association from the standard application page named Workflow.aspx, as shown in Figure 8-19. Recall that the user can navigate to the Workflow.aspx page by selecting the Workflow menu item from the ECB menu for an item or document.

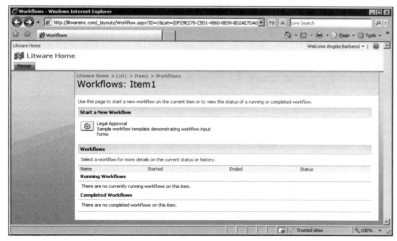

Figure 8-19   The Workflow.aspx page allows users to initiate workflow instances from any available workflow associations.

From the Workflow.aspx page, a user can click on the link to any available workflow association to start a new workflow instance. If the underlying workflow template is not configured with an initiation form, WSS automatically starts the workflow instance. However, when the underlying workflow template is configured with an initiation form, the user is then redirected to it.

In our scenario, click the Legal Approval link, which takes you to LitwareApprovalInitiation.aspx, as shown in Figure 8-20. You can see that the initiation form's input controls initially display the default values from the AssociationData property of the workflow association. This gives the user the ability to leave the default values as they are or make whatever changes make sense for the particular workflow instance being created.

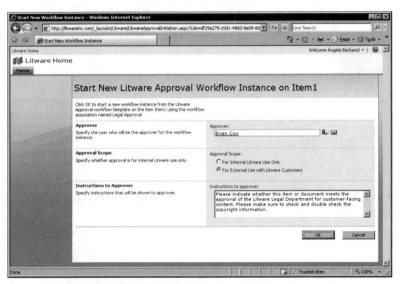

Figure 8-20 A custom initiation form gives the developer a chance to prompt the user for parameterization data that can be passed to the WF program when the new workflow instance is activated.

We want to make one minor point before moving on to discuss the implementation details of creating a custom initiation form. Custom initiation forms can be used only with workflow associations that allow the user to manually start workflow instances through the Workflow.aspx page. You cannot present the user with an initiation form in scenarios in which you have configured a workflow association to automatically start new workflow instances whenever a new item is added to a list or a new document is uploaded to a document library. These types of scenarios do not provide a natural flow to present the user with a custom initiation form and are therefore not supported by WSS.

Implementing a Custom Initiation Form

If you look inside LitwareApprovalInitiation.aspx, you observe that the input control tags and page layout are almost identical to those in LitwareApprovalAssociation.aspx. This makes sense because the association form is used to obtain default values for all workflow instances, and the initiation form then gives the user the opportunity to see these default values and optionally change them when starting a particular workflow instance.

LitwareApprovalInitiation.aspx relies on a code-behind base class named LitwareApproval-InitiationForm. The high-level structure for the LitwareApprovalInitiationForm class definition looks like the following code:

```
public class LitwareApprovalInitiationForm : LayoutsPageBase {
  // control fields
  // form-level variables
  protected override void OnLoad(EventArgs e) {...}
  protected void PopulateFormDataFromString(string AssociationData){...}
  protected string SerializeFormDataToString(){...}
  public void cmdCancel_OnClick(object sender, EventArgs e) {...}
  public void cmdSubmit_OnClick(object sender, EventArgs e) {...}
  protected override void OnPreRender(EventArgs e) {...}
}
```

The OnLoad method uses incoming parameters passed by WSS to create a new SPWorkflow-Association object. It then uses this SPWorkflowAssociation object to obtain association data from the current workflow association so that it can make a call to the PopulateForm-DataFromString method to initialize the form's input controls with default values. When the user changes the values within these input controls and clicks OK to start a new workflow instance, logic exists to call SerializeFormDataToString to serialize these data into a form-level variable named InitiationData. After that, there is a call to start the actual workflow instance.

When you need to start a workflow instance, you interact with an SPWorkflowManager object. The SPWorkflowManager object is exposed through the WorkflowManager property on the SPSite obect that represents the current site collection. The SPWorkflowManager object provides a method named StartWorkflow that does exactly what its name suggests.

```
Web.Site.WorkflowManager.StartWorkflow(ListItem,
                            WorkflowAssociation,
                            InitiationData);
```

Now take a moment to consider how the two workflow input forms you have seen so far interact with the WF program. You should realize that all of the code behind the association and initiation forms execute before the WF program starts running. It is not until the point at which the user clicks the OK button on the initiation form and the call to StartWorkflow is made that the WF program is called into action. At that point, code in the event handler of the OnWorkflowActivated activity of LitwareApproval.cs is able to retrieve the initiation data, deserialize them, and store them in fields defined within the WF program.

```
public class LitwareApproval : SequentialWorkflowActivity {

  // fields to store initiation data from initiation form
  public string Approver = default(string);
  public string ApprovalScope = default(string);
  public string ApproverInstructions = default(string);

  private void onWorkflowActivated1_Invoked(...) {
    // deserialize initiation data;
    string InitiationData = workflowProperties.InitiationData;
    XmlSerializer serializer =
              new XmlSerializer(typeof(LitwareApprovalWorkflowData));
    XmlTextReader reader =
              new XmlTextReader(new StringReader(InitiationData));
    LitwareApprovalWorkflowData FormData =
         (LitwareApprovalWorkflowData)serializer.Deserialize(reader);

    // assign form data values to workflow fields
    Approver = FormData.Approver;
    ApprovalScope = FormData.ApprovalScope;
    ApproverInstructions = FormData.Instructions;
  }
}
```

Custom Modification Forms

Once a workflow instance is in progress, you can supply a modification form that allows users to modify its state. When you properly integrate a modification form, the user is presented with a link on the WrkStat.aspx workflow status page, as shown in Figure 8-21. As you can see, the link to the modification form, Modify This Workflow With Custom Litware Form, is positioned under the standard information about the current workflow instance and above the task list.

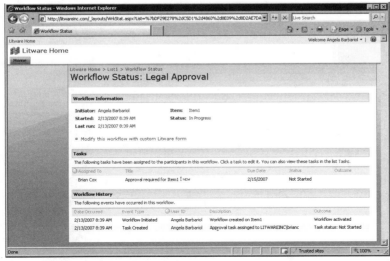

Figure 8-21   The WrkStat.aspx workflow status page displays a link for any active workflow modification.

When you create a workflow modification form, you can design it to display whatever input controls make sense for the modifications a user might want to make to a workflow instance in progress. The modification form used with the Litware Approval workflow template is shown in Figure 8-22. As you can see, it is designed to provide the user who initiated the workflow instance with an opportunity to change the approver, approval scope, and/or instructions while the workflow instance is still awaiting approval.

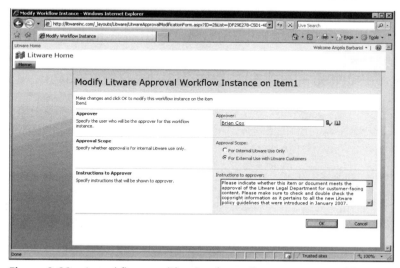

Figure 8-22 A workflow modification form allows users to modify a workflow instance while it is still in progress.

Implementing a Custom Modification Form

Let's revisit the elements that have been added to workflow.xml and that are used to configure a workflow modification form. The ModificationUrl attribute in the Workflow element references a specific .aspx file, which in this case is LitwareApprovalModificationForm.aspx. Another important element is nested within the MetaData element that defines a specific workflow modification, as shown in the following XML fragment.

```
<Workflow
  <!-- other attributes omitted for clarity -->
  ModificationUrl="_layouts/Litware/LitwareApprovalModificationForm.aspx"  >
  <MetaData>
    <Modification_c7a53c4e-ab25-450f-a595-ae2b380d7c3e_Name>
      Modify workflow instance with a custom Litware form
    </Modification_c7a53c4e-ab25-450f-a595-ae2b380d7c3e_Name>
  </MetaData>
</Workflow>
```

Though a workflow template can have only one workflow modification form, it can have more than one modification. Each modification is identified through a unique GUID and is defined using an element nested within the MetaData element that follows this form:

```
<Modification_SomeGuid_Name>
```

Inside this Modification element is text that is used to provide the caption for the link that the user will see on WrkStat.aspx. You have seen what needs to be set up in terms of declarative logic within the feature for the workflow template. However, the next section is somewhat tricky because you must add two different activities to your WF program to make the workflow modification work properly.

> **Tip**   Due to a bug in this version of WSS, any GUID used for a Modification ID must contain only lowercase letters. Things will not work properly if you use a GUID that contains uppercase letters.

First, you must add a method activity of type EnableWorkflowModification. This activity is used to make the modification active at a specific point within the life cycle of each workflow instance. Secondly, you must add an event activity named OnWorkflowModifed. This activity listens for the occurrence of modifications by users and responds by firing an event handler that executes whatever logic you provide.

You must decide at what point in time you want a modification to become active within the life cycle of a workflow instance. In the case of the LitwareApproval workflow template, the modification is designed to become active after the approval task is created so that workflow instance initiators can access the modification form while waiting for the approvers to do their work.

The technique for making a modification active requires creating an activity from the EventHandlerScope activity type supplied by the WF base activity library. You must then add a Sequence activity so that you can add several child activities inside the EventHandlerScope activity. Next, you should add an EnableWorkflowModification activity as the first activity that executes within the EventHandlerScope activity, as shown in Figure 8-23. The EnableWorkflowModification activity is a method activity that activates the modification and makes the link show up on the WrkStat.aspx page.

The next step is to set up the listener by using the OnWorkflowModifed event activity type. If you right-click the EventHandlingScope activity in the workflow designer, you notice various viewing options, including View EventHandlingScope and View Event Handlers. You need to switch over to the View Event Handlers to add and configure the OnWorkflowModifed activity.

Once you switch over to View Event Handlers, you can add an activity of the EventDriven activity type to the EventHandlingScope activity, which then makes it possible to add an event activity that acts as a listener. In the case of the Litware Approval workflow template, a single EventDriven activity contains the OnWorkflowModified activity. The main concept to grasp here is that the event handler for the OnWorkflowModified activity fires when the user updates information in the modification form and clicks the OK button.

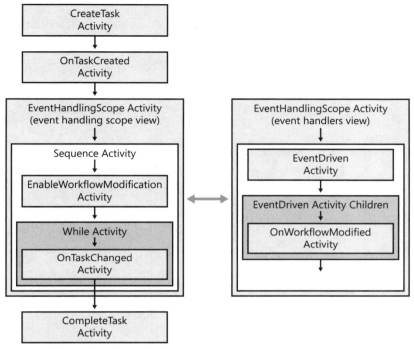

Figure 8-23   You can use an EnableWorkflowModification activity and an OnWorkflowModified activity within the scope of an EventHandlerScopeActivity activity to make a workflow modification active.

Each modification relies on a GUID and a correlation token. The GUID for a modification is hard-coded into the workflow template inside the workflow.xml file. When you add an EnableWorkflowModification activity and an OnWorkflowModified activity to a WF program to activate a modification, you must configure the ModificationId property of both activities with this GUID. You must also create a new correlation token and assign it to both activities. Note that you can create the correlation token by using the same technique you used with task-related activities. You should be able to see that the two modification activities in LitwareApproval.cs are configured with a correlation token named modificationToken. It is also important to point out that the OwnerActivityName for the correlation token named modificationToken is configured as the activity named eventHandlingScopeActivity and not the workflow program named LitwareApproval.

When you create a modification, you must add code to the WF program to pass any initialization data to the modification form that it needs. In our case, the WF program must pass the same data that the user enters on the initiation form. However, these data now exist only within the fields of the WF program. Therefore, the event handler of the Enable-WorkflowModification must serialize the form data again and assign them to a field named modificationContextData that is data bound to the ContextData property of the EnableWork-flowModifcation activity. This now makes it possible for code inside the modification form to retrieve these context data.

The LitwareApprovalModificationForm class defines the following fields as form-level variables.

```
// form-level variables
protected SPList List;
protected SPListItem ListItem;
protected SPWorkflow WorkflowInstance;
protected Guid ModificationID;
protected SPWorkflowModification Modification;
protected string ContextData;
```

The OnLoad event then supplies the logic to initialize these fields and retrieve content data passed by the WF program by accessing the ContextData property of the SPWorkflow-Modification object.

```
// Retrieve parameters passed by WSS
string paramList = Request.Params["List"];
string paramID = Request.Params["ID"];
string paramWorkflowInstanceID = Request.Params["WorkflowInstanceID"];
string paramModificationID = Request.Params["ModificationID"];
// Initialize form-level variables by creating WSS objects
List = Web.Lists[new Guid(paramList)];
ListItem = List.GetItemById(Convert.ToInt32(paramID));
WorkflowInstance = ListItem.Workflows[new Guid(paramWorkflowInstanceID)];
ModificationID = new Guid(paramModificationID);
Modification = WorkflowInstance.Modifications[ModificationID];
ContextData = Modification.ContextData;
```

Once the form initializes the data for the ContextData field, it can populate the input controls for the modification in a fashion similar to that used in the association and initiation forms. The final step in implementing the modification form is to add code behind the OK button that calls the ModifyWorkflow method on the WorkflowManager to pass the updated context data back to the WF program in a serialized form.

```
ContextData = SerializeFormDataToString();
Web.Site.WorkflowManager.ModifyWorkflow(WorkflowInstance,
                                        Modification,
                                        ContextData);
```

At this point, control is returned back to the WF program. The event handler for the OnWorkflowModified activity fires and allows your code to do whatever it needs to do with the updated context data. Note that you must data-bind the ContextData property on the OnWorkflowModified activity to a field within the WF program to obtain access to the data that are passed back from the modification form. Once you do this, your event handler can write the updated values from the context data into the fields of the WF program that are used to persist the data for the current workflow instance.

Custom Task Edit Forms

We have now reached the fourth and final type of workflow input form: the task edit form. You should design and implement a custom task edit form when you want to take over the user experience when it's time for a user to complete a task. In the example of the Litware Approval workflow template, a custom edit task named LitwareApproval-TaskEditForm.aspx, shown in Figure 8-24, is presented to users when they are ready to approve or reject an approval request.

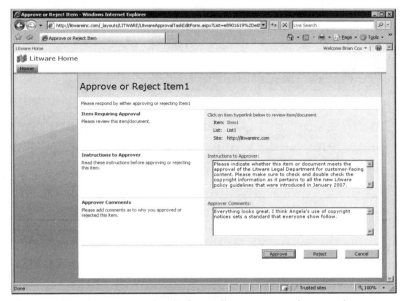

Figure 8-24   A custom task edit form allows you to take over the user experience when a user needs to complete a workflow-specific task.

You should see that there is an obvious benefit to using a custom task edit form. Instead of relying on the standard workflow task edit form, you can add extra command buttons, such as Approve and Reject, and direct the user's attention to the data and input values that matter to complete the task at hand. This can greatly help to streamline the human element when automating a business process, such as document approval.

Implementing a Custom Task Edit Form

Implementing a custom task edit form begins with creating a custom content type that inherits from the workflow task content type that is part of WSS. As you recall, we covered the basics of creating custom content types in Chapter 6, "Lists and Content Types." You should reread that section if you need a refresher on all of the details. The custom content type created for the Litware Approval workflow template is defined inside workflowTaskContent-Type.xml as follows:

```
<Elements xmlns="http://schemas.microsoft.com/sharepoint/">
  <ContentType
    ID="0x0108010084565D92BEFE4a75A28C2F658B7BECCA"
    Name="Litware Workflow Task"
    Group="Litware Content Types"
    Description="Create a Litware Workflow Task"
    Version="0"
    Hidden="FALSE" >
  <FieldRefs>
    <FieldRef ID="{e241f186-9b94-415c-9f66-255ce7f86235}" Name="Notes"
              DisplayName="Instructions"/>
    <FieldRef ID="{9da97a8a-1da5-4a77-98d3-4bc10456e700}" Name="Comments"
              DisplayName="Comments"/>
  </FieldRefs>
  <XmlDocuments>
    <XmlDocument
      NamespaceURI="http://schemas.microsoft.com/sharepoint/v3/contenttype/forms/url">
      <FormUrls xmlns="http://schemas.microsoft.com/sharepoint/v3/contenttype/forms/url">
        <Edit>_layouts/LITWARE/LitwareApprovalTaskEditForm.aspx</Edit>
      </FormUrls>
    </XmlDocument>
  </XmlDocuments>
  </ContentType>
</Elements>
```

The content type ID for the standard workflow task content type is 0x010801. Therefore, any content type that derives from this must use a value of 0x010801 as the first part of its content type ID. You can also see that this custom content type definition adds two extra fields named Instructions and Comments. These fields are used to store extra data in the tasks created to assist in the Litware approval process.

Finally, note the XmlDocument section at the bottom of the content type definition. This section demonstrates the technique used to integrate the custom task edit form into a workflow template. When a user chooses to edit an approval task, WSS presents the user with the LitwareApprovalTaskEditForm.aspx page instead of the standard workflow task edit form.

Code inside the OnLoad method of the LitwareApprovalTaskEditForm class is able to retrieve the instructions that were written into the task when it was created. There is also code behind the Approve and Reject buttons that call the static AlterTask method of the SPWorkflowTask class. This method accepts a HashTable of named properties and causes the event handler for the OnTaskModified activity within the WF program to fire.

```
Hashtable taskHash = new Hashtable();
taskHash["Comments"] = txtComments.Text;
taskHash["TaskStatus"] = "Completed";
taskHash["WorkflowOutcome"] = "Approved";
SPWorkflowTask.AlterTask(TaskItem, taskHash, true);
```

Choosing Between .aspx Forms and InfoPath Forms

We have walked you through the implementation details required to integrate all four different types of custom workflow input forms into a workflow template using .aspx files. As you can see, there are quite a few programming issues that you need to manage in the code that is written behind these .aspx pages. Now that you have seen what's required to integrate custom workflow input forms the hard way, it's important that you evaluate whether this approach is necessary for a given development scenario.

If you are developing workflow templates that run exclusively in a MOSS environment, you have the much easier option of building your custom workflow input forms by using the forms designer of Microsoft InfoPath 2007. The InfoPath forms designer provides you with a significantly more pleasant experience for creating the user interface for a workflow input form. More importantly, it also relieves you of the responsibility of writing any code behind .aspx pages. MOSS supplies standard .aspx pages and code for you. The only code you need to write when integrating InfoPath forms into a workflow template is the code that goes into the WF program that serializes data and passes them back and forth with the InfoPath forms.

While using InfoPath to create custom workflow input forms increases your productivity, there is an obvious catch. The workflow templates you create then have a dependency on MOSS and cannot run in any WSS farms that do not have MOSS installed. Creating workflow templates that integrate workflow input forms using .aspx is far more flexible because these templates can be deployed within any WSS farm whether MOSS has been installed or not.

Summary

The Windows Workflow Foundation (WF) is a framework for building reactive programs that includes its own programming model and a runtime environment that can load into whatever hosting application you want. The inclusion of reusable activities and the Visual Studio workflow designer provides a highly productive foundation for creating programs that automate long-running and episodic business processes.

WSS integrates with the WF in such a way as to hide the plumbing involved in initializing the WF runtime and persisting workflow instances to the content database. WSS also extends the WF to add a human dimension with elements such as task lists, workflow history lists, and workflow input forms. All in all, WSS and the WF together provide a great platform for building business solutions that automate common business processes, such as document approval.

While this chapter has provided you with an introduction to the WF and its integration with WSS, it has only scratched the surface of what you can do. We certainly encourage you to seek further reading and to continue on to more advanced topics, such as creating user-defined activities and developing state machine workflows for WSS-based business solutions. Now it's time to take the different types of WSS components that you have learned how to create in this book and discover how to package them into ready-made business solutions by using site definitions and solution packages.

Chapter 9
Solutions and Deployment

- Learn how to package components into site definitions.
- Learn how to deploy applications by using WSS features.
- Localize Web Parts, features, and site definitions by using Microsoft Visual Studio resources.
- Create installers for Enterprise and Commercial deployments by using solution packages.
- Create language packs for solution packages.

Introduction

Throughout this book, we have discussed how to design and implement features to define the structure, appearance, and functionality for various elements within a site. However, to this point, we have avoided a basic yet critical question about the origin of life in Microsoft Windows SharePoint Services (WSS). We begin this chapter by telling you the story of the birds and the bees and by answering the inevitable question, "Where do SharePoint sites come from?"

In a WSS environment, each and every site is created from a site definition. Therefore, we must first explain what a site definition is and show you how to create and deploy one. Along the way, we will also cover additional techniques for creating WSS features that depend on and aggregate other features.

The next part of this chapter delves into how WSS supports localizing language-specific resources, such as literal text strings, so that you can implement and deploy custom WSS components that target international markets. These localization efforts involve creating and working with resource files within Microsoft Visual Studio and integrating these resource files into your WSS features and site definitions.

Once you develop and test custom WSS components, such as features, site definitions, custom application pages, Web Parts, and localized resource files, the last step is to learn how to package them for deployment. The conclusion of this chapter introduces solution packages as the standard WSS deployment mechanism used to push components out to front-end Web servers in a staging or production environment.

Site Definitions

A *site definition* is the top-level component in WSS that aggregates smaller, more modular definitions to create a complete site template that can be used to provision sites. For example, a site definition usually includes a custom page template for the site's home page and can additionally reference external features to add support for other types of site-specific elements such as custom lists, secondary pages, and Web Parts. The value of creating custom site definitions is obvious. They enable you to develop site templates for creating new sites that act as prepackaged business solutions.

> **Tip**   While you can create and package list definitions and other components within a site definition, it's a best practice to package components within WSS features and then reference them from one or more site definitions.

In WSS, every site is provisioned from a specific site definition. This is true for all top-level sites as well as child sites nested within a site collection. Once a site is provisioned from a particular site definition, it picks up a dependency on that site definition that remains in effect for the lifetime of the site. A site's dependency on its underlying site definition can never be removed or changed, and the site definition must be installed and remain functional in the farm for the site to continue working properly.

Consider a scenario in which you create a custom site definition and deploy it within a particular WSS farm. Now imagine that you use this site definition to provision the top-level site within a new site collection. What would happen if you attempted to back up the site collection along with its top-level site by using the STSADM.EXE command-line utility and then restore it in another WSS farm? This would not work properly unless your custom site definition is installed in both farms.

Let's now move on to a discussion of how site definitions are structured and deployed. Similar to a WSS feature, a site definition is defined with a set of Collaborative Application Markup Language (CAML)-based files that are deployed within a named directory on the file system of each front-end Web server in the farm. Site definitions are deployed within the 12\TEMPLATE\ SiteTemplates directory and are referenced in the 12\TEMPLATE\<culture>\XML directory in WEBTEMP.XML files, where the <culture> folder is the locale identifier (12\TEMPLATE\ 1033\XML for US English).

WSS offers several pre-installed site definitions to provide users with creatable site templates out of the box. For example, a site definition named *STS* provides familiar site templates such as Team Site, Blank Site, and Document Workspace. You can always back up a site created from one of these site templates and restore it on another farm because the STS site definition is guaranteed to be pre-installed in any farm running WSS 3.0.

Tip It is recommended that you avoid making changes to any of the pre-installed site definitions that ship with WSS and Microsoft Office SharePoint Server (MOSS). However, you are free to create your own custom site definitions. Later in this chapter, you will also see that you can create custom WSS features that add extra functionality to the pre-installed site definitions supplied by Microsoft.

A site definition itself does not represent a creatable site template. Instead, a site definition contains one or more *configurations*, and these configurations are what appear to users as creatable site templates. Therefore, the STS site definition contains three different configurations: Team Site, Blank Site, and Document Workspace.

Tip When creating a new site by using the STSADM.EXE command-line utility or through custom code, you are often required to reference a site definition and one of its configurations by name. This is done by specifying the name of the site definition followed by the pound sign and the integer identifier of the configuration. For example, you can use STS#0 to reference the site template titled Team Site and STS#1 to reference the site template titled Blank Site. The following example uses one of these site template references when creating a new top-level site by using the STS command-line utility.

```
STSADM.EXE -o createsite -url http://litwareinc.com
                -ownerlogin LITWAREINC\Administrator
                -owneremail administrator@Litwareinc.com
                -sitetemplate STS#1
```

Remember to remove the line breaks between parameters when calling STSADM.EXE from either the command line or a batch file.

WSS provides several other pre-installed site definitions in addition to STS. A site definition named MPS contains five different configurations for the various Meeting Workspace site templates. Two site definitions are named Blog and Wiki, and each contains a single configuration for creating blog sites and wiki sites. Finally, a site definition named CENTRALADMIN provides the site template used to create the top-level site used in the WSS Central Administration Web application.

In a farm in which MOSS is installed, there are several pre-installed site definitions in addition to those normally included with WSS. MOSS uses these site definitions to provide site templates that add value on top of WSS by creating sites offering extended functionality in areas such as publishing, content search and management, business intelligence, and social networking. The fact that MOSS is so dependent on its own site definitions should provide you with a clear indication that developing custom site definitions is critical. This is what makes it possible to build real applications that are seen as complete business solutions on the WSS platform.

Tip As mentioned earlier, we recommend that you avoid making changes to any of the pre-installed site definitions that ship with WSS and MOSS. However, there is nothing stopping you from opening up the source files inside the site definitions on your developer's workstation and snooping around to see how they're built. Reverse engineering the pre-installed site definitions is a great way to learn about techniques that you can use when you build your own.

The Global Site Definition

WSS 3.0 introduces the *Global site definition,* which provides a common repository for site provision instructions required by every site definition. This new approach significantly improves the structuring of site definitions over the way things were previously structured in Microsoft Windows SharePoint Services 2.0, in which common provision instructions had to be included as redundant XML in each site definition. The Global site definition refactors more than 2,600 lines of required common components, such as *Base Types* and required *Galleries*, which were previously required in the ONET.XML file of every site definition.

The Global site definition is located at the 12\TEMPLATES\GLOBAL path. It contains the standard default.master page template along with instructions to provision an instance of default.master page into the Master Page gallery of every new site. The Global site definition also contains provisioning logic to create the following four site collection–scoped lists in every new top-level site:

- Web Parts gallery
- List Template gallery
- Site Template gallery
- User Information Profile list

Creating a Custom Site Definition

To create a simple site definition, create a new class library project. Similar to the feature projects introduced throughout this book, the *Site Definition* project is a class library project that is used for XML and ASPX editing and source control, whereas an install script is responsible for copying the files where they are needed for deployment. Later in this chapter, we will look at creating a WSS solution package for deployment that builds on this project format. We will also be localizing the site definition as it is built by using the Resources folder of the project.

At the top level of the project, create a RESOURCES folder and a TEMPLATE folder, which we will later deploy to the \\Program Files\Common Files\Microsoft Shared\web server extensions\12 folder, as was previously done with features. Next, create a folder structure as illustrated in Figure 9-1.

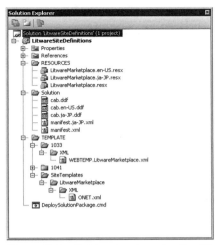

Figure 9-1 Folder structure for the Site Definition project

Inside the class library, create a SiteTemplates folder and a folder corresponding to your locale's identifier, which is 1033 for US English. Within the SiteTemplates folder, create a folder with the same name as your site definition, which in this example is LitwareMarketplace. Within the LitwareMarketplace folder, create an XML folder with an XML file named ONET.xml. The final folder structure should look like Figure 9-1.

The ONET.xml file serves as the high-level manifest for the site definition and references the components that are to be used. Generally speaking, all components that you want to be automatically provisioned within sites created from the site definition should be referenced from this ONET.xml file. You also want to add references to WSS features that define list types that you want to be available to users so that they can create new lists on demand. Our approach is to create an empty XML file and paste in certain elements from the STS Team site definition, while defining the core of the elements ourselves.

The base structure of the ONET site definition schema is shown in Listing 9-1. Note that we define this XML file to use the SharePoint XML namespace, which gives us assistance with the schema when editing the file in Visual Studio. (The pre-installed site definitions do not reference this schema, although it is inferred.)

Listing 9-1 The basic Site Definition project schema

```xml
<?xml version="1.0" encoding="utf-8"?>
<Project Title="My Site Definition"
        Revision="0"
        ListDir="Lists"
        xmlns:ows="Microsoft SharePoint"
        xmlns="http://schemas.microsoft.com/sharepoint/">
  <NavBars />
  <DocumentTemplates />
  <Configurations>
```

```
        <Configuration ID="-1" Name="NewWeb" />
        <Configuration ID="0" Name="Default">
          <Lists>
          </Lists>
          <Modules>
            <Module Name="Default" />
          </Modules>
          <SiteFeatures />
          <WebFeatures />
        </Configuration>
      </Configurations>
      <Modules>
        <Module Name="Default" Url="" >
          <File Url="default.aspx" NavBarHome="True" Type="Ghostable"></File>
        </Module>
      </Modules>
    </Project>
```

The basic structure defines core project attributes, navigation bars, document templates, configurations that group functionality, and modules that define files to be deployed—both static files and Web Part pages that can contain preconfigured Web Part instances upon page creation.

> **Tip**   Note that almost everything that can be defined in a site definition can also be defined in a feature. Features should be used for implementation, and site definitions should be used to aggregate features into user-creatable site templates. Both the Features element and the site definition Project element share common XML schema defined inside wss.xsd.

NavBars

The NavBars node defines navigation bars used in the site. These are optional items, but they are necessary if you're going to use the pre-installed SharePoint navigation bars. If you'd like to simply use the default navigation scheme in your site definition, copy the contents of this node from the STS site definition. If you are building custom navigation controls and want to bypass the SharePoint navigation user interface entirely, you can skip this node. Note that navigation bars included in this node also define the Quick Launch sidebar within the Team Site, which can also be accessed by code through the object model. To add a navigation element to the Quick Launch sidebar, add an additional NavBar element to the NavBars node. Following is an example QuickNav bar that you can add through CAML in the site definition. Note that the HTML within the Prefix, Body, and Suffix attributes is XML encoded. The name of the NavBar specifies the heading of the navigation section, and each NavBarLink node represents a hyperlink.

```
<NavBar Name="Site Pages"
        Prefix="&lt;table border=0 cellpadding=4 cellspacing=0&gt;"
        Body="&lt;tr&gt;&lt;td&gt;&lt;table border=0 cellpadding=0 cellspacing=0&gt;&lt;
tr&gt;&lt;td&gt;&lt;img src='/_layouts/images/blank.gif' ID='100' alt='' border=
```

```
0&gt; &lt;/td&gt;&lt;td valign=top&gt;&lt;a ID=onetleftnavbar#LABEL_ID# href=
'#URL#'&gt;#LABEL#&lt;/td&gt;&lt;/tr&gt;&lt;/table&gt;&lt;/td&gt;&lt;/tr&gt;" Suffix=
"&lt;/table&gt;"
        ID="1028" >

  <NavBarLink Name="Web Page 1" Url="SitePages/Page01.aspx" />
  <NavBarLink Name="Web Page 2" Url="SitePages/Page02.aspx" />
  <NavBarLink Name="Web Page 3" Url="SitePages/Page03.aspx" />
  <NavBarLink Name="Web Page 4" Url="SitePages/Page04.aspx" />

</NavBar>
```

DocumentTemplates

The DocumentTemplates node documents are used as document library default documents within the site. You typically reuse the content from the STS site definition for this node. To do so, simply copy and paste from the STS site definition to this node. Alternatively, you can provide your own document templates for each type of document. If you do not provide document templates, the site is still created, but the user is not able to create new documents by using the New button in Document Libraries.

Configurations

Configurations are the actual creatable site templates listed in the standard pages that WSS presents to users when they want to create a new site. Each site definition can contain zero or more configurations. Without a configuration, the site definition is abstract and cannot be created; however, it can contain common infrastructure definitions, such as the Global site definition. You'll note that you can reference components such as document templates in external site definitions, so you do not always need to have a configuration. The site definition can also have multiple configurations, but each configuration reuses the same modules, feature references, and lists. These named configurations must also be referenced in another configuration file, WEBTEMP.*.xml, to be available to Windows SharePoint Services. The following is a basic configuration inside the ONET.xml file that defines the Default configuration.

```
<Configurations>
  <Configuration ID="0" Name="Default">
    <Lists>
    </Lists>
    <Modules>
      <Module Name="Default"/>
    </Modules>
    <SiteFeatures/>
    <WebFeatures/>
  </Configuration>
</Configurations>
```

The configuration references all modules, lists, and default data that are created on site creation. To define lists within the configuration, specify the feature GUID of the list. You may need to browse the Features directory to locate this, or simply refer to the pre-installed site definitions. For example, the following List nodes specify that the Litware Customer List and Litware Vendor List be created on site creation at the site-relative Lists/Vendors and Lists/Customers URLs.

```
<!–Adds the Litware Vendor List -->
<List FeatureId="FBDECD96-62DC-48c8-8F0A-7B827A042FD9" Type="10001"
    Title="Litware Vendors"
    Url="Lists/Vendors" QuickLaunchUrl="Lists/Vendors/AllItems.aspx" />

<!-- Adds the Litware Customer List -->
<List FeatureId="FBDECD96-62DC-48c8-8F0A-7B827A042FD9" Type="10002"
    Title="Litware Customers"
    Url="Lists/Customers" QuickLaunchUrl="Lists/Customers/AllItems.aspx" />
```

You might wish to refer to the lists referenced within the STS Team site definition as well include instantiations of common lists, such as Announcements. You can override certain settings of the list, including the default data. To specify a default List Item, use the Data element of the list and include a Row element for each list item. You can use CAML data-defining or HTML-rendering XML within the list item, including dynamic tags such as <TodayISO/>, as long as the elements are escaped. The following code defines a default announcement that is created for the list instance that expires the same day it is created.

```
<List FeatureId="00BFEA71-D1CE-42de-9C63-A44004CE0104" Type="104"
     Title="Announcements"
     Url="$Resources:core,lists_Folder;/$Resources:core,announce_Folder;">
  <Data>
    <Rows>
      <Row>
        <Field Name="Title">
          $Resources:Litware,DefaultAnnoucementTitle;</Field>
        <Field Name="Body">
          $Resources:Litware,DefaultAnnoucementBody;</Field>
        <Field Name="Expires">&lt;ows:TodayISO/&gt;</Field>
      </Row>
    </Rows>
  </Data>
</List>
```

Within the configuration, you can also specify which features should be a part of this site collection or site. The SiteFeatures node lets you define features to be enabled for the site collection if the site is created as the site collection's top-level site. For site features, you want to include common infrastructure such as the BasicWebParts feature, as well as any additional infrastructure such as a feature that installs your company's custom .webpart Web Part entries in the Web Part gallery.

For features scoped to the site collection (Scope="Site"), you want to reference any custom features that are logically part of the site definition. The following code defines the basic Web Part feature that installs WSS Web Part entries in the site collection Web Part gallery and also the Team Collaboration feature that includes the basic WSS lists. Note that this feature does not create instances of the lists, but only enables their future creation on the site level.

```
<SiteFeatures>
  <!-- The Basic Web Parts feature installs the WSS Web Part entries. -->
  <Feature ID="00BFEA71-1C5E-4A24-B310-BA51C3EB7A57" />
</SiteFeatures>
<WebFeatures>
  <!-- The Team Collaboration feature includes the basic site lists. -->
  <Feature ID="00BFEA71-4EA5-48D4-A4AD-7EA5C011ABE5" />
</WebFeatures>
```

Configuration Modules

Modules are referenced in the configuration section to specify creation upon a specific configuration. They are not defined within the configuration, however, which means that several configurations can share the same modules. You can have references to as many modules as you like. For example, to include a single file Module named "Default" in the site configuration, simply reference the module in the configuration as follows:

```
<Configuration ID="0" Name="Default">
    <Modules>
        <Module Name="Default" />
    </Modules>
</Configuration>
```

Modules

We initially introduced Module elements in Chapter 3, "Pages and Design." As you remember, a Module element is a defined file set with nested File elements that are used to provision page instances from page templates. A Module element was also used in Chapter 4, "Web Parts," to demonstrate a feature that copies .webpart and .dwp files into the Web Part gallery. In addition to provisioning pages and Web Part description files, a Module element can also be used to provision many other types of files as well such as documents, images, and Cascading Style Sheet (CSS) files.

Because WSS 2.0 did not provide support for features, modules could be included only in site definitions. Therefore, modules were added to site definitions anytime there was a requirement to provision an .aspx page or copy a .dwp file into the Web Part gallery. With the introduction of features in WSS 3.0, it doesn't make sense to include the same number of modules inside a site definition. It's better to maintain the majority of your modules inside features instead. However, there are still times when you should use a module inside a site definition, such as when you need to provision a page instance named default.aspx from a custom page template to provide the home page for a new site.

As you remember from Chapter 3, the File element within a Module element provides the flexibility to prepopulate Web Part instances within a Web Part page as part of the provisioning process. You can also specify an alternate location for module files either from another installed site definition or from a feature. The following module specifies the home page from the STS site definition and specifies which list view Web Parts should be instantiated on the page.

```
<Module Name="Default" Url="" SetupPath="sitetemplates\sts">
  <File Url="default.aspx"  NavBarHome="True" Type="Ghostable">
    <View List="$Resources:core,lists_Folder;/
$Resources:core,announce_Folder;" BaseViewID="0" WebPartZoneID="Left" WebPartOrder="0" />
      <View List="Lists/Vendors" BaseViewID="0" WebPartZoneID="Left" WebPartOrder="1" />
      <View List="Lists/Customers" BaseViewID="0" WebPartZoneID="Left" WebPartOrder="2" />
  </File>
</Module>
```

Alternatively, you could also specify a page deployed in any folder under the path \\Program Files\Common Files\Microsoft Shared\web server extensions\12. Note that the referenced file does not need to be part of a feature or site definition, although you might want to make it part of a packaged feature that is part of a WSS solution package. The following Module element specifies Page01.aspx from the CustomSitePages feature (see Chapter 3) to be instantiated as "default.aspx" within the site.

```
<Module Name="Default" Url="" SetupPath="features\customsitepages">
  <File Url="default.aspx"
    NavBarHome="True"
    Type="Ghostable"
    Path="PageTemplates\Page01.aspx" />
</Module>
```

The most common use of the site definition module is to use either the pages defined in STS or custom pages that are defined in a feature or are unique to the site definition. In the latter case, you would simply include the page in the root of the site definition and would not specify the SetupPath attribute of the Module element. You would not rename the file by using the Url attribute of the File element.

Web Template Files

The last component of the site definition is the WEBTEMP file. The WEBTEMP file references configurations in the site definition's ONET.xml file. Each site definition solution you create should have its own WEBTEMP file, with the following naming convention: WEBTEMP.[solution].xml The WEBTEMP file has one Template node per site definition and a Configuration node for each configuration.

```
<Templates xmlns:ows="Microsoft SharePoint" >
  <Template Name="LitwareCustomer" ID="10003">
    <Configuration
        ID="0"
        Hidden="FALSE"
        Title="Litware Marketplace Site"
        Description="Create a Litware Marketplace site."
        ImageUrl="/_layouts/images/litware/LITWARE_PREV.PNG"
        DisplayCategory="Litware"
        RootWebOnly="false"
        SubWebOnly="false" />
  </Template>
</Templates>
```

Earlier in the chapter, we mentioned that it is actually the configuration and not the site definition itself that provides a creatable site template. The configuration defines a Hidden attribute that WSS uses to determine whether it should be shown to users on the standard WSS application pages used to create new sites. The Title and Description attributes are important for those configurations that will be presented to users as creatable site templates. The ImageUrl attribute can used to reference a graphic image that is shown to the user when the configuration is selected.

The DisplayCategory attribute allows you to add a custom configuration to one of the existing tabs already used by WSS, such as Collaboration or Meetings. MOSS adds two additional tabs of its own, Enterprise and Publishing. Assigning a unique value to the DisplayCategory attribute causes WSS to create a new tab to display your configuration to users, as with the Litware tab shown in Figure 9-2.

Figure 9-2   Configurations with a Hidden attribute value of false are shown to users as creatable site templates.

Finally, note that a Configuration element can contain two other attributes, RootWebOnly and SubWebOnly. Add the RootWebOnly attribute and assign it a value of true if you want to create a configuration that can be used only to create the top-level site within a site collection. Add the SubWebOnly attribute and assign it a value of true if you want to create a configuration that can be used only to create child sites within a site collection. For obvious reasons, both of these attributes cannot be assigned a value of true within the same configuration. When you use these attributes and assign a value of true, WSS ensures that the configuration is shown to users only at the appropriate times.

> ## Accessing CAML Schema Through the URL Protocol
>
> You can access the site definition project schema (localized ONET.xml file) for any WSS site for which you are an administrator by using the site-relative URL _vti_bin/ owssvr.dll?Cmd=GetProjSchema. When you access this URL, you are viewing a cached version of the parsed site definition, which contains the runtime values for the resource strings. You can also use this URL endpoint to access other CAML definitions, such as list schema, or to access list data. For more information, see the Software Development Kit (SDK) topic "Using the URL Protocol."

Adding a Site Provisioning Provider

WSS supports a component type known as a *Site Provisioning Provider* that can be configured to execute custom code during the site creation process. This makes it possible to add custom provisioning code to a site definition that complements CAML-based provisioning instructions by using the WSS object model to create site elements such as new pages, navigation menu items, and security groups. A Site Provisioning Provider can also be used to create portal-style sites that have a predefined hierarchy of child sites.

To create a Site Provisioning Provider, you must create a class that inherits from the SPWebProvisioningProvider class. This class must be compiled into an assembly DLL with a strong name and installed in the Global Assembly Cache (GAC) before it can be used. A site definition can reference a Site Provisioning Provider class from inside a configuration within the Web template file. The following example of the Web template file named WEBTEMP .LitwarePortal.xml is included in the sample code for this chapter within a Visual Studio project named *LitwarePortal*.

```
<Templates xmlns:ows="Microsoft SharePoint" >
  <Template Name="LITWAREPORTAL" ID="10004">

    <Configuration ID="0"
        Title="Litware Portal (LITWAREPORTAL#0)"
        Hidden="TRUE" />

    <Configuration ID="1"
        Title="Litware Portal"
        Hidden="FALSE"
        ImageUrl="/_layouts/images/litware/LITWARE_PREV.PNG"
        Description="Use this site template for a site with subsite."
        DisplayCategory="Litware"
        RootWebOnly="true"
        ProvisionAssembly="LitwarePortal, [full 4-part assembly name]"
        ProvisionClass="LitwarePortal.ProvisioningProvider"
        ProvisionData="Litware Portal Site" />
  </Template>

</Templates>
```

As you can see, there are two different configurations of the *LitwarePortal* site definition. The first configuration, named LITWAREPORTAL#0, is hidden and does not have an associated Site Provisioning Provider. However, the second configuration, named LITWAREPORTAL#1, is shown to users and is defined with a ProvisionAssembly attribute and a ProvisionClass attribute to reference a specific Site Provisioning Provider class. A third optional attribute, named ProvisionData, can be used to pass string data from the Web template file to the Site Provisioning Provider component.

Within the Site Provisioning Provider, you can override the Provision method to handle the site creation. The Provision method passes a single parameter of type SPWebProvisioning-Properties that provides you with access to the SPWeb object for the site being created as well as for the string-based provisioning data passed from the Web template file. Within this Provision method, you should call the ApplyWebTemplate method and pass a specific site definition configuration to process the CAML-based provisioning instructions. The following code is a starting point for creating a Site Provisioning Provider.

```
using System;
using Microsoft.SharePoint;

namespace LitwarePortal {
  public class ProvisioningProvider : SPWebProvisioningProvider {
    public override void Provision(SPWebProvisioningProperties properties){
      // apply template using a configuration
      properties.Web.ApplyWebTemplate("LITWAREPORTAL#0");
      // TODO: add extra code here to customize the new site.
    }
  }
}
```

Note in this example that the Site Provisioning Provider is configured to run on the configuration named LITWAREPORTAL#1, yet the call to ApplyWebTemplate is made using LITWAREPORTAL#0. This is important. You should never call ApplyWebTemplate on a configuration that has an associated Site Provisioning Provider. If you do, your code will be called recursively, resulting in an infinite loop of calls to ApplyWebTemplate. Instead, you should call ApplyWebTemplate on a configuration such as LITWAREPORTAL#0 that does not have an associated Site Provisioning Provider class. Therefore, site definitions that have Site Provisioning Providers must be created with at least two configurations, as in the LitwarePortal project example.

Another tricky aspect to writing a Site Provisioning Provider has to do with changing the security context before you begin to program against the new site using the WSS object model. After calling ApplyWebTemplate, you need to make a call to the RunWithElevatedPrivileges method to switch the code's execution context so that it runs as the SHAREPOINT\system account. Chapter 10, "Application Security," discusses the advanced security concepts involved with this example. At that point, we will cover the details associated with a call to RunWithElevatedPrivileges. For now, let us simply show you the code inside the Provision method of a Site Provisioning Provider that is written against the WSS object model to change the Title of the site and create two child sites below it.

```
public override void Provision(SPWebProvisioningProperties properties) {
  // apply template using a configuration
  properties.Web.ApplyWebTemplate("LITWAREPORTAL#0");
  // elevate privileges before programming against site
  SPSecurity.RunWithElevatedPrivileges(delegate() {
    using (SPSite siteCollection = new SPSite(properties.Web.Site.ID)) {
      using (SPWeb site = siteCollection.OpenWeb(properties.Web.ID)) {
        // update site properties
        site.Title = properties.Data;
        site.Update();
        // create child sites using Blank Site template
        site.Webs.Add("Child1", "Child Site 1", "",
                      1033, "STS#1", false, false);
        site.Webs.Add("Child2", "Child Site 2", "",
                      1033, "STS#1", false, false);
      }
    }
  });
}
```

Application Deployment Through Features

Features are the preferred packaging mechanism for SharePoint components. We have used features for deploying sample code throughout this book for the simple reason that they are easy to activate within existing sites and also have object and event models that are very powerful. A feature can be activated with a WSS site in five ways: through the Site Settings Web pages, the STSADM command line, site definition references, feature activation dependencies, or feature stapling. Because we have already looked at the first three options, we will now look at using feature activation dependencies and feature stapling.

Feature Activation Dependencies

Features can include *activation dependencies*. When WSS activates a feature that defines activation dependencies, it automatically activates any dependent feature that has already been activated. The TeamCollab feature that ships as a built-in feature with WSS provides a good example. The TeamCollab feature in and of itself provides no implementation. However, it defines activation dependencies on 19 other built-in features that define the collaboration lists and libraries in the Team Site.

Activating the TeamCollab feature forces the activation of these 19 other features that make all of the collaboration list types available such as Announcements, Contacts, Tasks, Events, and Document Libraries. As you can see, feature activation dependencies can be used to aggregate many features together into a common feature set that can then be activated and deactivated through a single high-level feature. Note that the STS site definition contains a Web feature reference to the TeamCollab feature so that all collaboration features are available within any new Team Site, Blank Site, or Document Workspace.

To demonstrate the use of feature dependencies, let's revisit the LitwareTypes feature from Chapter 6, "Lists and Content Types." We begin with a simple refactoring of the feature, in which we remove the list data from the feature in the VendorList.xml file. First, create a new feature called VendorListInstance within the same Visual Studio project. To do this, we create a folder called VendorListInstance within the Features folder and add a Feature.xml file with the following content:

```xml
<?xml version="1.0" encoding="utf-8"?>
<Feature
  Id="3295CBD4-9EA5-4811-8BCA-2CC4FA391177"
  Title=" Chapter 8: Vendor List Instance"
  Description="Demo from Inside Windows SharePoint Services"
  Version="1.0.0.0"
  Hidden="false"
  Scope="Web"
  xmlns="http://schemas.microsoft.com/sharepoint/">

  <ActivationDependencies>
    <!-- LitwareTypes Feature -->
    <ActivationDependency
        FeatureId="FBDECD96-62DC-48c8-8F0A-7B827A042FD9"/>
  </ActivationDependencies>

  <ElementManifests>
    <ElementManifest Location="VendorListInstance.xml" />
  </ElementManifests>
</Feature>
```

We create an ActivationDependencies node within the feature to define elements that will be enabled when this feature is added. Next, we move the ListInstance node from the VendorList.xml file to a new VendorListInstance.xml file within the VendorListInstance feature folder. VendorListInstance.xml should look like the following code:

```xml
<Elements xmlns="http://schemas.microsoft.com/sharepoint/">
  <ListInstance TemplateType="10001" Id="Vendors"
                Title="Vendors" Url="Vendors"
                Description="Litware Vendors"
                OnQuickLaunch="True" >
    <Data>
      <Rows>
        <Row>
          <Field Name="Title">Acme Corp, Inc</Field>
          <Field Name="FullName">Bob Jones</Field>
          <Field Name="WorkPhone">(813)345-5432</Field>
          <Field Name="Industry">High Tech</Field>
          <Field Name="CompanySize">101-1000</Field>
          <Field Name="ActivityNotes">They got the best widgets</Field>
        </Row>
        <!-- (Additional rows omitted for clarity) -->
      </Rows>
    </Data>
  </ListInstance>
</Elements>
```

We have created a feature that provisions a new list instance on activation. However, the feature is designed to force the activation of the dependent feature that defines the underlying list type when this is necessary.

Feature Stapling

A feature can also be used to attach one or more other features to a site definition through a technique known as *feature stapling*. For example, instead of creating a custom site definition, you can elect to create a custom feature to extend one of the built-in WSS site templates, such as Team Site or Blank Site, by automatically associating it with the Litware Types feature. You can extend a site template in this fashion by using a feature site template association.

To add the Litware Types feature to Team Site and Blank Site, you can simply create a new feature that associates the Litware Types feature with the site definition configurations identified by STS#0 and STS#1. The node that defines this relationship is the FeatureSiteTemplateAssociation node, in which the TemplateName parameter defines the site definition and configuration, and the Id parameter defines the feature that is added as part of the site definition. The Id parameter specifies the GUID of the feature to associate.

To use feature stapling, create a new feature to be used to associate one or more other features with one or more site templates. In the code samples for this chapter, we defined the new Feature folder named LitwareTypesDeploymentFeature in the Litware Types project in use since Chapter 6. This feature will only contain two files, the feature.xml file and the elements.xml file. Within the Elements node of Elements.xml, we created a FeatureSiteTemplateAssociation node for every site template to which we want to staple our feature. In this case, we want to staple the Litware Types feature to the Team Site (STS#0) and Blank Site (STS#1).

```
<Elements xmlns="http://schemas.microsoft.com/sharepoint/">
  <FeatureSiteTemplateAssociation
    Id="FBDECD96-62DC-48c8-8F0A-7B827A042FD9"
    TemplateName="STS#0" />
  <FeatureSiteTemplateAssociation
    Id="FBDECD96-62DC-48c8-8F0A-7B827A042FD9"
    TemplateName="STS#1" />
</Elements>
```

A feature created to perform feature stapling can be defined to be activated at any of the four supported activation scopes, including the scopes of site, site collection, Web application, and farm. For example, if you define a stapling feature at Web application scope, it provides a quick and easy way to activate the features being stapled within every Team Site and Blank Site in the target Web application. In the sample code for this chapter, we designed the stapling feature at farm scope. Once this feature is activated, it makes the Litware Types feature active within every Team Site and Blank Site in the farm.

Going one step further, we could associate the Litware Types feature with Global site definition configurations, which makes it available to all sites as opposed to only sites created from a specific configuration. The following elements manifest would associate the feature with the Global site definition configuration:

```
<Elements xmlns="http://schemas.microsoft.com/sharepoint/">
  <FeatureSiteTemplateAssociation
    Id="FBDECD96-62DC-48c8-8F0A-7B827A042FD9"
    TemplateName="GLOBAL#0" />
</Elements>
```

Attaching the Litware Types feature to the Global site definition configuration makes it globally active in all sites throughout the current WSS farm, including the Central Administration sites. This technique is powerful because it provides an approach to using feature stapling to make custom list types available to every site within a farm. You can also use it to import Web Part description files into the Web Part gallery of every site collection on a farm-wide basis.

Keep in mind that feature stapling can also be used to associate features that contain event handlers. For example, imagine that you want to run a piece of custom code anytime a new site is created on a farm-wide basis. You can start by creating a site-scoped feature with a FeatureActivated event handler. Then you simply need to create a second farm-scoped feature to staple the first feature containing the event handler to the Global site definition configuration.

WSS Globalization and Localization

Localization in WSS is based on *language packs* that are deployed as solution packages. Language packs include resources for specific cultures that are used to localize core solution packages. We will discuss solution packages and language packs at the end of this chapter, but we first want to provide some important background information about resource files, because you will want to use text defined in resource files within site definitions, features, and solutions to enable localization for specific languages and cultures.

By moving your literal text strings out into resource files, you can create WSS business solutions for the global market that can be deployed to multiple languages and cultures. Resource files also separate your text from your code, which can make editing a solution's literal text strings easier without the need to edit any CAML or .NET code.

For example, you could create an English solution and translate the resources into Japanese, and your solution would be deployable to Japanese markets without changing the core CAML XML files or any compiled code libraries. Site definitions and features can contain embedded resource references within their CAML, whereas Web Parts and compiled code can contain resources defined within assemblies. First, we will look at localization using resource XML files and compiled resources. We will then look at embedding the resources into language packs as we create solution packages.

Localization Through Resources

In .NET development, XML resource files can be used to embed resources into assemblies. In the case of ASP.NET, resources can be compiled at run time from XML resource files. Furthermore, the WSS runtime parses and compiles resources deployed in the installation's RESOURCES directory for use in WSS CAML files.

One of the key benefits of using resource files is that all of the language and locale-specific elements in an application or class library DLL, such as captions and user messages, can be factored out of your application code (including CAML). To do this, you need to create a separate resource file for each spoken language you must support. The actual resource file is a text-based file containing XML with a .resx extension. The following code displays an example of the XML data found inside a resource file with a single resource named Hello.

```
<?xml version="1.0" encoding="utf-8"?>
<root>
  <!-- schema omitted for clarity -->
  <resheader name="resmimetype">
    <value>text/microsoft-resx</value>
  </resheader>
  <resheader name="version">
    <value>2.0</value>
  </resheader>
  <resheader name="reader">
    <value>System.Resources.ResXResourceReader, System.Windows.Forms, Version=2.0.0.0,
Culture=neutral, PublicKeyToken=b77a5c561934e089</value>
  </resheader>
  <resheader name="writer">
    <value>System.Resources.ResXResourceWriter, System.Windows.Forms, Version=2.0.0.0,
Culture=neutral, PublicKeyToken=b77a5c561934e089</value>
  </resheader>
  <data name="Hello" xml:space="preserve">
    <value>Hello</value>
  </data>
</root>
```

When working with resource files in Visual Studio 2005, you also get the benefit of a strong-typed resource manager class that is generated automatically behind the scenes. For example, we can create a resource named LitwareControlStrings inside of the LitwareWebParts assembly in the Resources folder. It will have a single resource string named "Hello" with the text "Hello". We can also create a Japanese version, naming the resource file LitwareControlStrings.ja-JP.resx, and a US English–specific version named LitwareControlStrings.en-US.resx.

Within the Japanese resource file, you can copy and paste from the default resource, replacing the text value of the Hello string with "こんにちは." Paste the default resource file into the US English version, changing the "Hello" text to "Greetings". The LitwareControlStrings resource class has a ResourceManager static instance that returns either the correct string for the current locale or the default resource from the core assembly if a language-specific resource is not available. The following is an example of the Visual Studio–generated code for the Hello resource:

```
// Looks up a localized string similar to Hello.
internal static string Hello {
  get {
    return ResourceManager.GetString("Hello", resourceCulture);
  }
}
```

When you create resources in the class library, they must be named appropriately for the target culture. When you compile the assembly, Visual Studio automatically creates a locale folder for the resources. Because we created ja-JP and en-US localized resource files, Visual Studio compiles the *LitwareWebParts.resources.dll* satellite assemblies in the ja-JP and en-US subfolders of the compilation target.

When you create localized resources, it is also important to include default resources that are used in situations in which the localized resource for the current culture is not available. In this example, the Web Part solution running in an Australian localized installation would use the default resources (not the US English resources) because there are no Australian locale-specific resources.

> **Tip**   The Resource Generator for Visual Studio generates internal classes for strong-named resources; however, there are several Shared Source alternatives for generating public resource classes that can be shared between assemblies.

After learning the basics of localization, you should find it easy to include resources for all of your Web Part and event handler assemblies. Now that we have an assembly resource for the Web Part assembly, let's localize our HelloWebPart class. Instead of using the text "Hello" in the Web Part, we can read it from the resource that lets us easily localize and deploy our Web Part solution into multiple locales without changing any code. The following code block shows a new version of the HelloWebPart class that uses resources instead of the static "Hello" text.

```
using System;
using System.Web.UI;

namespace LitwareWebParts {

  public class HelloWebPart : System.Web.UI.WebControls.WebParts.WebPart {
    protected override void RenderContents(HtmlTextWriter writer) {
      writer.Write("{0} {1}",
        Resources.LitwareControlStrings.Hello, Context.User.Identity.Name);
    }
  }
}
```

Within site definitions and features, resources are not accessed through a compiled assembly when referenced from CAML, but are parsed at run time from the .resx file itself. However, you can still compile the resource if you wish to use it in any feature event receivers that are defined in the assembly. Within site definition or feature projects, place the resource in the Resources folder of the Visual Studio project. On your development machine, you can copy the Resources folder to the WSS Resources folder with a build event such as the following:

```
@SET RESOURCEDIR="c:\program files\common files\microsoft shared\web server extensions\12\
RESOURCES"
xcopy /e /y RESOURCES\* %RESOURCEDIR%
```

We will later package the resources into the solution package for deployment. To create localized resources for your custom WSS components, use Visual Studio to add a new Resources directory to your project. These resources will be copied to the RESOURCES directory and interpreted by the WSS runtime as it parses the CAML file's XML content. Note that the resources won't be accessible from a compiled assembly when created and deployed in this fashion.

Now that we've learned the basics of resources, in the Resources directory of the Litware Marketplace site definition, create a resources file named LitwareMarketplace.resx. We'll also create a Japanese version named LitwareMarketplace.ja-JP.resx. (Don't worry if you don't know Japanese, you can include placeholders for the interpreters to translate. We used AltaVista BabelFish to translate while writing this book.) This allows us to create a basic localized site definition for Litware that can be translated easily into other languages. Figure 9-3 displays the LitwareMarketplace.resx file containing the core string definitions Customer-ListTitle, DefaultAnnoucementBody, DefaultAnnoucementTitle, ServerEmailFooter, SiteTitle, and VendorListTitle.

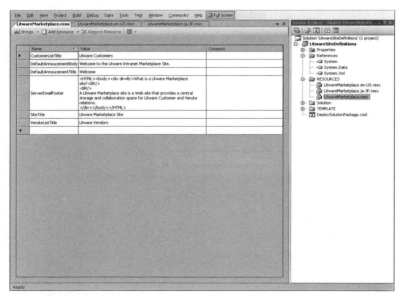

Figure 9-3 Visual Studio provides a resource file editor for working with resources, such as literal text strings.

Resources in SharePoint XML Files

After creating the .resx resource file, we can reference these resources in any CAML-schema XML files including site definition files, feature definitions, and list schemas. (The only CAML files you cannot localize are the prelocalized WEBTEMP files.) For example, instead of including a nonlocalized default announcement, we could create the following announcement in the site definition that can be created with the locale of the operating system upon site creation.

```
<List FeatureId="00BFEA71-D1CE-42de-9C63-A44004CE0104"
    Type="104" Title="$Resources:core,announceList;"
    Url="$Resources:core,lists_Folder;/$Resources:core,announce_Folder;">
  <Data>
    <Rows>
      <Row>
        <Field Name="Title">$Resources:Litware,DefaultAnnoucementTitle;</Field>
        <Field Name="Body">
            $Resources:Litware,DefaultAnnoucementBody;</Field>
        <Field Name="Expires">&lt;ows:TodayISO/&gt;</Field>
      </Row>
    </Rows>
  </Data>
</List>
```

Note that the resource format within CAML is $Resources:*ResourceFile,ResourceName*;, where *ResourceFile* is the name of the file and *ResourceName* is the name of the string within the file. The WSS runtime replaces this as it parses the CAML. Note that you can access the localized site definition (which is cached for the Internet Information Services [IIS] application lifetime) through the site-relative URL *_vti_bin/owssvr.dll?Cmd=GetProjSchema*.

> **Tip** For more background information on localization support in the .NET Framework and Visual Studio, read the following two MSDN columns written by Ted Pattison:
>
> *http://msdn.microsoft.com/msdnmag/issues/06/05/BasicInstincts/*
>
> *http://msdn.microsoft.com/msdnmag/issues/06/08/BasicInstincts/*

Deployment Using Solution Packages

Because SharePoint solutions are deployed on WSS or MOSS installations that range in size from a single standalone Web server to large enterprise server farms, there needs to be a mechanism to deploy them as a single unit. By deploying a single unit, we can have a supported, testable, and repeatable deployment mechanism. The deployment mechanism that SharePoint uses is the *solution package*.

Solution packages are critical components for deployment in enterprise or commercial scenarios and use the same Visual Studio project formats that you work with on your development box.

For all deployments outside of your development environment, you want to use WSS solution packages. Solution packages also enable your system administrators to create scriptable installs, an important requirement for many enterprise-class IT organizations.

It is also important to test solution package deployments in a controlled WSS environment (that is not the same as your development environment), such as a clean Virtual PC image, to test installation of the features, site definitions, assemblies, and configuration changes using solution packages. Solution packages are generally language neutral without localized resources, supplemented by solution language packs that contain the language-specific resources. First we'll look at solution packages and then at adding language-specific resources.

A solution package is a compressed .cab file with a .wsp extension containing the components to be deployed on a target Web server. A solution package also contains additional metadata that enables the WSS runtime to uncompress the .cab file and install its components. In the case of server farm installations, WSS is able to automate pushing the solution package file out to each Web server in the farm.

Solution packages are deployed by using two steps. The first step is installation, in which WSS copies the .wsp file to the configuration database. The second step is the actual deployment, in which WSS creates a timer job that is processed by all front-end Web servers in the server farm. This greatly simplifies the installation across farm servers and ensures a consistent deployment.

The .wsp file for a solution package can be built using the MAKECAB operating system utility by reading the definition from a .ddf file. The .ddf file defines the output structure of the .wsp file by referencing each file in its source location and its destination location in the .wsp file. This is one of the more tedious aspects of WSS development because you will likely need to create and maintain the .dff file by hand.

The metadata for a solution package is maintained in a file named manifest.xml that must be added to the root of the .wsp file. It is the manifest.xml file that tells the WSS runtime which template files to copy into the WSS system directories. The manifest.xml file can also instruct WSS to install features and assembly DLL as well as to add entries to one or more web.config files for SafeControl entries and code access security settings.

Solution Package for Deploying a Feature

To create a solution package for WSS deployment, we will simply create a .wsp file that includes the deployment files, schemas, and assemblies. The initial file that we create will be a Data Description File (DDF) that describes the files for the CAB archive. The DDF file for the LitwareTypes solution is defined in Listing 9-2. We can create the solution files, including the DDF and manifest, in the Solution subfolder of the Visual Studio project. Because the Litware Types feature is explicitly dependent on the LitwareFields project (both the assembly and the .ascx user controls), we can deploy the LitwareFields project as well as the LitwareTypes project in the same solution package.

Listing 9-2   A .ddf file defining the solution structure

```
DDF File for a Solution Package
; ** LitwareTypes.wsp (Pattison/Larson) **
.OPTION EXPLICIT        ; Generate errors
.Set CabinetNameTemplate=LitwareTypes.wsp
.set DiskDirectoryTemplate=CDROM ; All cabinets go in a single directory
.Set CompressionType=MSZIP;** All files are compressed in cabinet files
.Set UniqueFiles="ON"
.Set Cabinet=on
.Set DiskDirectory1=Package
Solution\manifest.xml manifest.xml
TEMPLATE\FEATURES\LitwareTypes\CustomerList.xml LitwareTypes\CustomerList.xml
TEMPLATE\FEATURES\LitwareTypes\feature.xml LitwareTypes\feature.xml
TEMPLATE\FEATURES\LitwareTypes\LitwareContentTypes.xml LitwareTypes\
   LitwareContentTypes.xml
TEMPLATE\FEATURES\LitwareTypes\LitwareCustomFieldSiteColumns.xml LitwareTypes\
   LitwareCustomFieldSiteColumns.xml
TEMPLATE\FEATURES\LitwareTypes\LitwareSiteColumns.xml LitwareTypes\
   LitwareSiteColumns.xml
TEMPLATE\FEATURES\LitwareTypes\VendorList.xml LitwareTypes\VendorList.xml
TEMPLATE\FEATURES\LitwareTypesDeploymentFeature\feature.xml
   LitwareTypesDeploymentFeature\feature.xml
TEMPLATE\FEATURES\LitwareTypesDeploymentFeature\Elements.xml
   LitwareTypesDeploymentFeature\Elements.xml
TEMPLATE\FEATURES\VendorListInstance\feature.xml VendorListInstance\feature.xml
TEMPLATE\FEATURES\VendorListInstance\VendorListInstance.xml VendorListInstance\
   VendorListInstance.xml
TEMPLATE\FEATURES\LitwareTypes\VendorListEventHandlers.xml FEATURES\LitwareTypes\
   VendorListEventHandlers.xml
TEMPLATE\FEATURES\LitwareTypes\CustomerList\schema.xml FEATURES\LitwareTypes\
   CustomerList\schema.xml
TEMPLATE\FEATURES\LitwareTypes\VendorList\schema.xml FEATURES\LitwareTypes\
   VendorList\schema.xml

TEMPLATE\XML\fldtypes_Litware.xml XML\fldtypes_Litware.xml
TEMPLATE\CONTROLTEMPLATES\CompanySizeFieldControl.ascx CONTROLTEMPLATES\
   CompanySizeFieldControl.ascx
bin\Debug\LitwareTypes.dll LitwareTypes.dll
bin\Debug\LitwareFieldTypes.dll LitwareFieldTypes.dll
;*** <the end>
```

Unfortunately, the manual process of adding the deployment files to the solution package is somewhat primitive. You must list each file explicitly in the .ddf file, including both the source file and its location in the .wsp package. Also confusing is the fact that the destination directory is not necessarily straightforward and may take some trial and error to get right.

Along with the .ddf file, you must also list each file in the solution manifest inside the Manifest.xml file. The solution manifest is created by using a Solution element and is shown in Listing 9-3. Every file that is to be processed during installation must be listed in the solution manifest. If a file is in the .wsp package but not in the manifest, the file is ignored.

Listing 9-3   Solution package manifest for the Litware Types solution

```
Litware Types Solution Manifest
<Solution SolutionId="47ACFA48-7846-499f-BD10-14D6A5C9C717"
    xmlns="http://schemas.microsoft.com/sharepoint/">
  <!-- A solution for Litware field types, content types and lists -->
  <FeatureManifests>
    <FeatureManifest Location="LitwareTypes\feature.xml" />
    <FeatureManifest Location="LitwareTypesDeploymentFeature\feature.xml" />
    <FeatureManifest Location="VendorListInstance\feature.xml" />
  </FeatureManifests>

  <TemplateFiles>
    <TemplateFile Location="XML\fldtypes_Litware.xml"/>
    <TemplateFile Location="CONTROLTEMPLATES\CompanySizeFieldControl.ascx"/>
    <TemplateFile Location="FEATURES\LitwareTypes\VendorListEventHandlers.xml"/>
    <TemplateFile Location="FEATURES\LitwareTypes\CustomerList\schema.xml"/>
    <TemplateFile Location="FEATURES\LitwareTypes\VendorList\schema.xml"/>
  </TemplateFiles>

  <Assemblies>
    <Assembly DeploymentTarget="GlobalAssemblyCache"
          Location="LitwareFieldTypes.dll" />
    <Assembly DeploymentTarget="GlobalAssemblyCache" Location="LitwareTypes.dll" />
  </Assemblies>

</Solution>
```

Like WSS features, solution packages also have a GUID that can be generated by using Visual Studio's Create GUID tool. The main elements to examine are FeatureManifests, Template-Files, and Assemblies. These define which features are installed, which template files to copy to the TEMPLATE directory, and which assemblies to install. Assemblies can be installed to either the GAC or to the local bin directory for one or more Web applications and are determined by the DeploymentTarget attribute of the Assembly node.

Feature manifests must be referenced from the feature folder in the FEATURENAME\ Feature.xml format. Note that the FEATURES\FEATURENAME\Feature.xml format is invalid. Directly referenced feature manifests (for example, CustomerList.xml in our source code example, but not schema.xml) are inferred from this location and copied automatically. Files that are not directly referenced from feature manifests (including items such as list schemas) must be explicitly installed by using the TemplateFile elements inside the TemplateFiles node. These files must include the full folder path from TEMPLATE, such as FEATURES\ LitwareTypes\CustomerList\schema.xml. The full manifest for the Litware Types, Litware Types Deployment Feature, and Vendor List Instance features is defined in Listing 9-3.

After creating the solution package .ddf and manifest files, you are ready to create the package. The DOS makecab command creates the .wsp file using the .ddf description:

```
makecab /f Solution\cab.ddf
```

After creating the .wsp file, you can install it by using the addsolution operation of the STSADM.EXE utility. This command causes WSS to copy the .wsp file into the configuration database, but it does not actually deploy it. To deploy the solution package, you can run the deploysolution operation.

```
stsadm -o addsolution -filename PACKAGE\LitwareTypes.wsp
stsadm -o execadmsvcjobs
stsadm -o deploysolution -name LitwareTypes.wsp -immediate  -allowGacDeployment -force
```

When you issue commands to the STSADM.EXE utility to deploy a WSP file, WSS runs these tasks asynchronously by using timer jobs. This makes solution packages a great way to deploy functionality across multiple servers in a server farm. The deploysolution operation of the STSADM.EXE utility can also be parameterized to start a deployment timer job at midnight when nobody's using the farm. This can be important because WSS issues an IISRESET command on each front-end Web server after it has deployed a solution package.

However, when creating deployment scripts, you might need to call the tasks in a synchronous fashion to deploy the package after adding it. Fortunately, you can use the execadmsvcjobs operation supplied by STSADM.EXE to kick off any scheduled jobs and wait for their completion. Use this command when writing aggregate commands in scripts to manage the installation and removal of solution packages. When you need to remove solution packages from the server farm during development, the following commands can be used:

```
stsadm -o retractsolution -name LitwareTypes.wsp -immediate
stsadm -o execadmsvcjobs
stsadm -o deletesolution -name LitwareTypes.wsp -override
stsadm -o execadmsvcjobs
```

Deploying the solution package installs the features inside, providing you with the equivalent of running the installfeature operation of the STSADM.EXE utility. However, installing a solution package does not activate a feature. Therefore, you must run the activatefeature operation of the STSADM.EXE utility or activate the feature through the standard WSS application pages to perform your testing.

Note that you can also load a solution package to the solution store without deploying it, in which case the solution would be available for deployment through the Central Administration Web site. The Central Administration site includes Solution Management pages that can be accessed from the Solution Management link on the Operations menu. The Solution Management page lists each solution that is installed, as shown in Figure 9-4. By selecting an installed solution, you can deploy a solution, retract a deployed solution, or remove a solution from the solution store. Removing the solution uninstalls it, thereby removing things such as SafeControl entries, GAC assemblies, and TEMPLATE-deployed files.

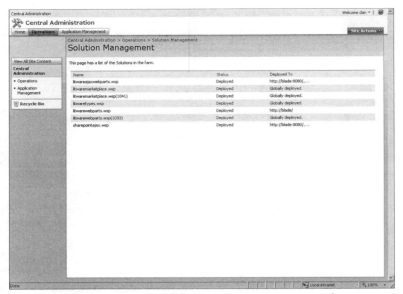

Figure 9-4   Once a solution package is installed, you can manage its deployment through the Solution Management pages of the WSS Central Administration site.

Solution Package for Deploying Web Parts

For our first Web Parts solution package, open the LitwareWebParts project. This is the same project that we created in Chapter 4, which includes the Web Part assembly as well as a feature for installing the .webpart files into the Web Part gallery. At the root level of the project, create a Solution folder with a cab.ddf file and a manifest.xml file. The cab.ddf file defines the layout and content of the .wsp file, which is a compressed .cab file containing the deployment files. The WSS runtime uses the timer service and the content database internally to deploy the solution package to all front-end Web servers using the .wsp file. The following code displays the ddf file for the LitwareWebParts.wsp solution package.

```
; ** LitwareWebParts.wsp (Pattison/Larson) **
.OPTION EXPLICIT      ; Generate errors
.Set CabinetNameTemplate=LitwareWebParts.wsp
.set DiskDirectoryTemplate=CDROM ; All cabinets go in a single directory
.Set CompressionType=MSZIP;** All files are compressed in cabinet files
.Set UniqueFiles="ON"
.Set Cabinet=on
.Set DiskDirectory1=Package

Solution\manifest.xml manifest.xml
TEMPLATE\FEATURES\LitwareWebParts\feature.xml LitwareWebParts\feature.xml
TEMPLATE\FEATURES\LitwareWebParts\elements.xml LitwareWebParts\elements.xml

TEMPLATE\FEATURES\LitwareWebParts\DWP\HelloWebPart.webpart FEATURES\LitwareWebParts\
   DWP\HelloWebPart.webpart
```

```
TEMPLATE\FEATURES\LitwareWebParts\DWP\RssViewWebPart.webpart FEATURES\LitwareWebParts\
    DWP\RssViewWebPart.webpart
TEMPLATE\FEATURES\LitwareWebParts\DWP\ContactViewer.webpart FEATURES\LitwareWebParts\
    DWP\ContactViewer.webpart
TEMPLATE\FEATURES\LitwareWebParts\DWP\UserControlHost.webpart FEATURES\LitwareWebParts\
    DWP\UserControlHost.webpart

TEMPLATE\CONTROLTEMPLATES\Litware\LitwareUserControl.ascx CONTROLTEMPLATES\Litware\
    LitwareUserControl.ascx

bin\LitwareWebParts.dll LitwareWebParts.dll

;*** <the end>
```

The manifest file in turn specifies the items in the solution for the WSS runtime. It specifies which files to copy to the TEMPLATES directory with the TemplateFiles node, which assemblies to deploy to the GAC, and which SafeControl entries to make.

```xml
<Solution SolutionId="DAE56AC0-97C7-4973-8704-DC3F6C48F4A4"
       xmlns="http://schemas.microsoft.com/sharepoint/">

  <FeatureManifests>
    <FeatureManifest Location="LitwareWebParts\feature.xml" />
  </FeatureManifests>

  <TemplateFiles>
    <TemplateFile Location="FEATURES\LitwareWebParts\DWP\HelloWebPart.webpart"/>
    <TemplateFile Location="FEATURES\LitwareWebParts\DWP\RssViewWebPart.webpart"/>
    <TemplateFile Location="FEATURES\LitwareWebParts\DWP\ContactViewer.webpart"/>
    <TemplateFile Location="FEATURES\LitwareWebParts\DWP\UserControlHost.webpart"/>
    <TemplateFile Location="CONTROLTEMPLATES\Litware\LitwareUserControl.ascx"/>
  </TemplateFiles>

  <Assemblies>
    <Assembly DeploymentTarget="WebApplication" Location="LitwareWebParts.dll">
      <SafeControls>
        <SafeControl Assembly="LitwareWebParts, [full 4-part assembly name]"
                  Namespace="LitwareWebParts" TypeName="*" Safe="True" />
      </SafeControls>
    </Assembly>
  </Assemblies>

</Solution>
```

To create the solution package by using the .ddf file, call the following from the command prompt or build event:

```
makecab /f Solution\cab.ddf
```

Note that the .ddf file in our example is coded to use the bin assembly, which must be configured as the Visual Studio build directory and built prior to this command.

STSADM.EXE Commands for Deploying Solution Packages

Similar to features, solution packages are deployed by using operations supplied by the STSADM.EXE utility. Before you can deploy the solution, you must install it. Installing the solution makes it available to the WSS server farm by placing it in the content database's solution store.

While this chapter has already shown you the basic STSADM.EXE operations involved in solution package deployment, we want to discuss a few additional parameterization options that are available to you. The following command installs the solution:

```
stsadm -o addsolution -filename package\LitwareWebParts.wsp
```

After installing the solution, it is available for deployment to any Web application on the server farm. To activate the solution, you must deploy it. The following command deploys the solution package after it is made available through the addsolution command:

```
stsadm -o deploysolution -name LitwareWebParts.wsp
```

There are a number of switches for the deploysolution operation. The important switches to know are allContentUrls, allowGacDeployment, and allowCasPolicies. The allow-GacDeployment switch is required where the solution package installs to the GAC, whereas allowCasPolicies is required where the solution package defines and installs custom security policies. The solution will not install at all without the required switches when CAS policies or GAC deployments are specified.

Solution Packages and Code Access Security

For Web Part assemblies (and any assembly running in the WSS Web application), we also want to specify the code access security trust levels that our Web Parts require. Many companies prefer to deploy their Web Part assembly DLLs inside the local bin directory for each Web application instead of using the GAC. This deployment style enables a company to run Web Part code within a sandboxed execution context that restricts what the Web Part code can do. By default, WSS configures the sandbox for Web Part assembly DLLs in the bin directory with a very restrictive trust level in which Web Part code is not allowed to access the hard drive of the local Web server or call into the WSS object model.

When you are creating a solution package for deploying Web Parts, it is a best practice to define the appropriate level of trust. This involves adding code access security configuration data into the solution manifest. If you don't perform this step, you'll find that your Web Parts work great on your development box, but fail miserably when deployed to production environments!

In the next chapter, we will discuss code access security in depth. You'll want to read that section to get a grasp on the importance of code access security in WSS as well as how to configure and secure your code with it. For now, we will focus on the basics of the solution package code access security configuration.

Before you test your final solution package, you want to prepare a clean test deployment environment, preferably with a virtual machine running in Microsoft Virtual PC or Microsoft Virtual Server. The test deployment environment should have either a clean installation of WSS or MOSS, or should have the configuration that most closely matches your target customer's environment. In most cases, you want to test your deployment both in WSS and in a MOSS installation.

> **Tip**   Virtual machine environments using Microsoft Virtual PC or Microsoft Virtual Server are our favorite tools for deployment testing. Undo disks in a virtual environment are too costly in performance penalties; therefore, we recommend creating a baseline test environment and backing up the virtual hard drive so that you can quickly restore the clean environment.

In the test deployment environment, make sure that the trust level of the web.config file is set as shipped to WSS_Minimal. Note that this is only for testing the solution deployment package and that it might break other custom Web Parts' functionality. Also ensure that the Web Part assembly (*LitwareWebParts* in this example) is not registered as Safe in the SafeControls section of the web.config because we will be setting that through the solution package.

> **Tip**   To ensure successful deployments and customer installations, make sure to test your solution package against a fresh WSS and MOSS environment (not just your development box)!

To define code access security in the solution package, add the CodeAccessSecurity element to the Solution element in the solution manifest.

```
<CodeAccessSecurity>
 <PolicyItem>
  <PermissionSet class="NamedPermissionSet" version="1"
       Description="Permission set for LitwareWebParts">
  </PermissionSet>
  <Assemblies>
  </Assemblies>
 </PolicyItem>
</CodeAccessSecurity>
```

Within the CodeAccessSecurity element, we can define the basic permissions required for our Web Part to run. We'll discuss advanced permissions in Chapter 10. For now, add the SharePointPermission class that allows our code to access the SharePoint object model. The following element adds the SharePointPermission permission to our assembly:

```
<IPermission class="Microsoft.SharePoint.Security.SharePointPermission,
     Microsoft.SharePoint.Security, Version=12.0.0.0, Culture=neutral,
     PublicKeyToken=71e9bce111e9429c"
     version="1" ObjectModel="True" Impersonate="True"
     UnsafeSaveOnGet="True" />
```

To specify the assemblies to which the code access security is applied, you can add nodes to the Assemblies element. You can add assemblies by either their simple name if they are deployed to the Web application or based on their strong name key. Using the simple name deployed by the Web application is preferable because it enables finer control over which assemblies are trusted and because all assemblies based on a common (corporate) public key are not treated the same. To add an assembly based on its simple name in the bin directory, use the following element syntax:

```
<Assembly Name="LitwareWebParts" />
```

Alternatively, you could use an assembly's public key. This is a bit trickier to obtain because you must use the .NET Framework SDK tool ILDASM to get the BLOB public key out of the assembly manifest. By using the CodeAccessSecurity element, we are defining a policy in which we allow our assembly to execute trusted code elements. At the WSS_Minimal and WSS_Medium trust levels, our assembly is not able to access the SharePoint object model unless we specify the permission defined by Microsoft.SharePoint.Security.SharePointPermission. Also, because the RSS Web Part makes Web requests (see Chapter 4), it would not be able to execute without the System.Net.WebPermission permission (defined in this chapter's sample code).

To ensure that our RSS Web Part allows access only to trusted locations, we could define more restrictive URL paths in the ConnectAccess node. We could also specify that this trust should apply to all assemblies signed with the Litware private key by choosing to trust the BLOB public key, obtained by loading the assembly's manifest by using the ILDASM tool. However, specifying fine-grained permissions per assembly is the most secure approach.

Solution Package for Deploying a Site Definition

In addition to Web Parts, the solution package also supports the deployment of site definitions. Site definitions can be much simpler to deploy through the solution package than through features because the required files and assemblies typically are previously deployed in features. To create a solution package for the Litware Marketplace site definition created earlier in the chapter, we will create a .ddf file referencing the ONET file, the WEBTEMP file, and the core resources.

```
; ** LitwareMarketplace.wsp **
.OPTION EXPLICIT      ; Generate errors
.Set CabinetNameTemplate=LitwareMarketplace.wsp
.set DiskDirectoryTemplate=CDROM ; All cabinets go in a single directory
.Set CompressionType=MSZIP;** All files are compressed in cabinet files
.Set UniqueFiles="ON"
.Set Cabinet=on
.Set DiskDirectory1=Package
```

```
Solution\manifest.xml manifest.xml
TEMPLATE\SiteTemplates\LitwareMarketplace\XML\ONET.XML LitwareMarketplace\XML\ONET.XML
TEMPLATE\1033\XML\webtemp.LitwareMarketplace.xml 1033\XML\webtemp.LitwareMarketplace.xml

RESOURCES\LitwareMarketplace.resx Resources\LitwareMarketplace.resx

;*** <the end>
```

A few additional solution manifest element types that are useful when deploying a site definition have not yet been discussed. First, the SiteDefinitionManifest node defines the location of the site definition. The child WebTempFile node defines the localized WEBTEMP file. You can add several of these elements to deploy to several different localized cultures from within the same solution package. The Location attribute of the site definition Manifest is a folder reference, in which case the XML\ONET.XML file is automatically deployed. Resources for the site definition can be deployed by using the RootFiles element, which defines files that are copied to the 12 folder. In our case, we are copying Resources to the 12\RESOURCES folder.

```
<Solution SolutionId="919974CF-F3A5-40a0-8829-849ECFB463CB"
      xmlns="http://schemas.microsoft.com/sharepoint/">

  <!-- A solution for the site definition "Litware Marketplace".
    Note: Litware Types is a prerequisite. -->

  <SiteDefinitionManifests>

    <SiteDefinitionManifest Location="LitwareMarketplace" >
      <WebTempFile Location="1033\XML\webtemp.LitwareMarketplace.xml"/>
    </SiteDefinitionManifest>
  </SiteDefinitionManifests>

  <RootFiles>
    <RootFile Location="Resources\LitwareMarketplace.resx"/>
  </RootFiles>

</Solution>
```

Web Configuration Changes

Certain scenarios exist in which deployment of your solution requires changes to one or more web.config files on the target front-end Web servers. As you have seen, a solution package provides you with an easy way to add SafeControl entries and CodeAccessSecurity entries to properly deploy Web Parts. However, this technique does not extend to other types of entries within the web.config file. This situation makes it necessary to find another approach when you need to modify the contents of web.config to deploy Application Programming Interface (API) components, such as custom HTTP handlers and HTTP module classes.

For example, to deploy the ASP.NET 2.0 AJAX framework to WSS 3.0, you need to add the *scriptresource.axd* handler to web.config. You might also need to add handler entries for other custom API endpoints, such as the opml.ashx handler from Chapter 5. (Note that you can use file extensions, such as .xml, for handlers in WSS 3.0 because all Web requests are processed through the .NET Framework.) In the AJAX Web Parts chapter (Chapter 5), we created an HTTP handler class to deploy the feed list as an OPML XML feed. To install this manually, we need to create the httpHandler node for opml.ashx on every IIS Web application in the farm. This process can become unmanageable over the life cycle of the server as new IIS Web sites are created and extended, especially in a farm configuration. The "no-touch" benefits of the solution package would be lost if your application depended on web.config modifications!

Fortunately, the WSS framework provides a way to manage both Web applications and web.config through the SPWebApplication class, which represents the IIS load-balanced Web application installed to the WSS server farm. This is an IIS Web application that is extended by WSS, which is also mapped to a WSS content database. It is virtualized across the server farm because you can extend arbitrary IIS sites to WSS Web applications, even on the same physical box. It can contain multiple site collections and can be accessed through the WebApplication property of the SPSite class.

> **Tip** SPWebApplication is a class with all types of fun and useful ways to administer the WSS Web application!

SPWebApplication is found in the Microsoft.SharePoint.Administration namespace, along with other classes used for administering the WSS environment, including the IIS servers that it runs on. By using classes in the administration namespace, you can manage the WSS environment as a single unit, regardless of the server farm configuration. For example, when you modify the web.config file through the WSS object model, it is modified across all instances of the WSS Web application, including multiple IIS sites that are extended with the WSS application across the server farm.

WSS also manages the state of the Web application so that changes made through the object model are applied to new servers added to the WSS farm as it is scaled out. For example, you might add an additional Web server six months after the initial WSS deployment. For each site on the new server, web.config contains multiple entries for SafeControls, HTTP handlers, and CAS policies, as well as assembly DLLs and other resources for your applications. With an approach that uses only the solution package deployment mechanism, these changes are all maintained by the WSS runtime and applied to the new server automatically.

To access the SPWebApplication, you can use any reference to the SPSite class, such as SPContext.Current.Site.WebApplication. Within a feature receiver, you can obtain a reference to the site collection through the SPFeatureReceiverProperties class and use that to access the SPWebApplication as in the following example.

```
public override void FeatureActivated(
        SPFeatureReceiverProperties properties) {
```

```
if (properties == null)
  throw new ArgumentNullException("properties");
SPWebApplication app = null;
SPSiteCollection site = properties.Feature.Parent as SPSiteCollection;
if (site == null) {
  SPWeb web = properties.Feature.Parent as SPWeb;
  if (web != null)
    app = web.Site.WebApplication;
} else
  app = site.WebApplication;
// Do something with the web application
}
```

The Web application has a collection called WebConfigModifications that it maintains in the content database and in each web.config for the application. The Web application's WebConfigModifications collection contains modifications to be applied across all instances of the IIS Web application across all servers in the farm. These modifications are encapsulated in the SPWebConfigModification class. SPWebConfigModification provides a way to make changes to web.config and can be used in a console application or feature receiver. Internally, the WSS runtime stores this information in the farm configuration database in the Objects table and uses XML-serialized objects to persist the class. This lets WSS reapply the objects to new web.config files as new sites come online. The properties for the SPWebConfigModification class are listed in Table 9-1.

> **Tip**   Use objects in the Microsoft.SharePoint.Administration namespace to manage your environments and avoid making manual changes to configurations in production environments.

Table 9-1   SPWebConfigModification Properties

Name	Description
Name	The relative xpath to the modification; used to locate the modification given to the root xpath from the Path property when removing the modification (also the constructor's name parameter)
Owner	The owner reference of the modification; used to track the modification in the content database; assembly's full name is recommended
Path	The xpath (also the constructor's path parameter)
Sequence	Specifies the ordinal sequence of the modification
Type	The SPWebConfigModificationType type of modification—either EnsureChildNode, EnsureAttribute, or EnsureSection
Value	The actual web.config element to insert

To test the SPWebConfigModification class, you can use a console application to administer the local server. To take this further, you could build an extension to STSADM by using the ISPStsadmCommand interface. ISPStsadmCommand is an interface that allows you to write custom STSADM commands. You can read more about extending STSADM through ISPStsadmCommand at *http://msdn2.microsoft.com/library/microsoft.sharepoint .stsadmin.ispstsadmcommand.aspx.*

A simple console application is included in Listing 9-4. This application adds an element to the WSS Web configuration through SPWebModification. Remember that this is a configuration change tracked and managed by WSS and the WSS configuration database over the lifetime of the WSS Web application, not just a modification to the web.config file. For simplicity, the values are hard-coded into the application in this example. To enable the WSS runtime to track this change, the Path property must be the xpath expression to the root node containing the child node, and the Name property is the xpath expression from the parent node to the new child node. The Name and Path properties are used primarily by WSS to manage the entry over the lifetime of the WSS Web application. On subsequent calls to ApplyWebConfigModification, WSS ensures that all of its modifications are applied or removed. If *Name* is incorrect on the initial add operation, the element can still be added, but WSS is unable to manage its removal.

Listing 9-4   Web Config Modification Console demonstrates simple use of SPWebApplication and SPWebConfigModification.

```
Web Config Modification Console
using System;
using Microsoft.SharePoint;
using Microsoft.SharePoint.Administration;

class Program {

  private const string ScriptHandler =
    @"<add verb=""GET,HEAD"" path=""ScriptResource.axd""
type=""System.Web.Handlers.ScriptResourceHandler, System.Web.Extensions""
    validate=""false""/>";

  static void Main(string[] args) {

    SPSite siteCollection = new SPSite("http://localhost");
    SPWebApplication webApp = siteCollection.WebApplication;
    SPWebConfigModification modification = new SPWebConfigModification();
    modification.Path = "configuration/system.web/httpHandlers";
    modification.Name = "add[@path='ScriptResource.axd']";
    modification.Value = ScriptHandler;
    modification.Owner = "ExampleOwner";
    modification.Sequence = 0;
    modification.Type =
      SPWebConfigModification.SPWebConfigModificationType.EnsureChildNode;
    webApp.WebConfigModifications.Add(modification);
    // To remove the modification:
    // webApp.WebConfigModifications.Remove(modification);
    webApp.Farm.Services.GetValue<SPWebService>()
    ApplyWebConfigModifications();
  }
}
```

The example code could be changed easily to remove the configuration change, as in the following example:

```
webApp.WebConfigModifications.Remove(modification);
```

The SPWebConfigModification class is perhaps most useful in the context of a feature receiver, in which case the SPFeatureReceiver passes an instance of the site context in the SPFeatureReceiverProperties object. Depending on whether the feature was installed at the site collection or site level, the feature receiver passes either an SPWeb or an SPSite reference. Using this technique, you can modify the configuration based on the activated feature, letting you package the SPWebConfigModification within the solution package. Following is the example FeatureActivated method of an example feature receiver, which adds the ScriptResourceHandler to the ScriptResource.axd path.

```
public override void FeatureActivated(
    SPFeatureReceiverProperties properties) {
  SPWebApplication app = null;
  SPSiteCollection site = properties.Feature.Parent as SPSiteCollection;
  if (site == null) {
    SPWeb web = properties.Feature.Parent as SPWeb;
    if (web != null)
      app = web.Site.WebApplication;
  } else
    app = site.WebApplication;

  SPWebConfigModification modification = new SPWebConfigModification();
  modification.Name = "add[@path='ScriptResource.axd']";
  modification.Path = "configuration/system.web/httpHandlers");
  modification.Value = @"<add verb=""GET,HEAD"" path=""ScriptResource.axd"" type=
  ""System.Web.Handlers.ScriptResourceHandler, System.Web.Extensions"" validate=""false""/>";
  modification.Owner = Assembly.GetExecutingAssembly().FullName;
  modification.Sequence = 0;
  modification.Type = SPWebConfigModification.SPWebConfigModificationType.EnsureChildNode;
  app.WebConfigModifications.Add(modification);
  SPFarm.Local.Services.GetValue<SPWebService>().ApplyWebConfigModifications();
}
```

Within the FeatureDeactivating method, you can remove the handler by using the following code, being careful to pass the same Name, Path, and Owner previously used.

```
public override void FeatureDeactivating(SPFeatureReceiverProperties properties) {
  SPWebApplication app = null;
  SPSiteCollection site = properties.Feature.Parent as SPSiteCollection;
  if (site == null) {
    SPWeb web = properties.Feature.Parent as SPWeb;
    if (web != null)
      app = web.Site.WebApplication;
  .} else
    app = site.WebApplication;

  SPWebConfigModification modification = new SPWebConfigModification();
  modification.Name = "add[@path='ScriptResource.axd']";
```

```
modification.Path = "configuration/system.web/httpHandlers");
modification.Value = @"<add verb=""GET,HEAD"" path=""ScriptResource.axd""
type=""System.Web.Handlers.ScriptResourceHandler, System.Web.Extensions"" validate=""false""/>";
modification.Owner = Assembly.GetExecutingAssembly().FullName;
modification.Sequence = 0;
modification.Type = SPWebConfigModification.SPWebConfigModificationType.EnsureChildNode;
app.WebConfigModifications.Remove(modification);
SPFarm.Local.Services.GetValue<SPWebService>().ApplyWebConfigModifications();
}
```

Using this strategy, you can create modifications to web.config and manage web.config files across the server farm through the use of feature receivers, and you can maintain a no-touch deployment strategy for your WSS solutions.

Language Packs

We have already looked at resources for localizing Web Parts, features, and site definitions. Language packs for solution packages enable the deployment of localized resources based on installed resources. Language pack solutions share the same Name and SolutionId as the core solution package, but they include only localized resources and are identified to STSADM by the *-lcid* switch. For example, for the LitwareWebParts.wsp package, we can create a Litware-WebParts.wsp package in an en-US folder with the same solution name and GUID identifier as the LitwareWebParts.wsp package. It will contain only the Resource files required for the localized solution. Listings 9-5 through 9-8 display the Litware Web Parts language packs for US English and Japanese.

Listing 9-5 The US English language pack CAB definition

```
US English Web Part Language Pack
; ** cab.en-US.ddf **
; en-US localized LitwareWebParts
.OPTION EXPLICIT      ; Generate errors
.Set CabinetNameTemplate=LitwareWebParts.wsp
.set DiskDirectoryTemplate=CDROM ; All cabinets go in a single directory
.Set CompressionType=MSZIP;** All files are compressed in cabinet files
.Set UniqueFiles="ON"
.Set Cabinet=on
.Set DiskDirectory1=Package\en-US
Solution\manifest.en-US.xml manifest.xml
bin\en-US\LitwareWebParts.resources.dll en-US\LitwareWebParts.resources.dll
;*** <the end>
```

Listing 9-6 The US English language pack solution manifest

```
<!-- manifest.en-US.xml -->
<Solution SolutionId="DAE56AC0-97C7-4973-8704-DC3F6C48F4A4"
    xmlns="http://schemas.microsoft.com/sharepoint/">
```

```
    <Assemblies>
      <Assembly DeploymentTarget="GlobalAssemblyCache"
         Location="en-US\LitwareWebParts.resources.dll" />
    </Assemblies>

  </Solution>
```

Listing 9-7   The Japanese language pack CAB definition

```
Japanese Web Part Language Pack
; ** cab.ja-JP.ddf **
; ja-JP localized LitwareWebParts
.OPTION EXPLICIT      ; Generate errors
.Set CabinetNameTemplate=LitwareWebParts.wsp
.set DiskDirectoryTemplate=CDROM ; All cabinets go in a single directory
.Set CompressionType=MSZIP;** All files are compressed in cabinet files
.Set UniqueFiles="ON"
.Set Cabinet=on
.Set DiskDirectory1=Package\ja-JP
Solution\manifest.ja-JP.xml manifest.xml
bin\ja-JP\LitwareWebParts.resources.dll ja-JP\LitwareWebParts.resources.dll
;*** <the end>
```

Listing 9-8   The Japanese language pack solution manifest

```
<!-- manifest.ja-JP.xml -->
<Solution SolutionId="DAE56AC0-97C7-4973-8704-DC3F6C48F4A4"
     xmlns="http://schemas.microsoft.com/sharepoint/">

  <Assemblies>
    <Assembly DeploymentTarget="GlobalAssemblyCache"
        Location="ja-JP\LitwareWebParts.resources.dll" />
  </Assemblies>

</Solution>
```

After defining the localized language packs, the commands to add them are the same as the core solutions except that the locale is identified by using the lcid parameter. The addsolution and deploysolution commands are used when deploying the LitwareWebParts.wsp language pack in the Package\en-US subfolder.

```
stsadm -o addsolution -filename Package\en-US\LitwareWebParts.wsp -lcid 1033
stsadm -o deploysolution -name LitwareWebParts.wsp -lcid 1033 -immediate -allowGacDeployment
```

The final build script for the Litware Web Parts project is used both on the development box and as a template for the deployment script for production release. It builds the Web Part solution package and language packs as well as adds and deploys the solution package. The complete build script is shown in Listing 9-9 and is available in this chapter's code samples.

Listing 9-9 The final Litware Web Parts build script

```
Litware Web Parts Build Script
if EXIST package\LitwareWebParts.wsp del package\LitwareWebParts.wsp

makecab /f Solution\cab.ddf
makecab /f Solution\cab.en-US.ddf
makecab /f Solution\cab.ja-JP.ddf

@SET SPDIR="c:\program files\common files\microsoft shared\web server extensions\12"

%SPDIR%\bin\stsadm -o deactivatefeature -name litwarewebparts -url http://localhost

%SPDIR%\bin\stsadm -o retractsolution -name LitwareWebParts.wsp -lcid 1033 -immediate
%SPDIR%\bin\stsadm -o execadmsvcjobs
%SPDIR%\bin\stsadm -o deletesolution -name LitwareWebParts.wsp -lcid 1033 -override
%SPDIR%\bin\stsadm -o execadmsvcjobs
%SPDIR%\bin\stsadm -o retractsolution -name LitwareWebParts.wsp -immediate -url
http://localhost
%SPDIR%\bin\stsadm -o execadmsvcjobs
%SPDIR%\bin\stsadm -o deletesolution -name LitwareWebParts.wsp -override
%SPDIR%\bin\stsadm -o execadmsvcjobs

%SPDIR%\bin\stsadm -o addsolution -filename package\LitwareWebParts.wsp
%SPDIR%\bin\stsadm -o execadmsvcjobs

%SPDIR%\bin\stsadm -o deploysolution -name LitwareWebParts.wsp -immediate
  -allowGacDeployment -allowCasPolicies -url http://localhost
%SPDIR%\bin\stsadm -o execadmsvcjobs

%SPDIR%\bin\stsadm -o addsolution -filename Package\en-US\LitwareWebParts.wsp
  -lcid 1033
%SPDIR%\bin\stsadm -o execadmsvcjobs

%SPDIR%\bin\stsadm -o deploysolution -name LitwareWebParts.wsp -lcid 1033 -immediate
  -allowGacDeployment
%SPDIR%\bin\stsadm -o execadmsvcjobs

%SPDIR%\bin\stsadm -o activatefeature -name litwarewebparts -url http://localhost
```

Localizing a Site Definition

Revisiting the site definition from earlier in this chapter, it is easy to add a Japanese language pack by adding a localized WEBTEMP file and a LitwareMarketplace resources file. For the Japanese language pack, the WEBTEMP file is localized and deployed to the locale directory TEMPLATE\1041\XML, and the resources are used by the site definition. Additionally, if you wish to make the resources available to custom application pages, you can use the ApplicationResourceFiles node in the solution manifest. The Japanese site definition language pack containing the .ddf file is shown in Listing 9-10, and Listing 9-11 contains the solution manifest.

Listing 9-10   The Japanese site definition language pack CAB definition

```
Japanese Site Definition Language Pack
; ** ja-JP\LitwareMarketplace.wsp (Pattison/Larson) **
.OPTION EXPLICIT       ; Generate errors
.Set CabinetNameTemplate=LitwareMarketplace.wsp
.set DiskDirectoryTemplate=CDROM ; All cabinets go in a single directory
.Set CompressionType=MSZIP;** All files are compressed in cabinet files
.Set UniqueFiles="ON"
.Set Cabinet=on
.Set DiskDirectory1=Package
Solution\manifest.ja-JP.xml manifest.xml
RESOURCES\LitwareMarketplace.ja-JP.resx Resources\LitwareMarketplace.ja-JP.resx
TEMPLATE\1041\XML\webtemp.LitwareMarketplace.xml 1041\XML\webtemp.LitwareMarketplace.xml
;*** <the end>
```

Listing 9-11   The Japanese site definition language pack solution manifest

```xml
<!-- manifest.ja-JP.xml -->
<Solution SolutionId="919974CF-F3A5-40a0-8829-849ECFB463CB"
      xmlns="http://schemas.microsoft.com/sharepoint/">

  <SiteDefinitionManifests>

    <SiteDefinitionManifest Location="LitwareMarketplace" >
      <WebTempFile Location="1041\XML\webtemp.LitwareMarketplace.xml"/>
    </SiteDefinitionManifest>
  </SiteDefinitionManifests>

  <RootFiles>
    <RootFile Location="Resources\LitwareMarketplace.ja-JP.resx"/>
  </RootFiles>

</Solution>
```

The final build script for the Litware site definition is shown in Listing 9-12. This build script incorporates the language resources built earlier in the chapter and includes default and Japanese language resources.

Listing 9-12   Final build script for the Litware site definition

```
Litware Site Definition Build Script
makecab /f Solution\cab.ddf
makecab /f Solution\cab.ja-JP.ddf

@SET SPDIR="c:\program files\common files\microsoft shared\web server extensions\12"

%SPDIR%\bin\stsadm -o retractsolution -name LitwareMarketplace.wsp
   -immediate  -lcid 1041
%SPDIR%\bin\stsadm -o execadmsvcjobs
```

```
%SPDIR%\bin\stsadm -o deletesolution -name LitwareMarketplace.wsp -override -lcid 1041
%SPDIR%\bin\stsadm -o execadmsvcjobs

%SPDIR%\bin\stsadm -o retractsolution -name LitwareMarketplace.wsp -immediate
%SPDIR%\bin\stsadm -o execadmsvcjobs
%SPDIR%\bin\stsadm -o deletesolution -name LitwareMarketplace.wsp -override
%SPDIR%\bin\stsadm -o execadmsvcjobs

%SPDIR%\bin\stsadm -o addsolution -filename PACKAGE\LitwareMarketplace.wsp
%SPDIR%\bin\stsadm -o execadmsvcjobs

%SPDIR%\bin\stsadm -o addsolution -filename PACKAGE\LitwareMarketplace.wsp -lcid 1041
%SPDIR%\bin\stsadm -o execadmsvcjobs

%SPDIR%\bin\stsadm -o deploysolution -name LitwareMarketplace.wsp -immediate -force
%SPDIR%\bin\stsadm -o execadmsvcjobs

%SPDIR%\bin\stsadm -o deploysolution -name LitwareMarketplace.wsp -immediate
  -force -lcid 1041
%SPDIR%\bin\stsadm -o execadmsvcjobs
```

Summary

In this chapter, you learned how to create site definitions and configurations to provide user-creatable site templates. You then learned how to attach features before or after deployment. These techniques should give you the basic skills you need to begin aggregating the WSS components you develop into prepackaged business solutions.

This chapter also examined working with resource files in Visual Studio to provide an effective approach for localizing WSS components. As you have seen, WSS 3.0 has added powerful support for localizing various types of resources that can facilitate developing business solutions that target international markets. The chapter ended by showing you how to package your components for deployment by using solution packages and language packs. That now brings us to our final chapter on security.

Chapter 10

Application Security

- Learn the basics of code access security and trust levels.
- Configure application trust levels by using solution packages.
- Understand WSS authentication and authorization.
- Work with WSS security classes and interfaces.

Introduction

Certainly, security is an important topic when designing and implementing a business solution with Microsoft Windows SharePoint Services (WSS). You don't want users who haven't been granted the proper permissions to be able to view or edit sensitive pages, items, or documents. At the same time, you need to ensure that users with the proper permissions can access what they need. Although WSS goes a long way toward providing out-of-the-box security features that allow site owners to configure access rights within a site collection, a WSS developer should know how WSS security works behind the scenes as well as how to extend the WSS security model with custom code.

WSS is very flexible in that it allows users to create and deploy content using Web Parts, thereby avoiding many of the formalities of traditional application development. Although allowing users to add Web Parts to pages on the fly is powerful, it also brings up security concerns because it allows end users (as opposed to administrators or developers) to decide what code runs behind a Web Part page. You have already seen how WSS employs SafeControl settings in the web.config file to ensure that users use only Web Parts that are preapproved by a farm-level administrator. WSS goes one step further when it comes to protecting the system from code within Web Parts that could be malicious or poorly written. The farm-level administrator is able to configure Web Part DLLs so that they run within a restrictive sandbox using trust levels and code access security.

The first part of this chapter covers code access security and shows you how to write and deploy Web Parts that might be deployed in a secure environment. The second part of this chapter discusses how WSS manages security contexts and user identities. As you will see, Web Part code runs under the security context of the current user by default. The application pool identity also plays a role, as well as the identity and trust of the Web Part code itself. Understanding these security contexts and their limitations helps you write effective code.

Trust Levels and Code Access Security

Code access security, commonly referred to as *CAS*, defines the execution permissions granted to a piece of code that runs in a *partially trusted* location. This concept is similar to user authorization, although it is the code and not a user account that is authorized. A partially trusted location does not fully trust the code that it contains and creates a restricted security context (that is, a sandbox) to isolate its code from the rest of the system.

Because the partially trusted location runs with restrictive permissions, it limits the attack surface of the system and is the most secure location from which to run code. The partially trusted location allows code to run in predefined security contexts without risk of compromising critical personal or corporate data. In WSS, each Web application's bin directory is a partially trusted location in which code access security is enforced. Because of this fact, it is the preferred location to deploy Web Part applications. The least trusted location is the most secure place from which to run your code. Likewise, code that is trusted the least is the most secure because it is less likely to compromise the system.

The most common misunderstanding about CAS policy is that developers often think the least-trusted code is bad because we don't trust it, and the code that we fully trust must be good. (We do trust it, don't we?) In fact, the opposite is true. Because we do not grant trust for an unknown functionality, we know that we *can* trust the code not to execute malicious operations beyond its scope of defined trust. It is similar to having a dog on a leash. If the dog is loose, it may or may not behave. Yet the cat across the street may be too difficult to resist even if the dog does behave 99 percent of the time. If the dog is on a leash, however, you can trust that it will not run into the street. It is more trustworthy because there is an element of control that forces it to behave, regardless of the cat across the street.

> **Tip**   Least-trusted code is the most *trustworthy* code.

The Global Assembly Cache (GAC) is a fully trusted location for WSS, as is the _app_bin location. (The _app_bin location is a special location for WSS infrastructure components that should not be used for custom code.) Certain WSS components, such as feature receivers and event handlers, must be deployed to the GAC, so you should create separate assemblies for Web Parts to enable deployment in the bin directory. You should also think of your Web Part assemblies as security containers, in which the CAS policy is applied to the entire assembly. You may wish to limit the scope of a Web Part assembly by the security that it requires. If you have Web Part code that requires an abnormal amount of trust, it may be better to isolate that component in a security-isolated assembly rather than raise the trust of the rest of your code.

> **Tip**   The Web application's bin directory is the preferred location for Web Part code because it has the most secure CAS policies. Web Part assembly DLLs that are installed in the GAC always run with full trust and cannot benefit from the ability to run code with partial trust in WSS.

CAS policies are aggregated into ASP.NET *trust levels*. Trust levels for the WSS Web application are defined in XML files and referenced in the Trust element of the web.config file. The trust level defines the amount of trust that is granted to predefined code groups running within the Web application context. This condition applies only to Web applications where code is deployed in the bin directory as a partially trusted code location. Code that runs as event handlers, admin console applications, or any other application outside of the Web application is not restricted and runs in *full trust*.

Default settings in the web.config for both WSS and Microsoft Office SharePoint Server (MOSS) run Web applications under a level of minimal trust. The custom trust levels that WSS defines and runs under are defined in the 12\CONFIG directory and include WSS_Minimal and WSS_Medium. These files are located at 12\config\wss_minimaltrust.config and 12\config\wss_mediumtrust.config. WSS also manages custom trust levels, defined as WSS_Custom, that are derived from solution package CAS policies. These CAS policy files are defined by the system by copying the most recent policy file and applying updates as needed. WSS maintains a change set per installed solution package. As a solution package is either deployed or retracted, it modifies the web.config of the Web site to which it is being installed.

Although most WSS developers tend to ignore CAS and the WSS trust levels by simply running in the full trust level or installing to the GAC, it is important to understand how WSS manages CAS because you might not be in control of the deployment environment. Although you can also bypass CAS entirely by running your assemblies in the GAC, this is not as secure as using controlled CAS policies. CAS policies affect not only your code, but all assemblies that might be available in the application. If you do not want to deal with CAS policies, it is better to install to the GAC than to set the trust level to full trust.

The benefit of strict CAS policies is that they allow the code to perform only trusted operations. For example, if you run in a restricted CAS policy (such as one derived from WSS_Minimal) that allows your code to call into the WSS object model, security demands within your code can prevent an untrusted assembly from using your code to call into the WSS object model. You can also have code that is allowed to make calls to certain trusted online XML data sources, such as security-scrubbed RSS feeds from NewsGator Online, while disallowing Web requests to unknown XML data sources by using the WebPermission's ConnectAccess property. CAS policies allow IT to use third-party components without enabling the same level of trust that is granted to internally generated code or limiting the context in which code can execute. Web Part solutions that contain feature receivers should place the feature receiver in an external assembly that can be GAC installed, thereby maintaining a restrictive CAS policy for the Web assembly.

Tip   Full trust escalates trust not only for your Web Part assembly DLL, but for all Web Part assembly DLLs.

The WSS_Minimal trust level denies code the right to execute certain calls or access certain resources such as Structured Query Language (SQL), Web requests, and even WSS object model access. These permissions are defined as CodeAccessSecurity classes and CodeAccessSecurityAttributes that are defined and demanded in the .NET Framework and Microsoft.SharePoint.Security.dll assembly. The WSS_Minimal trust level is the most secure, in which only Microsoft Web Parts and very basic functionality in custom Web Parts can execute. WSS_Medium is a common choice for most organizations because of its ease of development for Web Part developers, maintaining a balance of trust and ease of configuration. On the other hand, the default WSS_Minimal trust level is the most secure but requires more work to configure custom applications. As a SharePoint developer, you should always create components that can be installed to WSS_Minimal trust, with explicit trust policies documented and included in the solution package.

Tip   When using WSS_Minimal trust and solution-managed trust levels, WSS manages the trust levels and creates custom trust levels based on the original configuration and installed solution packages. This is the recommended approach to maintaining WSS trust levels.

Within certain environments, you may wish to switch the trust level from WSS_Minimal to WSS_Medium or even full trust. This can be a viable choice for initial development environments, but for commercial or enterprise applications, you want to ensure that your solution has the correct permissions to execute (and no permissions not needed to execute). You may often want to develop in full trust and switch to WSS_Minimal to test your solution package deployments.

Tip   As discussed in Chapter 9, "Solutions and Deployment," solution packages are the supported and recommended way to set custom security levels. Other than switching the trust level during initial development, editing and managing security manually in configuration files is not maintainable on large scales and is not a recommended practice..

To examine the security ramifications of code access security, we will examine the Security-WebPart code in Listing 10-1 that contains several security-sensitive calls, each of which demands a more sensitive security level. This Web Part runs in its entirety only in full or custom trust levels unless it is deployed to the GAC. For initial development (on the development box), we will deploy this assembly in full trust mode.

However, before deploying to a staging, quality assurance, or production environment, we want to create a solution package with the appropriate CAS policies. The LitwareSecurity Web Part project is included in the code samples and includes the Web Part in Listing 10-1. To see CAS in action, first deploy the LitwareSecurity assembly manually in full trust mode. Next, add an instance of the SecurityWebPart to the page. Running this Web Part in anything but full trust breaks the Web Part.

Listing 10-1   The example SecurityWebPart class demonstrates CAS security policies.

```
CAS Example: Security Web Part
using System;
using Microsoft.SharePoint;
using System.Security.Principal;
namespace LitwareSecurity {

  // An example Web Part demonstating CAS requirements
  public class SecurityWebPart : System.Web.UI.WebControls.WebParts.WebPart {

    protected override void RenderChildren(System.Web.UI.HtmlTextWriter writer) {
      // Runs in WSS_Minimal
      writer.Write(string.Format("Thread.CurrentPrincipal: {0} <br/>",
        System.Threading.Thread.CurrentPrincipal.Identity.Name));

      // Requires System.Security.Permissions.SecurityPermission
      //  with SecurityPermissionFlag.ControlPrincipal
      //  denied in the WSS_Minimal trust level..
      writer.Write(string.Format("Current user: {0} <br/>",
        WindowsIdentity.GetCurrent().Name) );

      // Requires System.Security.Permissions.SecurityPermission
      //  with SecurityPermissionFlag.ControlPrincipal
      //  denied in the WSS_Minimal trust level.
      using (WindowsImpersonationContext wic =
          WindowsIdentity.Impersonate(IntPtr.Zero)) {
        writer.Write(string.Format("Impersonated application pool user: {0} <br/>",
          WindowsIdentity.GetCurrent().Name));
      }

      // Requires Microsoft.SharePoint.Security.SharePointPermission
      // with ObjectModel = true
      // denied in WSS_Minimal, allowed in WSS_Medium
      writer.Write(string.Format("Current site: {0} <br/>",
        SPContext.Current.Web.Title ));

      // Requires Microsoft.SharePoint.Security.SharePointPermission
      //  with Impersonate=true
      //  denied in the WSS_Medium trust level,
      //  allowed in Full or custom permissions
      SPSecurity.RunWithElevatedPrivileges(          delegate() {
        writer.Write(string.Format("RunWithElevatedPrivileges user: {0} <br/>",
          WindowsIdentity.GetCurrent().Name));
      }
      );
    }
  }
}
```

To examine the effects of code access security, run this Web Part code in full trust and then reduce the trust levels to see what breaks. When reducing trust to WSS_Medium or lower, you will see an error message similar to the following:

```
The "SecurityWebPart" Web Part appears to be causing a problem. Request for the permission
of type 'Microsoft.SharePoint.Security.SharePointPermission, Microsoft.SharePoint.Security,
Version=12.0.0.0, Culture=neutral, PublicKeyToken=71e9bce111e9429c' failed.
```

Although we cannot grant the CAS policy for the assembly within the assembly itself, we can define it within the solution package and set it during the installation. During initial development, we might choose to simply run the Web application in full trust for rapid prototyping, but we want to sign the assembly and set its trust level explicitly before deployment. Within the assembly, we also request the security permissions it requires, which causes an early failure at deployment time rather than a more obscure runtime error. Failed permission requests cause the assembly not to load and provide details in the form of a System.Security.Policy.PolicyException, with a message stating something similar to "Required permissions cannot be acquired." By providing requests, we are letting the runtime know which permissions we require. The following example displays the permission request for the SharePoint permission.

```
[assembly: SharePointPermission(SecurityAction.RequestMinimum, ObjectModel=true)]
```

By specifying the security action RequestMinimum, we are letting the runtime know that this is a minimal permission grant required for the assembly to run correctly. We could also use the RequestOptional security action that lets the runtime know that we would like a certain permission, but our assembly will still run even though it may be less functional without this permission. For example, we may want to enable certain functionality that requires permissions to use the SQL client, but this is not required for all Web Parts. Within the assembly, we could specify this by using the following permission request.

```
[assembly: SqlClientPermission(SecurityAction.RequestOptional, Unrestricted=true)]
```

Likewise, if you want to refuse certain permissions from your assembly to take extra precautions to defend against luring attacks, you could use a RequestRefuse security action. The following permission refuses to allow the SQL client permission.

```
[assembly: SqlClientPermission(SecurityAction.RequestRefuse)]
```

Security requests from the assembly do not grant the permissions. They only let the runtime know that the permissions are required for execution. For the LitwareSecurity assembly, prior to creating the policy in the solution package manifest, we will first document the intentions and needs of the assembly by performing the correct permission requests in the assembly information file. The following permission requests define the required minimal permissions needed for the LitwareSecurity assembly as well as some optional permissions required for our SecurityDebugWebPart Web Part.

```
// Minimum permissions for the assembly to load:
[assembly: AspNetHostingPermission(SecurityAction.RequestMinimum)]
[assembly: SecurityPermission(SecurityAction.RequestMinimum,
  Execution=true)]
[assembly: SharePointPermission(SecurityAction.RequestMinimum,
  ObjectModel=true, Impersonate=true, UnsafeSaveOnGet=true)]

// Required by the optional Security Debug Web Part:
[assembly: EnvironmentPermission(SecurityAction.RequestOptional)]
[assembly: SecurityPermission(SecurityAction.RequestOptional,
  ControlPrincipal = true)]
```

After defining the permission requests, the next step is to configure the CAS policy for the assembly. We will do this through the solution package, first by signing the assembly with the Litware public key and then by defining security policy in the solution package manifest.

> **Tip**   For a refresher on solution packages, see Chapter 9.

You can modify the solution manifest file to grant the required CAS levels for your Web Part assembly DLLs. When defining CAS policies, you can define the trust based on the assembly's public key BLOB that is shared by all assemblies signed with your private key, or you can configure more granular trust based on the location of the assembly. Listing 10-2 shows a solution manifest that defines the permissions for Litware Security example code.

Listing 10-2   Security policy in the solution manifest

```
Litware Security Solution Package Manifest
<Solution SolutionId="75A16D0E-C8BA-43d6-9E50-D9C9CF4C7774"
    xmlns="http://schemas.microsoft.com/sharepoint/">
  <CodeAccessSecurity>
    <PolicyItem>
      <PermissionSet class="NamedPermissionSet" version="1"
          Description="Permission set for LitwareSecurity">
        <IPermission class="AspNetHostingPermission" version="1" Level="Minimal" />
        <IPermission class="SecurityPermission" version="1"
          Flags="Execution,ControlPrincipal,UnmanagedCode" />
        <IPermission class="Microsoft.SharePoint.Security.SharePointPermission,
Microsoft.SharePoint.Security, Version=12.0.0.0, Culture=neutral, PublicKeyToken=
71e9bce111e9429c" version="1" ObjectModel="True" Impersonate="True"/>
        <IPermission class="System.Security.Permissions.EnvironmentPermission,
mscorlib, version=1.0.5000.0, Culture=neutral, PublicKeyToken=b77a5c561934e089"
version="1" Read="UserName" />
      </PermissionSet>
      <Assemblies>
        <Assembly Name="LitwareSecurity" />
      </Assemblies>
    </PolicyItem>
  </CodeAccessSecurity>
  <Assemblies>
    <Assembly DeploymentTarget="WebApplication" Location="LitwareSecurity.dll">
```

```
        <SafeControls>
          <SafeControl Assembly="LitwareSecurity, Version=1.0.0.0, Culture=neutral,
PublicKeyToken=74bad7277fe0d19e"
          Namespace="LitwareSecurity" TypeName="*" Safe="True"/>
        </SafeControls>
      </Assembly>
    </Assemblies>
</Solution>
```

Note that within the solution manifest, each permission is defined in a NamedPermissionSet element. WSS creates a named permission set from this information. Within the permission set is a list of IPermission nodes, each of which defines a permission we are granting to members of this permission set. These IPermission nodes match the security requests we have already defined on the assembly. The three SharePoint permissions are also available in XML files in the 12\config folder. For a listing of the most common permissions used in WSS code, see the sidebar "Common Permission Definitions for WSS Applications" that follows.

Common Permission Definitions for WSS Applications

SharePointPermission   Defines permission to access the object model and permission to impersonate. ObjectModel, UnsafeSaveOnGet, and Impersonate are the optional properties that define the actual permission. UnsafeSaveOnGet specifies that the code has permission to update the database on a GET request. Note that this is also required for Web Service updates.

```
<IPermission class="Microsoft.SharePoint.Security.SharePointPermission, Microsoft
.SharePoint.Security, Version=12.0.0.0, Culture=neutral, PublicKeyToken=
71e9bce111e9429c" version="1" ObjectModel="True" Impersonate="True"/>
```

EnvironmentPermission   Defines permission to access the environment, including the current Windows user.

```
<IPermission class="System.Security.Permissions.EnvironmentPermission, mscorlib,
version=1.0.5000.0, Culture=neutral, PublicKeyToken=b77a5c561934e089" version="1"
Read="UserName" />
```

SecurityPermission   Defines permissions specified by the SecurityPermissionFlag enumeration including AllFlags, Assertion, BindingRedirects, ControlAppDomain, ControlDomainPolicy, ControlEvidence, ControlPolicy, ControlPrincipal, ControlThread, Execution, Infrastructure, NoFlags, RemotingConfiguration, SerializationFormatter, SkipVerification, and UnmanagedCode. The WSS_Minimal trust level grants the SecurityPermission with the only Execute flag to code running in the bin directory.

```
<IPermission class="System.Security.Permissions.SecurityPermission, mscorlib,
version=1.0.5000.0, Culture=neutral, PublicKeyToken=b77a5c561934e089" version="1"
Flags="Execute" />
```

> **AspNetHostingPermission**   Defines permission to access protected ASP.NET controls. This permission is granted in the WSS_Minimal trust level.
>
> ```
> <IPermission class="AspNetHostingPermission" version="1" Level="Minimal" />
> ```
>
> **WebPermission**   Defines permission to access Web resources, including Web services. The ConnectAccess element defines which URLs can be accessed.
>
> ```
> <IPermission class="System.Net.WebPermission, System, version=1.0.5000.0,
> Culture=neutral, PublicKeyToken=b77a5c561934e089" version="1">
>   <ConnectAccess>
>     <URI uri="http?://.*" />
>   </ConnectAccess>
> </IPermission>
> ```

The permissions defined in the solution manifest are applied to the custom permission configuration managed by WSS. The following permission set is generated from the solution package.

```
<PermissionSet class="NamedPermissionSet" version="1" Description="Permission set for
LitwareSecurity"
Name="litwaresecurity.wsp-75a16d0e-c8ba-43d6-9e50-d9c9cf4c7774-1">
   <IPermission class="AspNetHostingPermission" version="1" Level="Minimal" />
   <IPermission class="SecurityPermission" version="1" Flags="Execution,ControlPrincipal,
ControlAppDomain,ControlDomainPolicy,ControlEvidence" />
   <IPermission class="Microsoft.SharePoint.Security.SharePointPermission, Microsoft
.SharePoint.Security, Version=12.0.0.0, Culture=neutral, PublicKeyToken=71e9bce111e9429c"
version="1" ObjectModel="True" Impersonate="True" />
   <IPermission class="System.Security.Permissions.SecurityPermission, mscorlib,
version=1.0.5000.0, Culture=neutral, PublicKeyToken=b77a5c561934e089" version="1"
Flags="ControlThread, UnmanagedCode" />
   <IPermission class="System.Security.Permissions.EnvironmentPermission, mscorlib, version=1
.0.5000.0, Culture=neutral, PublicKeyToken=b77a5c561934e089" version="1" Read="UserName" />
</PermissionSet>
```

From the solution package, WSS modifies a copy of the WSS_Minimal permission set (or whichever permission set is referenced from web.config). For each solution package, a corresponding PermissionSet is created. The manifest GUID is applied to the solution package name, and a corresponding CodeGroup element is created. This code group is assigned to a permission set, and all code that matches its membership conditions is assigned this permission. In this case, the LitwareSecurity.dll assembly located in the bin directory is assigned to this permission set. The following code group is created from the solution package in the security configuration.

```
<CodeGroup class="UnionCodeGroup" version="1" PermissionSetName="litwaresecurity.wsp-
75a16d0e-c8ba-43d6-9e50-d9c9cf4c7774-1">
   <IMembershipCondition version="1" Name="LitwareSecurity" class="UrlMembershipCondition"
Url="$AppDirUrl$/bin/LitwareSecurity.dll" />
</CodeGroup>
```

The Listing 10-1 code example presented four methods that deal with identities and security. Each of these methods requires a specific grant of trust in order to execute. Because code access security is explicitly defined, it can be used to identify and audit security risks of an application. For example, we know that this assembly cannot be used to compromise a sensitive SQL database because we know it does not have the required permissions. Likewise, because this assembly does not have the System.Net.WebPermission granted, we know that it cannot be used to send data to remote Web endpoints regardless of any malicious code it could contain. Likewise, you could grant a restrictive System.Net.WebPermission that allows HTTP requests only to trusted endpoints, which enables the IT organization to limit its portal's attack surface by restricting executable code to predefined sandboxes. In security-sensitive environments, the manifest file of the solution package is an auditable asset that should be examined before deployment.

Troubleshooting Code Access Security

Before deploying your solution package, you want to test it against the WSS_Minimal trust level. To do this, set the trust level to WSS_Minimal and run your installer script. Then, place Web Parts from the package on a Web Part page. If your code has not been granted the correct permissions, its security demands will fail. In the Web browser, you may get a security exception stating that the request for a security permission failed. At this point, you can search for the permission type in a tool, such as the Microsoft Visual Studio Object Browser, to find the arguments for the permission type. WSS permissions are defined in the 12\config directory; however, you may need to search MSDN or the appropriate class library for the correct properties and syntax. In general, permissions take the form of <IPermission class="ClassName" Property="PropertyValue" />.

Next, examine the created permission set in the 12\config directory that corresponds with the WSS_Custom permission referenced in the web.config you are testing. Another common error is invalid configuration of the membership configuration. If you are not getting the expected results, check the IMembershipCondition element of your code group. For bin-deployed assemblies, this is either the public key BLOB from the signed assembly manifest or the URL of the assembly location, such as $AppDirUrl$/bin/LitwareSecurity.dll in our example. This URL is created based on the assembly name in the solution manifest (without the file extension suffix), which is the simple file name and not the strong name of the assembly. The solution package creates either UrlMembershipCondition references based on the file name or StrongNameMembershipCondition references based on the public key BLOB from the assembly manifest.

Tip Microsoft Visual Studio 2005 Team Edition for Software Developers contains code analysis tools to help you write more secure code. Analyzing your code with Visual Studio exposes and helps you fix common CAS-related security vulnerabilities.

Authentication, Authorization, and Identities

WSS does not perform any authentication on its own. Instead, WSS relies on either Internet Information Services (IIS) or the ASP.NET Framework to perform authentication. When WSS is configured to use *Integrated Windows Authentication*, IIS together with the operating system of the Web server authenticates the user against a Windows user account (which could be either a local or domain account). When WSS is configured to use *Forms Authentication*, an ASP.NET authentication provider authenticates the user against some other type of user accounts repository, such as a Microsoft SQL Server database.

Although WSS does not perform authentication, it does manage user identities and perform authorization. After authentication, WSS maintains a *user security token* that identifies the authentication mechanism and a list of groups and/or membership roles. WSS is able to read the groups and membership roles of the current user very efficiently at run time by examining this token. The structure of this token varies depending on whether the user is authenticated with Integrated Windows Authentication or Forms Authentication.

WSS supports the assignment of permissions to *security principals*. There are two types of security principals: *users* and *groups*. The WSS object model defines the SPPrincipal class that provides the base functionality for assigning permissions to a principal. SPPrincipal exposes the Roles SPRoleCollection property as well as the ParentWeb SPWeb property as WSS instantiates each principal in the context of a parent site. The WSS object model also defines two classes that derive from SPPrincipal—SPUser and SPGroup. These two classes extend this base class with their own unique methods and properties.

The request of an authenticated user runs under the content of an SPUser object and carries a security token. When you create an object reference to an SPSite site collection, WSS creates an instance of the SPUserToken and the SPUser. This always happens in the context of the site collection, and it is the user who creates the instance reference that WSS uses for authorization. As the code attempts to access resources, WSS checks this user's security token against binary access control lists (ACLs) to determine whether it should grant or deny access. An ACL is simply a data structure associated with a target WSS object, such as a site, list, or list item that tracks the rights of users and groups.

WSS objects may either use their own ACL or inherit the rights of a parent object. By default, most items within the WSS object model inherit parent ACLs. For example, a newly created document library inherits the ACL of its parent site. A newly created document automatically inherits the ACL of its parent document library. However, it's also possible to configure any document with its unique ACL to give it an access control policy that differs from other documents within the same document library. This can be done through either the user interface or custom code. To return the parent object containing the ACL used by any securable object in WSS, call its FirstUniqueAncestor property. To return the first parent SPWeb site that contains the ACL used by a child Web site, call the First-UniqueAncestorWeb property.

It is important to note that WSS manages users and groups and enforces authorization at the scope of the site collection. Rights assigned to a user in one site collection never affect what the user can do in another site collection. It is by design that WSS treats each site collection as its own independent island with respect to authorization and access control.

WSS stores and maintains a *user information profile* for authenticated users at the site collection level. The user information profile can be seen and updated by selecting the My Settings menu item command from the Welcome menu at the top right of the home page for a site. Remember that there is only one user information profile per user that extends across all of the sites inside. However, the user information profile does not extend across site collections.

Using Forms Authentication

The previous version of WSS supported authentication only against Windows accounts. This restriction created a tight coupling with Active Directory directory service that made WSS 2.0 less than ideal for extranet applications. Most companies also determined that the requirement to maintain user accounts in Active Directory made WSS 2.0 an impractical platform for creating Internet-facing sites that required authentication.

Microsoft ASP.NET 2.0 introduced the *Authentication Provider Framework*, which makes it possible to plug in and substitute various authentication provider components, each of which has its own unique implementation of the code required to authenticate users. A significant benefit to this new model is that an authentication provider can be written to authenticate user accounts that are maintained in any type of repository, such as a database or a Lightweight Directory Access Protocol (LDAP) provider.

ASP.NET 2.0 ships with out-of-the-box authentication providers that can be used to authenticate users against user accounts created in a SQL Server database or in Active Directory. However, the main benefit of the authentication provider model in ASP.NET is to promote flexibility. If a company wishes to maintain its user accounts in a different type of database or in any type of LDAP provider, it can commission a developer to write a custom authentication provider. Once written, the custom authentication provider can be plugged in and configured to provide the authentication plumbing required for ASP.NET applications.

WSS 3.0 is designed and implemented to support the ASP.NET authentication providers in addition to Integrated Windows Security. This is a significant step forward from the previous version of WSS because user accounts no longer have to be maintained in Active Directory. Companies should now see WSS 3.0 as a viable platform for building Internet-facing sites, including those that allow unknown Internet users to register themselves as members.

The easiest path to using Forms Authentication with WSS 3.0 is to use the AspNetSqlMembershipProvider class that comes as a standard component of ASP.NET 2.0. To get up and running, you or a system administrator must seek out the proper documentation to create an aspnetdb database in SQL Server and add the proper configuration data to the machine.config file and/or various web.config files on each front-end Web server.

Note that although WSS 3.0 supports ASP.NET authentication providers and forms authentication, it provides no components or features that assist with the creation or management of user accounts. For example, if you want to develop an Internet-facing site with a registration link that says, "Click here to create a membership account," you must then provide the code and user interface components that interact with the underlying authentication provider to create a new user account. Such code could be written into a standalone ASP.NET application or integrated into a custom application page or a Web Part.

> **Tip**   You should read the Security chapter of *Essential ASP.NET 2.0, Second Edition*, written by Fritz Onion and Keith Brown (Addison-Wesley Professional, 2007), if you would like more background information about how to interact with an ASP.NET membership provider or create your own custom membership provider.

WSS Security Context Versus Windows Security Context

When code runs within a custom WSS component, such as a Web Part or application page, it's important that you distinguish between two different security and authorization subsystems. There is both a WSS security context and a Windows security context. Let us provide a little more background to illustrate the difference.

As you know, WSS uses a user security token created by either Windows authentication or forms authentication to establish its own security context. This *WSS security context* is used to conduct access control checks in internal WSS objects such as sites, lists, and items. However, just because WSS adds it own authorization layer doesn't mean that the Windows authorization layer goes away.

The WSS components you write, such as Web Parts and application pages, often must access external resources. Access control to these external resources is controlled not by WSS, but instead by the Windows operating system itself, which means that you also must be aware of the current Windows security context as well as the WSS security context.

The standard web.config file for WSS Web applications has the following entry:

```
<identity impersonate="true" />
```

By setting the impersonate attribute to true, WSS instructs the ASP.NET runtime to process all requests under the Windows security context of the current user. When you write code for a Web Part or application page that attempts to access an external resource, such as a file system resource, database call, or Web service call, it runs under the impersonated Windows identity. This enables the Windows authorization subsystem (local or remote) to determine whether it should grant or deny access.

Understanding the Windows security context is fairly straightforward when you are using the default Windows Authentication provider because its identity is synchronized to the same user account as the identity of the WSS security context. However, things aren't so obvious when you are using forms authentication. Because forms authentication doesn't involve authenticating against a Windows account, the Windows security content takes on the identity of the IUSR_*MACHINENAME* account, or the account specified in the Authentication Methods dialog box of IIS (the same dialog box that enables IIS anonymous access).

> **Tip** Forms authentication impersonates the anonymous access Windows account. As credentials leave WSS and transition to the Windows authentication protocol, this anonymous user account is used.

Users and Groups

The WSS object model tracks user identities by using the SPUser class. If you want to access the SPUser object for the current user, you use the CurrentUser property of the SPWeb object associated with the current site. The following simple example shows you how to access some of the properties available through the SPUser class.

```
SPUser currentUser = SPContext.Current.Web.CurrentUser;
string userName = currentUser.Name;
string userLogin = currentUser.LoginName;
string userEmail = currentUser.Email;
```

The current user is always the user who was authenticated when the SPSite site collection object was created. If your code is running in the WSS Web site context, this is the user who authenticated to either WSS or the ASP.NET authentication provider. If your code is running in the context of a console application, the current user is the user whose Windows principal was used to create the initial SPSite reference. You cannot switch the security context of the site collection or its objects after it is created; it is always the user principal who first accessed the site collection that is the current user. We will look at elevation of privilege, delegation, and impersonation later in this chapter to further illustrate this point.

Assigning permissions directly to users is usually not a scalable and maintainable solution, especially across large enterprises with many users and sites. Besides the maintenance issues, as ACLs grow larger, they can bog down performance of WSS. This is not an issue unique to WSS, for it is the same issue solved by Active Directory users and groups.

WSS supports the creation of groups within a site collection to ease the configuration of authorization and access control. Groups are never created in the context of the site—they are always created in the context of the site collection and *assigned* to a site. For example, assume that we have a site located at /litware/sales, and that the /litware/sales site reference is the current context returned from SPContext.Current.Web. Given this environment, *site.Groups* would return the group collection of the sales site. This would be a subset of the groups available in the site collection, which is available through the site.SiteGroups property. For example, the following code would return the groups Team Site Members, Team Site Owners, and Team Site Visitors.

```
SPSite siteCollection = new SPSite("http://localhost/litware/sales/");
SPWeb site = siteCollection.OpenWeb();

foreach(SPGroup group in site.Groups){
  Console.WriteLine(group.Name);
}
```

Groups cannot directly be added to a site—they must be added to the site collection. If you try to add a group to the site's Groups collection, you get an exception stating, "You cannot add a group directly to the Groups collection. You can add a group to the SiteGroups collection." This situation occurs because the SPGroup is always *created* at the Site Collection level and *assigned* to the site. The following code is valid and adds the LitwareSecurityGroup to the site collection groups.

```
// Adds a new group to the site collection groups:
site.SiteGroups.Add("LitwareSecurityGroup", site.CurrentUser,
  site.CurrentUser, "A group to manage Litware Security");
```

However, this still does not associate the group with our site, nor would it be useful within the site without any permissions. To add the group to the site, create a new SPRoleAssignment by associating an SPRoleDefinition with the SPGroup, and then add that role assignment to the site, as in the following code sample:

```
SPGroup secGroup = site.SiteGroups["LitwareSecurityGroup"];
SPRoleAssignment roleAssignment = new SPRoleAssignment(secGroup);
SPRoleDefinition roleDefinition = site.RoleDefinitions["Full Control"];
roleAssignment.RoleDefinitionBindings.Add(roleDefinition);
site.RoleAssignments.Add(roleAssignment);
```

As with Groups and SiteGroups, multiple collections can be used to access site users. Table 10-1 lists user-related properties of the SPWeb site object and when to use them.

Table 10-1   SPWeb User Properties

Property	Description
AllUsers	Used to access any user who has accessed the site as a member of a domain group that is a site member or any user who is explicitly a member of the site. For example, the user Mike Fitzmaurice (LITWARE\mikefitz) may be a member of the LITWARE\sales group. If LITWARE\sales has access to the Sales site and Mike has visited the site (as a member of the LITWARE\sales group), he would be accessed through the AllUsers collection. Because it is the largest collection of users available (being a combination of the SiteUsers, Users, and group membership), you generally use the AllUsers collection when you want to access a user.
CurrentUser	Returns the current user who created the reference to the SPSite site collection. This is generally the user accessing the WSS Web site.
SiteUsers	Used to access the collection of users in the site collection. This is a subset of the AllUsers collection.
Users	The smallest collection of users, containing only the users explicitly added to a WSS site.

Application Pool Identities

The application pool identity plays a large role in WSS applications. Besides running the Web application, this account is used as the Windows account that connects to the WSS Content and Configuration databases and is the Windows account used when running code in the SPSecurity.RunWithElevatedPrivileges method. Although you can use an application pool identity of Network Services in a single-server deployment, it usually makes more sense to use a domain account. Using a domain account is a requirement in a Web farm environment where it's important for multiple processes running on different machines to all share the same identity.

Ideally, one account should be created to run only the Central Administration application and should be assigned the dbcreator and securityadmin permissions in the SQL database server. WSS assigns group membership to the IIS_WPG, Power Users, Users, WSS_ADMIN_WPG, WSS_RESTRICTED_WPG, and WSS_WPG security groups. These groups are required for the Central Administration system account, but they have more privileges than the actual WSS Web applications should be granted. With this administration account in place, WSS can manage the required permissions for additional accounts.

When you create a new Web application through the WSS Central Administration application, you should create it to run inside a new or existing application pool that is separate from the Central Administration application pool. Moreover, application pools for Web applications that are accessible to end users should be configured with a domain account that is not as privileged as the user account for the Central Administration application pool. For example, there is no reason why WSS code running within any application pool other than the Central Administration application pool would ever need to create a new content database or configure database security permissions.

Consider what happens when you create a new Web application through the WSS Central Administration application. When you do this, you get to determine whether WSS creates a new application pool for this Web application or uses an existing application pool. If you tell WSS to create a new application pool, you must supply the name and password of a valid Windows user account. When WSS creates the new content database, it grants this user account the dbowner role for that content database. WSS also grants the database roles public and WSS_Content_Application_Pools to this user account in the configuration database. You should note that user accounts that provide application pool identities must also be added to two local groups named IIS_WPG and WSS_WPG so that they have the proper permissions to access WSS system files as well as specific locations within the Windows Registry and IIS Metabase.

 Tip   Application pool identities could be local (machine) accounts if the machine is not a member of a domain.

SharePoint System Account

The SHAREPOINT\system account is an identity to which WSS maps internally when code is running under the identity of the hosting application pool. The SHAREPOINT\system account is not recognized by Windows because it exists only within the content of the WSS runtime environment. This enables WSS to use a statically named account for system-related activity regardless of whatever Windows user account has been configured for the hosting application pool.

For example, if you switch the application pool from LITWARE\SP_WorkerProcess1 to LITWARE\SP_WorkerProcess2, code running as system code still acts and is audited as the SHAREPOINT\system account. However, it is also important to realize that SHARE-POINT\system is not recognized by the Windows security subsystem. Therefore, code in WSS running as system code is recognized under the identity of the hosting application pool when it attempts to access external resources, such as the local file system or a SQL Server database.

Escalation of Privilege

The SPSecurity class provides a static method named RunWithElevatedPrivileges that enables code to execute as system code running under the identity of SHAREPOINT\system. This allows code to run in an escalated security context to perform actions as the system. This method should be used with care and should not expose direct access to system resources, but rather should be used when you need to perform actions on behalf of the system. The method is simple. You can either create a delegate to a public void method or simply write code within an inline delegate. The signature looks like the following:

```
SPSecurity.RunWithElevatedPrivileges(delegate()
{
  // Code runs as the "SharePoint\system" user
});
```

Code within the delegate runs under the Windows SHAREPOINT\system security principal. As covered in the previous section titled "Application Pool Identities," this account uses the application pool identity when passing credentials to external resources, but it uses the system account internally. However, if you use code similar to the following, you would notice a bug in your code that seems to indicate that the security context has not been switched.

```
// Bad code example:
SPSecurity.RunWithElevatedPrivileges(
  delegate() {
    SPListItem record = visitorList.Items.Add();
    // still the calling user:
    record["User"] = SPContext.Current.Web.CurrentUser;
    // uses authorization of the calling user, NOT the system:
    record.Update();
  }
);
```

To modify WSS content under the System credentials, you need to create a new SPSite site collection that generates a new security context for objects referenced from the site, as in the following example. You cannot switch the security context of the SPSite once it has been created, but must instead create a new SPSite reference to switch user contexts. The following code uses the system credentials to add a list item using the profile data of the current Web user:

```
SPSecurity.RunWithElevatedPrivileges(
  delegate() {
    using (SPSite site = new SPSite(web.Site.ID)) {
      using (SPWeb web2 = site.OpenWeb()) {
        SPList theList = web2.Lists["visitors"];
        SPListItem record = theList.Items.Add();
        record["User"] = SPContext.Current.Web.CurrentUser;
        record.Update();
      }
    }
  }
);
```

Code running with the escalated privilege should use a new SPSite object for code running as the system and use the SPContext.Current property to access the actual calling user's identity. The ElevatedPrivilegeWebPart shown in Listing 10-3 demonstrates the importance of the SPSite site collection object in generating a security context.

> **Tip** Create a new SPSite reference while impersonating to perform actions in the impersonated context.

Listing 10-3 The Elevated Privilege Web Part demonstrates the security context of the SPSite object.

```
Elevated Privilege and SPSite Example
using System;
using System.Web.UI.WebControls.WebParts;
using Microsoft.SharePoint;
using System.Security.Principal;
using System.Security;
using System.Security.Permissions;

namespace LitwareSecurity {

  [PermissionSet(SecurityAction.Demand)]
  public sealed class ElevatedPrivilegesWebPart : WebPart {

    protected override void RenderContents(System.Web.UI.HtmlTextWriter writer) {
      base.RenderContents(writer);
      SPWeb site = SPContext.Current.Web;
      // Impersonates SHAREPOINT\system:
      SPSecurity.RunWithElevatedPrivileges(delegate() {
        // The windows user is SHAREPOINT\system:
        writer.Write("Elevated privilege Windows user: {0}<br/>",
          WindowsIdentity.GetCurrent().Name);
        // The site context is still the calling user's:
```

```
       writer.Write("Elevated privilege user: {0}<br/>",
         site.CurrentUser.Name);
       // Open a new site security context using SHAREPOINT\system:
       using (SPSite siteCollection = new SPSite(site.Site.ID)) {
         using (SPWeb site2 = siteCollection.OpenWeb()) {
           // The new site context is now SHAREPOINT\system:
           writer.Write("New site elevated privilege user: {0}<br/>",
             site2.CurrentUser.Name);
         }
       }
     });
   }
  }
}
```

Elevated privilege is useful for either writing to read-only lists or using the application pool credentials to access Windows authentication–secured Web services. Listing 10-4 demonstrates the use of the system account to track visitors by writing to a read-only list. Regardless of the site privileges of the user, the system enters a visitor record in the Visitor list with the calling user's identity profile while using the system account security principal for authorization. Note that the use of the PermissionSet attribute's SecurityAction.Demand parameter forces a stack walk, ensuring that any code that is executing this method has the correct CAS policy.

Listing 10-4   The Visitor Tracker Web Part demonstrates the RunWithElevatedPrivileges security method.

```
Visitor Tracking with Escalation of Privilege
using System;
using System.Collections.Generic;
using System.Text;
using System.Web.UI.WebControls.WebParts;
using Microsoft.SharePoint;
using System.Security.Permissions;

namespace LitwareSecurity {

  [PermissionSet(SecurityAction.Demand)]
  public sealed class VisitorTrackerWebPart : WebPart {

    [PermissionSet(SecurityAction.Demand)]
    protected sealed override void OnLoad(EventArgs e) {
      base.OnLoad(e);
      SPWeb site = SPContext.Current.Web;
      SPUser user = site.CurrentUser;
      const string listName = @"visitors";
      SPList visitorList = null;
      foreach (SPList alist in site.Lists) {
        if (alist.Title.Equals(listName,
          StringComparison.InvariantCultureIgnoreCase)) {
          visitorList = alist;
          break;
        }
      }
```

```
        if (visitorList == null) {
          SPSecurity.RunWithElevatedPrivileges(
            delegate() {
              using (SPSite siteCollection =
                new SPSite(this.Page.Request.Url.ToString())) {
                using (SPWeb systemSite = siteCollection.OpenWeb()) {
                  systemSite.AllowUnsafeUpdates = true;
                  Guid listID = systemSite.Lists.Add(listName,
                    "Site Visitors", SPListTemplateType.GenericList);
                  visitorList = systemSite.Lists[listID];
                  visitorList.Fields.Add("User", SPFieldType.User, true);
                  visitorList.WriteSecurity = 4;
                  visitorList.Update();
                  systemSite.Update();
                }
              }
            }
          );
        }

        // Uses the SHAREPOINT\system creds
        SPSecurity.RunWithElevatedPrivileges(delegate() {
          using (SPSite siteCollection =
            new SPSite(this.Page.Request.Url.ToString())) {
              using (SPWeb systemSite = siteCollection.OpenWeb()) {
                systemSite.AllowUnsafeUpdates = true;
                SPList theList = systemSite.Lists[listName];
                SPListItem record = theList.Items.Add();
                record["User"] = user;
                record["Title"] = string.Format("{0} {1} {2}", user.Name,
                DateTime.Now.ToShortDateString(), DateTime.Now.ToShortTimeString());
                record.Update();
              }
          }
        });
      }
    }
  }
```

 Tip   The RunWithElevatedPrivileges method applies only to authorization, not CAS policy, and it requires the SharePoint security permission SharePointPermission to execute.

Delegating User Credentials

Within application code running in the WSS Web application, the code runs under the credentials of the application pool while impersonating the calling user. This condition enables WSS to secure objects, including sites, lists, and list items, by using the calling user's identity. Identity is configured automatically through the web.config setting <identity impersonate="true" />. This is true for both the Web application and Web service endpoints. When calling Web services, you can use this identity to authenticate to remote endpoints by setting the credentials to the Default Credentials. Note that to pass credentials to backend services, the WSS server must be set up with the rights to delegate Kerberos or NTLM credentials in Active Directory. For Web service requests to the same box, delegation is not required.

> **Tip**   Credential delegation can be tricky to set up and works differently when accessed from a remote box versus the local development server. When testing security delegation, be sure to use a remote box to access the WSS server.

The following code example uses the credentials of the current user to authenticate a Web request against a Web data source.

```
WebRequest xmlReq = WebRequest.CreateDefault(xmlUri);
xmlReq.Credentials = CredentialCache.DefaultCredentials;
```

In addition to the current user's credentials, you can access the application pool identity by using the SPSecurity method RunWithEscalatedPriveleges.

```
SPSecurity.RunWithElevatedPrivileges(delegate() {
  WebRequest xmlReq = WebRequest.CreateDefault(xmlUri);
  // Uses the app pool credentials:
  xmlReq.Credentials = CredentialCache.DefaultCredentials;
});
```

User Impersonation with the User Token

Two primary ways exist to create the SPSite as a security context. One way is to use the current Windows or Forms identity, which is the default method whether you are accessing the site from the WSS Web application or an administrative console. This is also the method used with the SPSecurity.RunWithElevatedPrivileges delegate—the current principal that happens to be SHAREPOINT\system is used to create the site security context.

The other way to create the SPSite is by using an SPUserToken object. The SPUserToken is the token created upon authentication. It references the principal of the user from either Active Directory or the identity store with its groups and roles. In the case of a Windows identity, this token is used to query Active Directory for the TokenGroups property. These tokens time out after 24 hours, making them a good candidate for system code that needs to impersonate users in the case of workflow actions or post-processing of list data that happens slightly after the original action (not days later). This token timeout value can be set by using the STSADM console. Using the user token in the constructor of the SPSite enables code to make changes to the WSS object model just as if the actual user were making the changes. Using impersonation is a security-sensitive operation that requires the SharePointPermission with the Impersonate property set to true.

You can request the token for any user in the system by using the UserToken property of the SPUser class (provided that your code has the SharePointPermission with the Impersonate rights). If the current user is not the user requested, WSS builds the token on the fly from the user's Security ID and group membership. You can then pass this token to the SPSite's contructor to create a new impersonated security context.

For example, let's revisit the list event receiver from Chapter 6, "Lists and Content Types." On creation of a Litware Company record in either the Vendor or Customer list, we will create an announcement with the credentials of the user who created the item. When this code runs, it is in the context of the SHAREPOINT\system account, and we don't have access to the actual credentials of the user who created the item. To create the item under the impersonated security context, simply obtain a user token from the SPUser profile that created the object and pass that into the SPSite constructor. When the item is inserted into the announcements list, it will be as if the impersonated user created the item even though the event receiver is running under the identity of SHAREPOINT\system.

```
public override void ItemAdded(SPItemEventProperties properties) {
  DisableEventFiring();
  string CompanyName = properties.ListItem["Company"].ToString();
  properties.ListItem["Company"] = FormatStringValue(CompanyName);
  properties.ListItem.Update();

  SPUserToken token =
    properties.OpenWeb().AllUsers[properties.UserLoginName].UserToken;

  using( SPSite site = new SPSite(properties.SiteId, token) )
  {
      using(SPWeb web = site.OpenWeb(properties.WebUrl))
      {
        SPListItem announcement = web.Lists["Announcements"].Items.Add();
        announcement["Title"] = properties.ListItem["Company"].ToString();
        announcement["Body"] = "A new company was added!";
      }
  }
}
```

Within this code sample, we are using the AllUsers property of the site. Users are available through a reference to the site (the SPWeb class). Three user collections are available within the site, and choosing which one to use may be confusing. The AllUsers property lists all users, including members of the site as well as members of domain groups that are members of the site. The SiteUsers property contains the users who are members of the site collection, and the Users property is the smallest group, containing only users who are explicitly members of the site.

Securing Objects with WSS

Objects in WSS are secured with the ISecurableObject interface, which is applied to the SPWeb, SPList, and SPListItem classes. Because of this, most objects of significance in WSS are secured with this interface, which is shown in Listing 10-5.

Listing 10-5   The ISecurableObject interface

```
Microsoft.SharePoint.ISecurableObject
[SharePointPermission(SecurityAction.LinkDemand, ObjectModel = true),
SharePointPermission(SecurityAction.InheritanceDemand, ObjectModel = true)]
public interface ISecurableObject {
    // Methods
    void BreakRoleInheritance(bool CopyRoleAssignments);
    void CheckPermissions(SPBasePermissions permissionMask);
    bool DoesUserHavePermissions(SPBasePermissions permissionMask);
    void ResetRoleInheritance();

    // Properties
    SPRoleDefinitionBindingCollection AllRolesForCurrentUser { get; }
    SPBasePermissions EffectiveBasePermissions { get; }
    ISecurableObject FirstUniqueAncestor { get; }
    bool HasUniqueRoleAssignments { get; }
    SPReusableAcl ReusableAcl { get; }
    SPRoleAssignmentCollection RoleAssignments { get; }
}
```

ISecurableObject provides a method for checking whether permissions exist as well as a method for demanding that the permissions exist. The first method, DoesUserHave-Permissions, is used to query for permissions, whereas the second method, CheckPermissions, throws a security exception if the permission does not exist. Because this interface is common throughout the object model, it is easy to learn how to use it throughout your code. For example, to check whether the current user has permissions to view list items, you can call the DoesUserHavePermissions method of the SPWeb class passing in the ViewListItems permission flag as follows:

```
SPWeb web = SPContext.Current.Web ;
if (web.DoesUserHavePermissions(SPBasePermissions.ViewListItems){
    // Enumerate lists
}
```

The SPList is also an ISecurableObject, which means that you can apply the same principles to check permissions on lists. To check the user's permission to view list items within a specific list, call the list's DoesUserHavePermissions method as follows:

```
foreach(SPList list in web.lists){
  if (list.DoesUserHavePermissions(SPBasePermissions.ViewListItems))
    // Process the list
  }
}
```

Likewise, the same method is available in other objects, such as the SPListItem class, which can be used to ensure that the user has permissions to the item or document.

```
foreach(SPListItem item in list.Items){
  if (item.DoesUserHavePermissions(SPBasePermissions.ViewListItems)) {
    // Process the list item
  }
}
```

To examine the ISecurableObject interface, we will examine code from the Litware OPML generator. The Litware OPML generator builds a list of feeds for the site collection by recursively walking the sites and lists. OPML is an XML format used for lists of XML feeds and is most often used for lists of RSS feeds. OPML feeds can be used with RSS aggregator software, such as NewsGator Enterprise Server or FeedDemon, to subscribe to a list of feeds. Alternatively, it can be used to build AJAX interfaces with XSLT and JavaScript as demonstrated in Chapter 5, "AJAX Web Parts." To build OPML for the current site scope, we will enumerate the current site and child sites while checking for permissions and writing nodes for items to which the user has read access. The full source code for the OPML generator is included in Chapter 5.

Within the code, we also want to track whether the current user is anonymous or authenticated. For anonymous users, we want to display only items that are available to the anonymous user. To check whether the anonymous user can access either the site or the list, use the AnonymousPermMask64 property. This permission mask contains the permissions available to the anonymous user. The following code enumerates child sites and calls the WriteSite-Feeds method when the user has permissions to view list items. First, we will check anonymous permissions if the user is anonymous. Secondly, if the user is authenticated, we will check the user's permissions against the ISecurableObject interface.

```
foreach (SPWeb childSite in site.Webs) {
  if (HttpContext.Current.User.Identity.IsAuthenticated == false) {
    if ((childSite.AnonymousPermMask64 & SPBasePermissions.ViewListItems)
        == SPBasePermissions.ViewListItems) {
      this.WriteWebFeeds(childSite, xw);
    }
  } else if (childSite.DoesUserHavePermissions(
      SPBasePermissions.ViewListItems))
    this.WriteWebFeeds(childSite, xw);
  }
}
```

The same code can be used against the SPList list object, as the following code demonstrates.

```
foreach (SPList list in site.Lists) {
  if (HttpContext.Current.User.Identity.IsAuthenticated == false) {
    if ((list.AnonymousPermMask64 & SPBasePermissions.ViewListItems) ==
        SPBasePermissions.ViewListItems)
      WriteListReference(xw, list);
  } else {
    if (list.DoesUserHavePermissions(SPBasePermissions.ViewListItems))
      WriteListReference(xw, list);
  }
}
```

Because we are using the DoesUserHavePermissions method, the code does not throw a security exception if the user does not have read permissions. Within the WriteListReference method, we could perform an additional security check to ensure that the user has permissions using the CheckPermissions method of ISecurableInterface, as in the following example. If this check fails, a SecurityException is thrown.

```
list.CheckPermissions(SPBasePermissions.ViewListItems);
```

Rights and Permission Levels

Rights within WSS are defined by permissions within the SPBasePermissions enumeration. This enumeration is a flags-based enumeration in which multiple permissions can be combined to create a permission set. SPBasePermissions are aggregated into more granular roles with the SPRoleDefinitions within the site context, in which permissions are role based. You will most likely assign a role when assigning permissions to a security principal; when validating rights for an action on a particular object, you will check the permission itself. To assign roles to a security principal, use the SPRoleDefinition class. By default, each site creates the following role definitions, exposing them through the Web's RoleDefinition property: Full Control, Design, Contribute, Read, and Limited Access. These roles, along with their aggregated permissions, are listed in Table 10-2.

Table 10-2   Default WSS Site Roles

Site Role	SPBasePermissions
Full Control	FullMask
Design	ViewListItems, AddListItems, EditListItems, DeleteListItems, ApproveItems, OpenItems, ViewVersions, DeleteVersions, CancelCheckout, ManagePersonalViews, ManageLists, ViewFormPages, Open, ViewPages, AddAndCustomizePages, ApplyThemeAndBorder, ApplyStyleSheets, CreateSSCSite, BrowseDirectories, BrowseUserInfo, AddDelPrivateWebParts, UpdatePersonalWebParts, UseClientIntegration, UseRemoteAPIs, CreateAlerts, EditMyUserInfo
Contribute	ViewListItems, AddListItems, EditListItems, DeleteListItems, OpenItems, ViewVersions, DeleteVersions, ManagePersonalViews, ViewFormPages, Open, ViewPages, CreateSSCSite, BrowseDirectories, BrowseUserInfo, AddDelPrivateWebParts, UpdatePersonalWebParts, UseClientIntegration, UseRemoteAPIs, CreateAlerts, EditMyUserInfo
Read	ViewListItems, OpenItems, ViewVersions, ViewFormPages, Open, ViewPages, CreateSSCSite, BrowseUserInfo, UseClientIntegration, UseRemoteAPIs, CreateAlerts
Limited Access	ViewFormPages, Open, BrowseUserInfo, UseClientIntegration, UseRemoteAPIs

Permissions are stored in the ACL for each ISecurableObject. These permissions are cached in the binary ReusableAcl property and define permissions for all users in the site collection on each object. These permissions are always accessed from the object (you will remember that object references always are accessed through the user and always contain permission information). The following code checks for permissions on the list object and, based on the AddListItems permission, decides whether to let the user add items.

```
if (list.DoesUserHavePermissions(SPBasePermissions.AddListItems)){
    // Let the user add an item
}
```

The full SPBasePermission is included in Listing 10-6 for your quick reference. You will see that there are both basic and advanced permissions that you can grant, not all of which are available as options in the user interface.

Listing 10-6 The SPBasePermission enumeration

```
SPBasePermission Enumeration
[Flags]
public enum SPBasePermissions {
// Has no permissions on the Web site.
EmptyMask = 0,
// View items in lists and documents in document libraries.
ViewListItems = 1,
// Add items to lists, add documents to document libraries.
AddListItems = 2,
// Edit items in lists, edit documents in document libraries.
EditListItems = 4,
// Delete items from a list or documents from a document library.
DeleteListItems = 8,
// Approve a minor version of a list item or document.
ApproveItems = 16,
// View the source of documents with server-side file handlers.
OpenItems = 32,
// View past versions of a list item or document.
ViewVersions = 64,
// Delete past versions of a list item or document.
DeleteVersions = 128,
// Discard or check in a document which is checked out to another user.
CancelCheckout = 256,
// Create, change, and delete personal views of lists.
ManagePersonalViews = 512,
// Create and delete lists, add or remove columns or public views in a list.
ManageLists = 2048,
// View forms, views, and application pages. Enumerate lists.
ViewFormPages = 4096,
// Allows users to open a Web site, list, or folder.
Open = 65536,
// View pages in a Web site.
ViewPages = 131072,
// Add, change, or delete HTML pages or Web Part Pages.
AddAndCustomizePages = 262144,
// Apply a theme or borders to the entire Web site.
ApplyThemeAndBorder = 524288,
// Apply a style sheet (.CSS file) to the Web site.
ApplyStyleSheets = 1048576,
// View reports on Web site usage.
ViewUsageData = 2097152,
// Create a Web site using Self-Service Site Creation.
CreateSSCSite = 4194304,
// Create subsites such as team sites.
ManageSubwebs = 8388608,
// Create a group of users that can be used anywhere within the site collection.
CreateGroups = 16777216,
// Create and change permission levels on the Web site and users and groups.
ManagePermissions = 33554432,
```

```
    // Enumerate files and folders in a Web site using Microsoft SharePoint Designer
    // and Web DAV interfaces.
    BrowseDirectories = 67108864,
    // View information about users of the Web site.
    BrowseUserInfo = 134217728,
    // Add or remove personal Web Parts on a Web Part Page.
    AddDelPrivateWebParts = 268435456,
    // Update Web Parts to display personalized information.
    UpdatePersonalWebParts = 536870912,
    // Grants the ability to perform all administration tasks for the Web site as
    // well as manage content.
    ManageWeb = 1073741824,
    UseClientIntegration = 68719476736,
    // Use SOAP, Web DAV, or Microsoft SharePoint Designer interfaces.
    UseRemoteAPIs = 137438953472,
    // Manage alerts for all users of the Web site.
    ManageAlerts = 274877906944,
    // Create e-mail alerts.
    CreateAlerts = 549755813888,
    // Allows a user to change his or her own user information, such as adding a picture.
    EditMyUserInfo = 1099511627776,
    // Enumerate permissions on the Web site, list, folder, document, or list item.
    EnumeratePermissions = 4611686018427387904,
    // Has all permissions on the Web site.
    FullMask = 9223372036854775807,
    }
```

Handling Authorization Failures with SPUtility

You will generally secure objects, including sites and lists, by using the ISecurableObject interface. If you need a simple check for permissions, you could also check properties of the current user, such as IsSiteAdmin, to ensure that the user is the site administrator. By default, the CheckPermissions method of the ISecurableObject throws a security exception and sends an access denied message to the user; however, you may wish to handle authorization failures yourself. The SPUtility class has several methods that are useful for handling authorization failures, including the SPUtility.Redirect method. The SPUtility.Redirect method can be used to send users to the access denied page by using the following syntax:

```
SPUtility.Redirect(SPUtility.AccessDeniedPage,
    SPRedirectFlags.RelativeToLayoutsPage,
    Context);
```

SPUtility also has a method that handles access denied exceptions and redirects the user to the access denied page. The SPUtility.HandleAccessDenied method takes an exception as a parameter and is used to handle SecurityExceptions.

```
try {
    // authorization code
} catch (SecurityException securityException) {
    SPUtility.HandleAccessDenied(securityException);
}
```

To check whether the user is a site administrator, you can use the EnsureSiteAdminAccess method of the SPUtility. If the user is not a site admin, WSS prompts for a site admin credential. If the site admin credential is not supplied, the user is transferred to the access-denied page. Alternatively, you can also check the current user's IsSiteAdmin property and redirect elsewhere.

Finally, SPUtility has a simple method to send an HTTP 401 (Access Denied) header to the user. To send a 401 to the user, enabling the user to either supply new credentials or end up at the access denied page, use the SendAccessDeniedHeader method, as in the following code.

```
try {
    // authorization code
} catch (SecurityException securityException) {
    SPUtility.SendAccessDeniedHeader(securityException);
}
```

Summary

In this chapter, you learned several techniques for securing WSS applications involving code access security (CAS), custom authentication, and authorization using securable objects. We first discussed the importance of using trust levels and CAS to run Web Part code in a more trustworthy fashion. At this point, you should be able to apply custom CAS settings to your Web Part code through solution packages so that it runs securely and reliably in least-trusted scenarios.

This chapter also discussed how authentication and authorization work within WSS sites. WSS tracks users at the site collection level with a user token that can be created by using either Windows authentication or forms authentication. This user token creates a WSS-specific security context that enables WSS to perform internal access control checks on WSS objects such as a sites, lists, and items.

However, it's also important to remember that the WSS components you develop often need to access external resources as well. This means that you must be aware of the current Windows security context as well as the WSS security context. This chapter also presented programming techniques involving elevation of privileges and user impersonation that can be used to change the WSS security content as well as the Windows security context.

Within WSS site collections, users are managed in terms of groups that can be assigned roles and permissions. Permissions and access control are based on securable objects, such as sites, lists, and items, that all implement the ISecurableObject interface. A securable object either provides its own unique ACL or relies upon the ACL of its parent. You have also learned how to write custom code against securable objects to ensure that the current user has the required level of permissions, and you now know how to create custom access control policies. The details of this chapter, along with the previous chapters, should give you a foundation for creating secure and reliable business solutions for WSS and MOSS.

Index

A

Access control lists (ACLs), 361
Action, 259
ActionUrl element, 58
ActivateFeature operation, 24, 335
Activation dependencies, 324–326
Active Directory, 362, 371
ActiveDocument object, 249
Activities property, 258
Activity, 257–258, 275–280. *See also entries for specific activity types*
Activity class, 257
Activity Library, 263
Activity types, 284–285. *See also entries for specific activity types*
Add A Workflow link, 283, 293
Add event, 209
Add From Existing Site Columns link, 188
$addHandler method, 139, 142
AddListItems permission, 375
Add method, 65, 223, 231, 244
Addsolution command, 338, 347
AddWrkfl.aspx, 283, 293–294
Ad-hoc workflow associations, 272
Administration utility. *See* Start Administrative Tools Internet Information Services (IIS) Manager
ADO.NET DataTable object, 56, 180
Advanced Settings page, 267
After events, 209
AfterProperties property, 213
AJAX components, 155
AJAX interface, 374
AJAX library, 134, 159–160
AJAX List View Web Part, 152, 167
AjaxWebPart base class, 155
AJAX Web Part library, building, 166–171
AJAX Web Part(s), 342
    architecture and Windows SharePoint Services (WSS), 147–148
    building, for Windows SharePoint Services (WSS), 155–173
    building rich Internet applications with, 136–155
    client-side connections for, 171–173
    creating JavaScript component with, 139–155
    defined, 133
    HTTP handlers as data sources, 150–155
    and JavaScript, 136
    object-oriented JavaScript with, 137–139
    overview, 133–134
    page life cycle, 134–136
    in SharePoint AJAX Toolkit, 165–166

    Web Service endpoints for ESS AJAX components, 148–150
    wiki Web Part for Windows SharePoint Services (WSS), 156–159
AllContentUrls switch, 338
AllFlags, 358
AllGacDeployment switch, 338
Allitems.aspx, 84, 92, 94, 283
AllItems.aspx list view page, 198
All Items view, 202, 206
AllowCasPolicies switch, 338
AllowPartiallyTrustedCallers, 105
AllowServerSideScript attribute, 72
AllUsers property, 365, 372
AllUsersWebPart element, 82–83
AltaVista BabelFish, 330
AlternateCSS property, 96–97
AlternateCssUrl property, 97–98
AlterTask method, 308
Always attribute, 72–73
And element, 183
Announcement content type, 196, 199
Announcements list type, 177, 180, 318, 324
Anonymous access, 3, 30
AnonymousPermMask64 property, 374
API. *See* Application Programming Interface (API)
API framework, 143
_app_bin location, 352
app_code directory, 104
Application map, 31
Application master file, 48, 83–84
Application page definition, 56
Application page(s), 47
    create custom, for document management, 226–229
    creating custom, 49–60
    difference between site pages and, 49
    performance and security issues, 48
    site page vs., 47–49
Application pool, 32–33
Application pool identity, 32–33, 366
Application Programming Interface (API) components, 341
ApplicationResourceFiles node, 348
Application security
    application pool identities, 366
    authentication, authorization, and identities, 361–371
    delegating user controls, 370–371
    forms authentication, 362–363
    overview, 351
    SharePoint/System account, 367–370

Application security, *continued*
  troubleshooting code access security, 360
  trust levels and code access security, 352–360
  user and groups, 364–365
  user impersonation with user token, 371–378
  Windows SharePoint Services (WSS) security context
    vs. Windows security context, 363–364
ApplyChanges, 114
ApplyCustomBrand method, 94
ApplyWebConfigModification, 344
ApplyWebTemplate method, 323
Approve button, 255, 270, 307–308
ArgumentException, 179–180
Array, 139
.ascx extension, 34, 41, 76–79, 129
.ashx extension, 34, 41
.asmx extension, 34, 41
ASP.NET AJAX-Enabled Web Site, 139
ASP.NET AJAX Update Panel, 137
ASP.Net application, 34
ASP.NET 2.0 Authentication Provider Framework,
    18–19, 361–362
ASP.NET compiler, 63
ASP.NET data binding techniques, 56
ASP.NET Framework
  ASP.NET pages, 34–35
  benefits of, 33–35
  developing reactive program using, 255
  HTTP Request Pipeline, 38–40
  implemented as ISAPI extension, 34
  master pages, 36–37
  to perform authentication, 361
  server-side control in, 74
  SharePoint development vs, 104
  Windows SharePoint Services (WSS) integration
    with, 40–49
ASP.NET 2.0 Framework, 257
ASP.NET GridView, 56, 121. *See also* specific controls
AspNetHostingPermission, 359
ASP.NET HTTP handler, 129
Aspnet_isapi.dll, 34
ASP.NET Master Pages, 17
ASP.NET page_load handler, 143
ASP.NET page parser, 44–46, 93
ASP.NET Register director, 75
ASP.NET Response object, 240–241
ASP.NET runtime, 363
ASP.NET server-side controls, 257
ASP.NET SiteMapPath control, 86
AspNetSqlMembershipProvider class, 362
ASP.NET TreeView control, 66–67
ASP.NET trust levels, 353
ASP.NET Web Part class, 102–103
ASP.NET Web Part class System.Web.UI.WebControls
    .WebParts.WebPart, 104

ASP.NET Web Part framework, 100
.aspx extension, 34–35, 41
.aspx file, 54, 76, 319
.aspx forms, choosing between, and InfoPath
    forms, 309
.aspx page parser, 46
Assemble DLL, 27
Assemblies element, 334, 340
Assembly DLL, 342
AssemblyInfo code file, 105
Assembly node, 334
Assembly Resource Handler, 129
Assertion, 358
Association data, 295
AssociationData property, 297–298, 300
Association form, 291, 293–299
AssociationUrl attribute, 292
Asynchronous data requests, 133
Asynchronous event, 209. *See also* Before events
Asynchronous JavaScript + XML. *See* AJAX
Asynchronous RSS Web Part, 116–118
Asynchronous Web Part processing, 116–119
@Assembly directive, 51, 56
AtlasScriptManager property, 165
Attach to Process, 110
AuthenticateRequest, 38
Authentication, 30, 361. *See also* Forms
    authentication
Authentication Methods dialog box, 364
Authentication provider, 18–19
Authentication Provider Framework, 362
Authorization, 5, 361–362
Authorization failures with SPUtility, handling,
    377–378
AuthorizeRequest, 38–39
Auto value, 72–73
AvailableContentTypes property, 200

B

Backward-compatibility Web Parts, 105, 107
BAL. *See* Base Activity Library (BAL)
Base Activity Library (BAL), 257–258, 263
Base Content Type, built-in, 199
BaseType attribute, 204
Base types, 177, 314
Basic Authentication, 3, 30
BasicPage content type, 199
Before events, 209–210
BeforeProperties property, 213
BeginRequest, 38–39
BeginsWith element, 183
Bind event handlers, 211–212
BindingRedirects, 358
Bin directory, 75, 340, 352–353
Blank site, 10–11, 312, 324, 326

BLOB public key, 340, 360
BlogComment content type, 199
BlogPost content type, 199
Blog site definition, 313
Boolean, 139, 298
Brown, Keith, 40, 363
BrowsableAttribute
Build Action Embedded Resource, 129
Built-in columns, 186, 224
Built-in fields feature, 186
Built-in field type class, 191
Built-in list types, 176–177
Built-in WSS field types, 190

C

CAB archive, 332
cab.ddf file, 336–337
CAL. *See* Client access license (CAL)
Calculated field type, 184
Calendar control, 35
Calendar list type, 177
Callback handler, 145, 257
CAML. *See* Collaborative Application Markup
        Language (CAML)
CAML data-defining XML, 318
CAML element, 207–208
CAML statement, 179–184
Cancel Handler, 275
CAS. *See* Code access security (CAS)
Cascading Style Sheet (CSS) file, 56, 85–86, 319
    best practices in site branding, 97–98
    branding Windows SharePoint Services (WSS) sites
            using, 95–98
    core.css, 95–97
    location of, 95
    SharePoint Designer for customizing, 15
    Windows SharePoint Services (WSS) 3.0 integration
            with, 17
CAS policies, 342
Catalog Zones, 81
Category attribute, 111
Central Administration application pool, 366
Central Administration Web site, 335–336
CENTRALADMIN site definition, 313
CheckPermissions method, 373–374, 377
Child sites, 5–9
Child WebTempFile node, 341
ChkShowHiddenLibraries, 222
Choice field type, 184
Chrome, 101–103. *See also* Web Part Verb
Citrus theme, 96
Class definitions, prototypes as, 138
Class registration, 138
$clearHandlers, 39
Client access license (CAL), 2
Client component template, 171

Client Script Manager, 104
Client-side connections, for AJAX Web Parts, 171–173
Client-side XSLT, 160–161
Close method, 238, 240–241
CLR. *See* Common Language Runtime (CLR)
CodeAccess SecurityAttributes, 354
Code access security (CAS), 104, 109, 338–340,
        352–360
CodeAccess Security class, 354
CodeAccessSecurity element, 339–340
CodeAccessSecurity entries, 341
Code activity, 260, 287
Code-behind approach, in custom application pages,
        52–55
CodeBesideAssembly, 282
CodeBesideClass, 282
Code Condition, 289
CodeGroup element, 359
Code view, 91, 274–276, 288
Collaborative Application Markup Language (CAML),
        19, 160
    basic query elements, 183
    create content type definition in, 197–199
    debugging through diagnostic logging, 185
    defined, 175
    defining custom list elements with, 184–185
    mixing CAML logic with some Windows SharePoint
            Services (WSS) object model code in
            Feature_Activated event handler, 225
    and site definitions, 312
Collaborative Application Markup Language (CAML)
        schema, 322
Columns, 14, 224. *See also* Fields; List Settings
Common Language Runtime (CLR), 256–257
Communications list type, 176
CompilationMode attribute, 72–73
Compiled page, 64
Completed, 283, 288
CompleteTask, 284–285, 305
Composite activities, 258
CompositeActivity, 258, 260
ConfigSections, 43
Configuration database, 2–3
Configuration element, 321
Configuration module, 319
Configurations, 313, 317–321
ConnectAccess node, 340
ConnectAccess property, 353
ConnectionConsumer attribute, 103, 124
Connection property, 171–172
ConnectionProvider attribute, 103, 124, 126–127
Console application, 260
Console.WriteLine, 261
Contact content type, 199
Contacts list type, 177, 324
Contains element, 183
Content, defining, with list schemas, 203–204

Content Control, create, 249–250
Content Controls feature, 246–247
Content database, 4
Content Editor Web Part, 100
Content element, 37
ContentLightup feature, 88–89
Content page, 36–37, 83
Content syndication, 208. *See also* Really Simple
    Syndication (RSS)
Content tags, 51
Content type definition, 197–199, 202
ContentType element, 197
ContentType field, 181
Contenttype/forms namespace URI, 203
Content Type Gallery, 200, 267
Content type ID, 198–199, 308
ContentTypeId object, 200
Content type item, 235–236
ContentTypes, 201, 204–205
Content type(s), 129
    binding event handlers to, 214–215
    columns within, 198
    defined, 17–18, 195
    define items with, 195–203
    in object model, 200–202
    overview, 195–197
    within package, 236
    See also individual types
ContentTypesEnabled property, 200
ContextData property, 306
Contribute role definition, 375
ControlAppDomain, 358
ControlAssembly, 91
ControlClass attribute, 91
ControlDomainPolicy, 358
Control element, 88–91
ControlEvidence, 358
Control Framework, 120
ControlId, 90
Control parameter, 160
ControlPolicy, 358
ControlPrincipal, 358
Control property, 157
Controls
    constructing pages with, 74–76
    constructing pages with user controls, 76–79
    designing site pages using, 74–83
    designing Web Part pages, 79–83
Control tag, 56
CONTROLTEMPLATES directory, 78
_ControlTemplates directory, 46–47, 120
_Controltemplates virtual directory, 78
ControlThread, 358
CopyTo method, 65
Core.css, 95–97
Correlation token, 285, 305

CorrelationToken object, 286–287
CorrelationToken property, 285–286
Correlator, 285
CreateChildControls method, 102–103, 105, 114,
    168, 192
Create Column page, 184
CreateEditorParts method, 105, 113, 172
Create GUID tool, 334
CreateListAssociation, 297
CreateListContentTypeAssociation, 297
Create page, 12–13, 176, 204
CreatePart method, 238–239
CreateRelationship method, 240
Create Site Collection, 9
CreateSiteContentTypeAssociation, 297
CreateTask activity, 284–287, 297, 305
CreateTask method activity, 291
Cross-Site Query, 121
Cscript.exe, 33
CssLink control, 85–86, 95
"Ctypes" feature, 197
Currency field type, 184
CurrentUser property, 364–365
CustomAction element, 23–25, 55–58, 226–227
CustomApplicationPages feature, 50. *See also*
    Application page(s)
CustomBranding feature, 88–89, 98
Custom controller components, 134
Customer element, 249
CustomerID property, 124
CustomerListTitle, 330
Customers list, 243
Custom helper class, 56
Customization, 14–17, 110–119
Customized content, defined, 175
CustomizedPageStatus property, 65
Custom List feature, 206
Custom list list type, 177
Custom Lists, 176
Custom List Type, 184
CustomMasterUrl property, 95
Custom menu, add, to ECB menu, 57–60
Custom page templates, 67–70
CustomSitePages feature, 67–69, 75, 87, 320
Custom trust levels, 353
Custom validation logic, 191
Custom Workflow Program Targeting Windows
    SharePoint Services (WSS) or Microsoft Office
    SharePoint Server 2007 (MOSS), 263
CustomXmlPart object, 249

D

Dashboard technology, 104
Data, separating, from presentation in Word 2007,
    247–250

Database call, 116
Data binding, 56, 246–252
Data-bound property, 260
Data Description File (DDF), 332–334
Data element, 318
DataLoaderCallback function, 160
DataLoader control, 160
DataLoader utility method, 164
Data node, 208
Data sources, HTTP handlers as, 150–155
DataStoreItem, 249
DataTable object, 121
Data View Web Part, 99–100
Date And Time field type, 184
.ddf file, 332–334
Debugging, 54–55, 113, 136, 185, 198
Debug menu, 110
Declarative Rule Condition, 289
DefaultAnnouncementBody, 330
DefaultAnnouncementTitle, 330
Default.aspx, 44–45, 81, 84, 92, 94
Default content, 37, 197
Default Credentials, 371
Default.master, 80–81
    components of, 85
    and creating custom template, 92
    customizing, 91
    defined, 84–86
    delegate control definition in, 88
    HEAD element of, 85–86
    navigation components defined in, 86–87
Default.master page, 314
Default policy, 47
DefaultTemplateName, 193
Default Web Site, 3–4, 29–30
Delegate, 367
Delegate controls, 85, 88–91, 257
Delegating user credentials, 370–371
Delete method, 65
DeleteTask activity type, 285
Deployment
    of application through features, 324–327
    of site definition, 312
    of solution package for feature, 332–336, 338
    solution package for site definition, 340–341
    using solution package, 331–346
    of Web Parts, 336–340
DeploymentTarget attribute, 334
Deploysolution, 335, 338, 347
Description, 22, 105, 204, 321
Designer view, 274–276, 285–289
Design role definition, 375
Design view, 91
Developer platform
    customization *vs.* development, 15–17
    development opportunities, 17–19

features, 19–20
    programming against Windows SharePoint Services
        (WSS) Object Model, 20–21
Developing provisioning components, 16. *See also*
        Event handler; Web Parts
Device driver, 32
Diagnostic logging, Collaborative Application Markup
        Language (CAML) debugging through, 185
Directive. *See* specific directives
DisableEventFiring, 214
Discussion content type, 199
Discussions list type, 177
DisplayCategory attribute, 321
Display mode, 116, 247
DisplayName, 197, 202, 204
Dispose method, 21
Div element, 157
DLL, 35
.doc extension, 41, 234
.docs file, 237–240
Document-based content type, 196
Document content type, 196, 198–199, 227, 267
Document libraries, 12, 58–59, 176, 324
    adding new file to document library, 221–229
    difference between, and standard Windows
        SharePoint Services (WSS) list, 218
    form libraries and Microsoft Office InfoPath,
        229–233
    New button in, 317
    Office Open XML file formats, 233–252
    programming against documents, 219–221
    saving .docx file in, 243–244
    SPDocumentLibrary class, 218–219
    use for entry, 58
    See also Lists
Document library instance, 224
Document library list type, 176
Document management, 226–229
Document Manager Assistance, 227
DocumentManager feature, 224, 227, 230, 243
Documents, 219–221, 268–269
DocumentTemplate, 317
DocumentTemplateUrl property, 225
Document Workspace, 324
Document Workspace site template, 312
Document.xml, 240
.docx extension, 41, 234–235
.docx file, 238, 240–244, 246
DoesUserHavePermissions method, 373–374
DOM. *See* HTML Document Object Model (DOM)
DOS makcab command, 334
DropDownList control, 190, 192, 194,
        218, 221
DWP directory, 108
.dwp extension, 107
.dwp file, 319

E

ECB menu, 57–60, 198, 226–229, 283
Ecma International, 233
ECM menu, 299
EditableControl, 138–144
EditableControl JavaScript class, 138
EditableControl object, 137
EditControlBlock, 58
EditControl expando property, 142
EditForm.aspx, 49
Edit Mode, 127–128
Edit mode, of content controls, 247
Editor Part, 105
EditorPart class, 113–114
EditorPartCollection object, 113
EditorPartCollection Web Part, 105
Editor Part control, 111
Editor Parts, 111–115
EditorPart Web Part, 105
Editory Zones, 81
Edit Page command, 14
ElementManifests element, 23
Elements.xml, 19, 23
Element type, 19
ElevatedPrivilegeWebPart, 368–369
"Embedded Resource," 128
Enabled property, 115
EnableEventFiring, 214
EnableWorkflowModification, 304–306
EnsureChildControls method, 103
EnsureSiteAdminAccess method, 378
Enterprise Content Management Starter Kit, 272
Enterprise Server, 209
EnvironmentPermission, 358
Episodic, 254. *See also* Reactive program
Eq element, 183
Error handling, 198
Escalation of privilege, 367–370
Esposito, Dino, 40
Essential ASPNET 2.0, 363
Essential ASP.NET 2.0, 40
Essential Windows Workflow Foundation, 263
Event activity, 285. *See also* specific event activities
Event content type, 199
EventDriven activity, 305
EventDriven activity children, 305
Event handler, 19, 35
  and activity consumers, 257
  adding, to feature, 2–28
  bind, to ItemAdded event, 231
  binding, to content type, 214–215
  to bring workflow instance back to life, 284
  create, when feature is activated or deactivated, 26
  defined, 209
  Generate Handlers menu item, 275

and timing of LogToHistoryListActivity activity, 280
  writing, 212–214
EventHandlerScope activity, 304–305
Event receiver
  binding event handlers to content type, 214–215
  blind event handlers to list instance, 211–212
  classes, 210
  defined, 209
  Event Sink concept, 210
  writing event handlers, 212–214
EventReceiver collection, 231
Event Receivers property, 212
Events, 259, 324. *See also* individual events
Event Sink concept, 210
Execadmsvcjobs operation, 335
Execute method, 257, 259
Execution, 358
ExecutionType property, 258
Expando property, 142
ExportWebPart method, 131
Extended Properties property, 288
Extensible HTML-based user interface, 14. *See also* Web Parts
Extensive StyleSheet Language Transformation (XSLT), 133

F

Farm, 2–4
Farm scope, 23, 88
Fault Handler, 275
FeatureActivated event, 68, 82–83, 87, 98, 225, 230
FeatureActivated method, 26, 212, 345
Feature activation, 19
Feature activation dependencies, 324–326
FeatureDeactivated, 26
FeatureDeactivating method, 345
Feature element, 281
FeatureId, 230
FeatureId attribute value, 224
FeatureManifests element, 334
FEATURENAME/Feature.xml format, 334
Feature property, 26
Feature receiver, 109
Feature(s)
  adding event handler to, 26–28
  to add menu item to Site Actions menu, 55
  application deployment through, 324–327
  create, 21–28
    deploy .ddl assembly, 27
    Properties property, 27
    ReceiverAssembly attribute, 27–28
    ReceiverClass attribute, 27–28
    SPFeatureReceiver, 28
  create custom page templates within context of, 67
  creating, for importing Web Parts, 108–110

element types defined by, 9
introduction to, 19–20
and site definitions, 316
solution package for deploying, 332–336
FEATURES directory, 19–22, 28, 318
FeatureSiteTemplateAssociation node, 326
Feature stapling, 326–327
Feature.xml, 19, 273–274
FeedConsumerID, 172
Feed Demon, 209
FeedDemon, 374
FeedListHandler class, 153–155
FeedListHandler XML REST, 168
Feed List Web Part, 125–127, 151–155, 167–171
FeedListWebPart, 172
Feed list Web Part, using SPGridView control, 121–122
Field, 185–186
FieldAdding method, 210
FieldDeleting method, 210
Field element, 208
FieldRef element, 183, 197
FieldRenderingControl, 191
Fields collection, 179, 205–206
Fields section, 205
Field type, 184, 190–195
FieldUpdating method, 210
File element, 69–70, 82–83, 93, 108–109, 195, 319
File instance, 69
FileNotFoundException, 178
File property, 219, 279–280
Files collection, 223, 244, 251
File template, 69
Final motivation, 8–9
FindParentElement function, 142
FireBug, 136
FirstName element, 249
FirstUniqueAncestor property, 361
FirstUniqueAncestorWeb property, 361
Folder content type, 199
Folders, 220. *See also* individual folders
Form authentication provider, 19
Form library list type, 176
Forms Authentication, 361
Forms authentication, 362–364
Forms identity, 371
Forms library, 229–233
Form (XMLDocument, or InfoPath form)
    content type, 199
FriendlyName, 105
Full Control role definition, 375
Full trust, 353–354

G

GAC. *See* Global Assembly Cache (GAC)
GAC assemblies, 335

Galleries, 12, 314
Generate Handlers, 275, 277–278, 286, 290. *See also*
    Event handler
GenericList template, 200
GenericWebPart wrapper, 102
Geq element, 183
GetContent(string), 145
GetContent(string.onSuccess.onFailed.userContext),
    145k
GetCurrent method, 155
GetElementById, 139
GetFeedProvider connection method, 172
GetFieldValue method, 126
GetFile method, 64
GetLimitedWebPartCollectionManager method, 130
GetList, 178
GetListFromUrl method, 178
GetListFromWebPartPageUrl method, 178
GetList method, 178
$get method, 139
GetNamedResource method, 129
GetSiteData method, 180–181
GetStream method, 239
GetToolParts(), 105
Ghostable, 70, 93
GhostableInLibrary, 70, 93
Ghosted page, 91
Ghosted state, 71, 79. *See also* Safe mode processing
Global.asax file, 39, 41
Global Assembly Cache (GAC), 27–28, 52, 75, 90, 136,
    190, 266, 322, 352
Globalization, 327–331
Global namespace functions, 139
Global site definition, 314, 317, 326–327
GridView control, 35
GroupBy element, 183
Group membership, 366
Group property, 109
Groups, 364–365
Groups collection, 365
Gt element, 183
GUID, 305
GUID identifier, 179

H

Handler entries, 341–342
Hashtable object, 223
HEAD element, 85–86
HeadlineMode property, 111–112
Hidden attribute, 22–23, 204, 321
HistoryDescription field, 279
History list, 18
Hosting Process, 263
HtmlControls, 129
HtmlDecode method, 161

HTML Document Object Model (DOM), 133
HTML layout, 50–51
HTML-rendering XML, 318
HtmlTextWriter class, 102
HttpApplication class, 38–39
HttpApplication object, 41–42
HttpContext, 39
HTTP handler, 150–155, 341–342
HttpHandler, 38–39, 42
HttpHandlers node, 155
HTTP headers, 241
HttpModule, 38–39, 42
HTTP module class, 341
HTTP Request Pipeline, 38–43
http://schemas.openxmlformat.org/
        wordprocessingml/2006.main namespace, 239
HTTP.SYS, 32–33
Hyperlink Or Picture field type, 184

I

IAsyncResult design pattern, 116
Icid parameter, 347
ICollection, 113
ICustomerProvider interface, 124
ID attribute, 197–198
Id attribute, 22–23, 281
ID "Placeholder," 164
IFeedProvider interface, 172
IfElse composite activity, 259
IFieldProvider, 126–127
IFrame, 100
IfThen, 258
IHttpAsyncHandler, 151
IHttpHandler interface, 151
IIS. *See* Internet Information Services (IIS)
IIS Administration tool, 29
Iisapp.vbs, 33
IIS Manager tool, 46
IIS metabase, 30–31, 366
IISRESET command, 33, 335
IIS Web application, 342–343
IIS Web server infrastructure, 29
IIS Web site
    administration utility, 30
    authentication and, 30
    defined, 3, 29
    ISAPI extensions and ISAPI filters, 31–32
    Windows SharePoint Services (WSS) integrates with
        ASP.NET at level of, 40
IIS worker process, 32–33, 262
IIS_WPG security group, 366
Image attribute, 204
ImageUrl attribute, 22–23, 321
Image Web Part, 100

IMembershipCondition element, 360
Impersonate property, 371–372
Import directive, 77
Indexed fields, 206
InfoPath forms, 271, 309
InfoPath form templates, 229
Infrastructure, 358
Inheritance, 138
Inheritance chain, 138
InheritsFrom type system function, 138
InInit method, 103
InitializeComponent method, 277
InitiationData, 301
Initiation form, 291, 299–302
In-line code
    custom application page containing, 50–51
    and safe mode processing, 71–73
    site pages do not support, 48–49
Input forms. *See* Workflow input forms
Install.bat file, 273–274, 282
Installfeature operation, 335
InstantiationUrl attribute, 292
Integrated Windows Authentication, 361
Integrated Windows Security, 362
IntelliSense, 21, 23, 51
Internet applications, 136–155
Internet Explorer method, 161
Internet Information Services (IIS), 361
Internet Information Services 6.0 (IIS), 3, 29
Internet Server Application Programming Interface
        (ISAPI) programming model, 31
IPermission node, 358
ISAPI. *See* Internet Server Application Programming
        Interface (ISAPI) programming model
ISAPI components, custom development of, 32
ISAPI extensions, 31–32
ISAPI filters, 31–32
ISecurableObject, 375
ISecurableObject interface, 152–153, 372–377
IsNotNull element, 183
IsNull element, 183
ISO international standards, 233
ISPStsadmCommand interface, 343–344
IsReusable read-only property, 151
Issue content type, 199
Issue tracking list type, 177
IsTargetLilbrary, 221
ItemAdded event, 209, 213–214, 231–233
ItemAdded method, 231
ItemAdding event, 212–213
Item-based content type, 196
Item content type, 199
ItemId token, 59
Items, 235–237, 268–269. *See also* specific item types
Items collection, 179–180, 220

ItemUpdated event handler, 214
ItemUpdating event handler, 212–213
IWebEditable interface, 102
IWebPartField interface, 125, 127
IWebPartTable interface, 125

J

Japanese language pack, 347–348
Japanese resource file, 328
Japanese site definition language pack, 348–349
JavaScript, 136. *See also* AJAX Web Part(s)
JavaScript application load event, 157
JavaScript component, 139–155
JavaScript event handler, 139
JavaScript files, 129–130
JavaScript proxy, 143
JavaScript serialized object, 145
JavaScript signature, 145

K

Kothari, Nikhil, 136

L

Language packs, 327–331, 346–350
LAYOUTS directory, 50, 291
_layouts directory, 46–49
LayoutsPageBase base class, 50–51, 53–54, 57, 295
LDAP. *See* Lightweight Directory Access Protocol (LDAP) provider
LDAP call, 116
LeadSheet.xsn, 232
Legal Approval Workflow association, 294, 299–300
Leq element, 183
LetterTemplate.docx, 250
Letter Template list, 243–244
Libraries list type, 176
Life cycle, for reactive program, 254
Lightweight Directory Access Protocol (LDAP) provider, 362
Limited Access role definition, 375
Link command, 19
Link content type, 199
Links list type, 177
Links List Web Part, 125, 127
List content type, 199
List data, 179–184
List definition, 19
List elements, 184–189
List index, 206
List instance, 19, 177–178, 207–208, 211–212
ListInstance element, 224–225, 230
ListItem entry, 218
List Reader component, 171

Lists, 13–14, 121, 208–209. *See also* Document library
List schemas, 203–204
List Settings, 13–14, 208–209, 266–267, 293
ListTemplated attribute, 211
List Template gallery, 218, 314
List token, 59
ListViewWebPart, 72
List View Web Part, 100, 169
List View Web Parts for Links List, 125, 127
Literal Control, 128–129
LoadFolderNodes method, 221
LoadXml method, 160–161, 164
LoadXsl function, 164
LoadXsl method, 161
Localization, 327–331
Location attribute, 58, 341
LogToHistoryListActivity activity, 279–280, 283
Look And Feel section, 12
Lookup field type, 184
Lt element, 183

M

MainPlaceHolder div, 143
MakeEditable method, 139
MakeFullUrl method, 223
Manifest.xml file, 332–334, 336
Mapping scheme, 48
@Master directive, 36
MasterPageFile attribute, 37, 68
Master page galleries, 176
Master Page gallery, 84, 92–94, 218, 314
Master page instance, 93
Master page(s), 17, 68–69
    create, 36–37
    create custom master page template, 92–95
    default.master, customizing, 91
    default.master, understanding, 84–86
    defined, 36–37, 83
    delegate controls, 88–91
    relationship between, and associated content page, 36–37
    SharePoint Designer for customizing, 15
    Windows SharePoint Services (WSS) navigation components, 86–87
Master Page template, create custom, 92–95
masterurl/custom.master, 95
masterurl/default.master, 68, 93–95
MasterUrl property, 93
Members Web Part, 100
MemoryStream object, 65, 223, 240–241, 243, 250–251
Menu, add custom, to ECB menu, 57–60
Menu command, 19
Message content type, 199
Metadata, for solution package, 332
Metadata column, 223–224

MetaData element, 303
Method activity, 285. *See also* specific method activities
Microsoft AJAX Library, 136, 142, 168
Microsoft ASP.NET AJAZ Script Library, 137
Microsoft 2.0 framework, 257
Microsoft InfoPath, 233
Microsoft Internet Explorer, 136, 233
Microsoft JavaScript library, 142
Microsoft .NET Framework, 257
Microsoft Office 2000, 234
Microsoft Office 2003 Edition, 233–234. *See also* Office Open XML file format
Microsoft Office InfoPath 2007, 229–233, 271. *See also* InfoPath forms
Microsoft Office Outlook, 209, 271
Microsoft Office PowerPoint, 233–234, 246, 264, 271. *See also* Office Open XML file format
Microsoft Office SharePoint Designer, 15
Microsoft Office SharePoint Server, 22, 176, 233, 272
Microsoft Office SharePoint Server 2007 (MOSS) Enterprise Edition, 2, 90, 233
Microsoft Office SharePoint Server 2007 (MOSS) licensing model, 2
Microsoft Office SharePoint Server 2007 (MOSS) Standard Edition, 2, 90
Microsoft Office Word 2007, 233, 246, 264
    data binding to Word content controls, 246–252
    document internals, 234–237
    and InfoPath forms, 271
    separating data from presentation in, 247–250
    See also Office Open XML file format
Microsoft.SharePoint.Administration namespace, 342
Microsoft.SharePoint assembly, 50–51, 56, 85
Microsoft SharePoint Designer, 100
Microsoft.SharePoint.dll, 20, 41, 77, 105
Microsoft.SharePoint.dll assembly, 80
Microsoft SharePoint Portal Server 2003, 83
Microsoft.SharePoint.Security.dll, 105
Microsoft_SharePoint.Security.SharePointPermission, 340
Microsoft.SharePoint.WebControls assembly, 121
Microsoft.SharePoint.WebControls namespace, 56
Microsoft.SharePoint.WebPartPages.Commumication namespace, 124
Microsoft.SharePoint.WebPartPages namespace, 80–81
Microsoft.SharePoint.WebPartPages.WebPart class, 124
Microsoft.SharePoint.WorkflowActions.dll, 271
Microsoft.SharePoint.WorkflowActions namespace, 274
Microsoft.SharePoint.Workflows.dll, 271
Microsoft SQL Server database, 361
Microsoft Virtual PC, 339
Microsoft Virtual Server, 339
Microsoft Visual SourceSafe, 16
Microsoft Visual Studio 2005 Edition, 237
Microsoft Visual Studio Object Browser, 360

Microsoft Visual Studio 2005 Team Edition for Software Developers, 360
Microsoft Web Part Page, 5
Microsoft Windows operating system, 233
Microsoft Windows SharePoint Services 2.0, 314
Microsoft Windows Workflow Foundation Step By Step, 263
MicroWiki list instance, 145
MicroWikiWebPart, 157–159
MIME content type, 241–242
Mngctype.aspx, 200
Model View Controller design pattern, 134
ModificationContextData field, 306
Modification element, 304
Modification form, 270, 291, 302–306
ModificationId property, 305
ModificationUrl attribute, 292, 303
Modify Web Part, 111
ModifyWorkflow method, 306
Module element, 69–70, 92, 108–109, 225, 230, 319–320
Modules, 319–320
MOSS. *See* Microsoft Office SharePoint Server 2007 (MOSS)
MoveTo method, 65
Mozilla, 161
MSBuil, 106
MSXML SMLDOM object, 161
Multiline TextBox, 115
Multiple Lines Of Text field type, 184
My Settings menu item, 362

N

Name attribute, 197, 204
NamedPermissionSet element, 358
Named placeholder, 36–37
Name element, 70
Name property, 259, 343–345
Namespace, 137. *See also* individual namespaces
NavBars, 316–317
Navigation components, of Windows SharePoint Services (WSS), 86–87
Navigation support, for application pages, 55–56
Neq element, 183
.NET AppDomain, 64
.NET Framework, 181
.NET Framework 3.0, 18
.NET 3.0 Framework, Windows SharePoint Services (WSS) 3.0 dependency on, 237
.NET Framework AppDomain, 34
.NET Framework Components, 274
.NET Framework SDK tool ILDASM, 340
.NET 3.0 packaging API, 250
Network Service account, 33
Never attribute, 72

NewForm.aspx, 49
NewHistoryListRequired, 298
NewItem.aspx, 84
New Project dialog box, 273
NewsGator, 209
NewsGator Enterprise Server, 374
NewsGator Online, 353
NewTaskListRequired, 298
New Web Parts page, 107
Next button, 293–294
No-compile mode, 64
NoFlags, 358
Notepad.exe, 77
Now element, 183
NTML credentials, 371
Number, 139
Number field type, 184

O

Object model, content types in, 200–202
Object-oriented JavaScript
    class registration and inheritance, 138
    functions as objects, 137–138
    global namespace functions, 139
    namespaces, 137
    prototypes as class definitions, 133
Objects, securing, with Windows SharePoint Services
        (WSS), 139, 372–374. *See also* individual objects
Office Excel 2007, 233–234, 246, 264, 271. *See also*
        Office Open XML file format
Office Forms Server, 233
Office Forms Service, 233
Office Open XML file format, 18
    data binding to Word content controls, 246–252
    generating .docx file, 237–240
    generating .docx files on server, 240–243
    motivation for, 233–234
    relationships, 244–246
    saving .docx file in document library, 243–244
    Word 2007 document internals, 234–237
OnClick event handler, 250
1HttpHandler interface, 38
ONET.xml file, 314, 317
Onion, Fritz, 40, 363
OnLoad event handler, 54, 220–221, 228
OnLoad method, 51–52, 102–103, 296, 298, 301, 308
OnPreRender, 102–103, 172
OnQuickLaunch property, 178
OnTaskChanged activity type, 284–285, 288–291, 305
OnTaskCreated activity type, 284–289, 291, 305
OnTaskModified activity, 308
OnWorkflowActivated activity, 275, 277, 280, 301
OnWorkflowModified event activity, 304–306
OpenBinary method, 64, 231
OpenBinarySystem method, 64

Open method, 238
Open Web Site command, 242
Operations menu, 335
OPML. *See* Outline Processor Markup Language
        (OPML)
Opml.ashx handler, 342
OPML XML feed, 342
OrderBy element, 183
Or element, 183
Outline Processor Markup Language (OPML), 160
Outline Processor Markup Language (OPML)
        endpoint, 150–153
OutputStream object, 240
OwnerActivityName, 286, 305
Owner property, 343, 345

P

Package, 235–237, 240
Package API, 237–238, 240, 250
Package class, 238
Package object, 238, 240
Package.Open, 241
Package relationship, 235
Package Viewer application, 248
Page class, 35, 102, 116, 151
Page directive, 295
Page ghosting, 45, 47, 63, 70
Page instance, 19, 45
Page life cycle, 134–136
Page.LoadControl method, 120
Page object, 151
PageParserPath element, 72–73
Page.PreRenderComplete method, 103
Page.RegisterAsyncTask, 116–118
Page template, 19, 45, 63, 67–70, 80–81. *See also*
        Master page(s)
PageTemplate nested directory, 69
Page Viewer Web Part, 100
Paragraph (p) element, 239
Parallel activity, 258
Parent-child relationship, 244
Parent property, 27, 259
ParentWeb SPWeb property, 361
Partially trusted location, 352–353
Partitioning sites, into site collections, 6
Part relationship, 235, 244, 249
Parts, 235–237
Path attribute, 69
Path property, 343–345
.pdf extension, 41
PerformSubstitution property, 129
Permission definitions, 358–359
Permissions and rights levels, 375–377
PermissionSet attribute, 369
Persistence Service, 262–263

Personalizable attribute, 111
Personalizable properties, 113
Personalizable Web Part, 105
Personalization, 14–15, 110–119
Personalization Scope, 114
PersonalizationScope.User, 114–115
PersonalizationScope Web Part, 105
Personalize This Page menu, 112
Personal storage, 15
Person Or Group field type, 184
Picture content type, 199
Picture library list type, 177
Placeholder, 36–37, 83. *See also entries for specific placeholders*
PlaceHolderAdditionalPageHead, 86
PlaceHolderMain, 51–52, 69
PlaceHolderPageTitle, 51, 86
PlaceHolderPageTitleInTitleArea, 51
PopulateFormDataFromString method, 298, 301
Populate Gallery button, 107
Post-build event, 110
Post content type, 181
Post-event build command line, 27
Power Users security group, 366
Pre-installed site definitions, 312–313, 315
PreRenderComplete event, 102–103
Presentation, separating data from, in Word 2007, 247–250
ProcessRequest method, 151
Programming ASP.NET 2.0 Applications: Advanced Topics, 40
Programming ASP.NET 2.0 Core Reference, 40
Project element, 316
Project tasks list type, 177
Properties collection, 224
Properties parameter, 26
Properties property, 27
PropertyCollectionBinder, 56
Property element, 91, 109
Prototype, as class definition, 138
Prototype property, 138
Provisioning, 5–6, 224. *See also* Site Provisioning Provider class
Provisioning components, 175–176
Provision method, 323
Public key, 340, 360
Public members, SharePoint.Ajax.XmlComponent, 165

Q

Queries, 8–9, 179–184
QueryString, 58–59, 227
QuickLaunchDataSource, 90
Quick Launch menu, 86–87, 90, 177
Quick Launch navigation section, 14. *See also* List Settings

Quick Launch sidebar, 316
QuickLaunchSiteMap, 90–91
QuickNav bar, 316

R

RadioButtonList control, 115
Reactive program, 253–256. *See also* Windows Workflow Foundation (WF)
Read role definition, 375
Really Simple Syndication (RSS), 208–209
ReceiverAssembly attribute, 27–28
ReceiverClass attribute, 27–28
Receivers element, 211, 214, 231
RegisterAsyncTask method, 116
RegisterClass, 138
Register directive, 75, 78–81
RegistrationId, 226
RegistrationID attribute, 58
RegistrationType attribute, 58
Reject button, 255, 270, 307–308
Relationship, 235–236, 240, 244–246. *See also entries for specific relationship types*
Relationship element, 236, 240
Relationship item, 235–236
R element, 239
_rels, 236–237
RemotingConfiguration, 358
RenderContents method, 74, 100–103, 157, 165
RenderContents() Web Part, 105
RenderingTemplate, 192–193
Render method, 103, 164, 172
RenderMode enumeration, 112
RenderMode property, 112
RenderMode.Titles, 116
RenderWebPart(), 105
Repeater control, 35
Replicator composite activity, 259
Representational State Transfer, 150
RequestMinimum security action, 356
RequestOptional security action, 356
RequestRefuse security action, 356
RequireSiteAdministrator property, 57
Resource class, 128–129
Resource files, 328–331
Resource folder, 330
ResourceManager static instance, 328
Resources, using, 128–130
RESOURCES directory, 328, 330
Response.Close, 242
Response.Flush, 242
REST architecture pattern, 150
Resumable, 254, 257. *See also* Reactive program
ReusableAcl property, 375
RevertContentStream, 65
Rights and permissions levels, 375–377

RoleDefinition property, 375
Roles SPRoleCollection property, 361
Root directory, 30
RootFiles element, 341
Root folder, 220
RootFolder object, 223
RootFolder property, 66
RootOfList content type, 199
RootWebOnly attribute, 321
RootWebOnly setting, 109
Router, 3
Routing workflow, 18
RSS, 160
RSS. *See* Really Simple Syndication (RSS)
RSS aggregator software, 374
RSS channel, 208
RSS feed, 374
RSS feed picker Web Part, 105
RSS feeds, 152, 208–209, 353
RSS (Really Simple Syndication), defined, 118
RssViewEditorPart, 113–114
RSS Viewer Web Part, 105–107
RSS View Web Part, 116, 121, 123
RssViewWebPart, 113, 131
RSS Web Part, 120, 125, 127, 340
RSS XML stream, 208
Rule Condition Editor, 290
Run (r) element, 239
RunWithElevatedPrivileges method, 323, 367, 369–370

S

SafeControl element, 74
SafeControl entry, 73, 76, 78, 106, 109, 335, 337, 341
SafeControls, 106, 339, 342
Safe controls, 73–76
Safe Mode Parser, 104, 120
Safe mode processing
    change behavior of, 72
    controls must be registered as safe controls, 75–76
    defined, 71
    ghosted state, 72
    in-line script, 71–73
    safe controls, 73–74
    scalability, 72–73
    security, 72
SaveBinary method, 64
SaveProperties, 105
Scalability, 47, 49, 72–73
Schema property, 126
Schema.xml file, 204, 206
Schmidt, Bob, 263
Scope attribute, 22–23, 181
Scribner, Kenn, 263
Script debugging tools, 136
Script Manager, 129, 142–144, 147, 155, 165

ScriptManager instance, 155
ScriptMethod attribute, 145
Script Reference, 142–144
ScriptResource.axd, 130
Scriptresource.axd handler, 341
ScriptResource.axd path, 345
ScriptResourceHandler, 345
ScriptService attribute, 143
SDK. *See* Software Development Kit (SDK)
Security, 18–19, 72
SecurityAction.Demand parameter, 369
Security configurations, 12. *See also* Users And
        Permissions section
SecurityException, 374
Security Exceptions, 104
Security framework, 100
SecurityPermission, 358
Security principals, 361
Security requests, 356
SecurityWebPart code, 354
SendAccessDeniedHeader method, 378
Sequence, 258
Sequence activity type, 289, 305
Sequence attribute, 204
Sequence property, 343
Sequential WF programs, 259. *See also* Windows
        Workflow Foundation (WF)
SequentialWorkflowActivity class, 276
SequentialWorkflowActivity form, 274
Sequential Workflow Console Application, 260
Sequential Workflow Library, 260, 272
SequentialWorkflow view, 275
SequentWorkflowActivity class, 260
SerializationFormatter, 358
SerializeFormDataToString, 298, 301
Server, generating .docx files on, 240–243
ServerEmailFooter, 330
ServerRelativeUrl property, 93, 222
Server-side control, 73–74, 76, 257
Server-side framework. *See* ASP.NET Framework
Server-side license, 2
ServerTemplate, 191
Service-oriented XML data sources, 134
SetConnectionInterface method, 127
SetPersonalizationDirty() Web Part, 105
Settings menu, 13
Settings page, 14
SetupPath attribute, 320
Set_Xml, 160
Shared Mode, 112
Shared storage, 15
Shared Web Part, 112
Share personalization scope, 111
SharePoint.Ajax.DataLoader method, 160
SharePoint.Ajax.JavaScript namespace, 160

SharePoint AJAX Toolkit, 136, 155, 159–161, 165–166

SharePoint.Ajax.WebParts.SmlWebPart, 166

SharePoint.Ajax.XmlComponent, 161–166

SharePoint.Ajax.XmlComponent JavaScript class, 165

SharePoint.Ajax.XmlComponent Public members, 165

SharePoint architecture

    application pools and IIS worker process, 32–33

    ASP.NET 2.0 Framework, 33–40

    creating custom application pages, 49–60

    ISAPI extensions and ISAPI filters, 31–32

    ISS Web sites, 29–31

    virtual directories, 30–31

    Windows SharePoint Services (WSS) integration with
        ASP.NET, 40–49

SharePoint Central Administration, 185

SharePoint 3.0 Central Administration menu, 9

SharePoint Designer

    creating ad-hoc workflow associations with, 272

    for customizing Cascading Style Sheet (CSS) files, 96

    for customizing Master Pages and cascading style
        sheets (CSS), 15

    make changes to default.master in, 91

    and page ghosting, 46

SharePointPermission, 339, 358, 371–372

SharePoint Requests, 181

SharePointSequentialWorkflowActivity, 274, 276

SharePoint Site Management section, 9

SharePoint site model, 100, 130–131

SharePoint site object model, 105

SharePoint Solution package, 104

SharePoint/system account, 367–370, 372

SharePoint Team Services (STS), 7, 320

SharePoint Tool Pane, 101

SharePoint WebPartPages namespace, 105

SharePoint workflows

    design goals of, 264–265

    fundamentals, 265–269

    workflow input forms, 270–271

SharePoint XML files, resources in, 331

Show Developer Tab In The Ribbon option, 246–247

Shukla, Dharma, 263

Signing key, 280

Simple List Extensions, 118

Single Line Of Text field type, 184

Site Actions menu, 11–12, 14, 23–25, 56–57, 184, 243

Site Administration, 11, 25

Site administrator, restricting application pages
       to, 56–57

Site branding, best practices in, 97–98

Site collection, 5, 88, 199, 281, 365

    importance of, 6

    partitioning site into, 6

    provisioning, 9–11

    purposes of, 6–9

Site Collection Administration, 11

Site Collection Features page, 283

Site collection-relative context, 51

Sitecollection token, 55

Site column, 17, 185–189

Site column definitions, defining, 185–189

Site Column Gallery, 188

Site customization, 11–15

Site definition

    adding site provisioning provider, 322–324

    Blog and Wiki, 313

    configuration modules, 319

    configurations, 313, 317–319

    creating custom, 314–320

    defined, 312

    DocumentTemplate, 317

    global, 314

    localizing, 348–350

    modules, 319–320

    NavBars, 316–317

    pre-installed, 312–313, 315

    and Site Provisioning Provider class, 322

    solution package for deploying, 340–341

    structure and deployment of, 312

    value of creating, 20, 312

    Web template files, 320–322

SiteDefinitionManifest node, 341

Site elements, 8–9

SiteFeatures node, 318

Site Features page, locate, 25

SiteGroups property, 364–365

Site icon, 97

SiteLogoUrl, 98

SiteMapDataSource, 90

SiteMapDataSource control, 87

Site membership, 18–19

Site pages

    default policy prohibits scripting in, 47

    difference between, and application pages, 49

    performance and security issues, 47

    vs. application pages, 47–49

Site Pages dropdown menu, 69

Site provisioning, 1–5

Site Provisioning Provider class, adding, 322–324

Site-relative context, 51, 55

Site scope, 88

Site Settings menu, 94

Site Settings page, 11–12, 19, 25, 48, 87, 96, 188, 200

Site Template gallery, 218, 314

SiteTitle, 330

site token, 55–56

SiteUsers property, 365, 372

SkipVerification, 358

SmallSearchInputBox delegate control, 88

SmallSerachInputBox, 89–90

Smart Part, 102

SMLHttpRequest object, 133

Software Development Kit (SDK), 18, 272, 281. *See also* Workflow Starter Kit
Solution element, 333, 339
Solution Explorer, 67–68
Solution Management page, 335–336
Solution package, 109
    and code access security, 338–340
    contents of, 332
    defined, 331
    for deploying feature, 332–336
    for deploying site definition, 340–341
    for deploying Web Parts, 336–340
    deployment steps, 332
    deployment using, 331–346
    importance of testing, 332
    metadata for, 332
    STSADM.EXE command for deploying, 338
    .wsp file for, 332–333
Solution Package installer, 160
Source file, 76–77, 274–276
SPBasePermissions, 375–376
SPContentMapProvider, 86
SPContentTypeId object, 202
SPContentType object, 200–201, 297
SPContext, 21
SPContext.Current property, 368
SPContext.Site.WebApplication, 342
SPCustomizedPageStatus, 65
SPDataSource class, 121
SPDataSource object, 121
SPDocumentLibrary class, 218–219, 228, 230
SPDocumentLibrary object, 59, 225
SPException, 178
SPFeatureReceiver, 28
SPFeatureReceiverProperties class, 26, 342
SPFeatureReceiverProperties object, 345
SPFile class, 220
SPFile object, 64–67, 130, 219, 224, 231
SPFolder class, 220
SPFolder object, 65–67
SPGridView control, 56, 102, 121–122
SPHttpApplication class, 41
SPHttpHandler, 43
SPItemEventProperties parameter, 213, 231
SPItemEventReceiver class, 231
SPLimitedWebPartCollection, 130
SPLimitedWebPartManager, 130–131
SPLimitedWebPart Manager object, 82–83
SPList, 218, 372, 374
SPListEventProperties parameter, 210
SPListEventReceiver class, 210
SPListItem class, 372–373
SPListItem Collection, 180
SPListItem object, 59, 179–180, 219
SPList object, 20, 59, 178–179, 218–200, 219, 228, 297
SPNavigationNode object, 87

SPNavigationProvider, 86, 91
SPPageParserFilter, 44–45
SPPrincipal class, 361
SPQuery object, 179–180
SpreadsheetML, 246
SPRequestModule, 44
SPRoleAssignment, 365
SPRoleDefinition, 365, 375
SPSecurity class, 367
SPSecurity.RunWithElevatedPrivileges method, 366
SPSite, 20–21, 342, 368
SPSite collection, 361, 364
SPSite constructor, 372
SPSiteDataQuery, 180–1881
SPSiteMapProvider, 86, 91
SPSite object, 223
SPSite reference, 345
SPSite site collection object, 368
SPUser class, 364, 372
SPUser object, 364
SPUserToken, 361, 371
SPUtility, handling authorization failures with, 377–378
SPUtility.HandleAccessDenied method, 377
SPUtility.Redirect method, 377
SPVirtualPathProvider, 44–46, 63, 93
SPWeb, 345, 372
SPWebApplication, 342–343
SPWeb class, 178, 372
SPWebConfigModification class, 109
SPWebManager, 100
SPWebModification, 344
SPWeb object, 20–21, 26–27, 223, 251, 364
SPWebPartManager, 80, 85
SPWeb property, 93, 97–98
SPWebProvisioning Properties, 323
SPWebProvisioningProvider class, 322–323
SPWeb site object, 365
SpWebUrl, 158
SPWeb user properties, 365
SPWinOePersistenceService class, 262
SPWorkflowActivationProperties object, 277
SPWorkflowAssociation object, 297, 301
SPWorkflowManager object, 301
SPWorkflowModification object, 306
SPWorkflowTask class, 308
SPWorkflowTaskProperties class, 286, 288
SPWorkflowTaskProperties object, 286
SPXmlContentMapProvider class, 86
SQL data type, 184
SQL-indexed name-value table, 206
SQL Server database, 2, 362. *See also* Configuration database
SQPRequestModule, 42
SQWeb object, 7
Src attribute, 79

Standard Edition, of MOS, 90
Stanek, William R., 169
Start Administrative Tools Internet Information
    Services (IIS) Manager, 30
Start button, 255
StartingNodeUrl attribute, 87
StartWorkkflow, 301
State machine WF program, 259, 263. *See also*
    Windows Workflow Foundation (WF)
StateMachineWorkflowActivity class, 260
State Machine Workflow Library, 260, 272
Static file, 316
Static tokens, 95
Storage, 105
StoreItemID attribute, 249
StreamWriter object, 223, 239
String, 139
StrongNameMembershipCondition references, 360
Strong-typed resource manager class, 328
STS. *See* SharePoint Team Services (STS)
STSADM, 343–344, 371
Stsadm.exe utility, 8, 24, 41, 67, 273, 282, 313, 335, 338
STSADM utility, 24
STS site definition, 312, 317
STS Team site, 318
SubWebOnly attribute, 321
Switches, 338
SyncChanges, 114
Synchronous event, 209. *See also* Before events
Sys.Application.add_load method, 143, 147
Sys.Net.WebRequest object, 160
System.ComponentModel namespace, 111
System content type, 199
System credentials, 368
System.IO, 238
System.IO.Packaging namespace, 238
System.IO.Stream object, 64
System.Net.WebPermission, 340, 360
System.Security.PolicyException, 356
System.Web assembly, 100
System.web.dll assembly, 35
System.Web.Extensions, 136
System.Web.IHttpHandler, 151
System.Web namespace, 136
System.Web.Script.Services namespace, 143
System.Web.UI namespace, 35, 129
System.Web.UI.ScriptManager class, 130, 155
System.Web.UI.WebControls.WebParts, 100, 102, 111,
    113, 124
System.Workflow.ComponentsModel assembly, 257
System.Xml namespace, 232, 234, 238–239

T

Table layout, 129
TagPrefix attribute, 56, 75

Target attribute, 236
Target zone, 82–83
Task, creating and waiting on, 284–291
TaskAfterProperties, 288
Task content type, 196, 199
Task edit form, 270, 291–292, 307–309
Task list, 18, 324
TaskListContentTypeId attribute, 293
TaskNotCompleted field, 289–290
TaskProperties field, 287
TaskProperties property, 287
Tasks list type, 177
TaskStatus field, 288–289
TeamCollab feature, 324
Team Collaboratioon feature, 318
Team Site, 312, 316, 324, 326
Template. *See* specific templates
TEMPLATE-deployed files, 335
TEMPLATE directory, 22–23, 67, 78, 96, 273, 293,
    334, 337
TemplateFile element, 334
TemplateFiles node, 334
TEMPLATEXML directory, 193
TemplateName parameter, 326
TEMPLATECONTROLTEMPLATES directory, 191
TemplateType, 224, 230
Templating framework, 100
TestData, 225
Testing, Workflow template, 280–284
TextBox, 115
TextBox control, 222
Theme control, 85–86
Themes, 96
THEMES directory, 96
Thread pool, 116
Thread synchronization, 32
Tielens, Jan, 102
Title attribute, 22, 321
Title property, 27
Today element, 183
TodayIso element, 183
Token, 55, 95, 285–286, 361, 363
TokenGroups property, 371
Tookit JavaScript library, 165
Toolbar.ascx, 129
Toolkit, 260
Tool Pane, 101
ToolPart, 105
Top-level Site, 7
Tracking list type, 176
TransformNode function, 161
Transitions, 259
TreeView control, 66–67, 220–221, 245
Trusted site, 118
Trust level, 104, 339–340, 353

Trust setting, 104
2007 Microsoft Office/suite, 234
TxtSmlUrl, 115
Type attribute, 70, 93, 195, 204
TypeName value, 76
Type property, 343
Type.registerNamespace method, 137
Type registration, 138

U

Uncustomized page, 65, 67
Unghosted, 46–47, 63–65, 91
Uniform resource identifier (URI), 235
UnmanagedCode, 358
UpdateAssociation utility method, 297
Update method, 27, 93, 178–179
UpdateTask activity type, 284–285
UpdateWorkflowAssociation method, 297
UrlAction element, 55–56, 227
Url attribute, 55, 58, 92, 227
Url element, 69
UrlMembershipCondition references, 360
URL protocol, 322
URL space, 30
U.S. English language pack CAB definition,
    346–347
UserContext object, 145
User Control (.ascx file), 102
UserControl class, 120
UserControl-derived class, 120
User Control Host Web Part, 120
User controls, 109
    constructing pages with, 76–79
    source file for simple, 76–77
    using, in Web Parts, 120–121
    and Visual Studio, 77
User credentials, delegating, 370–371
UserId property, 280
User impersonation, with user token, 371–378
User information profile, 362
User Information Profile list, 314
User interface, 5
User Mode, 112
User personalization, 111, 115
Users and groups, 364–365
Users And Permissions section, 12. *See also* Security
    configurations
User security token, 361, 363
Users property, 365, 372
Users security group, 366
User token, user impersonation with, 371–378
UserToken property, 372
Utility class, for resource access, 128–129

V

Validation controls, 35
Validation logic, custom, 191
Value property, 193, 343
VB Script macro, 33
VendorListTitle, 330
Verbs property, 123
Version attribute, 22
VersioningEnabled attribute, 204
Version numbers, 257
View Designer, 275
View Event Handler, 304
ViewEventHandlingScope, 304
ViewFields node, 206
ViewFields parameter, 181
ViewFields property, 180, 202
ViewListItems permission flag, 373
Views, 14, 206. *See also* List Settings; individual views
Virtual directory, 29–32, 46–47. *See also entries for*
    specific directories
Virtual_layouts directory, 48, 78, 83
VirtualPath attribute, 72
Virtual path provider, 44–46
Virtual server, *vs.* Web application, 4
Visual Studio, 21–28, 77, 110, 249, 330, 334
Visual Studio Extensions for Windows Workflow
    Foundation, 18, 260, 271
Visual Studio Templates, 272
Visual Studio Toolbar, 274
Visual Studio Workflow Designer, 260–261
_vit_bin directory, 46–47

W

Web application, 3, 342
    create, 41–46
    defined, 40–41
    overview, 40–41
    site collections within, 5–6
    standard web.config file for, 43–44, 73
    virtual directories within, 46–47
    virtual server *vs.*, 4
WebApplication property, 342
Web application scope, 23, 88
WebBrowsable, 111–114
WebBrowsableAttribute Web Part, 105
Web.config file, 38, 41–43
    defined, 34
    modify, for Web application to enable debugging
        support, 54–55
    requirements for ASP.NET AJAX, 156
    SafeControls section of, 339
    for Web application, 43–44, 73
WebConfigModifications collection, 343

Web configuration changes, 341–346
Web Content Management approval process, 18
Web Control, 74, 100–103
WebDescription attribute, 111
WebDescription Web Part, 105
Web Development Helper, 136
WebDisplayName attribute, 111
WebDisplayName Web Part, 105
Web page(s), 34–35, 74–79, 134–136. *See also* Web
    Part page
Web Part Application, 104
Web Part assembly, 338
Web Part chrome, 101
Web Part Client Control Registration Pattern, 157
Web Part connections
    connection provider and consumer Web Parts,
        124–125
    converting Feed List Web Part to IFieldProvider,
        126–127
    enabling connection to IFieldProvider, 127
    infrastructure of, 171
    introduction to, 124
    using resources, 128–130
Webpart extension, 107
Web Part feature, 318
.webpart file, 108–109, 319
Web Part framework, 104
Web Part gallery, 100, 106–110, 176, 218, 314, 318–319,
    327, 336
Web Part instance, 81–83, 319
Web Part Life Cycle, 103
Web Part management, 100
Web Part Manager, 111, 130, 172
WebPartManager control, 80–81, 100
Web Part menu, 127–128
Web Part page, 14, 316
    create, in ASP.NET 2.0 application, 80
    designed with one or more Web Part zones, 81–82
    designing, 79–83
    template for, 15, 80
    and Web Part zones, 79
WebPartPage class, 80–81
WebPartPage content type, 199
Web Parts
    ASP.NET AJAX components in, 155
    asynchronous Web Part processing, 116–119
    building blocks, 120–122
    built-in, 99–100
    connection provider and consumer, 124–125
    creating custom Editor Parts, 113–115
    creating feature for importing, 108–110
    customization and personalization, 110–119
    debugging, 110
    defined, 100

developing, for Windows SharePoint Services
    (WSS) 3.0, 105–108
example of, that loads User Control, 120–121
fundamentals of, 100–102
and ghosted state, 79
RenderContents method, 165
SharePoint development *vs.* ASP.NET development,
    104–105
site customization and personalization using, 14–15
support for customizing and personalizing, 79
using SharePoint's SPGridView Control, 121–122
using User Controls in, 120–121
WebControl basics, 102–103
as WebControls, 100
Web Part Verb, 123–124
working with, through SharePoint Site model,
    130–131
See also specific Web Parts
WebParts namespace, 125
Web Part solutions, 353
Web Parts solution package, 336–340
WebPartStorage, 105
Web Part technology, 5
WebPartToEdit property, 114
Web Part Verb, 123–124
WebPartVerbCollection, 123
.webpart XML file, 107
WebPartZone control, 80–81, 100–101
Web Part zone(s), 74, 79, 81–83, 104
WebPermission, 359. 353
Web Requests, 116
WebResource attribute, 129
WebResource.axd, 129–130
Web service equipment, 148–150
Web Service Proxies, 116
Webs property, 181
WEBTEMP file, 348
Web Template file, 320–322
Welcome menu, 362
WF. *See* Windows Workflow Foundation (WF)
WF assembly library, 260
WF Base Activity Library, 263
WF runtime, 256–257, 259–263
Where element, 183
While activity, 259, 288–291, 305
Wiki component, 139, 143
WikiControl, 138, 145–147
WikiControl AJAX component, 157
WikiControl JavaScript class, 144, 157
WikiControlTemplates, 157
WikiDocument content type, 199
WikiID, 157
Wiki page library list type, 176
WikiService endpoint, 148

WikiService Web service API, 144–145
Wiki site definition, 313
WikiWebService, 148
Windows Authentication provider, 364
Windows authentication-secured Web services, 369
WindowsBase.dll assembly, 237
Windows Explorer, 234, 248, 282
Windows Forms WebBrowser, 246
Windows identity, 371
Windows Program Files directory, 8
Windows Registry, 366
Windows security context, Windows SharePoint
        Services (WSS) security context vs., 363–364
Windows security token, 33
Windows Server 2003 operating system, 2
Windows Server 2003 Service Pack 1, 33
Windows SharePoint Services (WSS)
    AJAX architecture and, 147–148
    building AJAX Web Part Parts for, 155–173
    defined, 2
    as development platform, 15–21
    integration with ASP.NET, 40–49
    purpose of, 1–2
    securing objects with, 372–374
Windows SharePoint Services (WSS) 2.0, 83, 124
Windows SharePoint Services (WSS) 3.0, 237, 362
Windows SharePoint Services (WSS) 3.0 Central
        Administration application, 3–4, 41
Windows SharePoint Services (WSS) globalization,
        327–331
Windows SharePoint Services (WSS) list definitions,
        176–177
Windows SharePoint Services (WSS) lists, 176–179
Windows SharePoint Services (WSS) navigation
        components, 86–87
Windows Workflow Foundation (WF)
    activities, 257–258
    architecture of, 256–258
    creating, programs, 258–261
    programming model, 259–260, 262
    reactive programs, 253–256
    runtime, 261–263
    task and history lists, 18
    Visual Studio Extensions for, 18, 260, 271
Window.WikiControlTemplates array, 157
Word Options dialog box, 246
WordProcessingML content, 244, 246
WordprocessingML element, 249
Workflow.aspx, 268–269, 283, 299–300
Workflow association, 272, 283
Workflow association form, 270, 291, 293–299
Workflow.cs, 273–276
Workflow1.designer.cs, 273–275, 277
Workflow Developer Starter Kit, 272
Workflow ECB menu, 283

Workflow element, 265, 280–282, 292–293, 303
Workflow history list, 267, 269
Workflow initiation form, 270, 299–302
Workflow input form
    association forms, 291, 293–299
    initiation forms, 291, 299–302
    integrating, 270–271, 291–309
    modification forms, 291, 302–306
    task edit forms, 291–292, 307–309
    walkthrough using, 293
    See also specific forms
Workflow instance, 256, 259, 268–269, 283
WorkflowManager, 306
WorkflowManager property, 301
Workflow menu item, 268, 299
Workflow modification form, 270, 302–306
WorkflowPersistentService, 262–263
Workflow Properties property, 277, 280
Workflows, 18–19
    developing custom workflow templates, 271–291
    integrating workflow input forms, 291–309
    SharePoint workflows, 264–271
    Windows Workflow Foundation (WF), 253–263
    See also entries for specific workflows
Workflow settings, 266
Workflow Settings link, 283, 293
Workflow Starter Kit, 273–274, 281–282. See also
        Software Development Kit (SDK)
Workflow Status page, 269–270, 283
Workflow summary, 267
WorkflowTask content type, 270
WorkflowTaskContentType.xml, 308
Workflow task list, 267
Workflow template
    creating, 273–284
    defined, 265
    develop custom, 271–291
    to initiate new workflow instances, 267–268
    and input forms, 266, 270
    integrating workflow input forms, 291–309
    source files, 274–276
    testing, 280–284
    that uses InfoPath forms, 271
    Workflow Starter Kit, 273
    working with activities, 275–280
WorkflowToken, 286
Workflow.xml, 273–274
_wpresources virtual directory, 46–47
WriteContentToPackage method, 240
WriteListReference method, 374
WriteRssFeed method, 209
WriteSiteFeeds method, 374
WrkSetng.aspx page, 283
WrkStat.aspx, 269–270, 283, 302, 304
.wsp files, 332–334

WSS. *See* Windows SharePoint Services (WSS)
WSS Access Denied page, 57
WSS Activity Library, 257, 263
WSS Add Web Parts dialog, 109
WSS_ADMIN_WPG security group, 366
WSS authorization, 5
WSS Central Administration Web application, 313
WSS_Content_Application_Pools, 366
WSS Core Activity types, 263
WSS Create Site Collection page, 9–10
WSS_Custom trust level, 353
WSS_Full trust level, 104
WSS list, 148–150, 218. *See also* List
WSS list data, 175–184
WSS_Medium trust level, 104, 340, 353–354, 356
WSS_Minimal trust level, 339–340, 353–354, 358–359
WSS_Minimum trust level, 360
WSS object model, 82–83, 323, 342
WSS PeopleEditor control, 296
WSS Resources folder, 330
WSS_RESTRICTED_WPG security group, 366
WSS 3.0 RTM Web Services, 148
WSS runtime, 342
WSS SDK, 274
WSS security context *vs.* Windows security context, 363–364
WSS site, 5, 95–98
WSS-specific Pluggable Runtime Services, 263
WSS Web application, 342
WSS Web Part Gallery, 100
WSS Workflow Services API, 284–285, 287
WSS_WPG security group, 366
Wss.xsd, 23
W2wp.exe, 32–33
w3wp.exe process, 110
WYSIWYG editor, 100

X

XmlComponent, 161–166, 171–172
XmlComponent instance, 165
XmlComponent JavaScript class, 168
XML content, 203
XML Data Store, 246–252
XML data stream, 133

XML directory, 23
XmlDocument, 203, 230, 232
XmlDocument element, 214
XMLDOM object, 145
XML DOM parameter, 160
XML editor, 249
XML files, resources in, 331
XmlHttpRequest object, 133
XML parser, 234
XML property, 164
XmlReader, 232
XML schema, 232, 235, 316
XmlSerialization object, 251
XML-serialized object, 343
XmlSerializer class, 232, 297
XmlTextWriter, 151
XmlTransform method, 160–161
XML URL, 125
XmlUrl property, 111–112, 166
XML Web Part, 160
XmlWebPart, 166, 168
XmlWriter class, 239
XPath expression, 247, 250, 344
XSD.EXE command-line utility, 232
XslCompiledTransform class, 116
XSL property, 164
XSLT. *See* Extensive StyleSheet Language Transformation (XSLT)
XSLT DOM parameter, 160
Xslt file, 116
XSLT Pocket Consultant, 169
XSLTProcessor object, 161
XSLT style sheet, 160
XSLT technology, 169
XsltUrl property, 166

Y

Yes/No field type, 184

Z

Zero-based index, 179
.zip, 248
ZIP archive, 234–237

What do you think of this book?

We want to hear from you!

Do you have a few minutes to participate in a brief online survey?

Microsoft is interested in hearing your feedback so we can continually improve our books and learning resources for you.

To participate in our survey, please visit:

www.microsoft.com/learning/booksurvey/

...and enter this book's ISBN-10 number (appears above barcode on back cover*).
As a thank-you to survey participants in the United States and Canada, each month we'll randomly select five respondents to win one of five $100 gift certificates from a leading online merchant. At the conclusion of the survey, you can enter the drawing by providing your e-mail address, which will be used for prize notification only.

Thanks in advance for your input. Your opinion counts!

* Where to find the ISBN-10 on back cover

ISBN-13: 000-0-0000-00000
ISBN-10: 0-0000-00000-0

0 00000 00000

0 000000 000000

Example only. Each book has unique ISBN.

***Microsoft** Press*

No purchase necessary. Void where prohibited. Open only to residents of the 50 United States (includes District of Columbia) and Canada (void in Quebec). For official rules and entry dates see:

www.microsoft.com/learning/booksurvey/